European Media in the Digital Age

Visit the *European Media in the Digital Age* Companion Website at **www.pearsoned.co.uk/rooke** to find valuable **student** learning material including:

- Weblinks from the text
- Extended bibliography
- Author updates

PEARSON
Education

European Media in the Digital Age

Analysis and Approaches

Richard Rooke

Harlow, England • London • New York • Boston • San Francisco • Toronto
Sydney • Tokyo • Singapore • Hong Kong • Seoul • Taipei • New Delhi
Cape Town • Madrid • Mexico City • Amsterdam • Munich • Paris • Milan

Pearson Education Limited

Edinburgh Gate
Harlow
Essex CM20 2JE
England

and Associated Companies throughout the world

Visit us on the World Wide Web at:
www.pearsoned.co.uk

First published 2009

ISBN: 978-1-4058-2197-1

British Library Cataloguing-in-Publication Data
A catalogue record for this book is available from the British Library

Library of Congress Cataloging-in-Publication Data
Rooke, Richard.
European media in the digital age : analysis and approaches / Richard Rooke.
p. cm.
Includes bibliographical references and index.
ISBN 978-1-4058-2197-1 (pbk. : alk. paper) 1. Mass media—European Union countries. 2. Digital media—European Union countries. I. Title.
P92.E85R66 2009
302.23094—dc22

2008050625

10 9 8 7 6 5 4 3 2 1
13 12 11 10 09

Typeset in 10/13pt Minion by 35
Printed by Ashford Colour Press Ltd., Gosport

The publisher's policy is to use paper manufactured from sustainable forests.

For Joanne, Louise, Ewelina and Sylwia

Contents

Supporting resources

Visit **www.pearsoned.co.uk/rooke** to find valuable online resources

Companion Website for students
- Weblinks from the text
- Extended bibliography
- Author updates

For instructors
- Powerpoints containing extra graphics, tables and information to support the book

Also: The Companion Website provides the following features:
- Search tool to help locate specific items of content
- E-mail results and profile tools to send results of quizzes to instructors
- Online help and support to assist with website usage and troubleshooting

For more information please contact your local Pearson Education sales representative or visit **www.pearsoned.co.uk/rooke**

Preface, introduction and using this book

The new era of the media is a complicated affair with many layers, even diverse strategic levels, where a multitude of actors are changing the shape of how we see the world and how we see the mediators. Technology looms as a major cause. Equally, the creation of major media environments battling, competing with one another, is becoming the norm. For example, the corporation vs political institutional battle between Microsoft and the European Union (EU) will go down in the annals of business history.

The media nowadays is no longer a national concern but a trans-national one. Within this scene, an understanding of the continued developments of EU media policy is essential to media students and practioners alike if we are to react, at least in part, sensibly to the forces pushing us all toward a change in media behaviour. Perhaps even more than in the past, the media matters – economically, politically and socially – because it touches the core of our need to communicate.

Europe and the EU cannot be ignored in media terms because of the size and scope of its market. Understanding the present-day media scene therefore demands some knowledge of its European as well as its global context. International rules and regulations are changing the form of how the media is judged and how it behaves.

Changes are taking place in both production and distribution, and these are beginning to touch consumption. From new format newspapers, to digital TV and telephony on computers, countries are adapting to the new world in many different ways but, in the case of Europe, in a particular way through the institutions of the EU.

The media in any setting is of course imposing and important. It is so important in most modern societies, in one way or another, that we often assume that it is similar in its impact and its make-up. Commentators have often stressed this in referring to an intense media prominence, coining the phrase 'the power of the media'. In part there is truth here: the technology associated with the media is similar everywhere; even modes of production, to a certain extent, use similar practices and economic models.

The media collectively, as a source of information and values, is obviously deeply influential. This is the case in the EU market. Even so, when we look at the distribution and consumption within the media we find differences; within some media more than others, of course, but differences all the same. Who reads what and when, what is valued and what is not, whose news on what stage, how we watch and how we interpret the world around us, all depend on context.

There are signs of convergence across the globe in media delivery, including Europe, and there are a growing number of academic books and reviews dedicated to the subject of comparative media, the internationalisation of the media and regulation at the EU and international levels. At the same time, divergence of interpretation and differences in media provision are as normal as the forces that unite the media, and these too need to be explained and understood. It is in this way that we can know a little more about the power of the media.

In the political conglomerate known as the EU, there are signs both of convergence and of persistent divergence in media provision. At a time of complexity and diversity, major developments are now taking place: former certainties are coming to look more fragile.

The EU is beginning to set itself the task of creating a media architecture for its member states which has deep purposes and potentially significant outcomes for its citizens. This applies to both new areas of involvement, for example in the print industry (from 2005), and to the more settled policies in the audio-visual industries (from 1989).

What the EU is trying to shape in cultural and media terms is complicated though, because it acts on many levels and is not a state in itself with normal nation-statehood as its base. Therefore, the study of the EU media architecture is important as a case study because it shows the impact of both national provision *and* trans-nationalism (European and global) advancing at the same time.

Equally, the EU is no minor player, but a major economic and growing political power in the world and one which cannot as a unit be ignored. How the EU treats its media impacts upon on other major media players around the globe at corporate, national and trans-national levels. Add to this the new technology and the increasing power of diverse consumption and we are in the midst of a heady period of change.

Member states of the EU tacitly accept that the media is not only profit and entertainment; it is also important for their communities because it reinforces core cultural as well as political values. EU member states know that, on the one hand, the media is affected by cultural and political change, but on the other hand it can also influence public opinion and thus cultural and political assumptions. The media is therefore an important conduit of social, political and cultural coherence.

The media in Europe is thus to be analysed through two mirrors. First, it is a reflection of political and social forces which it reinforces and reorders. Secondly, it reflects and displays a wider entertainment and 'information' network beyond national constraints. Combining these two aspects provides for a specific communication network created for and used by Europeans.

This network is linked to the states that make up the 'new Europe' of the 21st century, all of whom have had previous national structures of production, delivery and consumption. Each has historic and constitutional concerns that also alter the way in which specific territories have developed their media. In Europe of all places you cannot escape the past, not even in the technology of the future.

Let us not forget, of course, that the media is 'big business', not only in national or European terms but globally. The media is invariably linked to economics and capital; sustaining sufficient demand for media to keep investment and continuity of production and the costs of distribution. The media has become an integral part of present-day Western economies, whether in the public sector or through private shareholders and business interests. Its economic influence is open to debate, but it is often put at between 2% and 5% of world GDP (in a wider definition of cultural products the OECD estimates possibly 7% of world GDP), but there are regional variations.

National governments in most Western European countries came to recognise the specific economic value of the media industries in Europe in the early 1980s. It became clear that some of the older industries, such as steel and coal, were becoming untenable. New industries were needed to create jobs and sustain the wealth of the nation. At the EU level, economic imperatives were the prime official mandate, and policy at the supranational level came to focus on economic imperatives which included the media.

The certainties of national or even regional economics, including the media, have become questionable. Europe, like so much of the globe, is now confronted with change: technological, social and even political. Some of our understanding of the media is also changing as theories are tested and reformed under the weight of new forces. As students of the media we need to observe, rethink and evaluate theory and relate it to any new forms of information and statistical analysis available to us. Equally we need to observe practice and ensure our thinking is related to what we perceive, and what we can measure.

We need verifiable research methods. In this book, you can explore these issues with a fresh mind and with renewed interest in a world as fascinating as it looks. Many of the topics are treated as introductory but, taken as a whole, they provide a range of analytical tools that help us understand a little more about the contemporary European media scene. This book does *not* set out to give us a definitive list of data, there are many sources available to us to do this, but establishes a base where we can develop our European media analysis and consider our approaches to some of the important topics in contemporary debate.

Reading: analysis and approaches – themes and boxes

Throughout the chapters you will note there are a series of reading and analysis aids placed in themes and boxes. These have been designed to help your reading of the text. They are designed to reinforce the 'benchmarks' laid down for teachers and students when we analyse and review the media in society. Therefore, they are tied to the 'learning objectives' and 'essentials' that head the chapters.

Themes

At the beginning of each chapter you will find a simple statement or series of statements around six themes. They should *not* be read as a given fact. They are more like a hypothesis (see Chapter 2) which needs to be proved, discussed, debated and then used in your own analysis of the subject. The ideas and approaches in this book are always to be considered with an open mind. This is important in higher education study and makes it distinct in so many ways from pre-university study.

The six themes are as follows, with an introductory comment in each. You will find that each chapter changes the commentaries to fit the subject area of the chapter.

Diversity of media

The 'media' is a diverse technology which is converging, but its diversity remains predominant even during a period of transition and for the foreseeable future. The media too is a collection of organisations, both public and private, changing over time, and often functioning differently in different countries.

Internal/external forces for change

The media is not only changing technologically, but also in a regulatory, political and economic way. In our analysis of the media we need to be aware of the internal media dynamic within the national industries but also mindful of the global, international, EU and even sub-national, local pressures that are pressing for change. This theme alerts you to this aspect and points to the internal, national dynamic and the external pressures forcing change.

Complexity of the media

The media is complex because of the way in which it is financed and how the economics are put together. This is often conveniently labelled as a discussion about public and private provision within societies. In the EU this is an important model and needs to be reflected upon. In the present era, however, the distinction between public and private sector broadcasting in particular is being blurred, with a mix of public and private finance being used to develop the 'old' media as well as the technologically 'new'.

Multi-levels

Media business and public broadcasting reform at global, national and local level is quickening. No longer is the nation state the only level at which the media interacts. The levels are often subsumed into what is called 'globalisation', whereas on the ground it is local and global as well as European levels which are in play.

European integrative environment

In the context of this book's investigation, one theme has been of major interest: the Europeanisation of the media market. Europeanisation is both a private and public sector concern and is political and economic and, in the long term, cultural. This theme alerts us to the process of European integration and its impact on us in matters cultural. As a term it is not meant to subvert the national but alerts us to a process whereby member states of the EU are bringing together their media and business policies in a form which is not only beyond the national into the global, but is uniquely European.

Cultural values

The media for most of us is not just a technology or a business but a content-laden communicator of cultural and social values: in a word 'content'. This theme reminds us throughout that the question of culture is ever-present in our analysis of the market place.

Boxes

There are five types of boxes in use in each chapter. They are not presented in a regular pattern but used in different chapters in different forms. The material encompasses both primary and secondary sources and should *not* be used as fact but as points to be approached in your own analysis of the subject. When you see an opinion, ask yourself, do you agree, or disagree, what alternative approaches can you take in using this material?

Case study

Related to the core text, each chapter has a series of case studies. They can be read on their own and can equally be used as a teaching aid in seminar or written work. They are best used of course in relating to the points raised in the text as a whole. They can also be referred to within the assignments and further reading and questions sections at the end of each chapter where necessary.

Point of view

Any analysis of a text demands a healthy critical eye at what is being argued. In most research and essay work, it is incumbent on us all to be aware that we need to engage in debate. Academics and practitioners of media markets disagree with each other, so there is a 'point of view' box that sketches different points of view.

This is supplemented by references within the text to important writers (e.g. McQuail, 1996) and a further reading list which is found at the end of each chapter. These only scratch the surface of analysis and writers on the subject, but they give us a way in to research.

Stop and consider

There is no more controversial subject than the role of media and society. All of us engaged in trying to understand its importance need to stop and consider different points of view and question our own thinking as we proceed. The stop and consider boxes help us do this and are reminders of how to approach some of the major ideas in the text.

Source(s)

The source box is similar to a point of view box and a case study box combined but with an emphasis on the importance of the source in our thinking. They have been chosen to illustrate the points in the text but often contain within them specific commentaries which may be useful either to describe or to analyse an aspect of the media.

Chapter summary

Each chapter ends with a summary box. These can be used for revision or debate. They are reminders of the major points within the chapter, alongside learning objectives.

Key terms

The study of the media, inevitably it seems, leads to the creation of what is sometimes called 'jargon', but the key terms are more than this. They are useful key words, often used as shorthand for a concept that lies behind them. The key terms give us a clear definition of what is meant behind the word or words used in the text. You will also find some of the key terms are actually described in the text itself, sometimes even in the boxes.

Discussion questions

A series of questions often useful for seminar or discussion groups, to help focus on the key arguments in the chapter.

Assignments

With a little more depth and needing a little more time, the assignment section poses questions which can be resolved either individually or within a work group. Refer back to the text, the learning objectives and the various boxes to come to some conclusions. Assignments are also useful for revision purposes.

Further reading

There was a time when much media research was book and review centred. This remains the case for important sources but is now complemented by up-to-date online resources. The market analyst nowadays needs the full range of sources and resources to help in analysis. This book can only touch the surface of some of this excellent work, but each chapter suggests some further reading that may help. At the same time, using creative research techniques and spreading our search for new and substantive work is one of the major skills required in developing the subject. It is *essential* that when using this book you step out from the stated commentary and compare and contrast its approaches with other work and other commentaries.

Online resources

Online resources are expanding rapidly. The list provided in each chapter points to well-known and in-depth web sites and online resources which, like the reading, can be usefully researched to widen your point of view and fine tune your tools of analysis.

You will not find an encyclopaedia-type list of data in these pages, although we have tried to give detail when we feel it relevant. It is important that you collect your own data from reliable databases: many of these can be found online, and that is why in many instances sources and source boxes have been used to extend your research.

References

The number of references within the text has been kept to a minimum so that the reading of the text is not interrupted. Remember in essay and exam work that using references and the debates *to the full* represents a very important part of not only academic but also market analysis. Remember this book is a text book, a study guide as much as it is a reference work. The content of this book could be seen as pro- or even anti-business or pro- or anti-private sector or pro- or anti-public service provision. There has been an attempt, however, to be neutral wherever possible, but it is in the nature of academic exploration that differences of view about the overall text will emerge. We hope, however, that you will find sufficient analysis and approaches to explore the media in Europe at a time of considerable change. Reading around the subject is, of course, always essential.

About the authors

Richard Rooke studied European Studies, a combination of political science, history and language, for his first degree at the University of Canterbury in Kent, where subsequently after four years' research in Paris and London, including teaching at the Institut d'Études Science Politiques (Sci-Po Paris), he was awarded his PhD from the Faculty of Humanities. He continued his teacher training during this period and was awarded a postgraduate certificate in higher education (Further Education) which he has used in a number of undergraduate and postgraduate settings over the past 20 years. He has taught at various institutions across the UK and Europe. He has been a visiting lecturer to the University of Liège, in Belgium; the Reims Management School in France; and a range of chambres de commerce 'écoles supérieurs' in France including IMEA in Besançon and ESC Dijon; he has taught on the Master's programme in European Public Administration in the postgraduate faculty of the Facchochschule Berlin (FHVR) Political Science Department in Germany and the Troisième Année (postgraduate) programme in European Management at EMLV Pôle Universitaire, Léonard de Vinci, in Paris. His present position is as a senior lecturer in social and policy studies at London South Bank University. He is the course director of a multilingual postgraduate Master programme in European Policy Studies collaborating with EMLV, LDV, Paris, France and FHVR, Berlin, Germany. His principal research interests include media policy, governance and policy development in the UK and at EU levels. He has undertaken consultancy work for the Home Office in the UK on public service management issues. He has recently written a chapter on 'Business and the changing public sector' in *The Business Environment: themes and issues* edited by P. Wetherly and D. Otter published by Oxford University Press (2008).

Contributor

Andrea Esser is a senior lecturer in media and cultural studies at Roehampton University, London. Her research interests include the sociology of television and the transnationalisation of the media, in particular in the context of European integration. Her work explores both the continuity of the market and the dynamics of change: socio-political, economic, and technological, alongside historical frameworks and changes in consumption. Her most recent publication is 'Audiovisual Content in Europe: Transnationalisation and Approximation', published in the *Journal of Contemporary European Studies*, 13:2 (2007). Before joining Roehampton University she worked in media consulting and publishing and lectured at Goldsmiths, UEL and LSBU.

Author's acknowledgements

Thanks are due to many, but I would like to mention those without whom this book would have been almost impossible. I am grateful to the many anonymous reviewers who read all or part of the book and whose commentaries were essential at all stages of the writing process. I am especially grateful to my supportive and very patient editor Andrew Taylor and colleagues Sarah Busby and Anita Atkinson at Pearson Education, thanks also to Lynette Miller (Permissions Editor), David Hoxley (Cartographer) and Linda Dhondy (Proofreader). As for my academic colleagues in the various institutions in which I have been privileged to ply my trade, my thanks go to them all for their help, conversation and advice. A special thanks to Brian Ardy, Robert Duplock, Jennifer Gibb and Helen MacFadyen whose guidance through some of the technical issues was invaluable. Other special thanks must go to Jean Seaton whose support so many years ago for the original idea of comparative European media work was the bedrock upon which this present work stands. My thanks to Julia my wife for the correction hunting and the ever present support. May I thank my colleagues and the European Commission for the invitation to attend the Information Society Network conferences at Exeter University in 2008 under the leadership of Alison Harcourt with a series of quite notable speakers including Robert Picard, Peter Humphreys, Tom Gibbons, David Levy, Colum Kenny, Adam Watson-Brown and others all of whom over the years have had an academic influence upon the author even though the interpretations and simplifications are, naturally, my own. My thanks also go to the decades of students and especially to all the 'media and policy studies' undergraduate and postgraduate students at London South Bank University who sharpened my teaching experience in this field. Needless to say, any of the omissions or failings in the text and the responsibility for the selection of material in the work are mine alone. Lastly and with much gratitude I would like to thank those who have allowed me permission to use copyright material throughout the text.

Publisher's acknowledgements

The publishers would like to extend their gratitude to Richard Rooke for all the dedication, enthusiasm and expertise he's poured into writing this book.

We would also like to thank the following academic reviewers for their generous and helpful comments, which have helped shape the manuscript:

Professor François Nectoux, Kingston University

Dr Mark Joyce, Southampton Solent University

Dr James Bennett, London Metropolitan University

Dr Tomas Coppens, University of Ghent

Robert Beveridge, Edinburgh Napier University

Dr Myria Georgiou, University of Leeds

and also thank Dr Andrea Esser for her contribution to the book.

We are grateful to the following for permission to reproduce copyright material:

Figures

Source 2.1 from *OECD Broadband Statistics, June 2005*, © OECD, 2005, www.oecd.org/sti/ict/broadband, Organisation for Economic Co-operation and Development (OECD 2005); Figure 3.1 from *Competitive Advantage: Creating and Sustaining Superior Performance*, The Free Press, a Division of Simon & Schuster, Inc. (Porter, M. E. 1985); Point of View 4.1 reprinted by permission of Hans-Bredow-Insitut; Source 4.3 from NACE Rev 2: CPA 2008, update June 2008, http://circa.europa.eu/irc/dsis/nacecpacon/info/data/en/index.htm, Eurostat, reprinted by permission of the European Communities; Case Study 5.9 from *Audiovisual Policy, 2001*, http://europa.eu.int/comm./avpolicy/index_en, reprinted by permission of the European Communities (European Commission, DG for Education and Culture 2001); Case Studies 8.5, 8.6, 8.7, 8.8 and 8.9 data from *World Press Trends*, reprinted by permission of World Association of Newspapers (WAN 2003); Case Study 8.11 reproduced from *World Advertising Trends 2002* with permission. Copyright World Advertising Research Center www.warc.com (WARC 2002); Source 9.4 based on ETS/EAO data in *EAO Yearbook 2002* and *EAO Yearbook 2005*, European Audiovisual Observatory (EAO 2002, 2005); Figure 10.1 from *Preparing Europe's Digital Future: i2010 Mid-term Review*, European Commission, reprinted by permission of the European Communities (EC 2008).

Tables

Table 3.1 from *The EU Publishing Industry: an Assessment of Competitiveness*, Pira International (Pira International 2003); Table 3.2 adapted from *EU Productivity and Competitiveness: an Industry Perspective. Can Europe Resume the Catching-up Process?*, © European Communities 2003, reprinted by permission of the European Communities (O'Mahony, M. and van Ark, B. eds 2003); Table 4.2 Television without Frontiers Directive adapted from *Europa 2007*, http://europa.eu/, European Commission, reprinted by permission of the European Communities (EU 1989, 1997); Point of View 7.1 adapted from *Global Entertainment and media outlook: 2002–2006 – Forecasts and economic analyses of 13 industry segments*, PricewaterhouseCoopers (PricewaterhouseCoopers 2002), cited in *Sector Futures: in Search of a Realistic Future*, © European Foundation for the Improvement of Living and Working Conditions, 2008, Wyattville Road, Loughlinstown, Dublin 18, Ireland, www.eurofound.europa.eu (EMCC 2004); Case Study 8.10 data from European Publishers Council, http://www.epceurope.org/, reprinted by permission of European Publishers Council.

Texts

Point of View 2.1 extract from Ignacio Ramonet, *Le Monde diplomatique*, January 2005, Le Monde diplomatique (Ramonet, I. 2005); Case Study 3.1 extract from Leader column, written by Neill Denny, Editor-in-Chief of *The Bookseller*, reprinted by permission of The Bookseller (Denny, N. 2005); Case Study 3.2 and Point of View 3.5 extracts from *Media Mergers*, DAFFE/COMP(2003)16, © OECD, 2003, pp. 8–10 and pp. 39–40, Office for Economic Co-operation and Development (OECD 2003); Point of View 3.3 extract from *Market Definition in the Media Sector – Comparative Legal Analysis*, European Commission, DG Competition, reprinted by permission of the European Communities (Bird and Bird 2002); Point of View 3.4 extract from European public film support within the WTO framework, *Iris Plus*, June, European Audiovisual Observatory (Herold, A. 2003); Point of View 3.4 extract from Application of EC competition policy regarding agreements and state aid in the audio-visual field, *Iris Plus*, June, European Audiovisual Observatory (Mayer-Robitaille, L. 2005); Case Study 4.6 extract from Audiovisual Media Services Directive from *Europa 2007*, http://europa.eu/, European Commission, reprinted by permission of the European Communities (EU 2007); Case Study 5.1 extract from EuroNews rebrands to take on rivals, *The Guardian*, 5 June, Copyright Guardian News & Media Ltd. 2008 (Sweney, M. 2008); Point of View 7.2 extract from *Books in France: Industry Profile*, June, Datamonitor (Market Business Line), Datamonitor Ltd. (Datamonitor 2008); Point of View 7.4 extract from European Commission, Communication from the commission to the council, the European parliament, the European economic and social committee and the committee of the regions on the Review of the EU Regulatory Framework for electronic communications networks and services, reprinted by permission of the European Communities (EC 2006); Point of View 8.2 extract from *Publishing in the Knowledge Economy: Competitive Analysis of the UK Publishing Industry*, Pira International (Pira International 2002); Point of View 10.1 extract from interview with André Lange, 17 January 2003, from http://www.obs.coe.int/about/oea/interview.html, accessed May 2008, European Audiovisual Observatory; Point of View 10.4 extract from EBU proposal for Amendments to the draft Amending Directive regarding the Framework, Access and Authorisation Directives ('Better Regulation') COM(2007)697 final, European Broadcasting Union (EBU) (EBU 2008); Point of View 11.1 extract from Digital media growing fast, study says, *Associated Press*, 4 June, used with permission of The Associated Press Copyright © 2008. All rights reserved (Mellgren, D. 2008); Case Study 11.1 extract from *The Consumer Experience – Research Report 07*, http://www.ofcom.org.uk/research/tce/ce07/, © Ofcom copyright 2007 (Ofcom 2007).

The Financial Times

Source 3.1 European media deals rise by 75%, © *FT.com*, 30 January 2007; Case study 5.5 Mecom predicts surge into black on cost cuts, © *FT Report*, 31 March 2007.

In some instances we have been unable to trace the owners of copyright material, and we would appreciate any information that would enable us to do so.

Abbreviations

AEJ	Association of European Journalism
AFP	Agence France-Presse
AFP	advertiser-funded programming
AP	Associated Press
AV	audio-visual
AVM	Audio-visual Media [Services Directive]
BBC	British Broadcasting Corporation
BT	British Telecom
CD	compact disc
COR	Committee of Regions
CSA	Conseil Supérieur de l'audiovisuel
CSIPA	Compte de soutien a l'industrie des programmes audiovisuels
CTV	cable television
DSL	digital subscriber line
DTV	digital television
DVD	digital versatile disc
EAO	European Audio-visual Observatory
EBU	European Broadcasting Union
EC	European Commission
ECREA	European Communication Research and Education Association
EEC	European Economic Community
EJC	European Journalists Centre
EMCC	European Monitoring Centre on Change
EPG	electronic programme guide
ESC	Economic and Social Committee
EU	European Union
GATT	General Agreement on Tariffs and Trade
GDP	gross domestic product
GNI	gross national income
HDTV	high-definition television
HBS	Household Budget Survey
IGC	Intergovernmental Conference
INSEE	Institut National de la Statistique et des Études Économiques
IPTV	internet protocol television
ISP	internet service provider
iTV	interactive television
iTVi	interactive television international
IVR	interactive voice response
MipTV	Marché International des Programmes de Television
MPEG	Moving Pictures Expert Group
NACE	nomenclature générale des activités économiques dans les communautés europèennes
NAICS	North American Industry Classification System
NAFTA	North American Free Trade Agreement
NVOD	near video-on-demand
OECD	Organisation for Economic Cooperation and Development
OFT	Office of Fair Trading
ONP	Open Network Provision
OSCE	Organisation for Security and Cooperation in Europe
PPP	purchasing power parity
PSB	public service broadcasting
PV	packet video
PVR	personal video recorder
PWC	PricewaterhouseCoopers
SMEs	small and medium-sized enterprises
SMS	short message service
SOFICA	Société Fiduciaire d'Expertise Comptable
SSNIP	small significant non-transitory increase in price
TBI	Television Business International
TEN-T	Trans-European Transport Networks
TNC	trans-national corporations
TRIPS	trade-related intellectual property rights
TWF	Television without Frontiers [Directive]
UCC	Universal Copyright Convention
UNESCO	United Nations Scientific and Cultural Organisation
UPI	United Press International
VOD	video-on-demand
WAN	World Association of Newspapers
WIPO	World Intellectual Property Organisation
WPPT	WIPO Performances and Phonograms Treaty
WTO	World Trade Organisation

EU member state abbreviations

AT	Austria
BE	Belgium
BG	Bulgaria
CZ	Czech Republic
DK	Denmark
DE	Germany
EE	Estonia
IR	Ireland
EL	Greece
ES	Spain
FR	France
IT	Italy
CY	Cyprus
LV	Latvia
LT	Lithuania
LU	Luxembourg
HU	Hungary
MT	Malta
NL	Netherlands
PL	Poland
PT	Portugal
RO	Romania
SL	Slovenia
SK	Slovakia
FI	Finland
SE	Sweden
UK	United Kingdom

Chapter 1

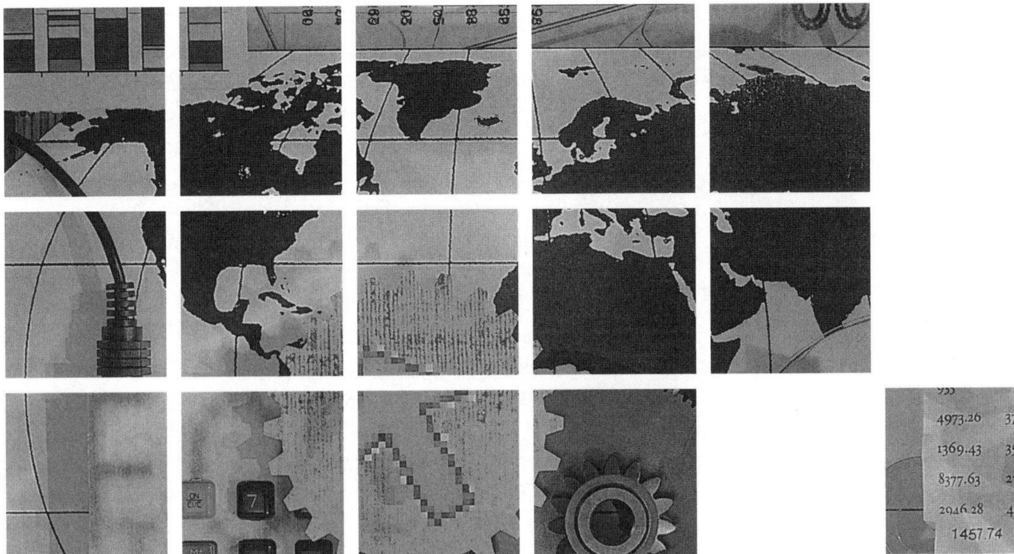

The EU and the media – EU media policy and globalisation

What this chapter covers

Learning objectives

When you have completed this chapter you will be able to:

- Understand some of the debates about globalisation and Europeanisation that provide working definitions and refinement as we review the media *in situ*.
- Appreciate that the EU media policy is not only evolving all the time but is an example of multi-factor policy development at many levels of interaction, from the global to the local.
- Outline the principal EU media policy agreements over the past 20 years and more.
- Identify the EU institutions and their decision-making that is bringing parts of the media policy together.

Themes

Below you will find a simple statement or series of statements around the six themes. They should *not* be read as a given fact. They are more like hypotheses (see Chapter 2) which need to be proved, discussed, debated and then used in your own analysis of the subject. The ideas and approaches in this book are always to be considered with an open mind; this is important in university study and is what makes it distinct from pre-university study.

Diversity of media

Many commentaries on the media will stress correctly the importance of viewing the media generically as if the media and its technology, for example, are the same anywhere. However, when we investigate the media *in situ*, within a context such as the EU, we notice differences and diversities which are just as important in our analysis as the similarities. In the EU this is most distinct in the press and publishing industries, but it can be found equally in the audio-visual sector.

Internal/external forces for change

Inside the EU the nation states (member states) will have ever-evolving national, legal and regulatory controls, which reflect a national point of view. Mergers and takeovers, for example, will occur within national settings. At the same time, European and global pressures, some technological, some regulatory and some legal, are also forcing change upon the market and the regulators.

Complexity of the media

More so than many geographical regions, the EU works through a public sector ethos as well as private industry. This is especially pertinent in the audio-visual television context, and it complicates the provision and even the distribution and consumption practices across the member states of the EU. In reviewing the media in the EU we quickly become aware of complexity within the market which is often centred on major debates about the public and private sector balance within given societies.

Multi-levels

National ways of thinking and controlling the media in the EU are the norm, although this is beginning to change. However, relying on our national knowledge is not enough to understand the reality of media provision across the EU. For example, in the press, regional newspapers often taken precedence in circulation figures over national papers, and this is a reflection of the social, cultural and even political shape that is the foundation for most EU states. In the market place, and the EU needs to reflect this, there are many layers of social cohesion, which are national, but also often sub-national at a regional and local level, as well as global.

European integrative environment

The EU is essentially an organisation designed to be economically integrative for its member states with a political aim of 'union'. The debates this throws forward, however, are often very contentious. In the field of media analysis there are heated arguments about the type of governance, effectiveness and efficiency that EU policy-making has created for the media: not least the battle about the degree of control that should be in the hands of the EU member states and their institutions on the one hand and the traditional national frameworks on the other. The evidence shows an uneasy consensus on these matters but step-by-step over the decades, the EU and its institutions have evolved into a more integrated view of the media, for the press and the audio-visual sectors.

Cultural values

There is no one 'European' culture or one set of 'European set-values', and this is reflected in press and national consumption, where the national, regional and differences of language hold sway. Nonetheless, with policies increasingly overlapping from the EU Single European Market, created from 1985–1993, media policies, such as the Television without Frontiers Directive, not only encourage diversity of provision but also lay down shared fundamental principles such as anti-racism, anti-discrimination, equal opportunities, right of reply, anti-ageism and shared business practices. All of these have their cultural sides to them and are, slowly, reshaping the cultural horizon of the EU member states.

Essentials

➤ To understand the contemporary media architecture in Europe and the EU means to understand a multi-national and cross-frontier world. In analysing its market, we need to look at both national and European levels of provision: it is a multi-layered system. As a collected group of societies within the global community, European markets are relatively sophisticated and, moreover, changing.

➤ Although there are forces that we can call loosely globalisation, pushing states together for trade and communication, there are also counter pressures that uphold cultural diversity and traditions. Not least, it is the declared aim of the EU, for example, to continue an integrative purpose. This has defined itself as different to other more loosely connected trans-frontier organisations such as the North American Free Trade Agreement (NAFTA). It too though wants to be a major trade player on the global stage, and therein lies the media industries' dilemma for European states.

➤ The media is inextricably linked to the markets, but it is also fundamental to political and cultural communication. The media is like a bridge between competitive products and cultures that, having been produced and distributed, are then consumed by societies but in their own context.

Introduction: the EU and the media in the 21st century

The European media market is large, profitable, rich and in the main technologically advanced. It has not reached comparability with the USA in media production, nor even South Korea in electronic networking, and its technological outreach varies, but its media and its engagement with the new media is overall impressive and growing. There are disparities across the member states but, taken as a whole, there is a rich diversity of provision and consumption of media products. This is not limited to the 'old' countries of the early European Community, but includes the northern Scandinavian states as well as the former communist societies of Eastern and Central Europe and the former more authoritarian societies of the south both on the Atlantic (Portugal) and the Mediterranean (Spain).

The media remains the prime organisation for the passing of information and often established values within societies. According to the European Commission (see Source 1.1), it is estimated that 98% of homes have access to television. Europeans engage with at least 200 minutes of TV 'spectating' each day, in addition to reading their newspapers, listening to their radios and watching films. **Europe** is now, like so many societies, launching itself into the world of gaming, web blogging, video on demand and the digitisation of IT platforms.

Source 1.1

EU institutions

This chapter will introduce some of the major institutions of the EU which are responsible for building and initiating media policy at an EU level. It is important to understand what is happening in these institutions if we are to understand, in part, the development of EU media policy and its relationship to national media. When you see an institution mentioned it is a good idea just to check and verify using its web site. Most will be covered through the official http://europa.eu/ web site. It is important to refer to the European Commission which initiates most proposals and then the two co-decision-making institutions: the European Parliament and the Council of the European Union representing the citizens and the nation states, respectively.

More than just living in an age of European integration and media policy-making, we appear to be living in an age where we can justifiably talk about an all-embracing 'information society'. This is not just a matter of entertainment or the idle gathering of news and information. Information is the key to business development, markets, products and employment, especially in what is called the 'new economy' of services. It is also the bedrock of communication, democracy, civic debate and pluralism. The media and its communication network can be seen as a key to modern societies and their economies.

Stop and consider 1.1

Does this concept of an 'information society' change your view of the media? Classically the media has been seen as something imposed from the top down – the producers and governments setting the agenda – or from the 'bottom up' – a reflection of consumer tastes. The information society seems to say that the media is not just about agendas or content but has as much to do with knowledge and communication built in to our economic system in a much deeper way. Is this right? What are the arguments for this and the arguments against? If the EU is redesigning our media system, for what purpose is it doing this? Could it be setting the agenda or creating a network which fuels the European economy?

The **EU** has been encouraging a redesign of the media for its member states. This has been a gradual process over the past decades. It applies to the telecommunications and audio-visual industries, including television and film, and the print industry, added to the agenda in 2005 and 2006, respectively. It includes the mundane of shopping 'rights' as well as the high fashions of advertising. The degree to which this design is working is hotly debated. Nation states still remain pivotal in the regulatory field and there are national constitutional differences across the EU. Yet, step by step, agreed practices are being implemented which are changing the architecture of the media. In an era of increasing global competition and growth in media products, this is seen as an essential part of a European (at least EU) response to global change.

In the minds of influential member states in the EU – the large, such as Germany, the UK, France and Italy, the small, such as Luxembourg, and the middle range, such as Denmark, Spain, Poland – the media's production, distribution and consumption are seen as a cultural bulwark, a defence and protection of what might be called European 'values'. The word 'civilisation' has even been bandied about. It is also a matter of business and political interests. The stakes are considered high.

Within its own boundaries, the EU is also a protector of what it calls 'cultural diversity': it tries to maintain the richness of its cultural heritage in language and political pluralism. Its members argue its case over, for example, intellectual property rights (the World Intellectual Property Organisation – WIPO). On a global scale, too, the EU aims to protect its culture, in particular against what some see as the 'hegemonic' position of US audio-visual products, a contentious issue at the earlier General Agreement on Tariffs and Trade (GATT) negotiations that is still an on-going negotiation within the World Trade Organisation (WTO).

So, over many issues the EU attempts to negotiate globally for its members. As an organisation it is also growing. The recent enlargement of the EU in 2005 with 10 more nations is the biggest since its creation and it can be reasonably predicted to reach 30 or more states in the near future. It participates directly in world trade rounds (WTO and WIPO notably) and bilateral talks with other international organisations (e.g. the Organisation for Economic Co-operation and Development – OECD). It is a player of some importance, not only for its members but also for those who are a part of the growing global media market; in the USA, India, China, Japan, Asia or Latin-America, for example. It is a participant at the UN on trade and development, and its member states equally participate in the long established Council of Europe (1949) where matters of culture are always on the agenda.

To help us understand the media in the contemporary era, this introductory chapter reviews the arguments about globalisation and integration in the EU in the light of its media policies. It also reviews the development of the EU as a political and regulatory area. The last section acquaints us, albeit briefly, with how polices are created at the EU level. Chapters 1, 2, 3, 4 and 5 should be used together as 'tools of analysis', even if at an introductory level, whereas the remaining chapters look at the media more directly and provide us with an 'indication' of some of the important contemporary issues. Combined they give us an insight into a fascinating media market.

The EU, globalisation and media

It is fashionable to talk about the impact of 'globalisation' on our media as well as on our lives in general. However, the quandary over the universality of service and diversity of context is no better exemplified than in our frequent and over-simplified use of the word 'globalisation'.

The trouble with 'globalisation' as a word or concept is that it is too broad, a catch-all for a whole series of forces changing the shape and structure of how the media is provided and produced, distributed and consumed. Some might argue that if globalisation is anything it is the continued march of global finance and capital, but that too would be to over-simplify. All of us lean toward the banner headline – the simplistic approach to a concept – because the words appear to express some underlying theme. Even so, to understand the dynamics we need to measure and categorise the workings of such 'broad' concepts.

Stop and consider 1.2

The James Bond series has often been seen as exemplar of a global 'product'. Sold round the world, it appears to be based on a series of universal values that seem to be 'global' and attract film-goers the world over. But it is estimated that half the production costs are earmarked for marketing, and the marketing of this 'global' product is 'localised' and bespoke to different parts of the world. In the case of a James Bond film how global then is it?

Check out a very interesting video case study created by the Open University *'Understanding society' series: 'Global Cultures'.*

This applies equally to the 'media' as a word, which is also self-evidently made up of different 'types' of media (film, radio, TV, newspapers and magazines) which react differently to globalisation because of new technology and the development of digitisation. Importantly too is the way in which they are consumed in socially different patterns. Inside the EU, differences of social behaviour, including consumption, have been the norm not the exception (see Chapters 8 and 11). In other words, media production, distribution and consumption are all 'variables', to use a statistical term, turned and twisted into forms by different societies and in different ways.

Globalisation also has its specific contexts, and in the EU there are other pressures acting upon the global forces, some internal and some external, which are also important for us. To understand this we need to unpick this process of change to make it more transparent, and illustrate what is happening in the EU as an example of how a regional global bloc reacts to the new. That means looking at the series of institutions at the EU level which impact upon the member states, and then at the national structures, which implement media policy and the many regional differences which impact upon it.

That said, most books dealing with the media concentrate on analysing it through 'national' systems, and this is for good reason. Most broadcasters and newspapers, for example, work through national regulation and definition and they are more easily defined (and controlled) than trans-national, cross-frontier forces. There is always the temptation to separate national systems from globalisation, when in fact they are intertwined.

'Globalisation' is, of course, as much to do with economics and technology as it is to do with politics. The media scene is certainly changing because of it. In capitalistic and economic terms, globalisation is clearer: financial markets and the use of capital are everywhere and in every facet of social inter-reaction. Indeed some say too much (Marxists), others not enough (liberals), and others welcome its wealth creation and cultural intermixing, its global creativity from Hollywood to Bollywood. Nowhere is this more obvious than in the music industry (MTV, etc.) and, increasingly, film production and consumption, not to mention TV scheduling. In press terms, often unsung and merely assumed, the large press agencies have been passing information around the globe since the 19th century let alone the 21st. Global forces of international trade are not new, but the technology of the new media is.

In technological terms globalisation is obvious and profound, not least in the bounding trans-national, digital, delivery platforms. This is altering consumption patterns: from analogue to digital, cable and satellite, from television to mobile, from newspapers to RSS feeds, from agencies to bloggers. Is technology the driving force behind the media? Some such as Marshall McLuhan (1967) or Ian Angel (2001) think so, to the point that technology might be seen as the prime source of change in society. It is difficult to see 'globalisation' truly functioning without technological drivers. Equally, Europeanisation is encouraged and promoted by better communication networks which are of a technological nature.

Technology intrigues and seemingly enlightens and empowers us. Applied technology and its outreach are potentially all-embracing. Enhanced interactivity and the cheap means of digital distribution on a global level, some argue, offer great potential for civic discourse and participation. Moreover, there is little that cannot be altered by technology in one way or another. This was the case in the past and it remains so in the digital age with arguably even more potency.

It is the consequences of finance-fed, capital-based, economic and technological change that increasingly fascinate and sometimes frighten contemporary societies. This in turn becomes of interest to societies' representatives: the politicians and therefore the regulators.

The 'media' is especially important because it contains the very building blocks of communication and culture that knit societies and communities together. Moreover, as the new technology blends with economic potential and the market is increasingly seen to be global (though some areas are more 'profitable' than others) rather than merely national, there will be pressures from providers, distributors and consumers alike to embrace the new opportunities. The regulation and law that encompasses change then needs to work on multi-national levels – international, cross/trans-national, national and regional, and even, in some cases, local forms.

The EU and localisation

The EU is made up of nation states participating in a joint venture for their own mutual interests. Equally the EU is made up of different types of nation states and communities, many of them distinctly local. Regional or local media provision can have two different meanings. Historically, it refers to a region within national boundaries. This is especially important in certain European countries, such as Germany or Spain in broadcasting, or Germany and France in the press, where there is a strong regional approach. However, the 'local' received a new impetus in broadcasting in the 1980s, when American channel operators, such as CNN, Discovery and MTV started to roll out their services globally. Their 'local feeds' often cross(ed) national borders, targeting language areas or culturally neighbouring nations such as the Scandinavian countries.

Stop and consider 1.3

How would you define 'local' media? Think of your own area and the media that is being generated for you: TV, newspapers, radio and film, and broadband services through telecommunications or mobile links. How much is local? It helps, perhaps, to think of this as the 'carriage' of services from the producers and especially the distribution system, on the one hand, and the 'content' which links into choice and the consumers on the other. The separation of 'carriage' from 'content' is the way that EU regulators are thinking about the future. Is this the way to think about the 'local' or are their limitations to this?

While the original approach had been to establish pan-European services, a trend called 'localisation' came to characterise the 1990s. One reason for localisation was advertising revenues. With too few financially strong international brands to finance the range of pan-European services, local opted-out advertising slots came to be offered to allow for smaller local companies to buy advertising space and thus add to the income of the pan-European broadcasters. A second reason for localisation was that channel competition in Europe was increasing manifold and trans-national broadcasters had to give their services some local identity if they were to compete successfully with local competitors. This was achieved by offering regional feeds, subtitled and dubbed, and with programme schedules reflecting local viewing habits. With increasing competition, trans-national broadcasters, moreover, started employing local presenters and investing in local productions.

Glocalisation

The localisation trend that has continued ever since also led to a rethinking of globalisation. While many commentators spoke of a reverse trend, arguing that differences in culture forestall trans-national or even global media services, the helpful Japanese term 'glocalisation' was picked up by the Anglo-Saxon marketing world and introduced to globalisation theory by Roland Robertson (1994). Glocalisation means 'global localisation', i.e. local diversification occurring within trans-national movements. Globalisation and localisation had become necessary complements: the former guaranteed power and synergies, the latter popularity with audiences (see Case Study 1.1). For cable operators, there is a greater range of potential advertising customers and, last but not least, appeasement of local media authorities.

The EU and 'Europeanisation'

In media terms in Europe, this multi-national, trans-national, 'glocal' movement and all the arguments and debates on its future are structurally complicated by another major factor: **Europeanisation.** Unlike the word 'globalisation', 'Europeanisation' is a process more easily defined, though no less complicated nor less debated. It is bound to the structures of the

Case Study 1.1

Localisation: MTV Networks Europe

MTV is the example par excellence of the ultimate inevitability of localisation. The broadcaster had entered Europe in 1987 with an English-language pan-regional service. While this approach proved successful enough in its initial years, with MTV gaining cult status across Europe, local competition forced it to adapt eventually. MTV started out broadcasting unscrambled, with cable operators paying no fees and revenues coming from advertising alone. However, like all other pan-European broadcasters, it found that advertisers interested in a pan-European reach were limited. The vast majority of advertisers could not afford pan-European coverage, or had products that were either available only locally or were branded differently across Europe. They needed local advertising possibilities. The pressure increased with the emergence of strong national competitors, such as MCM in France and VIVA in Germany, launched in 1989 and 1993, respectively. At first MTV remained reluctant to localise its successful global brand. Also, analogue transmission meant that it was costly to have to rent several satellite feeds. However, when it became clear that it was losing considerable audience shares to local competitors all over Europe, that it increasingly had to fight with local competitors over scarce cable space, and that the local advertising market was a multiple of the pan-European one, MTV finally began to localise in 1996. Digital transmission now made time-shifted transmission and local opt-outs possible and feasible. MTV started with four separate services (UK & Ireland; MTV Central, covering Austria, Germany and Switzerland; MTV European, covering 76 territories; and MTV Southern for Italy), and then rapidly followed with further local offers: MTV Nordic in 1998; MTV France, MTV Espana, MTV Holland and MTV Polska in 2000. Today MTV Networks Europe has regional channels in 26 different languages and considerable amounts of content are produced locally.

Author's thanks to Andrea Esser – see Chapter 9 – for this case study and the sections on EU localisation and Glocalisation.

political organisation now known as the 'European Union'. To understand what is happening in European media terms, the developments in the EU need to be understood by students, journalists, commentators, media providers, distributors and, perhaps oddly, less so by Europe's consumers than by its citizens.

The reason why the EU is important in media terms is not necessarily because of an overall integrated EU approach to the media as a supranational institution but rather because of the EU's other powers on the global stage, especially its bargaining position vis-à-vis other nations on trade matters. Media products are a part of global trade and, as a sector, have become increasingly important for the enormous value-added wealth they represent in economic terms. It is estimated that more 'profit' is made from the entertainment industries than from military hardware, and this is a phenomenon of the late 20th century which is accelerating into the 21st. The modern age has an insatiable demand for media products, and digitisation is bringing together different media outlets and marketing strategies to meet this demand.

The EU states have attempted to manage this change by a raft of economic policies, many of which touch the media industries. Most importantly, since 1985–1993, there has been the revamped economic policy of the European member states known as the Single European Market. This now encompasses all the states including the new enlargement of 2005 where 10 central European countries have now joined the existing 15 members of the EU to make a trading bloc of 25 countries, with two fairly recent additional members making 27. This is set to increase in the years to come.

More recently, in policy terms, this has been added to by what is known as the 'Lisbon Agenda' which sets out to make the EU an information-led, highly competitive, creative market, one to rival other major economic blocs. In the seeds of this policy the EU has tried to sow an integrative force that both protects and encourages media creativity. It hopes to enhance economic strength for all its members in a world which is changing through increased trade, capital-flow and digital strategies.

Stop and consider 1.4

There are many arguments about what the EU is, and what role it should play in the development of media policy. Most media policies in the past have sprung from national systems. If the EU is not a 'national' system, can it truly bring together the peoples of Europe in such a sensitive area as a media policy? When you are reading round the subject ask yourself, what does this writer, journalist, academic think about this question? You may find that arguments about European media policy are intrinsically linked with the issue of nationalism.

Defining and understanding the EU

What then is the EU if it is not a state? It will be no surprise to discover that commentators, academics, journalists and editors disagree about what exactly it is: some describe it as a super-power in the making; others as a federal form of state being born; and others as an intergovernmental organisation designed to prop up the nation states against growing global trade and competition from other major trading blocs. Some argue that it is an anachronism, a product of the Second World War and the cold war combined; an organisation designed as a bulwark against authoritarianism and the Soviet bloc which has served its purpose and needs to be dismantled.

There are some excellent analyses of the EU available, and some of these have been mentioned in the further reading and references sections, but here we want to analyse the fundamentals from a media point of view. Primarily, the treaties that have created the EU (see Source 1.2) and the integration process it engenders depend upon fundamental elements: trade combined with communication and political will. This is then established by agreement through international treaty. The media straddles all of these fundamentals and makes it an area of enquiry often different from others because it is a hybrid; it is both a product and a process which absorbs communication and information and entertainment, touching all social interrelations, including international relationships.

Source 1.2

The principal treaties that have created the EU

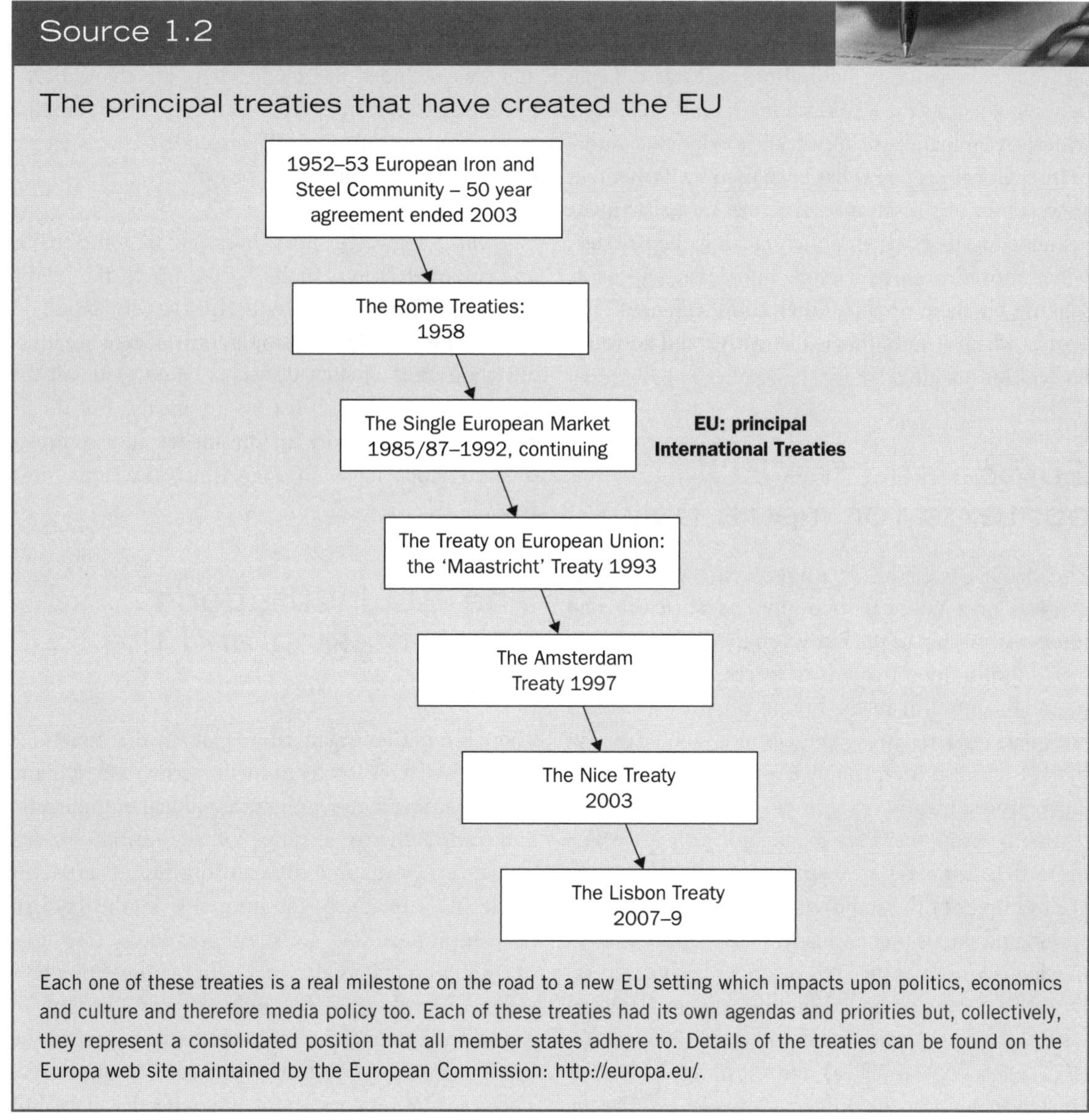

Each one of these treaties is a real milestone on the road to a new EU setting which impacts upon politics, economics and culture and therefore media policy too. Each of these treaties had its own agendas and priorities but, collectively, they represent a consolidated position that all member states adhere to. Details of the treaties can be found on the Europa web site maintained by the European Commission: http://europa.eu/.

In policy terms the media has lagged as a primary integrative policy choice. There are many arguments as to why, but two stand out: first, the reluctance of governments to give up their control of the media and second, a technology, principally analogue in audio-visual terms, that could be controlled relatively easily through licence and national territories. The new technological age and the Europeanisation of policy choices since the 1980s have changed all that. From the Single European Market onwards, media, telecommunications and the whole development of the 'information society' are coming increasingly to the fore in EU terms. Its potential for the integration of its peoples is tantalising and attractive in both business and political terms.

As the EU has changed and adapted, even grown from six primary nations to 25 in 2005 and 27 in 2007, and with the prospect of more growth in the near future, it has had to adapt to increasing global capital-flows and international trade. It has had to consider an accelerating level of technological change; changing economic and investment patterns; social change (urbanisation); greater linkages between societies on a cultural level; and a relatively wider dissemination of ideas, knowledge and information globally. The EU has been used by its member states as an organisational structure to assist in the bringing together of their policy-making. Step by step, it has moved towards a more integrated approach, soaking up these opportunities and challenges. The way in which it does this is distinctive and so too is its decision-making.

Europe and the EU: contexts for media policy

The media, any media, does not operate within either a social or a political vacuum. The structure and inter-relationship of the European media is reliant, in broad terms, upon two sets of forces. The first is the national control of media bound often by a defined national, legal territory, the second is a European market which is increasingly controlled by EU legislative procedures.

In EU terms there are a range of policies which unite the member states' approaches to the media. For example, for the audio-visual industries, there are specific proposals that enshrine the European market in what is known as the 'Television without Frontiers Directive' (1989, amended in 1997 and in 2005 onward), the new Audio-visual Directive (2005–2007) (EU, 1989a, 1997a, 2007a) and the range of polices created to support the 'information society'. On the latter, there is an all-embracing new initiative entitled 'i2010' dedicated to encouraging the new digital age across all the EU member states from broadband access to library provision. On top of this, there has been a profound review and a new set of consultative proposals for bringing together publishing interests.

There are directives (legal instructions from the EU) and a growing body of case-law at a European level touching upon both press and audio-visual policies. Even so, there remains no 'European Broadcasting Act' or 'European Press law' because, to all intent and purposes, the EU is not, and does not act like, a state. The EU assists the member states in converging or harmonising their laws and practices, and this includes the media. It is for the national parliaments to interpret and implement media policy, bearing in mind EU direction. This is where many of the complications, or even strengths, of EU policy originate.

Table 1.1 gives a quick overview of some major and minor decisions made by the EU in the media field: they form the base for further discussion in later chapters and are examples only. There are literally thousands of such decisions being made all the time. This is *not* a full list by any means, but shows the scope of EU work in the media and examples of the various stages through which decisions must pass.

The EU institutions, policy-making and the media

There is no other organisation globally that functions like the EU. This is why in media terms, where many of the member states' policies are linked both directly and indirectly to a range of EU initiatives, its influence is sometime difficult to assess. That is not to say it is relatively unimportant: in the field of telecommunications, technical standards, free flow of entertainment goods, legal rights, competition law, rights of workers in the industry and the flow of capital investment, the EU is an essential part of the European media architecture and cannot be ignored. There are arguments about how effective it is, but that does not mean we can ignore its presence.

At first glance, the complexity and the range of political and legal instruments that are re-creating the media scene can be confusing. Some of this comes out of the complexity of the EU itself: neither state nor nation, nor simply an international organisation. Some would say it is a new type of political organisation shaping itself to face the challenges of a new world trade order.

The EU functions through a mix of institutions. These too have been altered and added to over the years and at various levels. There is an EU-level (known

Table 1.1 EU regulatory activities in the media (examples)

Examples	*Description*	*Purpose*
1985–87 International Treaty: **The Single European Market** (EU, 1987)	Although not especially aimed at developing a media market, the impetus for new, widespread, economic trade growth touches all private sectors of business including broadcasting and print companies.	Widens the principles of market access and represents a move towards a harmonisation and standardisation of the regulatory environment to encourage trade and economic growth.
1989 **The Television without Frontiers Directive**. Amended and deepened in 1997 and 2007 to include new IT services (EU, 1989a, 1997a, 2007a)	Groundbreaking European initiative, attempting to create a more unified media market in audio-visual broadcasting for content, production, distribution and audience access.	Introduced new ground rules for media products, agreed principles on the protection of minors and developed support subsidies, e.g. EU MEDIA programme.
1989 **HDT** An example of technical convergence issues (EU, 1989b)	Council decision on high-definition television.	An early example of an EU technological response to new technology and potentially new markets.
1993 International Treaty: **The 'Maastricht Treaty'** (EU, 1992)	The Treaty on European Union, which entered into force on 1 November 1993, makes a specific reference to the audio-visual sector.	'. . . *the Community shall encourage co-operation between Member States and, if necessary, supplement their action in such fields as artistic and literary creation, including in the audiovisual sector* . . .'
1995 The Uruguay Round and the creation of the **World Trade Organisation**	The EU negotiates for its member states as a bloc.	'*The establishment of the first multilateral framework regarding trade in services (GATS) and the protection of trade-related intellectual property rights (TRIPS)*'[1]
1997 **Green Paper** (EU, 1997b) Followed in 2000 by (EU, 2000): and in 2002 by:	Proposal from the EU Commission regarding convergence of the telecommunication, media and information technology sectors. Regulation on unbundled access to local loop. New regulatory framework (see below).	An important reaction to the digital age in a series of measures leading into the 21st century.
1997 International Treaty: the **Treaty of Amsterdam** (EU, 1997c)	Protocol on the System of Public Broadcasting.	An extension of EU concerns to define what it considers to be 'core' EU public broadcasting values.
1999 International Agreement **'The Lisbon Agenda'**	A broad agreement within EU member states to enhance and intensify the EU single market and especially using new technology as a base.	'. . . *the most competitive and dynamic knowledge-based economy in the world, capable of sustainable economic growth with more and better jobs and greater social cohesion*'.[2]
2001 EU Council accords on film subsidies (EU, 2001)	Resolution on national aid to the film and audio-visual industries.	A major concern for many member states and as a document is an early indication of the EU support and defence for what it considers to be its 'cultural heritage'.

Table 1.1 continued

Examples	*Description*	*Purpose*
2002 New developments and %% proposals in **AV Policy**	The modernisation of rules of audio-visual services was launched with the Fourth Communication from the EU Commission (COM(2002)778 final) (EC, 2002). Framework Directive (EU, 2002a) Authorisation Directive (EU, 2002b) Access and Interconnection Directive (EU, 2002c) Universal Service and User's Directive (EU, 2002d) Data Protection and Privacy Directive (EU, 2002e) Radio Spectrum decision (EU, 2002f)	New agendas being set for the 21st century. A further broad proposal to include internet services within the remit of the audio-visual environment. It also tackles new questions over advertising policy. It lays down the coordination of policies including radio spectrum across the EU.
2005/06 New proposals for the **Print and Publishing Industries** (EC, 2005)	New proposals arising from the Commission's survey of the competitiveness of the EU publishing sector in a framework of media policy.	First major EU initiative into the private (mainly) corporate world of publishing and print industries within the EU.
2007/09 **The Lisbon Treaty** (EU, 2007b)	Following enlargement and debates about the EU 'constitution' an amending treaty that extends the powers of the EU into new areas of competence.	The decision-making system becomes more streamlined. The aim of this treaty is to extend and better coordinate policy-making at an EU level.
2005 **'i2010'**[3]	Carrying on from previous EU polices named e-Europe, this initiative measures, encourages and converges thinking on the digital age and the ways it may be accessed by EU citizens, public bodies and the like.	The integration of the communication network through the digital age is a very strong priority for the EU as it allows for greater communication between EU citizens, business and the body politic.
2005–2007 **The Audiovisual Media Services Directive** (EU, 2007a)	The Audiovisual Media Services Directive develops further areas for the member states of the EU such as advertising and world wide web and internet use.	From draft to reality. After many years of discussion and debate the EU extends the scope of the Television without Frontiers Directive into the digital age.

[1] (http://ec.europa.eu/avpolicy/ext/multilateral/wto/index_en.htm)
[2] http://ec.europa.eu/employment_social/knowledge_society/index_en.htm
[3] i2010 – see http://ec.europa.eu/information_society/eeurope/i2010/index_en.htm

as the 'Acquis Communitaire' or 'the EU'), national and, in some cases, regional levels of decision-making and control over the media.

The most important procedure for the media is the co-decision process where the European Commission proposes initiatives, and the Council of the European Union (representing the member states) co-decides with the Euro-MPs in the European Parliament. The resulting agreement is sent on to nation states to be made into national legislation. Although it appears cumbersome and bureaucratic at times, it has established itself as the *modus vivendi* of policy development. It includes a whole range of institutions embracing a range of organisations and interests, both professional and political, from associations to consultants, from lobbyists to ministers.

Source 1.3 indicates the principal institutions. In simple terms: the European Commission initiates proposals, the Council (which is a body divided between ministers – the Council of the European Union – and the heads of governments – the

Source 1.3

EU institutions

The following diagram illustrates the principal EU institutions. Emanating from the treaties that have created the EU, each institution may be visited online to explore their histories and powers of decision-making including their positions on media policy.

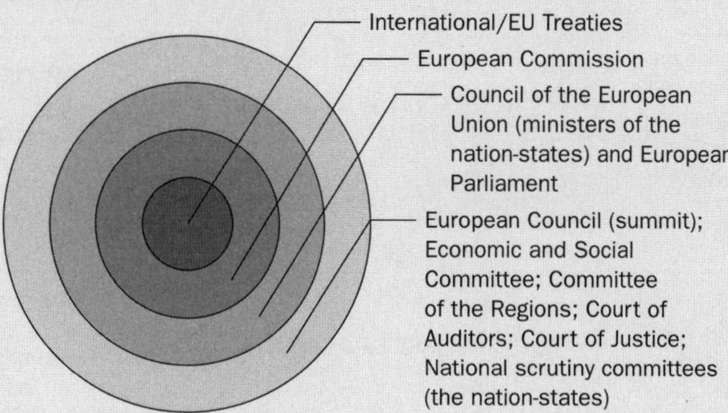

It is to be remembered, and it is often it seems forgotten in articles and general newspaper reporting, that decisions at the EU level are finally translated into national legislation through national legislatures, and this applies to media policy too. Moreover, the decisions made by the EU institutions are agreed by the member states through the Council of the European Union (ministers) before they are approved. The principal means used by the EU to convey its collective policies to nation states are the following types of rulings: directives, regulations, recommendations and decisions. Procedures may change if and when the new 'Lisbon Treaty' (2007–2009) or something similar is ratified with even more policy initiatives being added to the work of the EU, but the fundamental links between institutions remain the same.

European Council) co-decides with the European Parliament and, after due process, proposals are translated into law by the national parliaments. Other bodies are also consulted: the Committee of Regions (COR) and the Economic and Social Committee (ESC). Disputes are handled by the European Court of Justice.

The decision-making process is similar to national parliamentary processes: green and white papers; proposals leading on to different readings; and then final acceptance. The 'European' policy ordnances – directives, regulations, recommendations and decisions – are translated back into the national parliamentary systems and then adopted, controlled, implemented and policed by the nation states.

Disputes between corporations (e.g. Microsoft vs EU recently), interested parties, and even states can be handled by the European Court of Justice. Increasingly this EU institution is an important arbiter of the media, although the national provision is still tightly held by nation states, each fearful of losing control of media. The reasons for this fear are several: political control, institutional and organisational self-interest, control of markets and even creativity, elite interests, worries over 'political discourse' and plurality being some.

In many respects then, the EU is caught in a conundrum between on the one side, government acceptance of the 'realpolitik' of modern trade which demands cooperation and even integration at a

Source 1.4

Policy trails

When researching media policy, often the sources will be found in different policy initiatives. This is linked to what are known as 'policy trails'. The diagram below indicates how policies often inter-relate. It is sometimes very useful for us to create our own policy trail for our particular research topic.

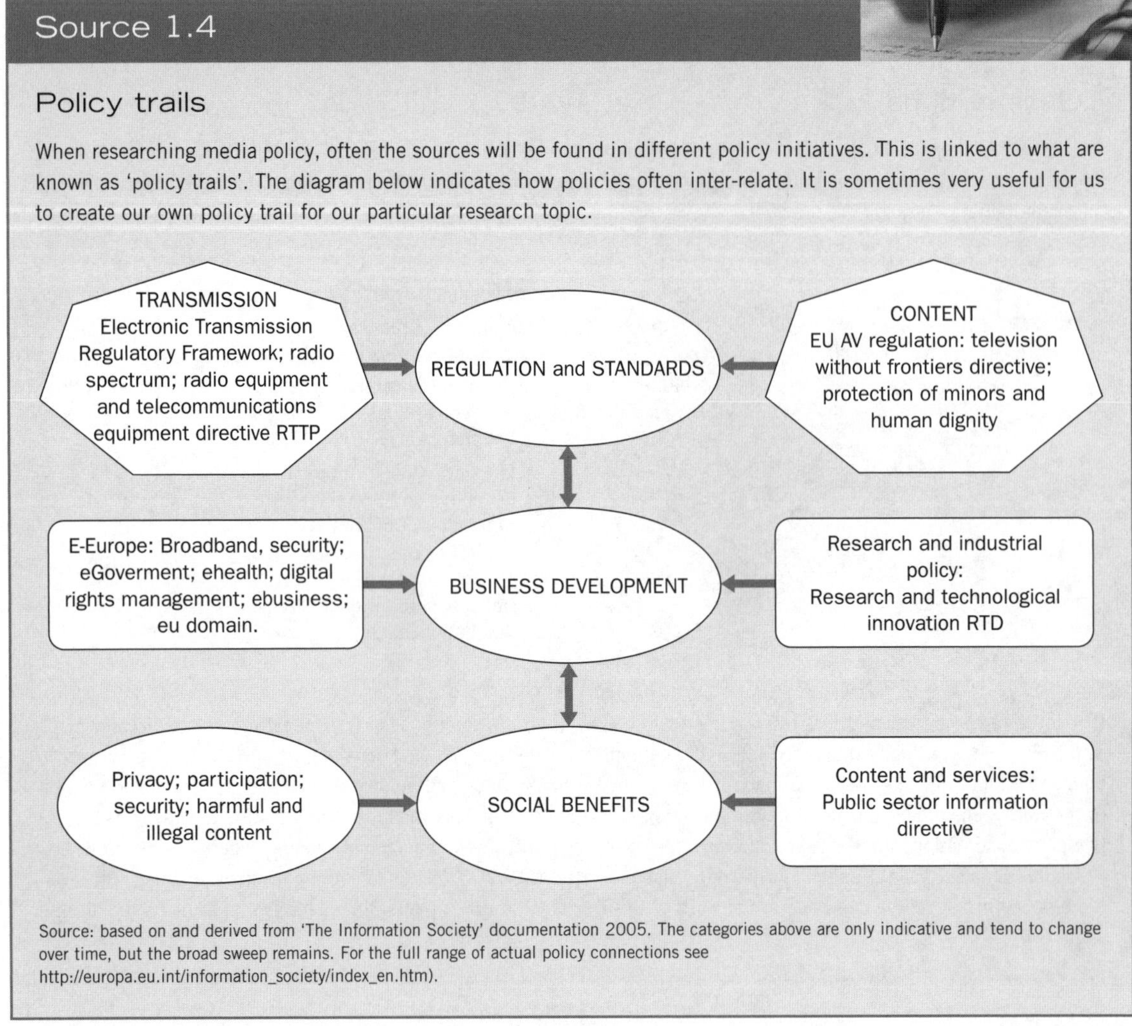

Source: based on and derived from 'The Information Society' documentation 2005. The categories above are only indicative and tend to change over time, but the broad sweep remains. For the full range of actual policy connections see http://europa.eu.int/information_society/index_en.htm).

trans-national level and, on the other side, governments and their political elites fearful of change within their nations and their communities. They argue that nation states have historical roots and deep-seated interests that should not be tampered with: their view is that the media should be national. They face a difficult task in a world where media corporations have been so keen, and now find it increasingly necessary, to distribute their products globally.

In broader terms, the EU attempts to link its proposals into policy trails, interconnected into an over-arching set of categories. These are interesting portals for research and an example is given in Source 1.4.

The structure of the EU

In line with greater integration, the structure of the EU has altered over the years, but at its core beliefs have remained founded on:

- the importance of public law (and legal processes) and the handling of disputes;
- the need for the codification of behaviour by rules and regulation;
- the creation of formal institutions which balance power between member states.

The purpose of the EU (and even its name) has changed over the decades. The early period saw a focus on post-war concerns, not least the reconstruction of a devastated Europe both in political and economic terms. This was primarily pushed forward by the creation of the European Economic Community **(EEC)** concentrating on two areas of economic formation: common policies on iron/steel/coal and then a focus on agriculture (1951–1986). Today, still, the agricultural sector absorbs over 40% of the EU's dedicated budget.

By the mid-1980s, however, the states of the EEC realised that they needed to adopt more common economic policies in a changing and competitive global market. They perceived threats to their own economic growth. This led toward the present 'process-developing' directives known as the Single European Market. This was adopted during the period 1985–1993. The creation of a single market is not an end in itself but is rather an impetus for change. It continues today and includes media and audio-visual policy/products as a part of its remit.

The Single European Market from 1985–1993 onwards together with and the Television without Frontiers Directive of 1989 (amended in 1997), plus the later Telecommunications Directive(s) and the Audio-visual Media Services Directive of 2007 (EU 1989a, 1997a, 2007a) is the foundation for much media policy. It has been absorbed into mainstream national provision, especially in audio-visual terms (film, TV, radio channels and spectrum availability, and e-products) although, as will be seen in Chapter 6, media policy is also beginning to touch upon the press and print industry.

Until 2003 the EU never targeted its policy-making directly at print and newspapers but worked upon these indirectly as a part of the continuing changes to competition law and the restructuring of the market. The purpose was to make markets more efficient and effective and, most importantly, work where necessary on a larger 'scale' while avoiding monopolies. This touched media ownership and cross-media provision. Principles such as the rights of reply became a part of European 'rights'. Changing the rules of trade meant building in 'economics' where comparative and competitive advantage (see Chapter 3) link with economies of scale for the mutual benefit of all: producers and consumers. The print sector was private in the main and was duly affected by such changes.

More important, politically, has been the debate on the maintenance of plurality and democracy in which the role of media is seen as crucial: healthy political societies, it is argued, need varieties of political views for two reasons: (i) to underline minority and national rights; and (ii) to ensure the balance of powers (and debates) that stand against authoritarianism – either of the left or the right.

However, it is important to note that from the early days of the EEC/EU, media and communication products, even education and culture, which are linked even if tentatively to media provision, were not a primary focus. It was argued that 'Europe', that is the European Community or now the member states, should have been aware much earlier of their cultural potential to work together in media and broadcasting terms. However, media provision does not necessarily derive from pure philosophy or an obvious economic rationale but the historical and ideological contexts in which it operates.

The after-effects of the Second World War still rumble on today, not only in the legislative framework of the nation states but also within the processes allied to the development of the EU. This is borne out by a close inspection especially of the press provision in each state where history has marked its scars upon the media landscape. Less so, but still dramatically, this can be seen in Public Service Broadcasting (PSB) systems across Europe which are national in form and rooted in national histories. Even so, some believe that perhaps we are now on the edge of a new European 'age': time will tell.

Other direct and indirect pressures on the EU media

There are indirect pressures upon the media, mostly imposed by the rules of the market, which govern ownership of single and cross-media, competition policies and the whole question of public sector provision and competitive private interests in the market. Much of what the media industry does fits with a wider economic framework. The media cannot escape the general economic culture of its time. If the economy goes global then the media will inevitably follow. It has been pointed out by many that economic pressures are gaining in influence and that politicians are increasingly powerless in a world dominated by trans-national corporations (TNCs) with the power to withdraw jobs and withhold taxes. Equally the media can go global, reaching beyond the national audience it might have previously normally serviced.

The media's ideological power, too, is said to be increasing in the meantime. The technology needed to make the media work is increasingly all-pervasive, some would say intrusive, in people's lives and there is a temptation to see the media as a 'power' unto itself. Some commentators argue vociferously that this is the case. In modern politics, for example, the importance of the media is often described in terms of the 'politics of spin' or media effects upon public opinion.

In past times, Greek philosophy highlighted the importance of 'rhetoric'; the ability to be convinced by an argument or a point of view. So these arguments are not new. What is generally accepted is that the media sets agendas, 'spins' the information into popular palatable messages for the benefit of its readers or viewers, politicians, political parties, interest groups or vested interests, or even for purely economic or social profit. Ownership matters too: who, and what policies and what horizontal or vertical structures the corporations may include are all in the hands of the owners and influenced by the pressures upon them to succeed.

Political interests are most important in media provision. It would be naive to think that the media in general, or the press or the news in particular, are without bias. This has been an area of enquiry which has occupied media analysts and academics for many decades.

Stop and consider 1.5

In the chicken and egg dilemma which is most powerful: the politics or the media? The legislators or the owners? It could be argued that it is the politics and the legislators because it is through the politics of a society that the media may be regulated, controlled and licensed. What are the counter arguments?

Most societies and their communities work through not only fixed, although sometime flexible, territories but also political organisations. Not only are they important in cultural, social and moral terms but, more pointedly, they work through creating regulation and law. Media organisations for convenience are often described legally as public or private and regulated as such; be that directly through media legislation or indirectly through other legal processes such as competition law for companies. There are ethical concerns established for public and private broadcasting, for civic society and for consumer rights. There are even ethical concerns relating to the individual such as libel, slander or privacy.

Exploring the political influences on the media, and taking Europe as an example, is not as easy as it may at first appear. The media varies in different settings. The influence of the media appears to be the same because of its obviously similar technological presence. Wherever you look you see the television set, plasma screen or HDTV, in almost every room in every house in every part of every country. So it appears the media is applied similarly everywhere. What is perceived in reality though is interpreted differently because of context and content, audience perceptions and even social assumptions. Market analysts and trans-national editors must take this into consideration at all times.

By its very nature, the media is manipulated by human activity, and therefore by the diverse nature of people and their societies and not least their politics. There is a continuous debate about the extent and influence that politics has on the media, and how much, conversely, the media changes the political 'discourse'. This debate goes to the heart of both the philosophical and theoretical considerations about the media in general and even its genre in practice.

Chapter summary

➤ The media operates not within a sectoral vacuum but in a definable political, social and economic framework. In Europe the framework is complicated and is working at many levels. To understand the media in Europe is to be aware of its production, distribution and consumption in terms not only of its genre, but also at local, regional, national, EU (European) and international levels.

➤ The political, social and economic framework in which the media operates is also subject to much debate and there are many models trying to explain its influence and impact. The contemporary student, researcher and media practioner need to have a background understanding of some of the models which are being used, such as globalisation, localisation, Europeanisation and even 'glocalisation'.

➤ Media can be seen as both a communication process and a product. Many academic disciplines may be used to investigate its power. Among these, the political and therefore regulatory world that surrounds it has to be understood as much as its cultural content.

➤ To understand how decisions are made at a political, policy level helps us to engage, individually, collectively and corporately, in the development of the media in a new era.

Key terms

The study of the media inevitably it seems leads to the creation of what is sometimes called 'jargon', but the words are more than this. They are useful key words often used as shorthand for the concept that lies behind them. The 'key terms' gives us a clearer definition of the meaning behind the word or words used in the text.

EEC: European Economic Community. The EU has gone through various stages of development. The acronym EEC, and sometimes EC (European Community), has been the most used until the Maastricht Treaty in 1993. The new Lisbon Treaty removes the use of the various definitions and coalesces the 'union' into one term for the future: the EU.

EU: a trans-national international organisation comprising a subset of European countries (member states) who agree on common policies, including areas such as television and audio-visual products.

Europe: a geographical space.

Note: these two terms are often used together. When reviewing statistical information it is good to check if the sample has mixed together those who belong to the EU and those who do not. There may be relative differences which need exploring.

Lisbon Treaty (2007–2009): linked to integrative development of the Single European Market and the Maastricht Treaty and other amending treaties (Amsterdam 1997 and Nice 2003) the present proposals to change procedures and policy developments in the EU are embraced by the new 'Lisbon Treaty'.

Discussion questions

1. To what extent should the media be regulated, and by whom? Should it be national providers or trans-national bodies such as the EU? Or should we reduce the level of regulation and allow ultimate consumer sovereignty to have freer rein? The arguments on all sides are profound.
2. Are we living through a period that might be called a new 'paradigm' of media provision? There is every indication that we are. What, for example, is the role of public broadcasting? How should it be funded? What should its future remit be? Certainly, European countries disagree on the way forward.

Assignments

1. Go to the following institutional web sites or library services and discover their attitudes and policies on media and then try to compare and find their definitions of the media: WTO, EU and member states inside the EU. For the latter you can use the excellent resources provided by the 'toolbox' of the European Journalists Centre, based in Maastricht.

2. Bearing in mind all the media in all its variety, list those media which are best suited for the following categories: 'global', 'European', 'national', 'regional', 'local' and 'glocal'.

Further reading

There are many dedicated journals that target research in the field. One of the best and most well known in the field of European integration and with a high reputation in the UK is:

- *Journal of Common Market Studies*, Blackwell Publishing.
- Also see *Journal of European Public Policy*, Taylor & Francis; *European Journal of Communication* and *Media, Culture and Society*, both Sage Publications.

As a start the following books are highly recommended:

Bondebjerg I., Golding P. (2004) *European Culture and the Media*, Bristol: Intellect.

Bulmer S., Dolowitz D., Humphreys P., Padgett S. (2007) *Policy Transfer in European Union Governance: Regulating the Utilities*, London and New York: Routledge.

Collins R. (2002) *Media and Identity in Contemporary Europe: Consequences of Global Convergence*, Bristol: Intellect.

D'Haenens L., Saeys F. (eds) (2001) *Western Broadcasting at the Dawn of the 21st Century*, Berlin: Mouton de Gruyter.

D'Haenens L., Saeys F. (eds) (2007) *Western Broadcasting Models: Structure, Conduct and Performance*, Berlin: Mouton de Gruyter.

Dinan D. (2005) *Ever Closer Union*, 3rd edn, Basingstoke: Palgrave Macmillan.

Hallin D., Mancini P. (2004) *Comparing Media Systems: Three Models of Media and Politics*, Cambridge: Cambridge University Press.

Harcourt A. (2005) *The European Union and the Regulation of Media Markets*, Manchester and New York: Manchester University Press.

Humphreys P. (1996) *Mass Media and Media Policy in Western Europe*, Manchester and New York: Manchester University Press.

Humphreys P., Simpson S. (2005) *Globalization, Convergence and European Telecommunications Regulation*, London: Edward Elgar.

Kelly M., Mazzoleni G., McQuail D. (eds) (2003) *The Media in Europe: The Euromedia Handbook*, London: Sage.

Levy D. (1999) *Europe's Digital Revolution: Broadcasting Regulation, the EU and the Nation State*, London and New York: Routledge.

Magnette P. (2005) *What is the European Union*, Basingstoke: Palgrave Macmillan.

McCormick J. (2005) *Understanding the European Union*, 3rd edn, Basingstoke: Palgrave Macmillan.

McQuail D., Golding P., Bens E. (2005) *Communication: Theory and Research: an EJC Anthology*, London: Sage.

Michalis M. (2007) *Governing European Communications: From Unification to Coordination*, Plymouth Lexington Books.

Nugent N. (2006) *The Government and Politics of the European Union*, 6th edn, Basingstoke: Palgrave Macmillan.

Sarikakis K. (2004) *Powers in the Media Policy: The challenge of the European Parliament*, Bern: Peter Lang.

Weymouth A., Lamizet B. (1996) *Markets and Myths: Forces for Change in the Media of Western Europe*, London and New York: Longman.

Online resources

http://www...

Our online resources are seemingly immense. The following is only an indication of major, important online organisations:

- *Datamonitor (Market Business Line)* www.datamonitor.com
- *DG Information Society* http://europa.eu/index_en.htm
- *European Audiovisual Observatory (EAO)* www.obs.coe.int
- *European Communication Research and Education Association (ECREA)* www.ecrea.eu
- *European Institute for the Media (EIM)* www.eim.org
- *European Journalism Centre (EJC)* www.ejc.net
- *Eurostat* http://ec.europa.eu/eurostat/
- *Hans-Bredow-Institute* www.hans-bredow-institut.de

- *UNESCO* www.unesco.org
- *United Nations Institute of Statistics* www.uis.unesco.org
- *World Association of Newspapers (WAN)* www.wan-press.org

Locate also the many national agencies available for statistics and reports on the publishing and audio-visual industries across the EU, e.g. *Ofcom* or *OFT* in the UK. The European Journalism Centre is a good start for this quest.

References

Angel I. (2001) *New Barbarian Manifesto*, London: Kogan Page.

EC (2002) *Fourth report from the Commission to the Council, the European Parliament, the European Economic and Social Committee and the Committee of the Regions on the application of Directive 89/552/EEC 'Television without Frontiers'*, COM(2002)778 final, Brussels, 6.1.2002.

EC (2005) Commission staff working paper. *Strengthening the Competitiveness of the EU Publishing Sector. The role of media policy*, Luxembourg: European Commission.

EU (1987) Single European Act, *OJ*, **L169**, 29.06.1987, 1–29.

EU (1989a) Council Directive 89/552/EEC of 3 October 1989 on the coordination of certain provisions laid down by Law, Regulation or Administrative Action in Member States concerning the pursuit of television broadcasting activities, *OJ*, **L298**, 17.10.1989, 23–30.

EU (1989b) Council decision 89/337/EEC of 27 April 1989 on high-definition television, *OJ*, **L142**, 25.05.1989, 1–2.

EU (1992) Treaty on European Union (Treaty on Maastricht), *OJ*, **C191**, 29.07.1992, 1–110.

EU (1997a) Directive 97/36/EC of the European Parliament and of the Council 30 June 1997 amending Council Directive 89/552/EEC on the coordination of certain provisions laid down by Law, Regulation or Administrative Action in Member States concerning the pursuit of television broadcasting activities, *OJ*, **L202**, 30.7.1997, 60–70.

EU (1997b) *Green Paper on the convergence of the telecommunications, media and information technology sectors, and the implications for regulation – towards an information society approach*, COM(1997)623 final, Luxembourg: European Commission.

EU (1997c) Treaty of Amsterdam, *OJ*, **C340**, 10.11.1997, 145–172.

EU (2000) Regulation (EC) No 2887/2000 of the European Parliament and of the Council of 18 December 2000 on unbundled access to the local loop, *OJ*, **L336**, 30.12.2000, 4–8.

EU (2001) Council Resolution of 12 February 2001 on national aid to the film and audio-visual industries, *OJ*, **C73**, 6.03.2001, 3–4.

EU (2002a) Directive 2002/21/EC of the European Parliament and of the Council of 7 March 2002 on a common regulatory framework for electronic communications networks and services, *OJ*, **L108**, 24.04.2002, 33–50.

EU (2002b) Directive 2002/20/EC of the European Parliament and of the Council of 7 March 2002 on the authorisation of electronic communications networks and services, *OJ*, **L108**, 24.04.2002, 21–32.

EU (2002c) Directive 2002/19/EC of the European Parliament and of the Council of 7 March 2002 on access to, and interconnection of, electronic communications networks and associated facilities, *OJ*, **L108**, 24.04.2002, 7–20.

EU (2002d) Directive 2002/22/EC of the European Parliament and of the Council of 7 March 2002 on universal service and users' rights relating to electronic communications networks and services, *OJ*, **L108**, 24.04.2002, 51–77.

EU (2002e) Directive 2002/58/EC of the European Parliament and of the Council of 12 July 2002 concerning the processing of personal data and the protection of privacy in the electronic communications sector, *OJ*, **L201**, 31.07.2002, 37–47.

EU (2002f) Commission Decision 2002/676/EC on a regulatory framework for radio spectrum policy *OJ*, **L108**, 24.04.2002, 1–6.

EU (2007a) Directive 2007/65/EEC of the European Parliament and of the Council of 11 December 2007 amending Council Directive 89/552/EEC of 3 October 1989 on the coordination of certain provisions laid down by Law, Regulation or Administrative Action in Member States concerning the pursuit of television broadcasting activities, *OJ*, **L332**, 18.12.2007, 27–45.

EU (2007b) The Lisbon Treaty, *OJ*, **C306**, 17.12.2007, 1–271.

McLuhan M. (1967) *The Medium is the Massage: An Inventory of Effects with Quentin Fiore*, produced by Jerome Agel, 1st edn Random House, reissued by Gingko Press, Corte Madera, CA (2001).

Robertson R. (1994) Globalisation or glocalisation, *Journal of International Communication*, **1**(1): 33–52.

Appendix

As an introduction to the EU see a variety of data given in Table 1.2 indicating:

- proportional wealth (GDP per capita);
- size of population, and hence audience reach;
- the primary languages used in the territory;
- the degree of social cohesion and migration, as an indicator of potential variations in audience;
- the degree of higher education spend as marker for a country's sophistication and potential creativity;
- the growing availability of Internet access (and the official figures are accelerating fast);
- the broadcasting and structural network: this allows us to see the development, complexity and size and geography of both analogue and digital networks.

The European Union (2008)

Table 1.2 Broad EU figures

	GDP per capita (2002 US$)	*Population (000s) (2003)*	*Languages major/minor*	*Immigrant population – % pop. migration (foreign born/foreign nationals) (2002)*	*Tertiary education US$ per student (2001)*	*Household access to Internet % (2002/3) (Cf figures in Chapter 11)*	*TV broadcast stations – the network*
EU 15	26 019	381 155	20 official languages (2005)	–/–			
Austria	28 872	8 067	German	–/8.8	11 274	46.0	10 (2001)
Belgium	27 716	10 372	Flemish, French	–/8.2	11 589	28.0 (2001/2)	25 (1997)
Cyprus	South 21 600 (2005 est.) North: 7 135 (2004 est.)	807	Greek/Turkish				South 4 North 4
Czech Republic	15 102	10 202	Czech	–/2.3	5 555	16.4 (2001/2)	150 (2000)
Denmark	29 231	5 387	Danish	6.2/4.9	14 280	59.0	26 (1998)
Estonia	16 400 (2005 est.)	1 300	Estonian	–/–			3 (2001)
Finland	26 495	5 213	Finnish	2.9/20	10 981	44.3	120 (1999)
France	27 217	59 768	French	–/–	8 837	28.0	584 (1995)
Germany	25 917	82 502	German	–/8.9	10 504	43.3	373 (1995)
Greece	18 439	11 036	Greek	–/7 (2001)	4 280		36 (1995)
Hungary	13 894	10 124	Hungarian	–/1.1	7 122		35 (1995)
Ireland	32 646	3 953	Irish Gaelic, English	–/4.8	10 003	33.6	4 (2001)
Italy	25 568	57 478	Italian	–/2.6	8 347	18.8 (2000/1)	358 (1995)
Latvia	12 800 (2005 est.)	2 300	Latvian				44 (1995)
Lithuania	13 700 (2005 est.)	3 400	Lithuanian				27 (2001)
Luxembourg	49 150	452	Luxembourgeoise	–/38.1			5 (1999)
Malta	18 800 (2005 est.)	397	Maltese				6 (2000)
Poland	10 846	38 195	Polish	–/0.1	3 579		179 (1995)
Portugal	18 434	10 449	Portuguese	–/4.0	5 199	21.7	62 (1995)
Slovakia	12 255	5 380	Slovakian	–/0.5	5 285		80 (2004)
Slovenia	20 900 (2005 est.)	2 000	Slovenian				48 (2001)
Spain	22 406	41 874	Spanish, Catalan, Basque	–/3.1	7 455		224 (1995)
Sweden	27 209	8 958	Swedish	11.8/5.3	15 188	53.3	169 (1995)
The Netherlands	29 009	16 224	Dutch	10.9/4.3	12 974	41.0 (2000/01)	21 (1995)
The United Kingdom	27 948	59 422	English, Scottish Gaelic and Welsh Celt	–/4.5	10 753	48.0	228 (1995)
New and Candidate Countries							
Bulgaria	9 000 (2005 est.)	7 800	Bulgarian	–/–			39 (2001)
Croatia	11 600 (2005 est.)	4 400	Croat	–/–			36 (1995)
Romania	8 300 (2005 est.)	22 200	Romanian	–/–			48 (1995)
Turkey	6 408	70 712	Turkish, Kurd	–/–		6.9 (2000/1)	635 (1995)

Sources: *CIA World Factbook* (https://www.cia.gov/library/publications/the-world-factbook/); BBC's Country Profiles (http://news.bbc.co.uk/1/hi/country_profiles/default.stm) which are based on data from the World Bank/UN, OECD, Europa.

Chapter 2

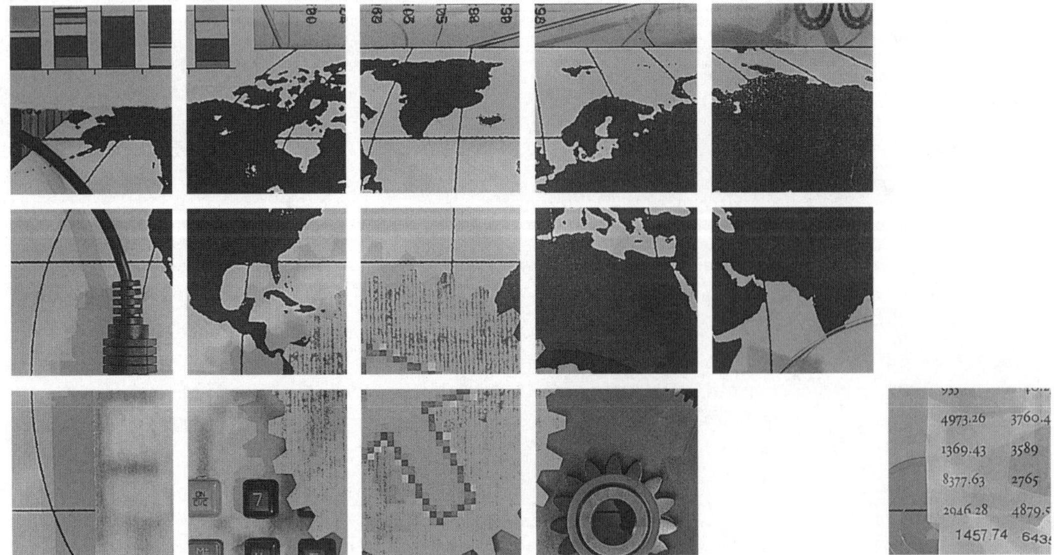

Understanding EU media through data – statistics

What the chapter covers

Introduction: the media and data

Sources

- *Classifying and gathering*

Statistics

- *Data*
- *Probability*
- *Statistical inferences*
- *P value, or 'the observed level of significance'*
- *Data description*

Preliminary investigation: are newspapers and print products in decline in the EU?

The context and the data questions: using qualitative methods

- *Politics*
- *Economics*
- *Social or societal factors*
- *Culture*
- *History*

Linear and non-linear ways of looking at data

Learning objectives

When you have completed this chapter you will be able to:

- Appreciate key statistical concepts that can be used in the assessment of the European media market.
- Outline and illustrate the debates surrounding market definitions in both global and European terms.
- Identify some of the keywords used by statisticians and the useful concepts they illustrate.
- Link statistical inferences to market analysis.

Themes

Below you will find a simple statement or series of statements around the six themes. They should *not* be read as a given fact. They are more like hypotheses which need to be proved, discussed, debated and then used in your own analysis of the subject. The ideas and approaches in this book are always to be considered with an open mind, this is important in university study and is what makes it distinct from pre-university study.

Diversity of media

Often it is only through strong statistical evidence that we can begin to understand the diversity of the media across the EU. Table 1.2 at the end of Chapter 1 shows us the degree of convergence and diversity in the EU member states in relation to size of populations, wealth (GDP), educational attainment and so on. All this data is important in measuring societies and their engagement with the media.

Internal/external forces for change

Measuring societies through data collection is an important aspect of statistical work, but so too are comparisons. As we shall see in Chapter 3 on economics, the data is often really valuable in comparative work, especially when we are beginning to review markets, media penetration and changes in consumer behaviour. At the same time, we need to know how debate and interpretation of statistics are used, and this is a very important part of our critical understanding. On the surface the data may seem to be reasonably clear, but underneath lie real dilemmas that are both interesting and in need of investigation.

Complexity of the media

In the major debates occurring across the EU about the role of the market in media provision, measuring activity gives us an indication of the media trends. This is where the complexity of the media can often be found. In newspaper publication, for example, private provision is normal, but there are many exceptions where some newspapers receive state subsidy (France and Luxembourg amongst others). In the broad sweep of analysis, is this relevant? Being so small a percentage of activity it is probably not statistically important for the EU overall, whereas the fact that newspapers are overwhelmingly controlled by the private sector is significant. However, this is not the case for public sector broadcasting, especially television in Europe which comes out of a public sector history. Herein lies a real quandary over the future of public broadcasting and its impact upon society. This has traditionally been measured by audience ratings. Assessing the impact of the media from both public and private sectors demands a careful balance of quantitative and qualitative views and this is where statistics can be an essential tool.

Multi-levels

The extent to which the media is seen to be developed nationally, trans-nationally and even globally often comes down to a judgement on percentages. The over-riding presence in the market of US audio-visual production, estimated at about 70% (see Chapter 11), is an important piece of evidence for policy-makers let alone advertisers. Measuring this aspect of the media again is a statistical need.

European integrative environment

The degree to which the EU member states' media has been integrated can be qualitatively judged but also, crucially, quantitatively measured. In all the heated debates about EU governance and the media, the data is very useful and is often a revelation in terms of European integration. We can measure, if we define properly, the amount of EU film-making, for example, and its reception by European consumers. We can judge where mobile use is being changed by EU policy-making on price per call by looking at correlations. Correlations can be used in many ways: minutes used by month of data collection linked to post-policy change or phone company implementation.

Cultural values

Measuring cultural values may seem difficult. However, with differences in language and consumer behaviour across the EU, these are also important elements that we need to reflect upon when using statistical arguments in addition to the standard qualitative literature-review based interpretations.

Essentials

➤ Media policy and media business decisions rely upon collecting and interpreting data. Misinterpretation and poor-quality judgement can spell make or break for a media product. From producers to consumers, we rely on data to decide what to listen to, what to read and what to watch and see. Equally making EU policy judgements and then interpreting them and translating the measures into the national context, all need some level of measurement and data analysis.

➤ Although this chapter is not designed to make us statisticians, data is increasingly used by the media analyst and the media practitioner. It is useful to have some critical background to the subject when we are judging trends, particularly when doing comparative work across the EU. This is the purpose of this chapter.

Introduction: the media and data

The media, both as an industry and as the principal conduit of opinion and information in society, relies on data for policy decisions and investment. So, in any modern society, or in the EU which is a collective group of societies, the media is often assessed statistically. Nowadays, we almost take this for granted, and it is an integral part of our political, democratic and economic lives. Moreover, in a mixed economy such as the European environment, the media functions like any other industry, thriving on competition and on audience and consumer reaction. Business data becomes, therefore, not only an important aspect of investment decisions but an essential part of the media analyst's world.

Good, up-to-date and accurate media analysis is often expensive. The 'information society' and 'information economics' are increasingly important in media circles, and in general our modern economies thrive on data (see Case Study 2.1). Modern economies function and profit from their use of information. Some would say that the media and service industries are often the keenest, most value-enhancing parts of modern economies. Therefore, the trend is toward more information-enhancing economics not less. Why? Because the media sector is likely to provide substantial profits as successful companies enter larger markets such as the EU single market, expand into global markets and develop a strategy towards the Europeanisation of media products within the EU.

So, gathering accurate and reliable data can often mean the difference between success and failure. Information and data are so important that often in the private sector and, interestingly, also in the public sector you will find access restricted as some data is 'confidential' or exclusive for commercial use. Nonetheless, there are available sources of high-grade information.

Why is this all so important? Advertisers need data to see whether their product is popular and whether it has been worth the investment. Consumers want to know what they can afford and whether they are receiving value for money. Politicians, policy-makers and local and national governments will want to know how their message is being received and whether or not it is considered to be truthful and relevant. Producers and broadcasters want to know when and how many people are watching, listening or reading. They need to gauge trends in the entertainment world so that they can invest in resources and new ideas. Launching a new product often comes down to data judgements: the 'number crunching'. In today's cut-throat business environment, data research and analysis is at a premium. Business competition dictates that companies keenly reflect on data analysis (see Case Study 2.2).

Sources

As with much information gathering, in present-day society there will never be one single source but rather a range of sources available to us. The real work comes in drawing the raw data together from the variety of sources in order to interpret what is

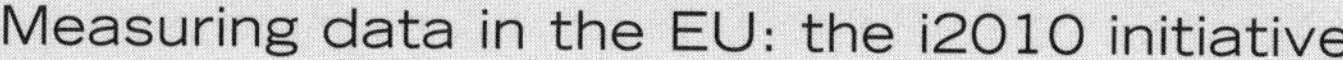

Case Study 2.1

Measuring data in the EU: the i2010 initiative

The EU is encouraging its member states to improve the engagement of their companies and citizens with the new communication networks that will dominate the competitive market and even public information networks in the 21st century. It has three main aims:

- Completion of the 'Single European Information Space' (theme 1)
- Strengthening 'Innovation and investment' in ICT research (theme 2)
- Achieving an inclusive 'European Information Society' that prioritises better public services and quality of life (theme 3)

To measure the success of the initiative, indicators have been drawn up to assess the impact of changed policy-making in each theme by gathering data. As an example, Theme 1 includes data on:

- Broadband coverage
  - % of population engaged with digital subscriber line (DSL) or upgraded cable
- Broadband take-up
  - Analysis of type of take-up depending on platform – cable, DSL, fibre, 3G, wireless connections
  - % of households with broadband access
  - % of households having access to Internet
  - % of enterprises with broadband access
- Speed and prices
  - Subscription numbers broken down by speed and cost including installation costs and monthly charges
- Multi-platform of access to the Internet
  - % of households with access to the Internet broken down by device: via packet video (PV), digital TV and mobile device.

Note how detailed the data is and how it relates to political and economic objectives. The drawing together of such data from the questionnaires has been framed in such a way as to relate to the question of how much take-up there has been of the new IT across Europe.

Source: *i2010 Benchmarking Framework* (i2010 High Level Group, 2006). See also http://ec.europa.eu/information_society/eeurope/i2010/benchmarking/index_en.htm.

Case Study 2.2

BT, BT Vision and soccer; France Telecom and on-demand services

This case study shows how important it is for companies to measure, forecast and assess the return on their investment. With much of the new IT, the investment is often large.

Sport is a high value, highly rated, TV content product, exploited by public and private service broadcasters around the world. Competition is keen for television rights, and the revenues associated with advertising and the profits from subscriptions are high. BT Vision, a part of BT plc, recently announced a 'top-up broadband service' for British soccer. The competition from the prime market share company, Sky, as a company, is tough, as it holds control of many of the premier games. BT Vision entered the market with lower subscription fees (10% of its competitors' packages in some cases) on the basis of a calculation of data and a new financial model on the back of the broadband new technology distribution system. Market research showed that up to 12 million homes were without pay-TV in the UK. There was a calculation that BT needed to take up a market share across the telecommunications network and break into other markets in other countries. Many of these homes, it was calculated, were unwilling to pay high subscription rates. It was a gamble, a financial risk in a very competitive market: the data appeared to indicate the risk was worth taking.

Source: BT gambles on broadband TV, *FT.com* (Parker, 2007).

France Telecom is also widening its broadband television-on-demand video content provision for its existing customers, off-setting its fixed line telephone revenue loss, with a resulting substantial rise in net profit to €3.3 bn (a 41% rise) for the first six months of 2007. In June, 2007, the group had 837 000 French subscribers rising from 577 000 from the end of 2006. Its telecom sales rose 2% to €25.9 bn. Data matters!

Source: France Telecom tunes into internet television, *FT.com* (Jones, 2007).

happening. Some of the most sensitive and detailed sources are held by specialist consultancies and private sector agencies whose job it is to collate and to provide for the media industry. There are also official sources, often located in government agencies. At the same time, there are many ways of gathering data.

Because the EU is a trans-national and a global institution, we need to explore the EU media with a range of sources in mind: international, EU-based, national and regional. The boundaries that are used to collate the information will be at times difficult to follow and not always easily compared, but it is worth persevering. Once understood, the relationships between different data can be significant and even ground-breaking.

Stop and consider 2.1

Is it that easy to collate information and data across frontiers? The simple answer is no. Often the data is defined differently, perhaps even not measured in the same way. Is it still useful to look at the data when it is perhaps only an approximation? If you were a public or a private broadcaster what would you think? Before answering this question it would be useful to look at some of the cross-frontier data that has been used by various reputable organisations – see Table 2.1.

When the world's two largest trading blocs, the EU and the USA, meet to negotiate a level playing field for their rival media, for example at the **WTO** (World Trade Organisation), arguments often emerge because the data is constructed differently. The stakes could be high in trade terms and consequently these arguments are fierce.

In other negotiations, even between EU member states, there may be a need to compare different national statistics to assess, for example, the effectiveness of state subsidies to public service broadcasters (PSBs). The ways in which PSBs are funded are very different in the EU member states. For example, BBC TV national broadcasting is known for its lack of advertising. This does not apply to its satellite service, BBC World, and across the EU most public broadcasters use advertising revenue as a part of their financial model.

It is interesting that the BBC financial model, free of advertisements, has not been taken up across most EU countries. France has recently stated (2008) that the time was right to do this, with President Sarkozy indicating that he would like to see a public broadcasting channel in France with no advertisements. There are many interpretations of why he appears to have launched such an initiative. Going to the

Table 2.1 Data gathering

Examples of data: quantitative and qualitative	*Source*	*Comment*
International	**OECD**	Excellent global statistics covering full range of economic activity.
EU and Europe-wide	Eurostat	The official source for EU data.
	Audio-Visual Observatory	Research publications.
	European Institute for the Media	Classifies itself as a 'think tank'.
National	Across the EU there a whole range of 'national' resources for media data: e.g.	
	OFCOM	UK regulator.
	Business Line (Datamonitor) and Mintel.	Examples of up-to-date business data companies.
Regional	See European Journalism Centre (EJC) in Maastricht	An invaluable source for comparing European media data and exploring national and regional sources of information. Relates to the European Institute of Media in the relevant sections.

sources and exploring the various issues is therefore important.

Classifying and gathering

Using and developing a bibliography of data-based sources is very important, and it depends of course upon the sector you are investigating. In the EU, to classify and gather means finding essential sources from both the national and the EU levels.

Moreover, the media is made up of various products that have been classified differently in the recent past. Film data can be different from television data (in terms of 'ratings' for example) which is different in turn from magazine readership and newspaper circulation figures. The modern age is also entering a digital age of 'convergence' which is blurring the distinctions between the media, making data collection more complex. For example, a film product is nowadays digitally constructed and used on 'TV' plasma screens, in multiplex digitally run cinema theatres or DVDs (even high-definition such as Sony's blu-ray technology) in specialised players or on laptops. Even newspaper web sites use the digital age to illustrate film trailers, boost their presence in the market, increase advertising revenue and, nowadays, even enter into TV-casting direct news-type programmes with short news items or stories direct to the public on screen.

Gathering accurate statistics is an essential tool of the EU, not just for media but for a whole range of data on society: economic, social or even political. It is so important that in order to join the EU, accession countries need to show that they are able to draw up accurate data on their society; for example, household spend on newspapers or broadband usage. This is a vital resource for the media industry which works in a growing European single market in goods and products, as we have seen from Chapter 1.

Statistics

So, what are statistics? Put in its simplest form, the study of statistics is the study of relationships. It could be the study of one series of data compared with another series of similar data (overall readership figures for example) or it could be one set of data compared with another set of data which may be related but different (overall readership and age of readership for example).

In the first case, we are looking at similar data. We can compare one country's readership of newspapers with another, counting the number of people who buy and read a newspaper and then comparing the data. Over time, we will be able to see whether one country's readership figures are decreasing, staying the same or rising. The reasons why this is occurring will of course depend on what has influenced the data.

In the second case, we are trying to understand if there is a relationship between data even if the data is different. We may want to compare the readership figures in a country not only through the raw figures of how many people read a newspaper, but looking also at how reading varies according to age.

In fact this is an important question. There is a general tendency for those under 25 to be less attracted to newspapers compared to the older population. Newspaper companies fear for the future as it is well-known that newspaper reading is a matter of habit and custom. If readers do not become used to reading newspapers early, they will not in the future become a regular revenue stream.

Not only does this have implications for long-term finance but it could also diminish the long-term political influence of a newspaper. This concerns newspaper owners, proprietors and shareholders, and those who work in the industry, because they need to attract advertisers and subscribers. As you will see later in Point of View 2.1 (p. 30), this has instigated a huge debate on the future of newspapers.

Stop and consider 2.2

When you are researching data and finding databases, you will find that much is made to look very 'scientific' and very clear as if the facts are the facts and no more. This can be very seductive. How do we guard against this? How do we improve our critical competence? How do we explain our doubts about the data?

The challenge with statistics is in the detail. The professional study of statistics is about trying to collate and compare accurately. By using complicated probability algorithms, statisticians judge and assess relationships. This chapter does not try to delve too deeply into the finer points of 'probability' assessment, although it is to be recommended as the investigation can be intriguing. For our purposes, a grasp of some of the basics will help in our assessment of the media market place and the other chapters in this book.

There are five introductory aspects of statistics that may be considered essential.

Data

Data comprises the raw information: the facts and the figures. Data can be both qualitative and quantitative.

- Qualitative data is any data or information which is not numerical: information gathered in interviews or related to documents or observations. Qualitative data though can be translated into quantitative material, and software such as *Nvivo* is designed among many other tasks to do this.
- Quantitative data is numerical – numbers. Software such as *Microsoft Excel*, *OpenOffice.org Calc* and *SPSS* is often used to draw together the numbers into categories and headings so that we can analyse, count and interpret the figures.

Stop and consider 2.3

How useful are numbers? For example, we can talk about the majority watching one programme rather than another, but perhaps the minority is richer, more influential and is truly the 'market' you are trying to impress! Why do TV audience figures (ratings) matter so much to public broadcasters and are they comparable to private broadcasters' interests in the figures? What are the differences in their views and why?

The data when it is collected into various categories is called the '**variables of study**', sometimes shortened to the '**variables**'. This is a way of classifying data into recognisable categories, for example one column for 'male' and one for 'female' readers.

Probability

When the data is brought together into columns and categories, **probability tests** (e.g. chance of a particular result occurring from the whole set of possible results, expressed as a proportion) are used to calculate the relationship between the data. There are strict and important rules for assessing probability, and much of the software (*Nvivo, Microsoft Excel* and *SPSS* for example) has been designed to do this work for statisticians. There are different approaches and calculations, and many ways of presenting the material.

Statistical inferences

Although the numbers and the information should be as accurately recorded as possible, when drawing conclusions from the detail, the data relationships are often developed through techniques called **estimation** and **hypothesis testing**, which are then used to make **statistical inferences**: a judgement on the relationship between the 'variables' used.

- **Estimation** refers to the technique, widely used, where samples are used to estimate what a given population might answer in its entirety if they were asked.
- **'Hypothesis testing'** is a method used to prove or not to prove the accuracy of a statement. An early tentative assumption is referred to as the **null hypothesis** (Ho), and its opposite, an **alternative hypothesis** (Ha). In most but not all cases, a 'null hypothesis' is used in a negative manner: in other words to show that there is no relationship between the categories or variables.

Stop and consider 2.4

Things are rarely black or white but usually somewhere in the middle: grey. So the saying goes. For statisticians, some relationships are truer, more inter-related, than others, but it depends what you are looking for. If you are a magazine publisher do you want to know, almost like fashion designers, where the readership's interests lie? Or are you more interested in finding the 'new' trend before your competitor? What is your priority?

P value, or 'the observed level of significance'

This is a figure used to express the validity, or significance, of a hypothesis. Assuming the 'null hypothesis' is accurate, it provides a figure (between 0 and 1) on the accuracy of the observed data we are researching. It allows the researcher to judge whether the 'significance' levels are at a level where the risk (probability) of mistakenly identifying a relationship when results that look like a relationship are really the result of chance (type 1 error) is acceptable. If the probability level is 0.05 (as is usual) the probability of this mistake occurring is up to 5 times per 100.

Data description

Data description is the term used for the way in which data and information is presented. There are many ways of depicting data using graphs and charts and the more imaginatively we inter-relate the information, exploring data pictorially, the more interesting the inferences that can be made. Most of us are used to standard x and y linear graphs, and finding the mean (the average), but the same material can be used in radar plots where the interesting visual presentation encourages us to look anew. Those used to drawing up data into *Excel* or *SPSS* will be acquainted with the many ways of displaying the same data. In *Microsoft Excel*, for example, there are standard buttons to depict columns, line charts, pie charts, area charts, doughnuts, scatter charts, stock, bubble and radar. In this book as a whole you will see some of these at work. Descriptive statistics are often classified as being 'tabular, graphical and numerical' presentations. Where there is only one variable being used this is known as **univariate methods** and where there is more than one variable, **multivariate methods**.

To this list could be added many other tools used by statisticians. But it is a good start.

No matter the accuracy of numbers there will be always interpretations and debates that surround the use of data. In the context of research methods exploring the debate is often as important as the raw material itself and, as with other more qualitative material, should always be a part of the researcher's approach to any question. This is included in what is often called the **literature review** in research work. To this we can add the **data review**: exploring the problems and difficulties of the data.

Preliminary investigation: are newspapers and print products in decline in the EU?

A reading of contemporary literature may lead one to believe that newspaper and printed products are in steep decline because of the introduction of new technology. Some people disagree. There are also contradictory signs: for example, let us turn to the data leading up to the 21st century. Household spend on published products in the 1990s appears to be up overall, but there is a suggestion that the 'spend' on newspapers may be diminishing. Point of View 2.1 shows how such arguments rage. The first source shows how variables are being used as factors to explain change. The second and third are very powerful and rely heavily on data and statistics. Who is right?

The question seems to have different answers depending on the data. When you value the print industry in terms of profit you find the figures generally are high and growing. However, the number of newspaper titles appears to be dropping. The number of mergers and takeovers in the industry appears to be up but, at the same time, commentators worry about the resurgence of what might be 'monopolies' in the EU and that a potential consequence could be a rise in prices.

This is a debate which has now come to the surface (see Point of View 2.1 again). Ultimately, of course, the answer will depend on what question you asked in the first place. The answer may concern the consumer more than the producer or vice versa. It may be more directed at the distribution network, as we have seen with the 'i2010' initiative. It is always good practice to discern from the data the question that is being posed and ask what is the purpose of the data and why it is being classified and gathered.

To explore the contemporary debate expressed in Point of View 2.1, let us set up a hypothesis from one point of view, which we can put to the test, and then validate some of the views being expressed above for the previous decade: a **null hypothesis** such as 'newspapers and printed products from a household spend are not in decline'. Using freely available data, it is possible to look at the preceding decade, starting in the 1990s, to establish trend lines. Moreover, we may start with a decade trend line with reliable statistics from a well-established source, Eurostat, for the period 1990–2000.

First, we need to know what variables might help us to answer the question. The newspaper and printing industry could be assessed using a supply-side or a demand-side evaluation. In the end, the

Point of View 2.1

How does the future look for the EU newspaper and paper industries?

Industries that involve themselves with the information society have traditionally relied on the print industry, sometimes known as the 'wood cluster': forest industry, paper-making, printing, packaging, graphic communication and publishing industries. In the heat of the new technology, some predict its downfall, but this is not how the industry sees the future (1):

> Demand for printed products is influenced by a number of demographic and economic factors such as population growth, composition of households, training and education as well as economic growth. The graphic industry, just like the publishing sector, is above all a supplier of products which disseminate information and knowledge and cater for leisure activities. Its role stems from its cultural, intellectual and educational vocation within the context of the exchange of ideas and information in democratic societies. Despite the low growth and population, the number of households and managerial jobs continues to grow as does the proportion of income available to education and information. All this continues to stimulate the demand from newspapers, magazines, periodicals and books. Consequently, the number of books printed has never been so high. New technologies have opened up new and ever growing markets, such as for computer manuals and educational material.
>
> [1] Source: European Commission, Enterprise and Industry, *Forest-based industries – printing* (EC, 2007). http://ec.europa.eu/enterprise/forest_based/printing_background_en.html.

Although the industry may point to a bright potential future within the European newspaper industry serious concerns are being expressed from highly reputable sources (2):

> For the first time for more than fifteen years . . . Le Monde diplomatic [sic] . . . which since 1990, has seen a regular increase in its circulation, and which, between 2001 and 2003, saw a record rise record in sales – higher than 25% – will undoubtedly face a test in a 2004 . . . with a drop in circulation of approximately 12%. The majority of the big national dailies of the national press show serious falls which will come to be often added to those already undergone in 2003. . . . The phenomenon is far from being just in France. The American daily newspaper International Herald Tribune, for example, saw its sales drop, in 2003, 4.16%; in the United Kingdom, Financial Times fell 6.6%; in Germany, over the five last years, circulation has dropped by 7.7%, in Denmark 9.5%, in Austria of 9.9%, Belgium 6.9%, and even in Japan, whose inhabitants are the largest purchasers of newspapers, the fall back was 2.2%. Within the European Union, during the last eight years, the number of sold daily newspapers fell by 7 million . . . On a worldwide scale, the subscription circulation of newspapers has fallen, on average, each year, by 2%. Some have come to wonder whether the newspaper industry would not be an activity of the past, a media of the industrial era, now in process of extinction.
>
> [2] Source: Final edition for the press, *Le Monde diplomatique* (Ramonet, 2005).

Not everyone agrees with this 'French position'. From the UK (3):

> Who said it was all over for newspapers? Who said the British media was in an unremitting cycle of dumbing down? The best circulation figures in the quality newspaper market since November 2002 would appear to refute both assumptions. Overall, sales in the quality market were up by 3.1% year on year. Yes, the picture is skewed by a frenzy of competition and promotional activity, but the outlook is rosy.
>
> [3] Source: The Abcs, *The Independent* (Burrell, 2005).

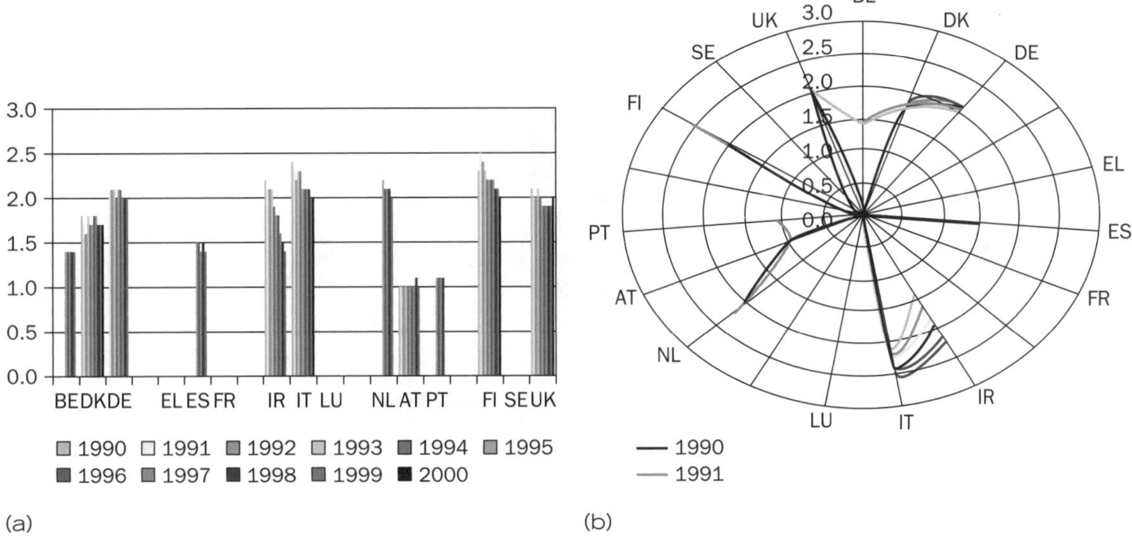

Figure 2.1 Outline % household spend on newspapers and print products EU-15, 1990–2000: (a) columns; (b) radar

Source: Eurostat.

demand-side is probably more important because it relates more closely to the consumer. One standard **variable** could be 'household spend' on these types of products. In other words, using the data on newspapers and print products we will investigate if there is a sufficient correlation in the data to validate the statement. In our case, based on our initial statement, we will investigate and see if we can prove that there is no significant relationship in the data (the Ho position) to counter the argument.

The initial set-up data for us to work on is presented in Figs 2.1a and b. We may accept the 'null hypothesis' in best statistical fashion if the data is seen to be between 95% and 99% significant and indicating that there is no decline. If this is not the case and we have 1–5% of the data pointing to a decline, we may accept the alternative hypothesis (the Ha position) that newspapers and printed products are in decline. In other words, newspapers and print products are in decline in Europe, the data proves there is a probability that something is causing change, and our variables indicate avenues of analysis that may help us to explain why.

In Figs 2.1a and b you will see an outline, in the form of a column chart and a radar chart of the same data, of the household spend on newspaper and print products in different EU countries. The sample suggests the range of percentage spend is from around 1–2.5% (1990–2000) depending on country.

We can see immediately that there are sizeable differences between countries, both in percentage terms and in trend terms. This is one of the advantages of using a simple column chart. The radar chart highlights this clearly but is more complicated than the column chart. How we depict data can be important.

Before dealing with the detail we need to see how the charts have been constructed and what they reveal and what they do not:

1. Household spend (the **data** in this case) on a media or any other product is often used in the industry and by economists. It shows almost immediately the interest and degree of confidence in a product as shown by the consumer's decision to buy it. It is also a major indicator of the buoyancy (or not) of any given economy and is often collated by governments and institutions analysing the economy.
2. By using household spend as a percentage we can make comparisons of similar household groups, within the same or between different societies. In this case it is a national comparison.

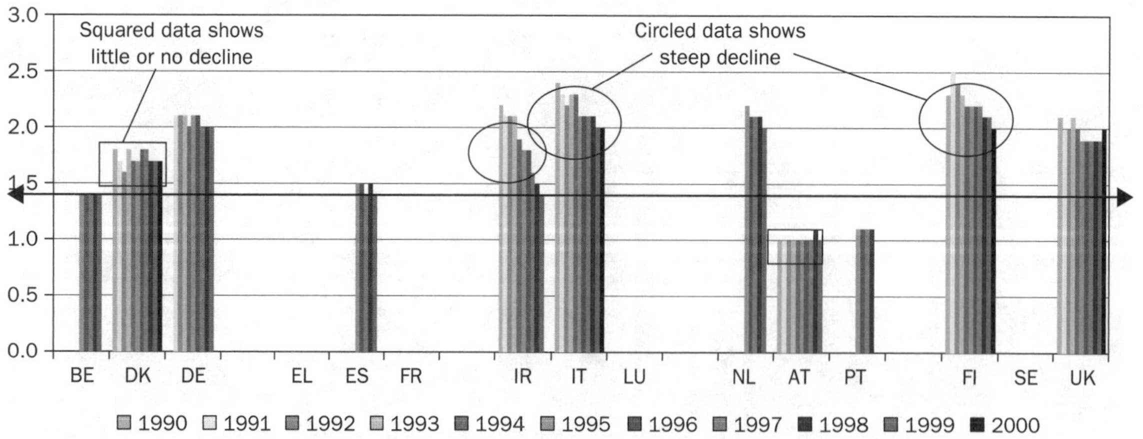

Figure 2.2 Outline % household spend on newspapers and print products EU-15, 1990–2000 – annotated

Source: Eurostat.

3. By setting down a parameter, in this case a time factor 1990–2000, we are able to see overall and specific trends in a given period where we can assess the various factors that might account for similarities and differences. The longer the trend the more well-founded is our judgement, although this is not always the case.

Therefore, from the start we have decided to use **multivariate methods**, with a series of **variables** that can be noted, as shown in Table 2.2.

Using **multivariate methods** means that we can try to bring the variables together into a recognisable pattern to explore consumer behaviour. We can then interpret the categories we are using and the variables, providing they are appropriate or useful. We can do this quantitatively and qualitatively.

We are using a sample of countries (the **estimation**) within the EU. Consequently, we will need to be careful in our assertions from or interpretation of the data. We must make sure that any **hypothesis** is statistically significant when using our **statistical inferences.** The gathering of data is often a snapshot at a given time. It is later when we string these snapshots together that we can make comments on trends.

Table 2.2 Variables

Variables
Country
Period (time)
Household spend

In making a relative judgement, it is often good practice to discover a mean or average figure. This allows us to see whether some countries are spending more than others but in a relative way: some countries being below the average and others above. A singular line, a linear expression, is used to illustrate this in Fig. 2.2.

There are limitations to linear depictions of data (see below), and a more detailed and rewarding analysis can be achieved by looking at clusters or individual trends before dealing with the overall. Inside the column-based graph, the circled data (Ireland, Italy and Finland) shows steep decline whereas the squared data (Denmark and Austria) shows little or no decline at all.

Even so, an average is still useful and could be used to compare, for example, the EU with US or Chinese data. From the sample, provided by our source Eurostat, the average household spend across Europe is just below 1.5% on newspapers and printed goods. Above average spenders include Ireland, Italy, Finland and the UK; below average include Portugal and Austria; Belgium and Spain are close to the average.

Nonetheless, from most of the chosen countries there has in fact been a decline in household spend on newspapers and print products over the 10-year sample: Ireland, Italy, the Netherlands, Finland and the UK. There is a minority which are static (Belgium, Spain, Portugal), some which have an erratic but overall small decline (such as Denmark) and one case (Austria) which has a small rise in spend levelling off in 2000.

The analysis does not stop here: some countries seem to be declining at different rates. For example, the Irish household spend on newspapers and print during this period shows a rapid decline from nearly 2.2% to 1.4% in 10 years, bearing in mind that this is not an 'absolute' graph we are looking at but percentages. The UK is also declining but its decline is much less, from about 2.1% to just under 2%. The country with the highest spend is Finland with 2.5% and, although it is in decline, it ends up above the average by 2000, with 2.0%. Again note we are dealing with percentages and not absolute figures.

We need to establish whether the original null hypothesis (Ho) has any validity. Out of 11 countries, only three showed no decline in household spend, with Austria marginally higher taken overall. Out of the 11 countries seven show a distinct decline in household spend on these products: almost 64%. This means that our original null hypothesis is inaccurate, i.e. is invalid, and we have to turn to the alternative. A decline is happening and needs further analysis to explain why, remembering at the same time that we now have evidence of a sample that indicates that household spend on these products may well be increasing and that this complicates our interpretation. To do this we need to look more carefully at the data and how it is depicted. No matter how good the quantitative data, it can be insufficient. This is why we need to turn our attention to qualitative analysis and interpretation of the statistics.

The context and the data questions: using qualitative methods

Data is normally collected for a purpose and in response to a question. The categories and classifications that define our data are also a part of a wider context.

A great deal of international, EU media data (e.g. Eurostat) reflects upon trade relations. At a national level, trade, supply and demand are important. Equally, a lot of the data will focus on consumer behaviour, production and distribution questions (e.g. Datamonitor). The variables chosen to illustrate the data will be related to the area of research. This is why, in qualitative terms, and as a start, the following list of issues often helps when reviewing work and studies of media data.

In our **qualitative evaluation**, which is an informed commentary on the data, we may include categories such as the following.

Politics

For example, relationships between private and public interests and political parties; media regulators at international as well as national, regional and local levels – see Chapters 1 and 4.

In our data on newspapers and print production, we noticed that one society had a stable, or even a slightly increased, household spend on newspapers: Austria. But note also that it lies very much below the average from our sample, indicating less interest in newspapers compared to other countries. Media analysts of Austrian society often comment on the stable, conservative nature of the Austrian consumer. This stability in the society is linked to the stability of its politics. A general truism is that the more crises there are affecting a society, the more interest there is in news and newspapers.

Economics

Rich and poor societies, modes of provision, supply and demand – see Chapter 3.

Irish consumption of print and household products showed a dramatic decline in percentage terms in the period of study. Economically, this was a period when Ireland was increasing its **GDP** and GDP per capita. Moreover, the political situation in Ireland was becoming more peaceful. This may explain the steep decline in consumer spend on print products, while the Irish consumer spent more on other media, or on other goods.

Social or societal factors

Relationships between people and social agendas, for example equal opportunities and the workplace – see Chapters 8 and 11.

The Irish case may also show us a society beginning to change, possibly rapidly. With economic and political alterations to the Irish scene, it is to be expected that social change will be another factor impacting on Irish consumer behaviour.

Culture

The roots of the culture – language, art, music, education and the nature of mass media in a society.

Another society from the data also shows a decline: Finland. Like Ireland, Finland in the 1990s went through a period of considerable political and economic change. Formerly bridging the ideological divide between Western and Eastern Europe, Finland, like many Scandinavian countries, invested heavily in the communication industries. In particular, Finland is one of the countries in the vanguard of the information economy and IT products.

History

The way things change in any given society and why.

Bringing together the political, economic and social factors into a broad analysis is the primary task of the historian. History matters in our analysis of the media. There is no more glaring example of this than the way in which the 1947 federal constitution of Germany, following the abuses of power associated with the Nazi period 1933–1945, is reflected in today's media organisations. Both its press and television are organised to counter any centralising power.

In addition, the German population and its historical tradition are deeply rooted in the world of literature. Germany has one of the highest figures for book readership, book purchase and newspaper circulation. Newspaper circulation is very regional in the main in Germany. The relatively small decline and the stability of household spend from the German data above may be indicative of this deeper, cultural, even historical, foundation to consumer spending.

By incorporating these factors into our analysis, we become more reflective and sympathetic towards our research materials, and our interpretation and assessment improve.

Stop and consider 2.5

In the above list, the category of ***technology*** *has not been included. It is discussed in detail throughout this book and is an important factor in our evaluation of the media and its trends. Is there an essential category difference between the above-mentioned five factors and the impact of technology? If so what? And if not, why? Should it be a 'sixth' factor? As a 'factor' is technology in the same league as the above categories?*

Linear and non-linear ways of at looking at data

Finally, data is usefully placed in the context of a mean or an average so that comparisons can be made. This is often depicted by a single, straight line: another example below, and one which is typical, shows how a straight line is based on plotted data. It is useful because it gives the analyst a simple 'mean' of the data, bringing the coordinates together. It could be used to show an average but equally a trend. This is often used in x–y graphs; a single straight line bringing together a series of numbers into what is known as a 'linear regression'. It is useful, but it has its limitations (see Source 2.1).

Although useful, the trouble with a single-line linear depiction like this is that it 'averages-out' the data. It does not necessarily provide us with the more accurate groups of data clusters or scatter structures which may reveal more than a simple single line does. In the above example, the scattered data is almost even throughout which may make us rely too heavily on the trend line or the linear summary and miss the finer points of analysis. Looking closely, some of the data appears in bunch-like formations and clusters which may call for further analysis.

The column work we used on EU newspapers and print products, 1990–2000 – Figs 2.1 and 2.2 – was

Source 2.1

OECD: Looking at data: collect, classify, summarise, present, analyse

The diagram below is only an extract from a long report by the OECD on the take up of broadband by different types of technology. In the original there are many symbols, but only four have been defined for us on the chart with precise symbols. In our investigation the point is not the individual detail in this case but how the various 'variables' have come together to give us a total picture. When we use multivariate analysis a single linear expression may not always help with our analysis of the data.

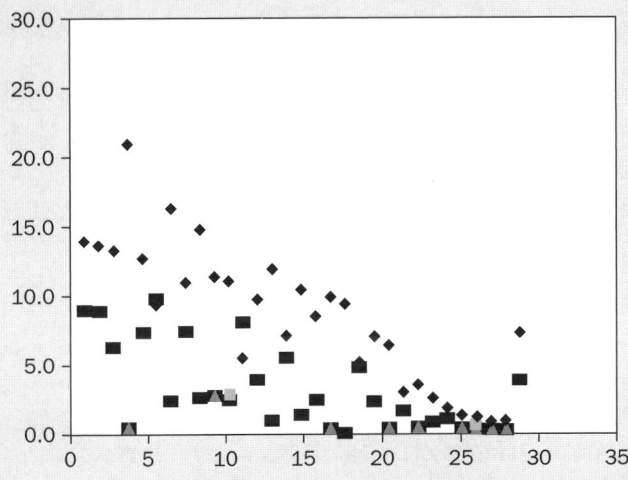

In this case the linear expression – the imaginary range of symbols (the four defined for DSL and cable take-up) – could 'average' all the points of the data. But note how some data are 'layered' and 'clustered' by the use of the different variables (DSL, cable, etc.); 'clusters' can be more important for our analysis than straight line trends.
Remember: The process of using statistics is often expressed as five phases: collect, classify, summarise, present and conclude (analyse).

Source: *OECD Broadband Statistics, June 2005* (OECD, 2005). www.oecd.org/sti/ict/broadband.

more clustered and probably more useful for our analysis, the circles and the squares if you recall. It provided clues to readership and household behaviour beyond the average or mean figures. This is where non-linear data, curved lines and radar graphs, for example, are often used, so that clusters become more perceptible. They are useful especially when working with comparative and quantitative analysis. When performing your analysis, it is good to reflect on both the linear and the non-linear approaches.

Again, non-linear regression options are available in programs such as *Microsoft Excel* or *Openoffice.orgCalc* and *SPSS*. The clusters and the shapes of scattered data are depicted in different ways and not in straight and linear expressions. This can be very useful as it avoids the over-use of simple, linear trend lines.

Chapter summary

The material is not designed to be a full coverage of the discipline but an introduction to some of the principal concepts that inform the debate on the modern EU media. In statistics:

- Depiction and interpretation is as important as data gathering.
- Hypotheses need to be checked and verified.
- In many cases, the evidence will need substantial qualitative judgement as much as quantitative analysis.
- The classification and categorisation of the data is most important and is linked to the research question you are exploring.

Key terms

Many of the technical terms have been explained in the text, but there are a few key terms or words which perhaps need some fine tuning:

BT: British Telecommunications – now, as with the rest of the telecommunication industries across the EU, a part of the private sector.

GDP: gross domestic product – a measure of national income often given in per capita (e.g. per 1000 population) terms so that relative comparisons can be made.

OECD: Organisation for Economic Co-operation and Development formed in 1961 with more than 100 countries participating – an invaluable source of statistics for Europe, the world and individual nations.

WTO: World Trade Organisation (formerly GATT – General Agreement on Tariffs and Trade).

Discussion questions

1. What essentially are statistics about and why are they used in the media industry so frequently?
2. Provide examples of both quantitative and qualitative analysis of a media industry. What are the essential differences?
3. Provide a list of all the qualitative factors that may be used to evaluate and assess statistics on the media. When you have made this list, justify your choice.
4. What is 'hypothesis testing', why is it useful and what are its limitations?
5. What is a statistical inference?
6. What is 'estimation' and why is it so useful?
7. Are 'linear regressions' useful in our analysis and how can we improve on presenting the data?
8. How should we measure, statistically, the impact of new technology on the media?
9. Why is media data so important for the EU? Try to think through this question bearing in mind the arguments in Chapter 1 and the details in the various industries from Chapter 6 through to Chapter 11: the chapters on production, distribution and consumption later in the book.

Assignments

1. Locate databases (OECD, Eurostat, Datamonitor, European Audio-visual Observatory, and so on) and draw together selected data for an analysis. Choose within the EU two or three countries as a sample of what is

happening within the EU, and compare across the nations media figures on a chosen topic you find of interest. Often this will depend upon what the database and the research report, for example, was designed to illustrate. Use the details in this chapter to (a) evaluate how the variables were created and (b) interpret the trends if they are available.

2. In looking at the trends in the media, and depending of course upon the sector, is there a real difference between 20th century and 21st century movements? If yes why and if not why not?

Further reading

There are many sources for statistics on the shelves of libraries, often of a very technical nature. This chapter is only an introduction and other more detailed work should be consulted. As a start we can use standard and reputable encyclopaedias such as *Encyclopaedia Britannica* or *Grand Larousse encyclopédique* where many of the above topics have been discussed in considerable depth.

There are also many standard works on statistics and many of them can be located in the 'Research Methods' titles. For example the Alan Bryman series across disciplines is particularly popular and is especially good at putting together both quantitative and qualitative approaches:

Bryman A. (2004) *Social Research Methods*, Oxford: Oxford University Press.

Bryman A. (2008) *Research Methods for Politics*, Oxford: Oxford University Press.

Bryman A., Bell E. (2003) *Business Research Methods*, Oxford: Oxford University Press.

Another easily read text is:

Robson C. (2002) *Real World Research*, Oxford and Cambridge: Blackwell.

A highly recommended and very readable text is:

Field A. (2000) *Discovering Statistics: using SPSS for Windows*, London: Sage.

A related field of course is economics and many of the statistical and economic issues of our era are investigated in the *Journal of Media Economics*, Lawrence Erlbaum Associates.

Online resources

http://www...

Most universities will provide online 'learning statistics' packages. These are highly recommended. One of the best resources in the UK is **intute** (formerly SOSIG) – http://www.intute.ac.uk/ – a portal open to all where you will be able to explore some of the best academic web sites across a range of disciplines, including learning about statistics. It includes a reference to the enormously interesting and informative StatSoft's *Electronic Statistical Textbook*.

References

Burrell I. (2005) The Abcs, *The Independent*, 17 October.

EC (2007) *Forest-based industries – printing*, Luxembourg: European Commission, Enterprise and Industry.

i2010 High Level Group (2006) *i2010 Benchmarking Framework*, Issue No. 1, Luxembourg: European Commission.

Jones A. (2007) France Telecom tunes into internet television, *FT.com*, 3 August.

OECD (2005) *OECD Broadband Statistics, June 2005*, Paris: Organisation for Economic Co-operation and Development.

Parker A. (2007) BT gambles on broadband TV, *FT.com*, 10 August.

Ramonet I. (2005) Final edition for the press, *Le Monde diplomatique*, January.

Chapter 3

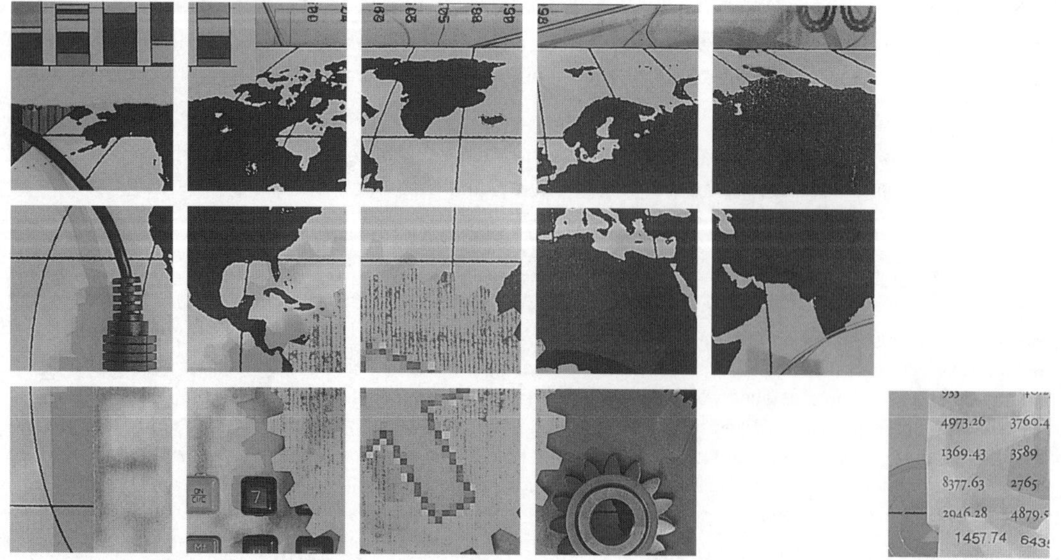

Understanding EU media through economics

What the chapter covers

- Introduction: economics and the media
- The macro and the micro
- Supply and demand of goods
- Price and costs (fixed and variable) and equilibrium
  - *Supply-side differences*
  - *Demand-side differences*
- Market definitions
  - *Economies of scale*
  - *Comparative and competitive advantage*
  - *Competition and monopolies*
  - *Mergers and takeovers*
  - *Horizontal and vertical integration, conglomerates and the 'value chain'*
  - *Ownership*
  - *Mono-media and cross-media ownership – the present*
  - *Profit motives: economic efficiency and the media market*

Learning objectives

When you have completed this chapter you will be able to:

- Define and use some of the key terminology and concepts used by economists working on the media.
- Apply key economic concepts to the development of the European media market in particular.
- Illustrate the debates surrounding market definitions in both global and European terms.
- Link competition policy to economic reasoning.
- Understand EU economic integration in terms of both media policy-making and the development of other market sectors.
- Specify some of the differences between public and private sector finance within the EU.

Themes

Below you will find a simple statement or series of statements around the six themes. They should *not* be read as a given fact. They are more like hypotheses (see Chapter 2) which need to be proved, discussed, debated and then used in your own analysis of the subject. The ideas and approaches in this book are always to be considered with an open mind; this is important in university study and is what makes it distinct from pre-university study.

Diversity of media

Most media in the EU is in private hands. This is the case for books, magazines, advertising media and the press, for example. Over one half, at least, of the broadcasting system is also in the private sector. The foundation of the private sector is market economics, and some would argue that all media including the public sector operates through similar economic models. So being aware of its operation in economic terms is crucial in our analysis regardless of the diversity.

Internal/external forces for change

The economics of the media is also in the hands of regulators who organise the market and its finances into a system which allows for competition and the operation of market forces. Nowadays those forces are at an EU and a global level and can be seen as a mixed dynamic between 'internal' EU and 'external' global forces.

Complexity of the media

The media is complex because of the way in which it is financed and how the economics are modelled. This is often conveniently labelled as a discussion about public and private provision within societies. Moreover, the distinction between public and private sector broadcasting, in particular, is being blurred, with a mix of public and private finance being used to develop the 'old' media and the 'new'.

Multi-levels

The economics of the media may be European and global but, due to its variety and complexity, it is also national, regional, local and sometimes 'glocal' in proportions. This makes the media, even in economic terms, a multi-level phenomenon.

European integrative environment

It is argued that the European integrative movement is built on the economics of self interest. As trade increases between communities, so the argument goes, the greater is the wealth created, benefitting all the member states. At the same time the degree of political integration is increased. The growth and occasional stuttering of media integration across the EU is in many ways the front-line debate between cultural roots and the power of transnational economics.

Cultural values

As the media operates as much culturally as economically, there is often a tension between the two ways of thinking about society, and this shows itself in different patterns of consumption: different languages and even different cultural norms are reflected in consumers' choice of media product. Yet, the apparent logic of economics appears to be a unifying process which is perhaps levelling the differences within the EU, even if this is happening at an evolutionary and not a revolutionary pace. Again, there are major debates on this topic.

Essentials

- Media products, in both the public and the private sector, need to be paid for by one method or another. In that sense, whether by licence or price and consumption, the media is a part of the study of economics. Due to some relatively recent pioneering work both in the USA and Europe, the study of media economics is increasing and becoming an important part of media analysis.

➤ As with other disciplines, the concepts used are often hotly debated, amended, and form the basis of a lively discussion (sometimes in research we use the words 'critical review') of the media for the contemporary era.

Introduction: economics and the media

As indicated, in this chapter we shall look at some economic concepts which are powerful tools in our analysis of media markets. This is not a full list of the tools used by economists, but they include key concepts which help us understand at least in part EU media policy (Chapter 1), its regulation (Chapter 4) and the new media agenda (see Chapters 6–11).

Like statistics, economic analysis depends on data collection and interpretation. How it is collected and categorised will influence our final analysis of the media market. In the end, the cornerstone of media economics is the study of the relationship between production, distribution and consumption.

Equally, the arguments about the power and influence of new technology often come down to questions about the data on investment, profit, resource allocation, cost and price. The change to new technology is undoubtedly altering, for example, the producer to customer relationship, and this demands new data so that we may understand contemporary media production and distribution as well as new consumer behaviour. This has led to considerable debate on the future development of the media industry as a whole.

There are major issues in media economics on such issues as capital flows (who owns the product if the finance is a co-production), negative integration in the EU (deregulation of markets as opposed to positive, subsidy-based developments) and the importance of mergers and takeovers and media ownership in the EU. In addition, there is considerable argument about horizontal and vertical integration of EU and global companies and their strategies. All these debates are rooted in economic models and concepts.

Economics is so taken for granted in some quarters that it is tempting to launch straight into the controversies without explaining some of the fundamental principles, but let us remind ourselves of some approaches. In other words, let us enter the debates as media analysts with some grounding in economic ideas and economic tools of analysis.

Stop and consider 3.1

*What is 'economics'? It might be useful for you to look up the word before we go any further. Is it a science? Is it a social science? How reliable as a discipline is it? Some of the key thinkers of the past such as Adam Smith (*The Wealth of Nations, *1776), Karl Marx (*das Kapital, *1867) and John Maynard Keynes (*The General Theory of Employment, Interest and Money, *1936) are still of relevance today. There are different schools of economic thought such as the 'Chicago school' and the 'Stockholm school'. Bear in mind that this chapter is only introductory and there is much more within the field to explore and investigate.*

The fundamental classification of economic activity into production and distribution and finally consumption is of course only a pointer to the way in which any economy works, but in media terms we can see it is useful. There are producers of the media in all its forms – films, television programmes, music – and these need some form of distribution. For example, there is analogue or digital broadcasting, the Internet, radio and mobile phones, the converging worlds of the audio-visual through multi-screen 'video' (see Chapter 10). Finally, there are the media outlets, such as shops or download sites, leading to the supreme arbiter of choice, the consumer.

Defining all these matters can be tricky. The consumer can be both an individual and a collective. Most EU state governments, for example, have tax revenues of almost 50% of gross domestic product (GDP) and are large spenders on and users of media products. This does not necessarily mean direct media ownership in most EU states but, because of the importance of public broadcasting, for example, governments will be actively involved, in some countries more than others, with the media market, its production and its distribution. This will obviously impact upon consumption.

The macro and the micro

Markets are constructed and then analysed, and to do this we need data. Economic data in any economy will normally be placed into two broad categories: micro- and macro-economic models. The macro refers to the totality of economic activity in a given area such as a nation: we refer to the macro-economy of Poland or France or Germany or the UK, for example. We can even talk about the macro-economy of the EU, although it is still more usual to talk in national rather than European terms.

When we review the European media economy as a sector, we often have to resort to national statistics first, make comparisons and see how the media overall is functioning in its national macro-economic setting, before investigating the European level. This is worth the effort too, as we can then relate the information to the wider European macro-economic scene, and are able to review the bigger picture.

The micro-economy is the study of the smaller aspects of the macro-economy: how individuals, or companies or organisations or corporations decide in their own economic interests through choices. It is a study of market mechanisms.

The two models, of course, inter-relate: the general well-being of an economy will have a marked impact on the micro-economic choices that people, including media companies, make. Equally, macro-performance is driven by a plethora of micro-choices. The study of economics is therefore complex but also fundamental; it is not a perfect science but a matter of perceptible trends and our interpretation of them. Recently the study of media economics has come to the fore with very interesting work coming out of the USA (for example, the work of Professor Robert Picard) which we can apply in the EU context. There are several economists across the EU (for example, Gillian Doyle in the UK, Gustafsson in Sweden, Knoche, Kopper, Heinrich and so many others in Germany, and so on: see Heinrich and Kopper, 1997). Each of the member states will have their own academic and practioner economic consultants, and using them is of great advantage in our analysis of the present-day media. On a wider economic stage the work of Michael Porter is often cited (see Point of View 3.1), and his work is not only fascinating but often used in the media industry, as we shall see later.

Supply and demand of goods

In simple terms a market is driven by both the supply of and the demand for goods. Goods could mean fuel

Point of View 3.1

The work of Michael Porter

Michael Porter, a world renowned economist, has recently been redefining the relationship between the macro- and micro-economic factors. His work was used in the recent Pira report (2003) on the media for the **European Commission**, where it was quoted:

> But Porter goes on to argue: '. . . The central challenge in economic development, then, is how to create the conditions for rapid and sustained productivity growth. Stable political/legal institutions and sound macroeconomic policies create the potential for improving national prosperity. But wealth is actually created at microeconomic level – in the ability of firms to create valuable goods and services using productive methods.'

Note how the report pays respect to the work of Porter on broad economics, and note too how it helps analysts to think through media developments inside the EU from a policy and an economic point of view.

Source: Pira International, *The EU Publishing Industry: an Assessment of Competitiveness*, p. 32 (Pira International, 2003). See also EC (2005).

and food, but also a media product such as a film. As we shall see later, factors of consumption (audience factors, for example) are almost like hierarchies of choice (c.f. **Maslow's hierarchy of needs**) perhaps transforming the goods on offer into a selected range of goods from essentials to luxuries.

Different societies may have different priorities and this is reflected in the choices they make, including their media preferences. For example, some societies will prefer soap operas over documentaries, sport over news. Nonetheless, in the Western world, including the EU, there are broad tendencies which show some convergence of choices.

Stop and consider 3.2

Are consumers all the same? Obviously there are differences but how much? Should we treat consumers as universal human beings with similar needs or do we think of them in a context – in a market which is special to them like their nationality or language groups or religious communities. Stop and consider this in terms of the many nation states and their consumers that make up the EU.

Consumer choice, which provides demand, will therefore depend on social and societal pressures, and on what is available to the consumer. Different societies may have different needs. Within the EU there is much economic and social diversity to be found among the nation states. However, the EU economy overall, the macro-economy of the EU nations, has shown steady economic growth, with what appear to be normal downturns along the way. Wealth has grown in the main throughout the EU. Thus household spend on the media in general, and media products in their entirety, is also on the increase; of course noting that some newspapers and some print products are declining somewhat in certain countries.

Within the market there has been a shift to embrace and spend on new technology, from mobiles to computers, to high-definition televisions. Broadcasting, broadband companies and technologically-driven companies, from hardware to software, have seen marked increases in value and corporate wealth over the decades in Europe as a result.

Price and costs (fixed and variable) and equilibrium

Price is central to the operation of markets, because it operates to reconcile supply and demand and determine output. The demand for (sales of) a product is likely to be negatively related to the price. As the price of a product falls sales will increase because it can be substituted for other products and because it can more easily be afforded. The supply (production) of a product is likely to be positively related to the price. As the price of a product falls, production will decrease as it becomes more difficult to cover the costs of production. The movement of price up and down will lead to changes in supply and demand leading to an 'equilibrium' where the amount consumers want to buy is equal to the amount producers want to sell at the current price.

All goods and services compete for consumer expenditure, but it is product 'substitutability' (see Case Study 3.1) that allows for product competition and choice for consumers and links similar type products to the same market. One of the big developments in media has been the extent to which different media can fulfil similar functions, for example CDs and iTunes downloads. Thus the demand for CDs is sensitive to the price and availability of downloads. This is why reports for the European Commission make such a play of 'substitutability'. It is on this that much of the media analysis, in economic terms, is based – the way in which competition in supply based on costs interacts with demand to determine price and output: the nub of market economics.

The price will be determined of course by a myriad of factors including costs of production, rules and regulations of the market and taxation. For an example of how costs are calculated in one part of the media production chain, see Table 3.1. It is an extract which was used recently in a report on the competitiveness of the EU publishing sector. Using the figures below we can begin to make comparisons and deduce comparative and competitive advantages across member states.

Bearing in mind the need to recover the costs of product development, producers and distributors are

Case Study 3.1

Comparing a film with a book in times of recession

The following extract is fascinating as it emerges from reflections within the UK book industry and shows how comparisons can be made between different media: the 'substitutability' of a product. Ask yourself: is this how you think about choosing a media product – the amount of time you are entertained by it? It is an interesting question.

> Of all retail sectors, books has been least affected by the recent slowdown, with three factors combining to save the day. One: better product, particularly from Dan Brown. His phenomenal success has boosted the whole market and got new people interested in reading. Although a work of fiction, perhaps his book also ties in with this consumer need for authenticity – he is purporting to show the secret 'truth' behind Christianity.
>
> Two: more retailing, better retailing. New retail channels, especially the internet but also the supermarkets, have made books more widely available – and cheaper. Meanwhile, book retailers have started to successfully copy proven retail techniques from across the high street: multibuys, category management, January sales.
>
> Three: free advertising. Richard and Judy have spent a year using their mass market appeal to push reading. Not only have their efforts transformed individual titles, they have spawned a wave of book-related TV that will hit the screens this spring.
>
> Going forward, the outlook for books is surprisingly robust, with all three stimulants to the business in play. And it is important to remember that although the froth has been blown off the top of the consumer boom, the economy is still in robust shape, with growth nudging 3% this year.
>
> Books hold up in a recession, or in this case a cooling-off period, so the saying goes. Eight hours of reading begins to look like good value in home entertainment compared to a two-and-a-half hour DVD for a similar price. Paperbacks in particular offer great value for money. If booksellers can get their value proposition right, capturing the cautious consumer pound should be a breeze.

Source: *The Bookseller*, 10 February (Denny, 2005).

sensitive to the cost price factor. They will wish to match supply and demand at a sufficiently high price to profit from the product; or low enough, in some cases, depending on competition, to encourage sufficient demand. Few businesses can finance a steady stream of losses.

Meeting and creating demand is an essential ingredient in the media industry, but so is pricing and controlling the costs. When supply and demand reach a balanced relationship, it is known as the 'equilibrium' or the 'equilibrium price'. This may alter if either supply or demand is changed.

The cost of a product will be determined too by a whole range of factors which for economists can be fixed or variable, depending upon how long it takes to adjust them. 'Fixed costs', which are difficult to change quickly, will be costs such as interest on capital invested in buildings (theatres, studios) and

Table 3.1 EU media competitiveness (newspapers)

Country	*Sector/cost*	*Paper and printing %*	*Content (acquisition and editing) %*	*Distribution%*	*Marketing and administration%*
Austria	Newspapers	30	20	20	30
Finland	Newspapers	28	26	21	26
Ireland	Newspapers	30	45	9	16
Italy	Newspapers	40	40	10	10
Luxembourg	Newspapers	28	40	5	27
Sweden	Newspapers	15	20	30	40
United Kingdom	Newspapers	28	10	12	20

Source: Pira International, *The EU Publishing Industry: an Assessment of Competitiveness*, p. 100 (Pira International, 2003). See also EC (2005).

distribution networks (cables, masts), depreciation of machinery (cameras, audio equipment, printing presses) and administrative costs.

With many media products such as song performance and films the major costs involved, the production costs, are fixed; the distribution costs once the product is made are very low. So the more people who see a film the lower the average cost of production. This has many interesting implications. It shows why successful films are so profitable and the unsuccessful so unprofitable. It makes pricing difficult, particularly for distribution as DVDs/downloads. It is also why copyright is so important and piracy so profitable.

Variable costs can be adjusted relatively quickly as market circumstances change. These are wages and raw material costs (silicon, plastic). They are directly related to the volume of production and can be changed as production changes.

An important cost would of course be the labour costs. The amount of these costs per unit of output depends upon wage levels and how much each worker produces, or productivity. The USA is often taken as a benchmark for productivity. Taking US productivity as 100 it can be seen (Table 3.2) that average EU productivity in manufacturing is significantly lower with no relative improvement. (It is important to realise that US and EU productivity is rising, but the EU is not catching up.) By contrast, in printing and publishing, from being significantly lower than that of the US in 1979–1981, productivity has grown much more quickly in the EU and in 1999–2001 was over one third higher than that in the USA.

Some media products have price mechanisms which vary according to the type of product. This is sometimes known as 'continuous media production' (newspapers, general broadcasting) on one side or 'single media production' on the other (songs, films). Newspapers, for example, can only work as a product if they are continuously produced; building a readership and revenue stream over the long-term. A film, however, is often seen as a single one-off product in terms of the income it brings in; even if the means of producing films is linked to more continuous processes.

In contemporary definitions of the media, a distinction is often made between media content (information) and distribution (companies or processes). The media in this sense is a hybrid of many products. This is similar to the idea that the media works in a 'dual product market' (Picard, 1989, p. 17) serving both content users and advertisers. Unpicking the various strands of economic activity is the work of the economist and the accountant.

A media product can have in-built variations to its value and price. It is not an easy supply and demand relationship. For example, a song covered by copyright is the same within any market, but who sings the song may also settle the price the consumer pays, because one singer is more popular than another. The selling of 'valuable' and sought-after tickets at popular concerts (or any entertainment event) even becomes 'news', often reported in the press. It is interesting to note that the EU has and will continue to take initiatives in this area.

Table 3.2 Productivity in manufacturing and printing and publishing USA and EU

	1979–81	*1994–96*	*1999–2001*
Printing and Publishing	67	120.3	134.5
EU-14 (all manufacturing)	84.6	88	80.3
US	100	100	100

Source: Adapted from European Commission, *EU Productivity and Competitiveness: an Industry Perspective. Can Europe Resume the Catching-up Process?* (O'Mahony and van Ark, 2003).

Stop and consider 3.3

Can a media product be compared to any other product or is the media 'special'? Can we compare an 'Arctic Monkeys' concert on the one hand with a 'Rolling Stones' concert on the other? What do the ticket price differences reflect: popularity for these tickets or different market segments associated with different types of consumer? There are arguments here as we shall see. Look at 'supply-side differences', point 3 below.

Because media products are both culturally content-laden and technologically closely linked to distribution, there are strong arguments to suggest that media production and consumption are different to other economic sectors, sufficiently so that they change the 'economics' and the economic management of these sectors. Economists could disagree with this view but, as a starting point, these arguments are interesting and can be used in our analysis of the media (Picard, 2002, 2005).

Supply-side differences

1. Because of the initial overall costs and policy restrictions on creating media corporations, competition in the industry is much less when compared with other products or other production processes. This makes for a more monopolistic structure, distorting the normal forms of competition which govern supply and demand, price and equilibrium.
2. As the media is essentially created through content, media industries often follow non-economic criteria – cultural and social aims rather than economic ones. This is often used to justify public broadcasting, again distorting the market.
3. Producing media content often relies on people whose motives go beyond competitive salaries (an important price-cost mechanism) and may be more about artistic goals or celebrity-seeking than the norms that dictate wage bargaining.
4. The media by its nature is 'virtual', 'digital' in the present-day era; therefore the distribution mechanisms and costs are different to physical products.
5. Copyright and patents are indicators of the intellectual property that is a crucial feature of media products. At the same time, such products are prone to piracy and forgery; this changes the nature of the product and how we consume it and also impacts upon price.

Demand-side differences

1. On the demand side there is said to be a high degree of 'unpredictability' of success. A media product relies on taste and culture, even fashion: factors difficult to predict and quantify.
2. Media products, even single products, are often used in different ways. For example, a motion picture may be shown in a cinema theatre, sold in the supermarket on a DVD for home entertainment or even sold for TV showing. All of this complicates the revenue relationship and our economic understanding of what constitutes 'demand'.
3. Media products are also so numerous that no one consumer could consume all the content. In effect, there is an over-supply of content which signals choice for the consumer, but increases the risk of failure and distinguishes media from other products. Over-production of imaginative products is often needed to ensure success. In evaluating demand, this factor is important as the 'big' successes pay for the failures and ensure continuity of production.
4. Some aspects of media demand are built on loyalty and repetitive audience behaviour. In other words, the media, working through a narrative such as a soap opera, creates an emotional relationship over a period of time which alters the behaviour of the consumer in ways that are more complex than with less creative products.
5. Media products are often wide-ranging, and this means that consumers pay for a product that they do not totally consume. For example, in Europe the average viewer may watch television programmes for 3.5 hours a day, whereas the choice and output operates 24/7. A newspaper reader may buy a newspaper in its totality, but only read those sections in which he or she is interested. All of this complicates the economic calculations and market analysis.

Market definitions

As such, and no matter the arguments about the media being a 'special' case, economists are trying to develop EU market definitions for legal and competition practice (see Points of View 3.2 and 3.3) so that we may judge how media products compete with each other. This is especially important in the EU market which relies so heavily on cross-national trade for wealth creation and employment. This is why detailed discussions on market definitions were a recent priority for the European Commission. Point of View 3.2 indicates the principal arguments for delineating the European media market. Recent thinking in the EU on media definitions has been expressed as follows:

> Market definition is primarily an analytical tool to help identify, in a systematic way, the competitive constraints faced by an undertaking. The purpose of defining the relevant market is that of identifying those proper products in which we include services whose suppliers are capable of exerting effective competitive pressures on each other and of constraining each other's behaviour.
>
> (European Commission, DG Competition, *Market Definition in the Media Sector: Economic Issues*, p. 2 (Europe Economics, 2002))

See Point of View 3.2 below for an extension of this view.

Point of View 3.2 was a part of two major investigations commissioned for the EU; one on market definitions and one on regulation. An extract from the latter is given below (Point of View 3.3). They are a useful starting point for the contemporary debate on market trading of media products in the EU, not necessarily easy reading but they remain important and worth the effort. Point of View 3.2 tries to illustrate this by showing a small extract and then using keywords to expose how markets and competition between products are constructed.

Economies of scale

Media production is often characterised by 'economies of scale' – an increase in the volume of production can result in lower average costs. The golden age of Hollywood was characterised by large studios using their expensive lots (sets and sound

Point of View 3.2

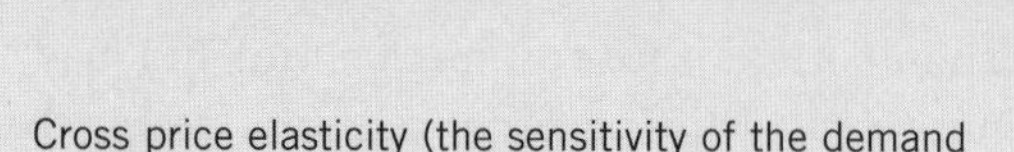

Market definition – economic issues

The language of economics can be difficult but once unpicked and defined allows us to enter the debates about the industry.

> . . . the evidence required by traditional techniques for market definition . . .
> (a) Methods based on a direct assessment of substitutability, including transport cost, diversion ratio and cross price elasticity analyses;
> (b) Residual demand analyses, which underpins the most direct form of empirical application of the SSNIP test; and,
> (c) Methods based on the analysis of market outcomes, including price correlation and stationarity tests, shock analysis, price concentration and profitability analyses.

Key words and definitions:

- Substitutability (the degree to which we can substitute one product for a similar product, thereby allowing us choice, and leading toward competition);
- Diversion ratio (how much demand switches from one product A to its substitute, when the price of B falls);
- Cross price elasticity (the sensitivity of the demand for one product A to a change in the price of its substitute B);
- Residual demand (the demand assumed to be present by a producer for its products bearing in mind competitors);
- SSNIP test ('Small Significant Non-transitory Increase in Price' – the smallest market in which a monopoly might be able to raise price);
- Price correlation (the relationship between prices of different products, i.e. do the prices change together);
- Stationarity tests (a different statistical method testing for common price changes);
- Shock analysis (looking for similar price changes when dramatic changes occur, within a data analysis);
- Price concentration (relationship between price levels and the number of firms in the industry);
- Profitability (profits as a percentage of price or assets).

Source: European Commission, DG Competition, *Market Definition in the Media Sector: Economic Issues*, p. 125 (Europe Economics, 2002).

Point of View 3.3

Market definition – legal issues

This extract may seem daunting but has real value for us as analysts of the media market. It allows us to see the debate and the need for accurate definition in the media industry. Note too that the extract reminds us that economics cannot be divorced from questions of regulation or business practice or even, in the EU context, national cultural sensitivities.

> . . . 4. . . . Media services are of a particular nature. They relate to the freedom of expression, and thereby to diversity and pluralism, which explains why most European countries have special media ownership control regimes. Media also interferes with the cultural field and represents a means for promoting national or transnational cultural and social values. It is therefore all the more necessary to determine the playing field boundaries for the undertakings that are active in the media sector, in order to make sure that the regulations which aim at promoting objectives other than a fair and feasible competition may be applied uniformly and take into account new forms of transmission . . . 5. Even that sensible context, regulatory and competition authorities now face the challenge to duly integrate a time dimension in their market definition appraisal, while remaining consistent. . . . That challenge is not to be missed if competition authorities want to play their role as a watchdog of the healthy evolution of markets, the promotion of the appearance of new players and the overall supervision of the concentration and consolidation process, while preserving the specificity and sensitiveness of the media sector. A coherent and uniform methodology for market definition is thus needed so as to ensure a consistent treatment of all media players throughout the EU, to promote legal certainty and to enhance trust in the competition and regulatory authorities . . .

Source: European Commission, DG Competition, *Market Definition in the Media Sector – Comparative Legal Analysis*, pp. 5–6 (Bird & Bird, 2002).

stages) and equipment intensively to produce films at relatively low cost.

Of course there may be limits to this process, often referred to as 'diseconomies of scale'. In theory, enlarging an organisation may mean it can become bureaucratic and less responsive to the market. This is a particular problem in the creative industries. Together with technical change, this has meant that today many films are produced outside the traditional studios. However, because of the system of distribution of films and the ability to spend on advertising and promotion the large studios still dominate the film market.

Comparative and competitive advantage

Traditionally economists viewed international trade and competition as being based on the relative efficiency of production, i.e. differences in productivity, but then it was recognised that allowance had to be made for differences in wage levels between countries. So, it is often argued, Germany is probably more efficient at producing most products than Poland, but Poland's wages are a fraction of those in Germany. Hence Poland will produce and export products where its relatively low productivity is offset by lower wages and will import products where this is not the case. This is known as 'comparative advantage'.

In modern economies, comparative advantage, based as it is on the idea of competition based on price, is inadequate for the products of today where price is only one factor among many influencing demand. This is particularly the case in the service industries which are so important in modern economies; for example, media production and success is often associated with social imagination and creativity.

Thus more widely defined competitive advantages will derive from society more generally, their populations (workers and consumers), education, skills, creativity, culture, etc. To signal this, the notion of 'competitive advantage' has been developed (Porter, 1985).

The concept of 'competitive advantage' is useful because it allows us to conceptualise how success in media products might be achieved. Porter calls the production process the 'value chain', emphasising the importance of different stages and of the process that connects them together. The value chain also indicates that all stages do not have to take place within an individual company, as was once usually the case (the studio system of film production). This leads to the idea of clusters both of competing firms and of their related industries in generating competitive advantage. Porter saw these clusters as localised in an area (Hollywood) but, with technical change, the value chain can span national borders. Porter's work indicates the importance of companies and clusters of companies for competitive success. Not only large companies but small companies and new companies are vital for sustaining economic growth (Porter, 1985).

Competition and monopolies

In the end, media products work through supply, demand, trade advantages, equilibrium prices and costs. Markets especially work through forms of competition that embrace private and public, company or corporate media (see Case Study 3.2) and the convergence of the regulation of markets. Increasingly, within the EU the market is being redefined by agreement between EU states, and this includes, broadcasting and other media sectors.

Competition, in one form or another, is essential for the effective operation of markets. In economic terms we can use two fundamental aspects of competition to help us understand a market. First, we need to understand that economists define 'competition' in different ways. On the one hand, there is 'perfect competition'. This is a concept which imagines an extremely competitive free market where individual suppliers and consumers have no power to influence the price because the number of companies/consumers is so large. On the other hand, economists define markets as 'imperfect competition', where suppliers can influence the prices because they have a significant share of production. The second is closer to the reality of the market, but the first helps us to

Case Study 3.2

Network markets in the EU since the 1980s

In a succinct, carefully constructed article, Jacques Pelkmans illustrated the development of EU network markets (telecoms, postal services, air transport, rail, gas and electricity) since the 1980s. Although critical of EU strategy and management, he highlighted the importance of the EU as a catalyst for market change, showing the synergy between sectors, including media:

- Stage 1: First EU measure, be it a directive or a competition decision in the sector.
- Stage 2: Combination of remaining monopoly elements, allowing access and regulation.
- Stage 3: Competitive network markets, combining regulation and competition policy.

Source: Making EU networks competitive (Pelkmans, 2001).

EU liberalisation: recent, gradual, unseen, complex

	1980–1985	*1985–1990*	*1990–1995*	*1995–2000*	*2000–*
Broadcasting	Stage 2*	Stage 3*	–	–	–
Telecoms	–	–	Stage 1	Stage 2	Stage 3
Postal	–	–	Stage 1	Stage 2	–
Electricity	–	–	–	Stage 1	–
Gas	–	–	–	Stage 1	–
Air transport	Stage 1	Stage 2	Stage 3	–	–
Rail transport	–	–	Stage 1	–	–

* For a more detailed view of EU regulatory concerns for broadcasting refer to Chapter 4.

Point of View 3.4

WTO and the EU concern on 'cultural products'

The following two extracts show the degree of concern and debate that surrounds global and EU trade in the film industry. It is good to review these types of comments and locate the commentary in your own critical analysis.

> Feature film as both a very influential and the most vulnerable of the media is a primary preoccupation of European, both national and EU, cultural policies. The financial support it receives yearly from the public sphere around Europe reaches more than €1 billion allocated by the national and regional funding bodies and more than €80 million granted by the Pan-European funds, MEDIA and Eurimages. The WTO certainly impinges upon cultural policies, which has been demonstrated in the Canadian periodicals case, widely criticised for being insensitive to cultural values. It concerned a dispute between the United States and Canada over measures introduced by the latter in order to protect the national magazine industry as a medium of Canadian ideas and a tool for the promotion of Canadian culture. The US objected to the measures as being restrictive and protectionist and initiated a WTO dispute settlement procedure, which led to an unfavourable ruling for Canada. In this way the case raised the vital issue of the significance of culture under the WTO system, and its limits.

Source: European Audiovisual Observatory, European public film support within the WTO framework, p. 2 (Herold, 2003).

> . . . the (European) Commission has announced firstly that it is to undertake consultations with a view to reforming state aids for film and television production, and secondly that the specific criteria required for the aids in question only remain valid until the 30th of June 2007. It is in this context of reform that article 151 EC is important, in as much as it requires the community institutions to take cultural aspects into account in their actions under other community policies. It is therefore essential that, in applying the principles of free competition, the community institutions take into consideration the cultural variable when it is a matter of agreements between audiovisual undertakings and state aid in the audiovisual field . . .

Source: European Audiovisual Observatory, Application of EC competition policy regarding agreements and state aid in the audio-visual field, p. 2 (Mayer-Robitaille, 2005).

explore the underlying laws (trends) of economics (see Point of View 3.4).

There is an opposite of competition: monopoly. A monopoly can be considered as either good or bad depending on your political and philosophical point of view. By, definition monopolies are companies that produce products that have no close substitutes. Pure monopolies can exist where there is a complete nationalisation of the media and therefore no competitive pressures: a state-run national radio for example. They may often be created through suppression of the free market. In reality nowadays they are rare; plurality of media ownership is seen by the EU as vital for democracy. Therefore, most 'real' markets tend to be imperfectly competitive, rather than perfectly competitive or pure monopolies.

In the immediate past, the 20th century, when European state television broadcasting was prime and paramount in media markets, the oligarchic, monopolistic tendencies were obvious. In a previous era, in the mid-19th century, newspapers were a good example of 'oligopoly': few titles but large circulations. Even today the trend toward media concentration in newspapers across EU member states is akin to the 19th century, albeit technologically different. Since the 1980s and into the 21st century, we have witnessed more media competition because of digital convergence. Nowadays newspaper and broadcasters' content will compete on the web (Internet) and through a range of competing telecommunications internet service providers (ISPs).

Nevertheless, the question – does the consumer of media products have a real choice? – is still being asked. New technology, economic growth and growing markets have hastened the process of trade within the EU. Access to products seems to be growing. Even globally the rules of trade have widened and deepened and are in theory less monopolistic. Also, market rules are becoming less national and trans-national (see Chapter 4), and this too is widening the market. Even global trade rules emanating from the WTO are embracing new media products as well as other sectors. This trend is apparent, although there are profound debates on how far normal trade rules should apply to 'cultural' products.

Major media producers are responding to what they see as a new demand by enlarging their product range. This is pushing them toward mergers and takeovers, which are occurring across the EU and across the globe. Over-concentration of product manufacture of course can be a concern, especially if the companies become oligopolies (see below). This lies beneath the EU sensitivities regarding global, open trade of audio-visual products. The battle lines, it appears, have been drawn over the issue of expanding markets, and this will be a contentious issue for the foreseeable future (see Source 3.1).

Mergers and takeovers

The word oligopoly applies to competition in industries where a small number of producers have a large share of the market. Potentially, this gives individual companies the power to control the market. In media terms this may lead to an over-bearing influence on policy development and market direction. Oligopoly is different from 'monopolistic competition', where there are many sellers (producers) making differentiated products. It is characterised by uncertainty and interdependence between firms because each firm's actions affect the market and its rivals. Thus the outcome of one firm's decision depends upon its rival reactions, so competition and the price mechanisms do not function properly. This can lead to high prices, poor-quality products or both. Oligopoly is often at the heart of the discussions and debates about mergers and takeovers within the media sector (and others sectors too) across Europe and globally.

'Mergers' implies the bringing together of companies or businesses in a voluntary fashion, whereas 'takeovers' (acquisitions) are a hostile taking over of one company by another. In both cases there may be good financial reasons for the action (see Source 3.1). Often the reasoning is based on the economies of scale. The aim is to lower production costs, enhance product development and pass on the price advantage. Hopefully, too, there are product quality improvements for the consumer. The result would be a boost to income and profit for the producer who gets it right. Mergers are a high-risk strategy with many, if not the majority, ending in failure, e.g. AOL, Time-Warner. There are also darker sides to the business game. There may be a wish to remove a competitor and to create a monopolistic position.

Source 3.1

Estimates of merger and acquisition activity in the EU market

It is useful to access good journalistic sources of media material such as this, e.g. *Financial Times, Handlesblatt, Les Echos* and other similar publications in the EU are important sources of knowledge.

> the number of media merger and acquisition deals in Europe, including the UK, rose 12% in 2006 to 175 transactions, compared with 156 in the year before. The value of the deals rose to €43 billion, closing in on the level seen in 2000, which saw 186 deals valued at $52 billion, according to PricewaterhouseCoopers . . . In 2006, private equity groups accounted for 44% of the value of deals in European media. Private equity firms were behind three of the four largest deals in Europe. VNU, the Dutch group, was bought by a group of six firms including Thomas H. Lee and Blackstone; Pages Jaunes Groupe of France was bought by KKR; and Germany's ProSiebenSat.1 was bought by KKR and Permira. . . . newspaper groups were notably more keen to purchase online companies amid concerns about traditional advertising revenues, while marketing service companies are expected to continue to look for pure play digital agencies . . . elsewhere both private equity and large media companies look for growth through media acquisitions in emerging markets. Axel Springer bought big stakes in both Dogan TV in Turkey and Polsat in Poland . . . Mecom, the UK listed group, bought Orkla Media, which has newspaper assets from the Netherlands to Poland, from its Norwegian parent in a deal worth €876 million . . .

FT Source: European media deals rise by 75%, *FT.com* (Terazono, 2007).

Point of View 3.5

Defining the media market – 'media mergers'

1. Market definition is a particularly difficult and time consuming exercise. Nevertheless, market definition and market share analysis is as necessary in reviewing media mergers as in reviewing any other mergers.
2. Due to significant first mover advantages and two-sided market effects, media markets sometimes manifest positive feedback cycles and downward spirals that need to be taken into account when predicting the effects of a merger.
3. In two-sided media markets, one cannot assess the impact of the merger on one side without taking into consideration effects on the other. Difficult trade-offs might be unavoidable.
4. Vertical integration and associated risks foreclosure can be an important concern in some media mergers. Remedies in problematic cases are often behavioural in nature as competition authorities try to eliminate anti-competitive effects while permitting the parties to reap substantial efficiencies.
5. Media mergers could affect content diversity and quality, and could do so in ways that present competition authorities with awkward trade-offs.
6. The difficulties inherent in measuring diversity and quality, and in predicting how a merger might affect them is not a good justification for ignoring them in merger review. This is especially true if there is little or no sector regulation dealing with these matters.
7. Economic welfare and pluralism are separate rather than coterminous goals, and there could be difficult trade-offs that need to be made between them in media merger reviews. Competition authorities will tend to protect pluralism whenever they block anti-competitive media mergers, but even media mergers not harming competition may sometimes harm pluralism.
8. There are at least two ways to deal with the issue of potentially diverging economic welfare and pluralism in media mergers, but there is no consensus on which is best.

Competition authorities could pay attention to economic welfare, media regulators to pluralism; or competition authorities could pay attention to both – the latter view is usual within EU member states.

Key words and definitions:

- Market share (the percentage of sales in a market which one company or enterprise accounts for);
- First mover advantages (where producers have a natural advantage by being the first to produce a new product – competition is initially non-existent);
- Two-sided media markets (where media producers gain revenue from advertising and product sales);
- Vertical integration (see below);
- Economic welfare (the standard of living of society in terms of the goods and services people can consume).

Source: OECD, Directorate for Financial, Fiscal and Enterprise Affairs: competition committee, *Media Mergers*, pp. 8–10 (OECD, 2003).

It is for this reason that many, if not most, states have rules on market competition which restrict or control mergers and takeovers within the private sector. Before the EU was formed, this was solely in the hands of the nation states. Since the creation of the Single European Market, the rules for mergers and takeovers have taken on a national and a European dimension. At both national and EU level the purpose of this control is to ensure that no 'dominant position' can result from a merger or a takeover. The precise definition of what constitutes a company or business 'dominant position' within a market depends upon EU and national law and court rulings.

A recent OECD round-table discussion considered media mergers in the light of changes to media technology. The evidence they drew upon was global and included a submission from the European Commission. The OECD documents (see Point of View 3.5) highlight that an agreed control of mergers is necessary if democratic principles are to be upheld. Once again the extract contains key words which we need to use.

Horizontal and vertical integration, conglomerates and the 'value chain' (Porter, 1985)

Mergers (and takeovers) can be of three kinds: horizontal, vertical or conglomerate. Horizontal mergers are when a company merges with another at the same stage (similar product range for example) of production (e.g. News Corporation taking over the *New York Times*). This allows for 'economies of scale': one large factory creating DVDs rather than two smaller ones.

Vertical mergers are when the stage of production is different (a TV broadcaster buying a TV programme producing company, a film studio buying a chain of cinemas). The economic reasoning for the merger will often be a perceived advantage for savings and efficiencies by integrating the production process. Such mergers can also be defensive, making it more difficult for new competitors to emerge.

Conglomerates are mergers where the companies or businesses are essentially in different markets. They are often encouraged for financial or capital reasons, allowing for cash hungry companies to be associated with cash-flow rich companies and for diversification allowing for greater risk management of new products or initiatives.

In most cases, the justification for a merger or takeover or conglomeration is efficiency and 'value-added' gain to benefit both producer (more profit) and consumer (lower price). At the level of the firm, the 'value-added' is often dissected into what Porter (1985) called a 'value chain'. His standard 'public domain', copyright approved diagram, often adapted and used, is shown in Fig. 3.1.

Notice how firms' activities are broken down into a chain of activities, each of which can be defined and measured and a calculation made of the 'value' in each. This is not the place to deepen this important, and in this case very simplified, economic analysis; but for those who want to explore this approach, Porter's work is highly recommended. Moreover, many market analysts are now beginning to add this type of evaluation in media market analysis. For example, the well-known data analysis from 'Datamonitor' (MarketLine Business Information Centre, MBIC) has started using this approach in its analysis of media markets.

As part of the Porter analysis of how companies have to evaluate their operations, regulation plays its part. In the EU, rules, regulations, law and judgements on competition policy try to maintain stability and dynamism within the market place. This is not easy. The shift to a larger European Single Market, including media products, has both its supporters and its detractors. Consequently the debate on how markets should operate is unending.

In an important case in the mid-1990s, the question of vertical (and an implied horizontal) merger came to light and led to an EU ruling. The case was commented on by some of the leading specialists in the field: Humphreys and Lang (1998), De

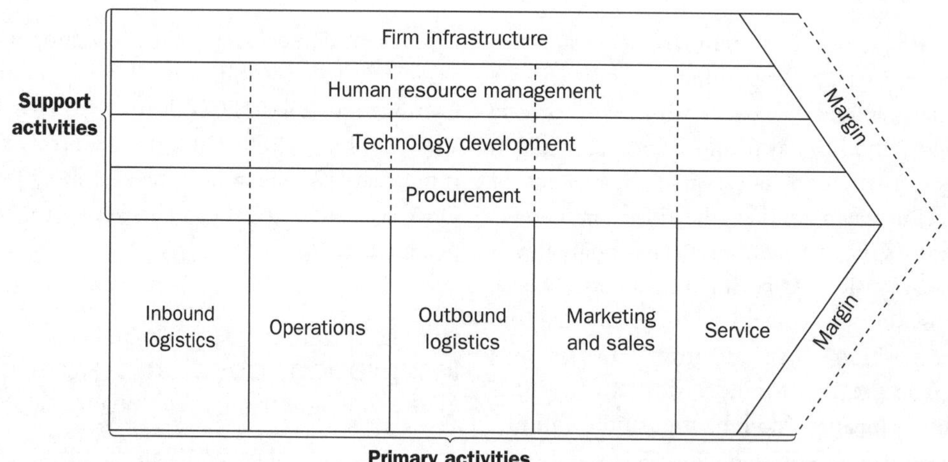

Figure 3.1 M. Porter: value chain

Source: Reprinted with the permission of The Free Press, a Division of Simon & Schuster, Inc., from *Competitive Advantage: Creating and Sustaining Superior Performance* by Michael E. Porter. Copyright © 1985, 1998 by Michael E. Porter. All rights reserved.

Case Study 3.2

The power of the regulator to stop a perceived 'dominant position': Bertelsmann

The following extract is detailed but once again worth the effort. It shows the importance given to competition rules within the EU.

> In March 1994, Bertelsmann, Kirch and Deutsche Telekom proposed to form a joint venture, MSG Media Service. It was reported that: The new company . . . will initially focus on providing pay-TV and pay-per-view services and eventually video-on-demand and TV-shopping services to the 14 million households wired up by DT's cable television network. While the joint venture will not provide any content services, other media companies will become its clients to transmit their own movies, home-shopping and other programming. In 1994, Bertelsmann had interests in book and magazine publishing, book clubs, printing, music publishing, sound recording and commercial television. It was also active in foreign markets and made about 6% of its turnover outside Germany. Its arch rival Kirch was the leading German supplier of feature films and television programming and was active in commercial television. Kirch also had interests in pay-TV suppliers outside Germany. Deutsche Telekom was the incumbent telecommunications operator in Germany and was also the owner and operator of 'nearly all the German cable-television networks.' At the end of December 1994, the European Commission blocked this joint venture because of concerns arising in three vertically related markets:
>
> 1. Technical and administrative services for pay-TV and other payment-financed communication services in Germany – the Commission concluded that MSG would acquire a 'durable dominant position' in this market;
> 2. Pay-TV – the Commission deduced that: If MSG held a dominant position on the market for technical and administrative services, this would considerably strengthen the position of Bertelsmann/Kirch on the downstream market for pay-TV. It would have to be expected that the setting-up of MSG would give Bertelsmann and Kirch a durable dominant position on the market for pay-TV.
> 3. Cable networks – the Commission deduced that: It can be expected that the proposed concentration will in the long-term also adversely affect to a considerable extent effective competition on the market for cable networks in Germany. . . . There is a danger that, by jointly operating the pay-TV structure together with the leading pay-TV suppliers, Telekom will strengthen its position as a cable network operator in such a way that, following liberalization, competition in the cable network market will be substantially impeded and thus Telekom's dominant position safeguarded.

Source: OECD, Directorate for Financial, Fiscal and Enterprise Affairs: competition committee, *Media Mergers*, pp. 39–40 (OECD, 2003).

Streel (2002) and Kovacic and Reindl (1997). In Case Study 3.2 we see an argument presented by the EU for its decision to block a proposed takeover by the German media giant Bertelsmann (1994).

Ownership

Media barons, the owners of newspapers or the proprietors of TV stations, are themselves interesting, often the focus of media limelight. However, in economic terms it is what the 'owner' does that is important: managing products through costs and competition. It does not necessarily make a difference whether they are private individuals, boards of governors, shareholders or an annexe of a government ministry. It is the decisions they make that matter. The simple truth is that the rules of economics apply to all, no matter who the owner is. Owners may decide to compete or collude (not compete) in a market, whether they are a state broadcaster or a private firm. It all depends on the regulation and rules, such as competition policy, mergers and 'dominant position', as well as their management competence.

In certain instances there can be agreements not to compete, but only in exceptional circumstances is collusion in cartels legal. However, if an owner takes up a dominant position, this can be unhealthy in economic terms and dangerous in media terms because of propaganda and attacks on the principle of political pluralism.

There is one, often cited, fundamental difference in ownership: the difference between private and public corporations. A view of these arguments can be found in various chapters throughout this book. The European (and EU) tradition has been, and will continue to be, a mix of both public and private provision. This is a debate about nationalisation and public broadcasting, and about privatisation and private sector provision. Can economics help our assessment of the two sectors?

The argument for nationalised industries is chiefly that they represent special sectors of the economy which need two seemingly contradictory economic aims to be satisfied. First, they need high levels of investment (with natural economies of scale that allow for efficiencies of mass and large-scale production) and they need to control pricing for the consumer so as to be socially inclusive and because they are in a monopoly position. Second, a media product can be deemed essential for social and political stability, or even the general well-being of a society. In the past, major sectors of the economy were regarded in Europe as 'natural' sectors for national control and regulation: energy, water, social housing, transport, telecommunications, postal services, health and media in the form of public broadcasting.

Nonetheless, over the past decades across Europe, within the EU, there has been growth in private participation. This can be seen in sectors formerly linked to nationalised media organisations, a process called, in a sweeping generalisation, 'privatisation'. Privatisation has taken many shapes and forms across the EU and has been managed by a variety of governments in different ways.

Creating a European Single Market has increased the convergence of policy development, especially through rules on competition and through external tariffs, albeit not yet VAT and national tax levels. There remain marked debates about the future of EU tax policy given the widening participation in the Euro-zone and its common monetary policy across most EU nation states. Even countries outside the Euro-zone, such as the UK, Sweden and Denmark, need to bear in mind the tax policies of their EU partners. All of this impacts on national economies and thereby the media.

Stop and consider 3.3

The EU does not have agreed 'harmonised' VAT rates on products including media products, so there will be distortions of consumer behaviour created by different national tax rates. When you are looking at the media product data in economic terms, it is good to stop and consider how important tax regimes are in influencing consumer behaviour. Overall data such as this can be found in the OECD and in national statistical resources.

As can be seen from Chapter 4 there has been a growth of media regulation and market influence exercised by the institutions of the EU on the member states. This is having an impact on the way in which the media market is developing. For public service broadcasters (PSBs), the growth of privatisation threatens their remit at a time when governments are highly conscious of demands on the public purse.

Competition is also becoming keener. Technology is allowing the telecommunications market to flourish, grow and interconnect across the EU and beyond, and new media players (Microsoft, Google, Tiscali and Yahoo) are entering the field creating, but also competing for, advertising revenue. This too touches on the traditional role and public service remit as they are now independent distributors of media content. Most of the present-day debate in the EU about the future of the media revolves around the role and importance of and the possible market share between the private and public sectors.

It appears that the EU has settled on a broad compromise to preserve PSBs but equally to drive forward integrative media policies within the EU to establish economies of scale. This they hope will mean that EU media organisations will be able to compete with other major, cross-national media producers such as the USA and the new economies – potentially powerful, national media markets such as India, Brazil and China.

The former deeply rooted national PSBs within the EU are faced with noticeable difficulties: tax revenue and increased investment is limited while their private sector competitors have access to European and even global capital markets. Besides, the private sector companies have a strategy of growth through mergers and takeovers, using private capital, shareholding and stock markets. This is normally denied by statute to PSBs or nationally controlled media outlets.

Moreover, how much tax the EU can directly take out of the European economy for integrative purposes (1.24% of EU **GNI**) is restricted by the member states. Media policies remain a fine balance between private and public sector interests, and this is reflected in the EU's economic regulation of the media. Some critics of the EU position point to the EU's encouragement of deregulation in the media (sometimes known as 'negative integration'), but to achieve integration of the market the EU has little recourse to 'positive' (subsidy-based) initiatives.

Mono-media and cross-media ownership – the present

One of the major controls placed upon the private and the public sectors is the regulation of cross-media ownership by EU nation states. It varies throughout the EU and there are different practices in each country, but even here, technology, and in particular the digital revolution, has impacted on the markets and the rules that control them. This has created a deeper synergy allowing for greater cross-media ownership. The strict divide between telecommunication, broadcasters (radio and television), newspapers and internet service providers is breaking down. This has opened the market up to more mergers and takeovers and a greater degree of conglomeration activity, meaning greater horizontal and vertical integration (mergers) challenging the mono-media and cross-media divide.

What is the present cross-media scene like? In global terms (based on revenue), there are eight major media conglomerates, two of them (indicated in bold) are European: General Electric, Time Warner, Walt Disney, **Vivendi Universal (EU)**, News Corporation, **Bertelsmann (EU)**, CBS and Viacom. All of them perform across frontiers and all of them are owners of cross-media groups: from TV to Internet, from publishing to film, from radio to telecommunications. There are also what are called mono-media companies: those who dedicate their competence to one field of activity.

Both cross- and mono-media are subject to rules and regulations on ownership. In regulatory terms, they face international, EU and national levels of control. To work in the EU is to understand and follow the rules in this multi-level framework (see Chapters 1 and 4 and Source 3.2).

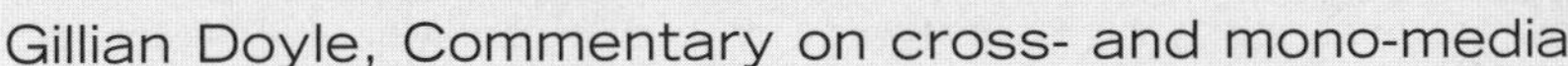

Source 3.2

Gillian Doyle, Commentary on cross- and mono-media

One of the leading lights in the UK on media economics is Gillian Doyle. Recently she researched the economic case for mono- and cross-media ownership. Her views are contested, but they are relevant to contemporary thinking on the issue:

> Since the early 1990s, regulators across the globe have faced increasing pressure from media firms to liberalise domestic media and cross-media ownership restrictions. Based on empirical research carried out in the U.K. . . . Findings suggest that, although factors other than size will affect performance, there is generally a strong and positive correlation between the market share and the operating profitability of firms involved in either television or radio broadcasting or newspaper publishing. But, with regard to cross-media ownership of television and newspapers, there is no compelling evidence that diagonal integration brings about inherent synergies, economies of scope or other economic benefits. Thus, whereas a variety of economic efficiency gains may be available to justify a relaxation of restrictions over monomedia expansion, few such benefits can be found in support of deregulating cross-ownership of television and newspapers. (Abstract)
>
> Source: The economics of monomedia and cross-media expansion: a study of the case favouring deregulation of TV and newspaper ownership in the U.K. (Doyle, 2000).

Nonetheless, and from 2000, the growth of cross-media ownership appears to be on the rise – see below. The synergy is often expressed as 1 + 1 = 3, based on putting two companies together making them more efficient and more profitable, e.g. by reducing duplication. Economies of scope – combining two activities in one company – will mean that activities can be carried out more efficiently.

Table 3.3 Corporations and media platforms

Sector: Companies/group	*TV*	*Film*	*Radio*	*Cable*	*Telecoms*	*Online*	*Publishing/print*
General Electric	●	●		●		●	●
Time Warner	●	●			●		●
Walt Disney	●	●	●			●	●
Vivendi Universal	●				●		●
News Corporation	●	●	●			●	●
Bertelsmann	●	●	●			●	●
CBS	●		●			●	
Viacom	●	●	●			●	●
Clear Channel	●		●				
Gannet	●						●
Cox	●		●		●		●
Tribune	●		●				●
The Hearst Corporation	●		●				●
The Washington Post Company	●		●				●
New York Times Company	●		●				●
Comcast	●					●	
Advancenet				●	●		●
Cablevision	●				●		
McGraw-Hill	●						●
CanWest Global	●		●				●
Scripps	●						●

Source: Based on data from Who owns the media, 2006? *freepress.net*, http://www.freepress.net/ownership/chart/main.

Major companies with a cross-media agenda are emerging as important global players (see Table 3.3). They all compete with one another at corporate, capital and financial levels; the fortunes of such companies vary from year to year. Many will lose, many will gain, many will be merged or taken over.

There are also mono-media major players who specialise in media services, building corporate partnerships or links with other major industry players, such as Microsoft, Yahoo or Google. There are specialist telecoms companies moving into printing and publishing and, conversely, some of the bigger players are listed in Table 3.4.

Profit motives: economic efficiency and the media market

Producing profit, based on products and services, is the lifeblood of markets, but equally the general well-being of the global, international, European and national economies is important too. The media industry, like so many parts of the modern economy, is inter-related and inter-dependent. Levels of employment, spending power (e.g. household spend), economic growth, inflation, capitalisation and entrepreneurial culture are some of the many aspects of the overall economy which impact on the media industry.

As a general truism and as an example, the media is tied neatly, some say perversely, to the advertising sector: if it falters, and it generally does when the economy dips, so too do the media companies. The public sector (PSB), being financed differently, is less sensitive to economic conditions. However, across the EU most PSBs also rely on advertising revenue (the BBC national broadcasting is one of the exceptions in some parts of its business model), and they are therefore vulnerable to any drop in advertising expenditure.

The degree of risk in the market can be cushioned by the 'wealth', or by the investment, innovation and successful branding strategies of the big 'private' players, and that is why Table 3.3 is so intriguing. It does not mean that these global players are bound to succeed; bad management and tactics can always lead to failure. However, being able to spread their financial risk and rely on cross-media provision can help them survive. The message appears to be: the digital age and new technology can help if companies diversify and develop their product range.

Table 3.4 Media players

	TV	Film	Radio	Cable	Telecoms	Online	Publishing/print
Adelphia					●		
Verizon					●		
AT&T					●		
BellSouth					●		
Reed Elsevier							●
Pearson							●
Knight Ridder							●
Hachette Filipacchi (Lagardere)							●

Source: Based on data from Who owns the media, 2006? *freepress.net*, http://www.freepress.net/ownership/chart/main.

Chapter summary

➤ This chapter highlights important tools of economic analysis that may be applied to the media.

➤ The material is not designed to be a full coverage of the discipline of economics but an introduction to some of the principal concepts that inform the debate on the modern media.

➤ Economics can be used to explore and interpret the media within the EU.

➤ The principles of economics underline many of the key decisions made in the development of the EU.

➤ In the EU economics is an integral part of the integrative movement, and this is impacting on media policy as well as other sectors.

Key terms

Many of the key terms have been dealt with in the text, but there just a few other terms used that might need some more consideration:

European Commission: this EU institution has the sole power to propose Europe-wide legislation. Look at Chapter 1 for the decision-making process that is at play. This will include the role of the euro currency and the position of the European Central Bank in its development.

GNI: similar to GDP (gross domestic product), this is a measure of a country's total value, but also taking into account income and payments from and to other countries.

Maslow's hierarchy of needs: emanating from a famous psychologist, the needs of individuals are put into a series of normally five sets of needs that embrace categories such as physiological, safety, love and belonging, esteem and what was termed 'self-actualisation'. In simple terms, the hierarchy works as we move through the factors, satisfying each layer of need before embracing the next.

Discussion questions

1. In terms of media analysis, how important among the many factors that impact upon the media is the 'economics' and economic modelling?
2. In the EU is it useful to think in macro-economic or micro-economic terms? What are the advantages and disadvantages of thinking about EU media in this way?
3. What is 'substitutability' and why is it important in media economics?
4. What role does 'price' play in media economics and why is this significant, especially in the EU single market context?
5. Economics works through supply and demand, but some commentators have argued (Picard) that the media and its economics are different to other products. Enumerate these differences (the factors) on the supply side and demand side citing EU examples. Can you find arguments against these points?

6. What is the difference between comparative and competitive advantage? Think of media examples in the EU.
7. How do we avoid monopolies in the media and why is this important for the EU media market?
8. What is the difference between a merger and a takeover? Use EU examples to illustrate your answer.
9. Who should own the media and why? In your answer reflect on why the majority of media in the EU is in private hands.

Assignments

1. Using data and material from a reliable source such as the European Journalism Centre draw up a synopsis of the macro-economy of an EU member state and then evaluate the micro-economy of the media sector within the national economy. Assess its importance and its general economic trends.
2. When you have completed Assignment 1, do the same for another EU member state and then compare the two countries.
3. When you have completed Assignment 2, look at the macro-economy in EU terms from a reliable source such as OECD or Eurostat. As well as looking at the micro-economy of the media sector you are interested in at an EU level, compare your results to the national findings you have created in the previous assignments.

Further reading and references

Aubry P. (2000) *European Audiovisual Observatory*, The 'Television without Frontiers' Directive, Cornerstone of the European Broadcasting Policy.

Begg D., Dornbusch R., Fischer S. (2005) *Economics*, 8th edn, London: McGraw-Hill.

Bird & Bird (2002) *Market Definition in the Media Sector – Comparative Legal Analysis*, Luxembourg: European Commission, DG Competition.

Burda M., Wyplosz C. (1997) *Macroeconomics: A European Text*, 2nd edn, Oxford: Oxford University Press.

Chang B-H. (2004) Consumer evaluations of cable network Brand extensions: a case study of the Discovery channels, *Journal of Media Business Studies*, **1**(2): 47–70.

Denny N. (2005) Leader column, *The Bookseller*, 10 February.

de Streel, Alexandre (2002) European Merger Policy in Electronic Communications Markets: Past Experience and Future Prospects, Mimeo, draft 4 September 2003; downloaded on April 26, 2003 from: http://intel.si.umich.edu/tprc/papers/2002/99/EuropeMergerPolicy.pdf and cited in OECD (2003) *Media mergers*, DAFFE/COMP(2003)16, p. 39.

Dobrev S.D. (1999) The dynamics of the Bulgarian newspaper industry in a period of transition: organisational adaptation, structural inertia and political change, *Industrial and Corporate Change*, **8**(3): 573–605.

Doyle G. (2000) The economics of monomedia and cross-media expansion: a study of the case favouring deregulation of TV and newspaper ownership in the UK, *Journal of Cultural Economics*, **24**(1): 1–26.

Doyle G. (2002) *Understanding Media Economics*, London: Sage.

Doyle G. (2002) *Media Ownership*, London: Sage.

EC (2005) Commission Staff Working Paper. *Strengthening the Competitiveness of the EU Publishing Sector. The role of media policy*, Luxembourg, European Commission.

EMCC (2003) *Sector Futures: The Future of Publishing and Media*, Dublin: European Foundation for the Improvement of Living and Working Conditions.

EMCC (2004) *Sector Futures: Publishing and Media: Balancing the Interests of Producers and Consumers*, Dublin: European Foundation for the Improvement of Living and Working Conditions.

EMCC (2004) *Sector Futures: In Search of a Realistic Future*, Dublin: European Foundation for the Improvement of Living and Working Conditions.

Ernst and Young (2007) *Competitiveness of the European Graphic Industry*, Luxembourg: European Commission.

Europe Economics (2002) *Market Definition in the Media Sector – Economic Issues*, Luxembourg: European Commission, DG Competition.

Fu W.W. (2003) Multimarket contact of US newspaper chains: circulation competition and market coordination, *Information Economics and Policy*, **15**: 501–519.

Graham A. (2001) The assessment: Economics of the internet, *Oxford Review of Economic Policy*, **17**(2): 145–158.

Gulyas A. (2003) Print media in post-communist east central Europe, *European Journal of Communication*, **18**(1): 81–106.

Ha L. (2003) The economics of scholarly journals: a case study in a society-published journal, *Learned Publishing*, **16**(3): 193–199.

Harcourt A. (2004) Institution-driven competition: The regulation of cross-border broadcasting in the EU, *EUI Working papers*, RSCAS No. 2004/44, European University Institute.

Heinrich J., Kopper G. (eds) (1997) *Media Economics in Europe*, Dortmund and Berlin: Vistas.

Herold A. (2003) European Public Film Support within the WTO Framework, *Iris Plus*, June, Strasbourg: European Audiovisual Observatory.

Holznagel B. (2000) The Mission of Public Service Broadcasters, *International Journal of Communications Law and Policy*, **5**: 1–6.

Humphreys, Peter and Matthias Lang (1998) Digital Television between the Economy and Pluralism, Chapter 1 of Jeanette Steemers (ed.) *Changing Channels: The Prospects for Television in a Digital World*, John Libbey Media, 1998, and cited in OECD (2003) *Media mergers*, DAFFE/COMP(2003)16, p. 39.

Kovacic, William E. and Andreas P. Reindl (1997) Entertainment Industries, New Technologies and Antitrust, unpublished manuscript but cited in OECD (2003) *Media mergers*, DAFFE/COMP(2003)16, p. 40.

Lange A. (2005) *The Financial Situation of Television Companies in the European Union (1999–2004)*, September.

Mayer-Robitaille L. (2005) Application of EC competition policy regarding agreements and state aid in the audio-visual field, *Iris Plus*, June, Strasbourg: European Audiovisual Observatory.

McChesney R.W. (2000) The political economy of communication and the future of the field, *Media, Culture and Society*, **22**: 109–116.

McQuail D., Siune K. (1998) *Media Policy: Convergence, Concentration & Commerce*, Zurich: Euromedia Research Group, London: Sage (reprinted 2001).

Mintel (2007) *National newspapers – UK – November 2001*, London: Mintel Group.

OECD (2003) *Media Mergers*, DAFFE/COMP(2003)16, Paris: Organisation for Economic Co-operation and Development.

O'Mahony M. and van Ark B. (eds) (2003) *EU Productivity and Competitiveness: an Industry Perspective. Can Europe Resume the Catching-up Process?*, Luxembourg, European Commission.

Pelkmans J. (2001) Making EU network markets comcpetitive, *Oxford Review of Economic Policy*, **17**(3): 432–455.

Picard R.G. (1989) *Media Economics: Concepts and Issues*, London: Sage Publications.

Picard R.G. (1997) *The Newspaper Publishing Industry*, Needham Heights, MA: Allyn & Bacon.

Picard R.G. (2002) *The Economics and Financing of Media Companies*, New York: Fordham University Press.

Picard R.G. (ed.) (2005) *Media Product Portfolios: Issues in Management of Multiple Products and Services*, Mahwah, NJ: Lawrence Erlbaum Associates.

Pira International (2003) *The EU Publishing Industry: an Assessment of Competitiveness*, Luxembourg: European Commission.

Porter M.E. (1985) *Competitive Advantage*, New York: Free Press.

Porter M. (1998) *The Competitive Advantage of Nations*, New York: Free Press.

Reding V. (2007) The convergent publisher – print media in the broadband economy, Speech, Publishers Forum, Brussels, 6 December.

Skouras T., Avlonitis G.J., Indounas K.A. (2005) Economics and marketing on pricing: how and why do they differ?, *Journal of Product & Brand Management*, **14**(6): 362–374.

Terazono M. (2007) European media deals rise by 75%, *FT.com*, 30 January.

Towse R. (2005) Alan Peacock and Cultural Economics, *The Economic Journal*, **115** (June): F262–F276.

WAN (1999) Strength in numbers: the challenges for newspaper advertising, READY Report, Paris: World Association of Newspapers.

Wetherly P., Otter D. (eds) (2007) *The Business Environment: Themes and Issues*, Oxford: Oxford University Press.

There are many journals in the field and of course we cannot forget the *Journal of Media Economics*, Lawrence Erlbaum Associates, for many of the more technical approaches.

Online resources

http://www..

A good starting point to create your own website list is intute: follow the instructions and the various disciplines and record the sites as you go: http://www.intute.ac.uk/. There is also a whole range of encyclopaedias covering many of the topics listed in this and other chapters.

Chapter 4

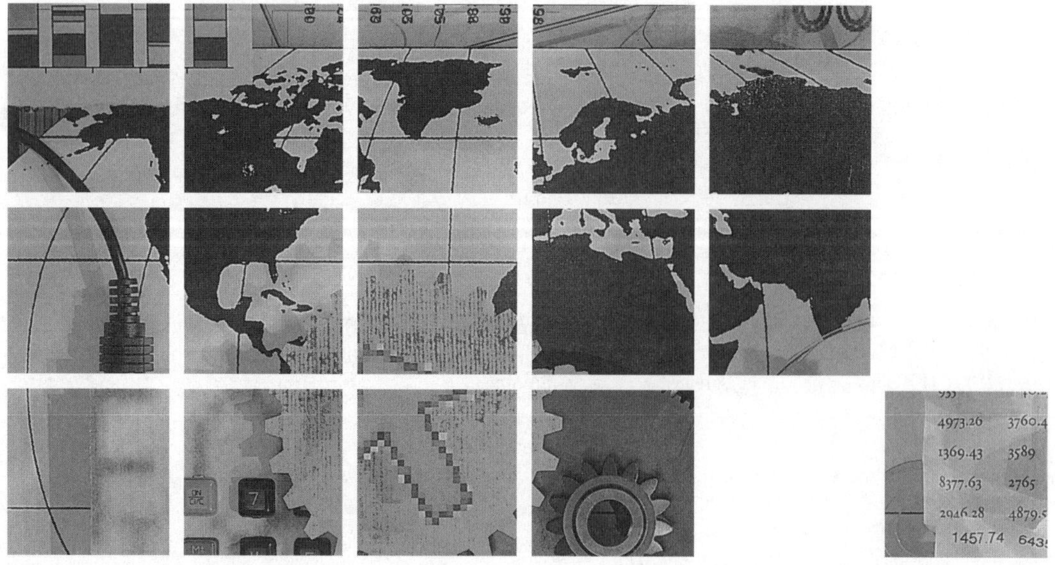

EU politics, regulation and media legislation

What the chapter covers

- Introduction: regulation and the regulators
- The EU regulatory debate
- The European regulatory context
  - *European scheduling*
  - *The European mediascape – now and in the immediate future*
- Public vs private
  - *Money and investment*
  - *European history*
  - *Digital delivery*
  - *Research work*
  - *How to categorise the regulatory frameworks*
  - *Using regulations and assessing their importance*
  - *National vs trans-national regulation*
  - *European convergence between states*
- International rules and the EU
  - *The extent of international regulation*
  - *Copyright and intellectual property*
  - *Patents*
- EU regulatory development – key areas
  - *The Hahn Report 1983*
  - *The Bangemann Report 1994*
  - *The Television without Frontiers Directive (TWF), 1989, revised in 1997 and 2005 onwards*
  - *The Single European Market 1987–1993 and TWF 1989 onwards*
  - *Mergers, acquisitions and takeovers, monopolies and competition policy and state subsidies*
- Moving on into the 21st century
  - *The Lisbon Agenda 1997, eEurope (2002–2006) and i2010*
  - *Open Network Provision (ONP) 1998*
  - *EC regulatory framework for electronic communication and services (convergence) 1999–2002*
  - *Policy frameworks*
  - *The Audio-visual Media Services Directive (AVM) 2007 onwards*
  - *Reaction to EU media policy and regulatory change*
  - *Company reaction to policy changes*
- EU member state national regulation
- Regulation, deregulation, self-regulation and co-regulation
- Conclusions and more questions

Learning objectives

When you have completed this chapter, you will be able to:

- Relate the media scene to the regulatory framework set in place by the EU and the individual countries and other similar types of organisation, e.g. WTO, EU or European nations.
- Understand that conflicts of interests are often linked to regulation, law and the politics behind different regulatory frameworks.
- Recognise that while media 'regulations' across the EU are often diverse, they are often similar too.
- Draft a thumbnail sketch of the principal international, EU and trans-national regulations.
- Identify the range of competing views about the changing media regulatory landscape at the many levels of governance (national, European, international and even regional).
- Examine how political and economic pressures impact upon the picture of the changing media global services.

Themes

Below you will find a simple statement or series of statements around the six themes. They should *not* be read as a given fact. They are more like hypotheses (see Chapter 2) which need to be proved, discussed, debated and then used in your own analysis of the subject. The ideas and approaches in this book are always to be considered with an open mind; this is important in university study and is what makes it distinct from pre-university study.

Diversity of media

The 'media' is a diverse technology that is in the process of converging. Even so, its diversity remains predominant within organisations, both public and private, changing over time and often functioning differently in different countries.

Internal/external forces for change

The media is not only changing technologically, but also in a regulatory, political and economic way. In our analysis of the media, we need to be aware of the internal media dynamic within the national industries but also mindful of the global, international, EU and even sub-national, local pressures that are pressing for change. This theme alerts you to this question and points to the internal, national dynamic and the external pressures forcing change.

Complexity of the media

The media is complex because of the way in which it is regulated and how the rules are put together. This is often conveniently labelled as a discussion about public and private provision within societies. Moreover, the distinction between public and private sector broadcasting, in particular, is being blurred, with a mix of public and private regulatory initiatives being used to develop the 'old' media and the 'new'.

Multi-levels

Media business and public broadcasting reform at global, national and local level is quickening. No longer is the nation state the only level at which the media interacts. The levels are generally subsumed into accepted notions of globalisation, whereas on the ground, it is local and global as well as European levels that are in play.

European integrative environment

In the context of this book's investigation, one theme has been of major interest: the Europeanisation of the media market. Europeanisation is both a private and public sector concern and is political and economic and, in the long term, cultural. This theme alerts us to the process of European integration and its impact upon us in matters cultural. As a term it is not meant to subvert the national but alerts us to a process whereby member states of the EU are bringing together their media and business policies in a form which not only goes beyond the national into the global, but is uniquely European.

Cultural values

The media for most us is not just a technology or a business but a content-laden communicator of cultural and social values: in a word 'content'. This theme reminds us throughout that the question of culture is ever-present in our analysis of the market place.

Essentials

This chapter provides an overview and an introduction to the most important international, national and EU media legislation. Understanding media regulation is often a specialist field of activity. The present era embraces some very technical subjects such as cross-border assimilation of legislation, foreign ownership, the softening of ownership concentration legislation, provisions for the continuation of public service broadcasters (PSBs), and programming quotas in television together with copyright and patents. Although this chapter cannot investigate these in depth, they are sufficiently important that we need to have some background information if we are to get to grips with the contemporary media scene. The work in this chapter has three broad themes:

➤ The background to international media regulatory regimes.

➤ The evolution and context of EU media regulation.

➤ A discussion of some of the debates that surround new media regulations.

Introduction: regulation and the regulators

The competition between big technology companies such as Microsoft and Google may dominate the information technology headlines, but eventually the battle for the new media agenda and the impact of the new technology on the media will settle on the law and regulation. It will be the legal factors that define the market and its operation.

Media law and regulation can be seen as the bridge between politics, economics and the media industry which is in both private and public ownership. For example, the introduction of agreed principles across the member states in the EU on protecting children against unacceptable content or the common acceptance of a model of a private and public duopoly model different to that of the USA speaks volumes about the direction of the European media market.

The EU regulatory debate

In regulatory terms, the EU offers us an insight into two fundamental present-day concerns:

1. There is increasing concentration of private sector global players who, if they continue unchecked, may take up monopolistic positions. For example, the EU has recently fined Microsoft for apparent abuse of position with its software. Equally, US products in the audio-visual (**AV**) business comprise over 65% of all production (Lange, 2001), especially in television products. This could damage both nationally-based and more community-oriented media companies and corporations, and distort not only competition but also public service broadcasting.
2. The media has such a powerful voice that if concentration continues it may well threaten 'pluralism' and the healthy exchange of political ideas, restrict 'freedom of speech' by restricting content breadth and undermine democratic values.

Some argue that 'regulation' at whatever level – national, European and even international – is important in stemming the new tide of media concentration. Nevertheless, new technology opens up a myriad of opportunities for small and medium-sized companies, and even individuals, to share and develop new ideas and make profitable companies (Pay-Pal, Stylewriter, Skype, etc.). Do we over-worry about media monopolies in a world as diverse as ours? The Internet, the web, allows a potentially huge growth in peer-to-peer sharing of culture and ideas on the back of the profits that mass markets and the new technology offer.

The European regulatory context

It is of course recognised across the EU that the press, the print and the audio-visual industries are faced with technological convergence. This is demonstrably changing the delivery platforms upon which both media producers and consumers rely. The previous distinctions between the different types of media, which were both technological and legal, are beginning to blur. Not surprisingly in such an atmosphere, law and regulations play an important part in the 'mediascape'. The EU states though have often reacted with some difficulty because of differing political agendas.

Creating a public service broadcasting system at an EU level has not yet been possible. The thrust for trans-national European media production (Bertelsmann AG, Vivendi Universal and Pearson plc are good examples in the private sphere) has been in the main resisted by states and national PSBs. As such, PSBs remain a matter of member state and not EU responsibility. The BBC before the recent charter changes in 2004/05 is a good example, with a strongly held view, at least in public, that national rather than European public broadcasting is best for maintaining standards. The BBC marshals strong arguments to support this view, which are seen, in some quarters, as serving its own self interest, it being one of the best funded PSBs in Europe.

There is no European public broadcasting regulatory system akin to the national systems, only the semi-advisory group the European Broadcasting Union (EBU), or the consultative 'Conseil de l'Europe' or background organisations such as the Organisation for Security and Co-operation in Europe (OSCE) and the Organisation for Economic Co-operation and Development (OECD). There is no defined single organisation for media policy or public sector broadcasting in Europe and it is uncertain if there is a political will to create one in the near or even the medium-term future. Nevertheless, a European media 'public' space fed by inter-related public and private broadcasters is not only technologically possible, but appears to be evolving.

Differences of view and responses to change are the norm inside the EU: compare the changes to the BBC charter, which take place every ten years, with the proposed broadcasting alterations in France (2008–2009) that appeared like lightning on the scene as an initiative from President Sarkozy and his team.

There are Europe-wide organisations that are beginning to pull the market (at least in data) together: the European Audio-visual Observatory, Eurostat, various media institutes such as the Institute of European Media and even academic research groups such as the European Communication Research and Education Association (ECREA).

The EU has now created an almost one-stop portal within the EU Commission for Audio-Visual policy (**DG** X: Information, Media and Culture) and, importantly, the publishing industries are now included. Furthermore, the private sector and its international and European strategic research for placing products, from games at Ubisoft, to satellite provision, to shared technical harmonisation for mobile communication, is creating new market opportunities and expectations at the same time.

European scheduling

Besides, the private sector as it grows, acquires and merges, shares scheduling, programming and resources is creating a European network intrinsically. Even in the 'public sector' there are examples of cross-border initiatives such as the Franco-German **ARTE** broadcasting organisation. Created to form a cross-national broadcasting venture, ARTE began broadcasting in 1993 and is primarily aimed at German and French speaking audiences. Although not a major market share programmer, ARTE is reputably one of the most innovative and culturally alive forms of television in the world. Other PSBs would dispute this of course.

There is much sharing of data and new techniques even in the publishing world. The press, photographic and specialised **press agencies** such as Havas, Reuters and **AFP** have brought together news and information for almost a century and a half. They feed stories to both press and broadcasters. Increasingly, they are offering their products to a wider audience and direct through the web. They form a network with other agencies, the American **AP** and **UPI** agencies but also Chinese and Russian agencies, creating a global source of journalism and journalistic resources which feeds the 'global' news screens of our present age.

The European mediascape – now and in the immediate future

For the Europeans this background shapes the European political and economic project and its mediascape. This is where the EU institutions, who are pushing for greater integration, and the nation states, who are clearly trying to preserve national interests, display political tension. This tension shows itself in the policy-making of the last few decades and is discussed briefly below.

In simple terms, there is the media on one side and the wider political forces on the other. These interests include the corporations, the states, lobbying associations, including unions, and an impressive mixture of other groups all representing the interests of the many (the consumers) and often the demands of the few (the producers).

As might be expected, compromise and incremental development is beginning to hold sway rather than a major shift in the balance of the media in Europe. There is strong agreement that the future of the media in Europe will preserve a relative balance between public and private provision (see Case Study 4.1 for an interesting angle on the Euronews channel). This will maintain a fundamental distinction between Europe and the USA.

Nevertheless, most players concede that the public service remit needs further definition to justify its special financial position in the market. Some say this should be linked to consumer choice; others encourage the public sector to be more community, nationally, culturally and innovatively inspired to safeguard national and cultural distinctiveness. What appears to be emerging, across the EU, is the call for a 'public service value' test and an established, transparent, provable 'remit' for PSBs.

The **digitisation** of the new delivery technology, however, is difficult for states to control. The market place will be different in the future, as the number of media players changes and the choices, at least from a consumer point of view, multiply.

The debates rage on, not least over the question of whether the media has fulfilled or should fulfil the democratic demands of diverse European societies (Harcourt, 2005). The jury is out. However, the trends suggest increasing trans-nationalism, with a core 'national' public service. The state broadcasting

Case Study 4.1

Euronews

As an example of European-type scheduling, the case of the channel 'Euronews' is revelatory both for its ups and its complex downs. More important, it represents the continued attempt to create a true EU-formed rather than national-based 'news' delivery outlet for EU citizens. Its aims are ambitious (2007):

> Euronews wishes to show its viewers, on a daily basis, Europe as it is: richly diverse and complex . . . Ambition and impartiality are the guiding principles that will shape the channel's coverage of current events in and outside the European Union . . . A national focus is now too narrow for informing the public and debating the issues. Euronews is tracking the emergence, out in the field, of a genuine European public arena.
>
> Source: Euronews annual statement of commitment to viewers, http://www.euronews.net/en/services-ue/.

So far in audience reach it has not attained the heights set for itself. Its description of itself though is more upbeat (2007):

> **euronews** is the **leading international news channel** covering world news from a **European perspective**. Launched in 1993, **euronews** today is a multi-lingual (English, French, German, Spanish, Italian, Portuguese, Russian and Arabic), **multi-platform news service**. . . . **euronews** remains the only multilingual news channel broadcasting simultaneously in 8 languages to a global audience.
>
> Source: http://www.euronews.net/en/the-station/.

Even so, bounced from the public to the private it landed on the scene in 2006 with what may be defined as a public–private mix that is innovatory. Its future of course depends upon the market place and political will. (See also Chapter 5.)

systems are adapting, throughout the EU in some cases, fast. There is a continued argument over who or what is creating the shift, but the EU organisation is playing its part in this field through influence and pressure, a part which should not be over-estimated but, equally, should not be underestimated either.

Public vs private

State broadcasting has always seen itself as a bulwark against the worst excesses of private media, often considered politically to the 'right', with bias toward the corporate world, although in content terms this is often difficult to prove. It is agued that the public interest should be safeguarded by bolstering the PSBs. With this comes a licence that normally allows governments to control or at least supervise the media channels. Theoretically, the 'public' system should be free of the normal competition between companies because of its special public service role in society.

In Germany, for example, the state broadcasters are obligated by constitutional law to be pluralistic in approach, stretching their news reports and stories across the political spectrum. This is why the FRAG case (see Case Study 4.2 on p. 68) was so important.

The private sector has always maintained that this is a system that leads to a public sector which is an unfair competitor: supported and bankrolled by taxpayers' money and guaranteed by government decree or charter. These are old arguments. The BBC in the 1920s faced this type of debate. First created as a company in the private sector in 1922 (The British Broadcasting Company Ltd) it was re-created in 1927 as a public sector corporation run by governors and a charter, the British Broadcasting Corporation.

The present debates are important and have increased in intensity in the present e-led era. So many of the proposed regulatory decisions revolve around the relationship between the public and private sectors. What are the PSBs for, and are they in reality any different from any other media corporation? Should or can they be preserved? Are the private large trans-national companies a threat or not? What is the role of regulation and its relationship to production, distribution and consumption? These are old questions but in a new context. The following subheadings indicate the direction of some of these questions.

Money and investment

Some suggest it all comes down to arguments about money and investment, and the role of the state in modern economies – in particular, the new 'mediascape' raises a question about the taxation system. How much should be spent on public service interest (such as PSBs) and how much should be left to the private sector, economic competition and innovation? Tax relates to state subsidies and political control. It raises the question of to what extent media content should reflect public interest if it remains primarily national in outlook. These questions will occupy the states in the EU in the near and medium future. Whatever the outcome, the role of the state public broadcasting systems is under review. It is not surprising, therefore, that nothing is occupying the mind of the EU public broadcasters more than the future of the public broadcasting system itself. One way or another, the emergence of the digital age within an era of Europeanisation and globalisation is changing their world and ours with it. Europe in general remains wary of creating a 'global' media-regulatory world because it is trying to protect its media in the interests of its culture and economy, whereas in the USA many argue that the media should be treated as any other economic sector and open to competition.

Although at times disputed, the argument has run thus: the larger the market, the better the use of the available resources. Making markets larger provides for economies of scale and enables comparative and competitive advantage (see Chapter 3). This is especially the case for the private sector media industries. Equally, this is important for those countries with larger consumer populations and a history of media production. The UK, France, Germany and Italy are in the vanguard, but there are also other EU countries such as Spain and Poland trying to break into global markets. The UK has the widest lineage in the EU and remains one of the key host countries for global media companies outside the USA.

European history

In another way, the debate is about European history itself. There is a fear of the renewal of anti-democratic forces supported by a popular, media-led, potentially chauvinistic or even communist leaning or capitalist élite-led agenda. The shadow of Hitler and Goebbels, Stalin and Franco and the role of propaganda within the media and in the past remains a presence. This accounts for some sensitivity about the prominence of US multi-national, corporate and broadcasting power. Finally, yet importantly, it colours people's views on the question of international and European regulation.

Private companies, international competition in production and distribution and audience and readership shifts in demand are challenging the position of PSBs in most societies across Europe. For example, a recent report (UK Ofcom, 2006) points to a new generation (16–24 age group) of media and telecommunications consumers that are PC-literate, digitally-led and are not loyal to any accepted television channels.

Digital delivery

However, this is nothing compared to the potential new era of digital delivery. New technology means the state broadcasters' power over media distribution (especially television-type imaging but also the wider audio-visual), through state control and licences, is threatened. You can see this on web portals and internet downloads in all its forms: web pages, podcasting, film and media readers, cable or satellite, PC TV and wi-fi distribution techniques.

State broadcasters are not just competing with the increasingly merged private broadcasters but also the large and increasingly privatised telecommunication networks. There are also the new 'kids' on the block, the digital giants: Microsoft, AOL, Google, Yahoo, Tiscali and Orange (taking over Wanadoo). In an era when the 'information society' impinges on all economies, the question of intellectual property and copyright, let alone piracy of goods, is increasingly important.

Research work

Where do we turn for some of the latest commentaries and research? The latest work coming out of the Hans-Bredow-Institut research group, for example, is a good resource to understand how media regulations play a part in the modern media framework (Hans-Bredow-Institut, 2005; Prosser, 2008). They along with others have been doing important work for the European Commission and are a serious resource for us to use.

The Oxford Media Law group (1992, now known in terms of 'Programme of Comparative Media Law' – see online resources below) is another. The Institute of Information, Telecommunications and Media Law is yet another. More important perhaps, every nation state will have regulatory bodies. To develop our knowledge it is always good practice to look at national bodies responsible for regulation. Many of them try to define the media–society relationship.

In the Hans Bredow model (Point of View 4.1), the state is responsible for an overall legal and regulatory framework through parliament and international agreements. The state responds to the needs of its citizens who occupy the position of the civil society. At the same time, they react to changes in the economy and therefore the market, which link them to producers, distributors and the consumers. The media, private and public, forms a central position in the communication network between all the parts of society. Equally, the media as companies or corporations have their own interests in maintaining investment, profit, audience reach, influence and employment.

How to categorise the regulatory frameworks

When we use the EU model of decision-making transposed on to the system, however, we need to multiply these relationships by the number of participant member states. The 'state' in this sense becomes not only the nation state but the collective as represented by the EU institutions. This means the media and its regulation have to be defined in a multi-layered way. The types of media regulation

Point of View 4.1

Hans-Bredow-Institut – media and civil society

To illustrate a contemporary debate and in a recent report for the European Commission, the Hans Bredow researchers neatly described societies as made up of a triangle of the state, and what they call civil society and then the market (2005).

Sitting between the state, civil society and the market is the media: a place and a channel that allows the parts to communicate with one another. Equally, the media, they also contend, is also a self-interested organisation, acting as a body separate from both government and people, but joined inextricably to both.

Source: Hans-Bredow-Institut: drawn from various reports but especially *Interim Report Study on Co-regulatory Measures in the Media Sector* (Hans-Bredow-Institut, 2005), http://ec.europa.eu/avpolicy/docs/library/studies/coregul/interim_rep.pdf.

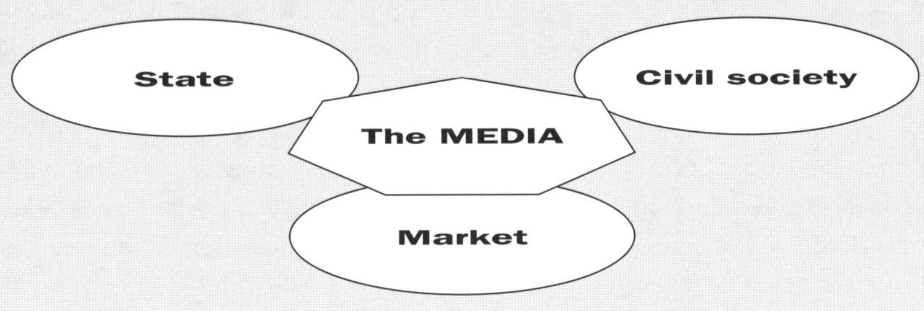

Hans Bredow describes across Europe are classified in the following manner:

- law(s) by parliament(s) and state bodies, plus the EU decision-making process;
- market regulations that include property, consumers and advertisers at national and European levels;
- associations, even lobbying groups, bringing citizens and other interest groups together;
- media self-regulation through journalists, codes of practice and professional business conduct, again at national and European levels.

Stop and consider 4.1

In all of this, the importance of legal definitions looms into focus. For example, should there be a legal difference between individual blogging or bloggers or comments found on My Space *and the edited work of a journalist working in a public broadcasting system, say the* BBC *or* FrTV *or major press agencies such as* Reuters*? Most of all perhaps, can 'we' as consumers distinguish between the public and private sectors and does it matter? These are questions we will need to come back to. Certainly, we need to 'stop and question' these fundamental issues.*

The core difference between the 'blogger' and the professional journalist is accountability and responsibility. The BBC journalist has strict guidelines to adhere to, for example, producers' guidelines, while the blogger has none. The law normally reflects this difference.

Equally, the reader will need to know whether the writer has taken into account such issues as impartiality, accuracy, balance, code of practice or libel law.

Using regulations and assessing their importance

Nevertheless, a word of caution about regulations: technological innovation often outstrips the plans of the rule-makers. In politics, creating rules and laws often imposes on and shapes our world, but equally the change they seek is often overtaken by innovation and new practices on the ground.

Therefore, when weighing up the media rules, we need to see them in practice: the consumption, reception and use of the media in different settings. If we do this, we discover again that in the EU there is much diversity within the market place, but there are also trends. Later chapters of this book, dealing with the production, distribution and consumption of the media, are dedicated to this and should be read alongside this section (from Chapter 6 onwards).

National vs trans-national regulation

Apart from the press and print industry, which in the main has been in private hands in Europe, the audio-visual network since 1945 has been mostly governed by the state or state agencies framing behaviour through national control. Broadcasting was a particular concern of the state. Most countries adopted a different approach to the print and AV industries, arguing that they functioned differently. The press was left in private hands because there was sufficient choice available to the consumer to reflect differing opinions. The AV side was initially controlled by the state or the public sector because the technology was expensive and choice more limited and because its visual, live format was potentially more influential.

Later, most countries in the EU, although there are exceptions of course, adopted a duopoly in AV, a mixture of PSBs and private broadcasters, though the latter were also content-managed by national regulation. In the era of analogue distribution networks, this was something states found reasonably easy to do.

The FRAG case (Case Study 4.2) shows us that there were and are differences of provision, depending on the history and politics of each nation state. There are still many varieties of control across the EU. Amongst other cases, and ones that include the trans-national aspect of the media market, are the Sacchi and Debauve cases of 1974 and 1980, both of which are seen as very important landmarks in the development of EU media regulation (see Case Study 4.3).

In the 1980s with the support of the EU, the member states embarked on an experiment to open their borders to encourage, but also protect, their creative industries. In so doing, the states gave up some of their own regulatory control to share content approaches and allow for market development. They targeted the television market first, which then came to embrace, systematically, most audio-visual provision.

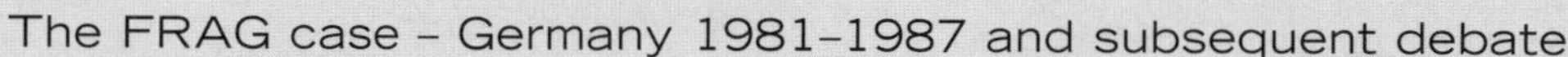

Case Study 4.2

The FRAG case – Germany 1981–1987 and subsequent debate

A previous attempt to establish private broadcasting in West Germany had failed before the German constitutional court in 1961. The possibility of a monopoly and the need under German Basic Law to allow for pluralistic news were seen to be threatened. However, another attempt from 1981, known as the FRAG case, overturned this ruling.

In legal jargon, a later ruling included this comment which reveals the national pressures surrounding legislation that arise when dealing with the media in Europe:

> The question of who is to receive one of the scarce resources for broadcast programming must therefore not be left to chance or the free play of market forces. It is also not enough when the decision is left to the unbridled discretion of the executive. This would not be compatible with the proviso of law (cf. BVerfGE 33, 303 [345 f.] – Numerus clausus). Rather, the legislature itself must define the prerequisites under which access is to be granted or denied, and it must establish a fair procedure for deciding on this. The mandate of equal treatment can be fulfilled without great difficulty within the framework of a system that allows broadcasting times to be allocated or, if need be, proportionately reduced.

Source: FRAG case (BverfG, 1987).

Case Study 4.3

Sacchi and Debauve

Sacchi was a cable operator in Italy in 1974 who claimed that the national broadcasting system was unfairly taking advertising revenue away from the private sector. Although the courts found against the company, the European Court of Justice specified that broadcasting signals were an economic activity. This brought the sector into the jurisdiction of the European market and hence its courts.

The 1981 *Debauve* case established that no broadcasting signal could be restricted because of national origin. This opened up the market for all member states in broadcasting and was another landmark case.

These two cases added to the impulse toward the Television without Frontiers Directive of 1989.

For a good review of these cases in context see Harcourt (2004).

The modern era, moving away from analogue provision to digital, is facing a whole set of new challenges and opportunities. As consumers buy into digital technology, both the producers and the distributors are moving in the same direction. Europe as a whole, as with other global players, is going digital. Overall this means a shift from less state control to greater choice for the consumer and, in many respects, less regulation through the state. New regulation means laying down principles and frameworks, while the new technology of 'digitisation' has hastened the process at both a global and European level.

European convergence between states

Later, and more indirectly, the EU institutions started to issue advice and gather data even on the print industry, mainly because of concerns over cross-media ownership; where publishers were involved in AV as well as print production. There is no print or publishing directive equivalent to the Television without Frontiers Directive, although general legal restraints in most societies in the EU exist: media legislation deals with libel and slander (for example, the UK), and privacy laws (for example, France, see Case Study 4.4) or personal respect (for example, Germany).

Case Study 4.4

Law cases: privacy and freedoms

In France, privacy is not explicit in the 1958 Constitution (creating the fifth republic). But a ruling in 1994 in the French constitutional court said that 'privacy' was 'implicit' in the constitution.

Privacy laws always lead to debate. In November 2005, the French magazine *Paris Match* was ordered to pay €50 000 in damages to Prince Albert of Monaco following a cover story about his son.

This led the lobby group Reporters Sans Frontières to write (2006):

> We hope Paris Match will take this case to the European Court of Human Rights. French law is one of the most restrictive in this area. The German courts ruled against Prince Albert in the case he brought against a German newspaper for running a similar story to Paris Match's. And the ties between two people are not usually seen as restricted to the private domain in Britain. An international court should rule on this issue.
>
> Source: Concern about privacy laws after Prince Albert wins ruling against Paris Match, *Reporters Sans Frontierès*, 6 January 2006, http://www.rsf.org/article.php3?id_article=16109.

A more official line can be found in French Embassy attitudes to the whole issue of privacy and French law (2007):

> In France, as in many other countries, invasions of privacy have become widespread, aided by advances in science and technology as well as abetted by the claim that 'the

Case Study 4.4 (continued)

public has a right to know' and justified by the principle of freedom of expression. Freedom of expression is enshrined in article 11 of the Declaration of the Rights of Man and of the Citizen – part of the corpus of constitutional law – and in the European Convention on Human Rights. . . .

The value to society of information on the private life of public figures is obviously undeniable where it has the potential for public enlightenment. But a just balance needs to be found between what can be publicized, in deference to the principles of freedom of expression and of information, and what has to be safeguarded from excessive public curiosity, so as to avoid infringing the individual's right to privacy and right to his or her picture (photograph or drawing), both of them rights of personality.

Source: French Legislation on Privacy, 2007, http://ambafrance-us.org/spip.php?article640.

International rules and the EU

Creating trans-national regulation is not new, and the EU works in a global media context where regulation has been a part of the scene for many decades. For example, the first major global treaties date from as far back as the 19th century. Therefore, to think of the trans-national regulation of ideas and the trade in published or media goods as a new phenomenon would be inaccurate. There have always been important international rules, for example on intellectual property and copyright.

The extent of international regulation

What is different today is the scale and extent of international and European regulatory regimes. Surprisingly, this does not necessarily mean more regulation but new levels of regulatory policy. The modern era embraces more sectors than the past: audio-visual policy, radio, telecommunications, ownership, advertising and the internet. In addition, this is a time when the role of regulation is being discussed at national, international and EU levels and is a reflection of a new digital and globalising era.

Copyright and intellectual property

Historically, copyright and intellectual property was at the core of international concern and this is a good place to look at principles and case law. Table 4.1 is not a full list but an illustration of some of the important, sometimes contested, features of the international regulatory regime:

Patents

Intellectual property has been a part of the international scene for a long time. This has included patents (the registering of ideas) and was a part of the 1883 Paris Convention. Even so, the patent regimes in individual countries remain very important, usually with a long history of development, and they are complex. Their primary purpose is to allow the development of new ideas while protecting those who have developed them.

The overall context of world trade in ideas and published goods is an important aspect of how nations respond to international media trade. The EU responded as we can see above with its own copyright directive, the EU Copyright Directive (2001), covering all member states. There has been another directive recently created, specifying its rationale:

> **Directive on measures and procedures to ensure enforcing intellectual property rights** (2004/48/EC): 'This Directive seeks to create equal conditions for the application of intellectual property rights in the Member States by aligning enforcement measures throughout the Union. It also aims to harmonise Member States' legislation in order to ensure an equivalent level of intellectual property protection in the internal market.'
>
> (EU, 2004)

Copyright and patents are one area of activity, but the EU nowadays goes beyond such measures. Like national regulators before it, the EU legislates

Table 4.1 International agreements: intellectual property (examples)

Regulatory development	*Description*
1883 The Paris Convention and 1886 Berne Convention	In the 19th century protecting an author's work, either economic or creative, was nationally bound. At the instigation of the French writer Victor Hugo, and in 1886, the Berne Convention changed this. Various bureaus were created to oversee the internationalisation of these regulations and are the forerunner of the WIPO and WTO organisations that exist today. The USA was in the past reluctant to participate, arguing that protection should be 'term' defined and not associated with the lifetime of an author.
1952 UCC or Universal Copyright Convention	Set up by the United Nations the UCC embraced developing nations and the Soviet Union. The latter argued that previous conventions were too 'Western' in approach, and by that they meant 'capitalist'.
1961 Rome Convention or the Protection of Performers, Producers of Phonograms and Broadcasting Organisations	Until this convention authors held most copyright or ownership of intellectual property. This convention, in response to new technology such as tape recording, provided for copyright protection of producers, including broadcasters and performers.
1994 TRIPS (WTO) Trade-Related Aspects of Intellectual Property Rights	The Agreement on Trade-Related Aspects of Intellectual Property Rights applies to all members of the WTO. It remains the most comprehensive, and often most contested international agreement. Perhaps most importantly, the WTO agreement, springing out of the former GATT rounds, provides for disputes and sanctions for participants.
1996 WIPO Copyright Treaty and 1996 WIPO Performances and Phonograms Treaty (WPPT)	Both the USA and the EU abide by the principles of these WIPO agreements but have amendments (extensions) to their clauses. In essence, and again in response to the new IT technology, this provides protection for computer programs.
1998 (USA) Digital Millennium Copyright Act. EU Copyright Directive (2001)	These two laws spring out of the TRIPS and WIPO agreements, and form the base for much of the trans-Atlantic trading, and contestations, in media products between these two blocs.

how the European media market operates within its 'single market', and what relationship it has in general to the 'outside' market: by definition, markets beyond its borders and customs and external tariff control. This has not happened overnight. It has been evolving over the past few decades and is constantly evolving. For the latest changes to copyright inside the EU regarding performers as well as authors, see http://ec.europa.eu/news/culture/080220_1_en.htm and http://ec.europa.eu/internal_market/copyright/index_en.htm.

EU regulatory development – key areas

More than just seeing the media as a product, in the 1980s EU regulators began to argue that the media played an important role in helping to create the 'European identity' and further EU integration. Some landmarks in its development are described below.

The Hahn Report 1983

Following an important legal ruling at the European Court of Justice – the Debauve ruling 1980 – various political parties (mainly on the left) published reports emanating from the European Parliament. They called for two new media initiatives: protecting state broadcasting and checks and balances on media concentration and monopolies. A second report called for the creation of a pan-European broadcasting channel. The latter was taken up by what is known as the Hahn Report, in 1983.

The Bangemann Report 1994

The debate about the future of the European media had not yet ended, and the call for regulation in mergers and takeovers in such a sensitive area as media policy continued through the 1980s and into 1992–1994. The Bangemann Report, in effect there was more than one report, is seen as seminal, because it strongly argued that this was not the time for restriction of markets but, on the contrary, a moment to put 'faith in market mechanisms'. In addition, it argued that Europe should embrace 'the information society' as a means to increase the EU's global competitivity. It also considered that media ownership should not be measured by content, or by channels, or even by the number of media owners, but by market share.

The Television without Frontiers Directive (TWF), 1989, revised in 1997 and 2005 onwards (EU 1989, 1997, 2007)

Depending on how you interpret the next moves, the European Commission, already deeply involved in creating a single market (potential and real unemployment in Europe was growing, as was competition from the USA and Japan), began to embrace the media. The EU from 1993, and the EC even before this, was already proposing technical harmonisation of standards to support the market in the important telecommunications sector.

The EC equally understood the importance of the media industry within the overall economy and launched an initiative in the media sector known as the 'Television without Frontiers' proposal. There was a Green Paper in 1984, later annexed in to the White Paper 'Completing the internal market', 1985, which was then accepted as a directive in 1989. This was then approved by the member states in the 'Council'. The latter was the 'Council of Ministers', later to be named the 'Council of the EU' – see Chapter 1. It remains the most important media broadcasting directive on the present scene. Table 4.2 summarises the fundamental sections of the Television without Frontiers Directive and introduces us to the language of EC directives. Proposed changes, including e-services, are given in the section on EC regulatory framework below (see p. 74).

The Single European Market 1987–1993 and TWF 1989 onwards

These rules for European television listed in Table 4.2 were very much a part of the European drive to create a single market, both in its timing and its thinking. Nevertheless, the TWF initiative was also linked to other factors. Even so, in many respects the heady mix of the Hahn Report and the Bangemann Report, the creation of convergence between telecommunications and the media, the harmonisation of standards including radio and new projects such as HDTV, all emanate from the thinking behind and the momentum of the Single Market.

Yet, creating a functioning 'Single Market' in the media along with other products was always going to be problematic because of political, linguistic and economic differences in the EU. Its purpose was and is to boost the European economy, increase jobs and employment and uphold peaceful inter-state negotiations on trade.

As well as differences, it has often been argued that media products have a lot in common culturally, and should be brought together for their own protection. The Single Market's main targets were private industries as opposed to public services. Even so, as many of the broadcasting and almost all the print industries were in private hands, the Single Market's influence on the EU media market was bound to increase.

The EU specified major areas of corporate concern that were to touch the media industry in one way or another. Not least, it encouraged companies to grow and merge. Nevertheless, this was to be completed in a controlled manner, linking regulation of competition policy with regulations on mergers and takeovers with an over-riding pressure to reduce state subsidies.

Table 4.2 Television without Frontiers Directive – key areas

Principles and purposes	*Definitions*
Its regulations to apply across the EU to all members states and permit access of member states' products between and across frontiers	'Every member state must regulate the transmissions of broadcasters under its jurisdiction in accordance with its national law but the reception or re-transmission of a broadcast from one member state is not to be restricted in any other member state. The only exception concerns services which infringe the protection of minors' provisions in Article 22.'
Promote distribution and production of TV programming within the EU	'Member states are required to ensure that services, where practicable, transmit a majority of European material excluding news, sports events, games, and advertising and teletext services. At least 10% of such transmissions must consist of European works made by independent producers. These requirements are to be achieved progressively.'
Promote advertising standards	'Advertisements must be clearly identifiable between programmes or in natural breaks. Advertising of tobacco and prescription medicines is banned and limited on alcoholic beverages. Minors must be protected. Programme sponsors must be identified and may not influence the scheduling or content of programmes or encourage the purchase of products or services. News and current affairs programmes may not be sponsored. Spot advertising is limited to 15% of daily transmission time and to 20% in any one-hour period.'
Protect political pluralism	–
Protect minors (violence and pornography in the main)	'Member states must prevent broadcasters under their jurisdiction from broadcasting programmes which might seriously impair the physical, mental or moral development of minors, particularly those involving pornography or gratuitous violence.'
Provide for 'right of reply'	'Asserts a right of reply or "equivalent remedies" for anyone whose legitimate interests have been damaged by an assertion of incorrect facts in a TV programme.'
Copyright	'Harmonization of copyright rules across Europe'
Protect major (national) in the main 'sporting' events from exclusive coverage.	–

Source: Television without Frontiers Directive (EU, 1989, 1997). Adapted from European Commission, *Europa 2007*, http://europa.eu/.

Mergers, acquisitions and takeovers, monopolies and competition policy and state subsidies

To subsidise or not to subsidise? – that is the question at the heart of EU media regulation.

> **Stop and consider 4.2**
>
> *It is often said that the newspapers are free of state interference because they are not subsidised. This is in relative terms true, but there are countries that do provide tax incentives, postal preferences or other subsidies for their press industries. Notably, there is assistance given in Luxembourg and France (see Chapter 6). What are the arguments for and against subsidising the media in Europe?*

The rules and regulations for company mergers, acquisitions and takeovers and the rules on monopolies and bad practice are complicated and usually hotly contested. The case of the alleged Microsoft 'bundling' of software material and its resulting fines (2006) imposed by the EU is now part of media folklore. There are many other legal media cases although many do not make the headlines. Case law in this area dates back a long while and is worthy of study by students and practitioners alike.

Forming market rules has always been a central core of the purpose of the EU. The rules and regulations for mergers, acquisitions and takeovers are designed to counteract what is seen as monopolistic or competitive advantages that would be harmful to the consumer.

In the past, much of this control was national in form and it remains so in policing and legal procedures. Yet, in a global market, the EU has assumed power and interest in the media legal field. The rules for mergers, both horizontal and vertical, apply across firms in general in the EU. The EU member states enforce and translate the rules into national legislation.

What this means in practice is increasing pressure on individual states and regions to become more transparent across the sectors from banking to subsidy. At present, there are many diverse practices across the EU which some might argue is 'unfair' and tends to distort economic competition and accountability.

Moving on into the 21st century

The Lisbon Agenda 1997, eEurope (2002–2006) and i2010

Developing the European economy remains a priority for all EU member states: this is both practical and strategic. As the media is such an important part of Western economies, it cannot remove itself from these wider economic initiatives. This is the case with what is known as the new 'Lisbon agenda', and the increasing emphasis on the 'information society'. This has meant developing a whole gamut of directives to include not only the private sector but also services provided to and by the public services. The media and communication industries are playing an important part in this initiative. This can be noted in policy trails or frameworks developed by the European Commission. The Lisbon Agenda of 1997 together with the development of the i2010 initiative (see Chapter 1) has re-emphasised the importance of the grand strategy (see Point of View 4.2).

Open Network Provision (ONP) 1998

This directive opened up the access to telecommunications services in the EU, especially telephone services (voice telephony). The driving force behind this innovative directive was the use of the Single Market (internal market) initiatives, as opposed to using competition law which was used in the Television without Frontiers Directive (Harcourt, 2005). The 'regulatory framework for electronic communications and services' directives later enhanced this.

EC regulatory framework for electronic communication and services (convergence) 1999–2002

Where there is greatest European agreement is in technological convergence, making sure that the EU system performs across borders. During the 1990s

Point of View 4.2

EU positions and grand strategy? The Lisbon Agenda and the Berlin Declarations' broad visions for the future

We have seen that the EU is built in part on economic dynamics and political unity, but with continued support for diversity. The recent declarations by the EU, the grand strategies we might call them, have had a direct impact on many aspects of future policy but also more generally on the media:

Lisbon Agenda (2000): To make the EU by 2010

> the most competitive and dynamic knowledge-based economy in the world, capable of sustainable economic growth with more and better jobs and greater social cohesion.

> Source: European Parliament, Lisbon European Council 23 and 24 March 2000, http://www.europarl.europa.eu/summits/lis1_en.htm#6. See also http://ec.europa.eu/employment_social/knowledge_society/index_en.htm.

Berlin Declaration (2007):

> In the European Union, we are turning our common ideals into reality: for us, the individual is paramount. His dignity is inviolable. His rights are inalienable. Men and women enjoy equal rights. We are striving for peace and freedom, for democracy and the rule of law, for mutual respect and shared responsibility, for prosperity and security, for tolerance and participation, for justice and solidarity.
>
> Source: http://europa.eu/50/docs/berlin_declaration_en.pdf.

and beyond, the EU was increasingly aware of the need for harmonisation of technical standards across the telecommunications sector. There was a series of directives (often called a 'Framework' and related to 'policy trails' – see below) aimed at achieving this. Because of convergence, all of them impinged on media policy:

- Framework Directive:

  > The Framework Directive provides the overall structure for the new regulatory regime and sets out the policy objectives and regulatory principles.
  > (EU, 2002a)

- Authorisation Directive:

  > Under the 2002 *Authorisation Directive*, Member States can no longer use the instrument of individual licences to regulate the sector. They are required to establish a general authorisation for all types of electronic communication services and networks, including fixed and mobile networks and services, data and voice services, broadcasting transmission networks and services.
  > (EU, 2002b)

- Access Directive:

  > The Access Directive (2002) sets out the terms on which providers may access each others' networks and services with a view to providing publicly available electronic communications services.
  > (EU, 2002c)

- Universal Directive:

  > The Universal Service Directive deals with the obligation to provide a basic set of services to end-users.
  > (EU, 2002d)

- Data Protection Directive:

  > The Privacy Directive establishes users' rights with regard to the privacy of personal data.
  > (EU, 2002e)

There were also two other important initiatives during this period: the 'radio spectrum decision' (EU, 2002f), which was pan-European in form, and the Cable Ownership Directive (1999), separating cable company activity from telecommunications, to encourage competition (see also Case Study 4.5).

Case Study 4.5

Telecoms

Bringing the telecoms industry together within the EU context has not been easy but in fact complex, as you will see if you read the two recommended articles below. The fundamental problem was not technological but regulatory. Across the EU, the member states had different rules and regulations governing telecommunications. This was exacerbated by the fact that most telecommunication industries were state-owned and bound closely to political, national agendas, not market, orientated trans-national markets. The difficulties in creating a single market in telecoms have been recognised even by the European Commission:

> . . . in Europe, all these significant new opportunities are being slowed down by regulatory uncertainty and by a lack of scale in the European internal market. In fact: there is no internal market for electronic communications. The internet may see no borders, communications services may be the most powerful force for a 'global village' or a 'world that is flat' but broadband – and also mobile – services stop at frontiers in Europe or are offered under completely different rules and conditions once one crosses a border. This creates a big challenge for European policy makers. Our system of 27 national markets is slowing us down, the very least we need is greater consistency in the application of regulation. The regulators that lack full independence and the remedies that are not always imposed in a timely manner or which appear to be ineffective create distortions of competition from one geographic market to another. The playing field is not level for operators that have a European footprint – already today around one third of telecoms revenues are cross-border.
> Source: Viviane Reding (Commissioner), speech (Reding, 2007).

See also two very interesting and thoughtful articles to deepen the argument: Humphreys (2006) and Pelkmans (2001).

Policy frameworks

At an EU level, as we have seen, there are two main audio-visual, regulatory, policy areas: television and telecommunications. Since 2007, the field has included a new 'audio-visual' media directive in response to technological and media change. However, looking beyond these specific directives there are other connected initiatives that influence the media sectors. Nowadays, there is interconnectedness between policy areas: 'eEurope' for example and the 'Information Society' bring together policy development in the private and the public sectors. This goes beyond the narrow definitions of media policy.

In reviewing regulatory policies at EU level, from the past to the present, it is often good to build policy trails: noting how one policy links to another (see Source 4.1). The one suggested below is rudimentary and from 2002 but shows how, at any given moment, policy development is always related to wider concerns. Sometimes they are called 'frameworks'. Below, the 2002 (Information Society) and 2007 (Framework) EU priorities have been classified showing linkage, change and continuity (see Source 4.2).

In this policy trail, the driving factor was the EU emphasis on the importance of the 'information society' (from 1999): a designation which embraced new ways of looking at contemporary economies (see Chapter 3) and the new technology of the modern era. Linking its many policy areas together, the EU was able to locate a network or trail of initiatives which would enhance not only the Single Market, but also the political and social aims of the EU. From the boxes, we can see that there are relationships being developed between political, social and economic directives: from social affairs, to education, to telecommunications to e-business.

Source 4.1

EU policy trails

When seeking out EU media policy developments, especially in regulatory terms, it is good to follow the criss-cross pattern of policy-making. Below is a 'trail' of polices created from 2002.

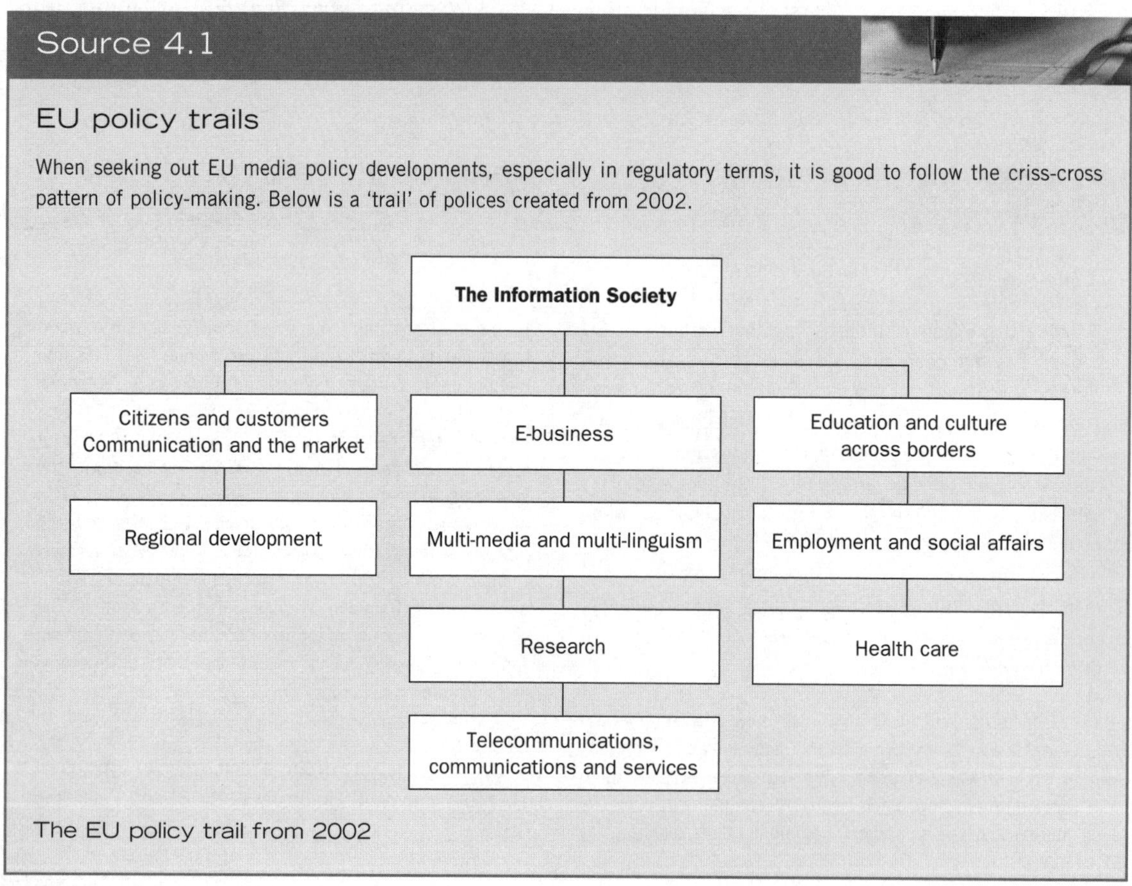

The EU policy trail from 2002

Source 4.2

EU frameworks

When seeking out EU media policy developments, especially in regulatory terms, it is good to follow the criss-cross pattern of policy-making. Below is a 'framework' of polices created from 2007.

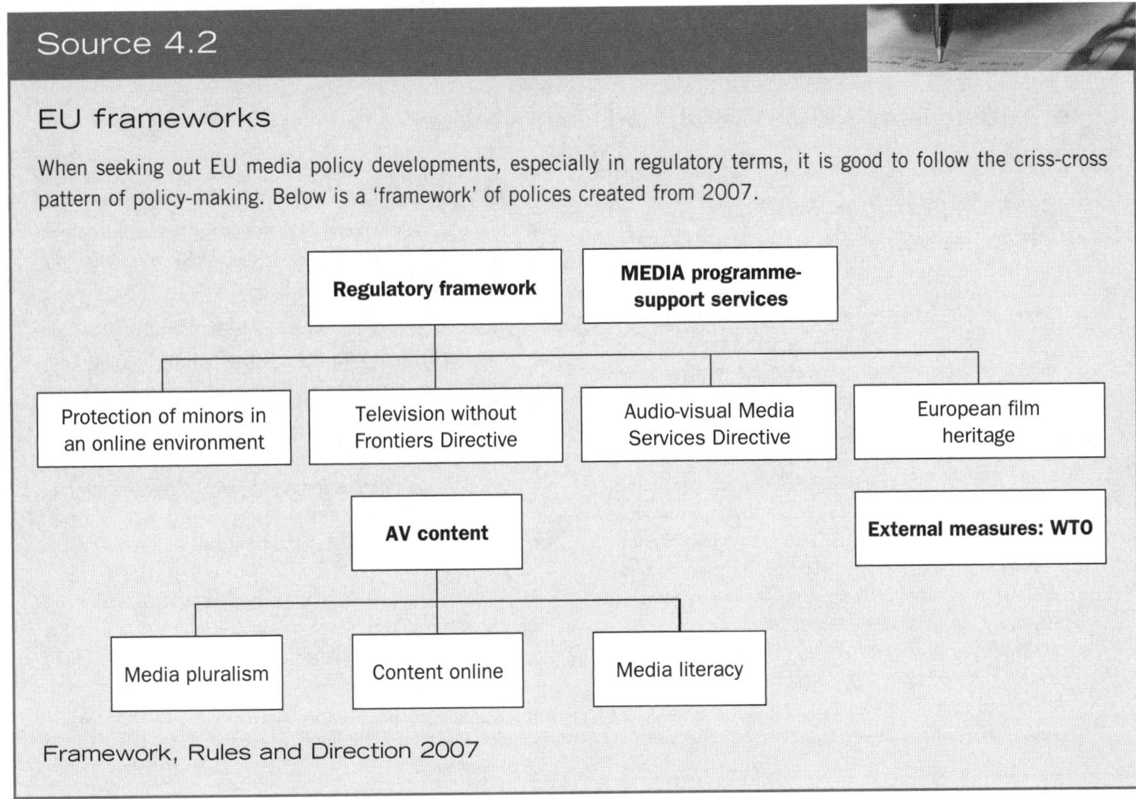

Framework, Rules and Direction 2007

The EU 'frameworking' or policy development is especially important for nation states. In the framework above, we can place specific directives into a more complete pattern. Like policy trails the frameworks give coherence to policy development. The degree to which they are successful remains a part of the debate.

Member states will interpret the overall approaches, translating them into their own national regulations. Nevertheless, the EU Court of Justice has the right to over-ride the national courts of appeal if there are conflicts. It is the inherent power bestowed on the European Court of Justice that oversees the relevant media rules, not just at a cross-national but now also at an EU level. Increasingly the EU is providing detailed and readily transparent details through their web portal on these issues. Case law on competition cases can be found at the European Court of Justice web site and is revealing.

The strength of a single legal European 'voice' in media terms is also important because the EU represents its member states in many of the international trading arenas (WTO, WIPO and OECD). The media industries pay heed to this strengthened position of the EU institutions, as they work the market within the EU and other international market places.

The Audio-visual Media Services Directive (AVM) 2007 onwards (EU, 2007)

The newest proposals for regulatory change are the EU response to new technology. Adding to the range of key developments comes the new 'Audio-visual' Media Services Directive. It amends and updates the Television without Frontiers Directive. In essence, it extends the provisions on 'television' to the Internet. It treats the AV screen – web and internet – in similar fashion to the TV screens of the past. It moves the regulatory control into an e-era, which will dominate the 21st century. You will notice that the TWF Directive lays down principles, which are then translated back

Case Study 4.6

The Audio-visual Media Services Directive 2007

The principal proposals for the AVM Directive extend the 'Television without Frontiers' Directive:

> As it stands, the directive requires member states to co-ordinate their national legislation in order to ensure that:
>
> - there are no obstacles to the free movement of television programmes within the single market;
> - television channels, where practicable, reserve at least half their broadcasting time for films and programmes made in Europe;
> - safeguards are in place to protect certain important public interest objectives such as cultural diversity;
> - governments take action to ensure that a broad public has access to major events, which therefore cannot be restricted to pay-TV channels only. This provision refers mainly to international sporting events such as the Olympic Games or World Cup football;
> - governments take measures to protect minors against violent or pornographic programmes by scheduling them late at night and/or by limiting access through a technical device built into the TV control handset;
> - parties unfairly criticised in a television broadcast have the right of reply;
> - the maximum volume of advertising that channels can carry during a given period (measured in minutes per hour or per day) are fully respected.

The proposed changes, which were submitted to the European Parliament and the EU Council of Ministers for approval, retain the basic principles in the directive but seek to:

- Extend its cover to include new media services, such as video-on-demand, or services provided over the internet or mobile phones;
- Allow more flexibility in the timing of advertising spots on TV;
- Allow indirect advertising through product placement – where broadcasters can charge for featuring a branded product in a programme. This is allowed in the United States, but is so far illegal in Europe.

Source: Audiovisual Media Services Directive (EU, 2007). European Commission, *Europa 2007*, http://europa.eu/.

into the legal systems of the nation states. This is the case with the extension of these principles, such as the use of product placement, for the Audio-visual Directive (see Case Study 4.6).

During its development, the Audiovisual Media Directive 2007 has been very contentious in certain quarters. This is often the case in EU regulatory matters.

Reaction to EU media policy and regulatory change

EU media policy-making is often praised and damned all in one breath. It is 'good', it is argued, because it pulls the market together. However, it sometimes imposes upon member states and their traditional way of handling the media. Nevertheless, nation states cannot draw away in the modern global era from some level of harmonisation of their approaches. The European market place has, as we have seen, a common commercial policy and therefore an overarching economic background (the Single European Market). This includes the media. It allows the media market to work within a given set of rules no matter how difficult this may be. Even so, some may say that EU media policy can be too prescriptive, general and insensitive to the diverse communities it serves. It is also criticised for being too deregulatory, too open to the market and not making exceptions to the identity issues that surround the media.

These arguments are hard-hitting even if the EU has a broader, state-wide accepted, legal integrative purpose set down by international treaty accepted by all member states. There are even European directed programmes to encourage media integration, for example the EU's MEDIA Programme. Though taken as a whole at an EU level, they remain financially modest at €671 bn (2007–2013). The new MEDIA programme (see Case Study 4.7) has three objectives, interesting because they show political as well as economic aims for national and trans-national cooperation.

Case Study 4.7

Media investment by the EU

Often cited as an example of EU subsidy, the new MEDIA programme is designed to encourage EU content. The question is – does it provide the customer with 'value-for-money'?

MEDIA III: The global objectives of the programme are to:

(a) Preserve and enhance European cultural and linguistic diversity and its cinematographic and audiovisual heritage, guarantee its accessibility to the public and promote intercultural dialogue;

(b) Increase the circulation and viewership of European audiovisual works inside and outside the European Union, including through greater cooperation between players;

(c) Strengthen the competitiveness of the European audiovisual sector in the framework of an open and competitive European market favourable to employment, including by promoting links between audiovisual professionals.

Source: EU decision concerning the implementation of a programme of support for the European audiovisual sector (MEDIA 2007 (EU, 2006)).

Despite the arguments about whether forming the EU is a 'good or bad' objective, integration and policy convergence is occurring. No nation state is an island in media technological terms, and it would be a mighty economic risk to separate the communication structure from one state and another in the modern era. Nation states may wish to build forms of protection through media-related state subsidies for example, or attempt to create quotas for products, but the pressure is to open up not close markets. In the end the media works on long-term trends not short-term ones, and the long-term trend is for access and growth.

Company reaction to policy changes

In broad terms, what has this meant for companies working within the media industries?

- Companies have had to adapt and harmonise the products for an EU market.
- Their strategic concerns embrace a wider EU market which gives them both opportunities and competitive risks.
- Organisationally they have often needed to alter and consider trans-national imperatives as well as their national or local markets.
- There is often a private–public mix that needs to be managed and the rules understood on both sides.
- They must adapt to changing technological demands.

From 2005/06, the EU Commission has proposed further developments to the regulatory framework for telecommunications (see Humphreys, 2006; Humphreys and Simpson, 2005).

EU member state national regulation

Beneath the level of the major global and EU players is the medium and smaller sized corporate media world. This is the bedrock of the industry. For example, it is calculated that there are 97 000 companies working in the publishing industry, 80% of which have fewer than 50 employees (Pira International, 2003). They operate across borders depending on their product and their function. This section of the media though often works more at a national or regional level, and is often a mix or a relationship between private and public concerns.

Both the public sector and the private are controlled by a regulatory regime that is both European and national. Some companies will also be cross-media, but many are not. Law or rules emanate from the different state constitutions, parliamentary processes, procedures and pressures.

State constitutions working within the EU are therefore an essential part of the trans-national policy-making in media regulation because they enact the law, and embrace cultural and political as well as legal precedents. Where the EU cannot go in regulation, the nation states can. National systems are often incrementally 'conservative' by nature, but they respond to change because of 'democratic' and economic pressures. However, how do we compare, review, and draw together all the diverse national provision in the EU in to one picture?

First, we make definitions. The principal market definitions of the industry are defined in Europe by what is known as the NACE classification (in the USA there is something similar entitled NAICS). Market definitions normally follow the market and its changes, such as Internet provision or tele-shopping, and therefore are constantly being updated. A recent descriptive diagram of how the different systems interact is given in Source 4.3.

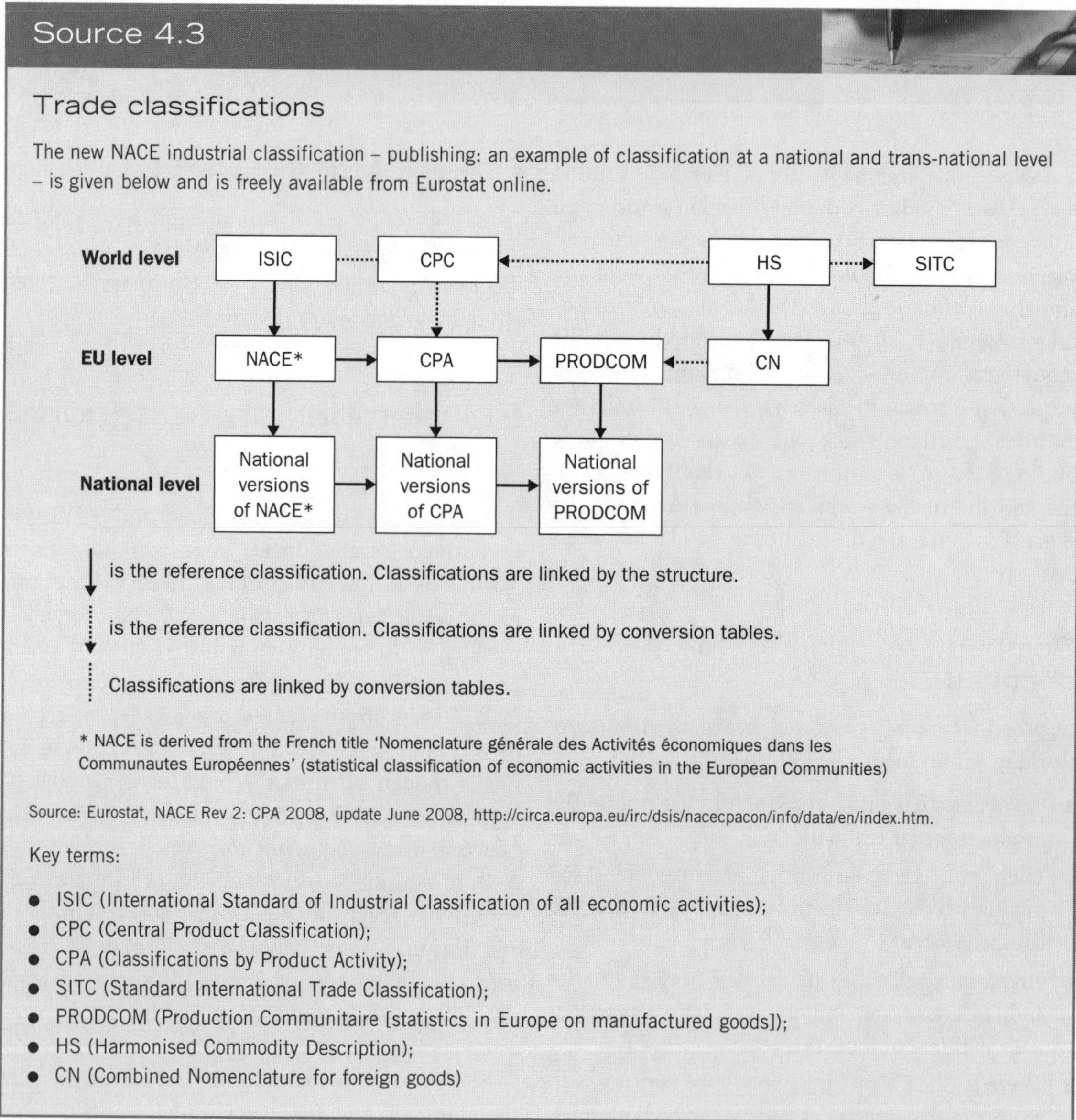

Source 4.3

Trade classifications

The new NACE industrial classification – publishing: an example of classification at a national and trans-national level – is given below and is freely available from Eurostat online.

Source: Eurostat, NACE Rev 2: CPA 2008, update June 2008, http://circa.europa.eu/irc/dsis/nacecpacon/info/data/en/index.htm.

Key terms:

- ISIC (International Standard of Industrial Classification of all economic activities);
- CPC (Central Product Classification);
- CPA (Classifications by Product Activity);
- SITC (Standard International Trade Classification);
- PRODCOM (Production Communitaire [statistics in Europe on manufactured goods]);
- HS (Harmonised Commodity Description);
- CN (Combined Nomenclature for foreign goods)

Second, we start to find ways of comparing the market, its provision and how it is regulated. Comparative analysis of the different national regulatory media regimes in the EU reveals an extensive array of legal arrangements. Some countries are highly regulated relative to others that are partly or even non-regulated. In this frame, the EU has developed an overarching approach as we have seen above, which is praised by some but heavily criticised by others.

Picking out the important differences in the detail is not easy, but in methodological terms this can be done by using comparative general themes. To help us draw together the shape of national regulation in the EU the regulatory themes shown in Tables 4.3 and 4.4 are useful and have been used by important recent research in the field. At the same time the tables indicate how intricate research in the field often can be, where the categories and the variables, the questions asked by researchers, can be different bearing in mind the objectives of the report or enquiry.

The EU then is a complex place, and the regulatory regimes on the ground within the EU remain at the level of detail different from one another. Report after report has shown how intriguing but intricate it is to bring the EU data together. Fine judgements have to be made in comparing one system with another. Nevertheless, no matter the complexity, it is the working reality of the present-day media within the EU. To grasp it is to understand the European media market and its direction. This also means that

Table 4.3 EU regulation comparative research (examples)

Source: Regulation Comparative Work: Areas of recent comparative media research	*Description*
Media ownership and legal controls	Ownership of the media has always been a highly charged affair. Where there is one owner or limited choices, fears of monopolies and propaganda are always present.
Working of competition law including corporate dominance	Worries also exist if corporations become over-present in a market. A lot of regulation has been used, successfully and not so successfully, to counter this.
Transparency of data	Research nowadays demands data. In the field of media research, this can be expensive as media advertising revenues are keenly fought for and having the latest data can offer an edge in a very competitive market.
Working conditions journalists – codes of practice	If journalists are not relatively free to be independent and publish what they find, transparency and accuracy suffer. Most societies check and regulate to ensure that journalists have basic and in some cases additional freedoms for information gathering.
Self-regulation through press councils and associations	In both the press and AV, self-regulation of the media also means that it usually reports on cases of abuse. Those societies that use self-regulation often have associations of agencies reporting on this state of regulation and abuses of power.
Proportion of PSBs vs private	In Europe, the exiting duopoly varies from state to state, but is a model of media provision that often needs scrutiny, especially in terms of what is often referred to as 'proportionality'.
Extent of media pluralism – internal/external	Assessing how much 'pluralism' is being maintained in society is important and there is research work across the EU in this area.
Freedom of speech	Most EU societies will have representatives assessing the degree and practice of freedom of speech. Reports on their activities are always useful.
Relative differences between press and AV	The historical divide between the press and the audio-visual may be coming to an end, but EU states will often have different research depending on the type of media in question.
Technical definitions	Technical convergence is very important in the digital age, and research on the technical aspects of convergence is often reported.

Table 4.4a Examples of EU regulation comparative research projects – market definition

Market	*Products*	*Resources*
AV services	Books	Eurostat research and measurement based on NACE
Cinema	Newspapers	EU Commission (print industry)
DVD/video	Journals/periodicals	Consultation document research and enquiry
TV	Sound recordings	
Sound recording	Other (photos, posters works of art)	
Radio		
Video games		

Table 4.4b Example of EU regulation comparative research project – market assessment

Project	*Research areas*	*Resources*
Competitor assessment	Labour productivity	EU Commission (print industry)
	Productivity growth	Consultation document research and enquiry
	Specialisation index (competitive advantage) – production/consumption	
	Trade openness	
	Media time, e.g. TV 48%, radio 28%, newspapers 13%, internet 10%, mags 8%	

we need to be aware of the debate that surrounds the modern media.

Regulation, deregulation, self-regulation and co-regulation

The future regulation of the media industry in all its forms is a major preoccupation at the present time. The Hans-Bredow-Institut has been advising that future developments lie in what has been called 'co-regulation': a halfway house between regulation and deregulation. Co-regulation is a means of allowing forms of self-regulation to sit alongside other regulatory statutory regimes. Most importantly perhaps, it allows the EU mediascape to embrace existing regulatory schemes across the many member states while allowing them to evolve under the umbrella of the EU.

Differences may be necessary in terms of media rules, it is argued, to embrace the existing diversity. For example, you can allow for different rules for different types of media, i.e. the press is normally self-regulatory while national broadcasting is much more regulated. Some of these ideas were expressed recently in a seminar in Brussels:

- Allow for co-regulatory systems to implement directives.
- Distinguish clearly between co-regulation and self-regulation.
- Self-regulation is defined by the absence of state interference into this regulatory process.
- Regulatory theory underpins the specific strengths of self-regulation.
- Room for pure self-regulation where a co-regulatory system is in place. Self-regulation can further the development of professional ethics.
- However, under the jurisprudence of the European Court of Justice the complete absence of state regulation is not sufficient for a Member state to comply with European directives.
- Regard protection of minors and advertising content regulation as suitable fields for co-regulatory measures.

(Prosser, 2006)

Conclusions and more questions

At the heart of the present EU media debate lies the question of media regulation: who, when and why. Alongside these debates are the new calls for wider EU media deregulation of the media, arguing for change to happen ever more quickly. All of this has raised difficult questions.

1. To what extent and for what purpose do we regulate in the era of new technology?
2. Should the market be more open to cross-border free competition or remain more the choice for nation states?
3. Can the EU, or even the nation states, control the global forces pushing for change? Do they want to? Who decides? The questions do not stop there.
4. What about freedom of expression and human rights?
5. What are the differences between collective organisations that write in the name of the public and the more individual statements from citizens found on the web?

No matter the questions, the new mediascape reflects a new form of communication-network in the making. The major players, working at a global, international, European and even national level, can see this and the 'global', trans-national profits (or influence) that it represents.

To find some of the answers we need to go to other chapters for ideas and Chapters 6–11 for some further details to back up our views and arguments.

Chapter summary

➤ The reality of media change in Europe is that it is being 'globalised', 'internationalised', Americanised, Europeanised and localised all at the same time. This changes the former national regulatory networks, but not completely.

➤ The networks are growing, interlocking, as they adapt, not being replaced but being amended as they develop. Even so, as with politics in general, the EU media sector is wedded to the nation states that socially and culturally define and finally police the system.

➤ The nation states remain vital in regulatory terms. At the same time, there appears to be a convergence of general rules and principles that are now jig-sawed into international, European and trans-national frameworks. The media regulatory world is changing.

➤ The lawmakers, the 'European' regulators, then remain national but European-advised at the EU institutional level. They use the instruments of policy-making as we have seen in Chapter 1: directives, regulations, recommendations and orders. Even so, the future demands even greater transparency of the media landscape if progress is to be made toward a more cohesive market.

Key terms

Many of the following acronyms are used in various chapters across the book but are added here as reminders. The great majority of key terms in this chapter are discussed in the text above.

AFP: Agence France-Press – major agency player along with Reuters in Europe.

AP: Associated Press – leading US-based global press agency.

ARTE: European Cultural (TV) channel with European partners but primarily Franco-German in origin.

AV: audio-visual – shorthand for the combined visual and radio forms of broadcasting.

Digitisation: the technical process that allows the conversion of digital signals into many forms of AV format.

DG: Directorate General – usually associated with the various portfolios held within the European Commission. DG X refers to 'Education, culture and communication'.

Press agencies: specialist agencies that collate and then provide to the wider industry. They have been a key part of European press and publishing industries since the 19th century. Their role in the communications network has not been given the importance it merited. Most national and even cross-national media use them extensively.

UPI: United Press International – major US-based global press agency.

Discussion questions

1. Name three trans-national European companies operating inside the EU.
2. What is ARTE and why is it important in audio-visual cultural terms inside the EU?
3. Is the creation of a channel called 'Euronews' in any way valuable for European consumers?
4. What is the relation between media and society according to the Hans-Bredow-Institut?
5. What was the significance of the *Sacchi* and *Debauve* case law in 1974 and 1981, respectively?
6. In international, trans-national terms how important are copyright and patent regulations?
7. What are the essential differences between the Hahn (1983) and Bangemann (1992–1994) Reports?
8. What are the essential elements of the 'Television without Frontiers' Directive 1989 and amendments 1997?
9. What are the essential elements of the EC regulatory framework of electronic communication and services?
10. What are the essential elements of the Audiovisual Media Services Directive 2007?

Assignments

The following questions could be assignments – they go to the heart of many of the debates and there are no easy answers.

1. Have the regulators and the regulatory regimes kept up with the changing scene?
2. Have the EU and its members states coped with the problem of global even national media monopolies and the perceived attack on political pluralism?
3. Have the nation-states of the EU and/or the EU itself been able to keep the diversity needed for healthy democratic practices?

Further reading

Bulmer S., Dolowitz D., Humphreys P., Padgett S. (2007) *Policy Transfer in European Union Governance: Regulating the Utilities*, London and New York: Routledge.

Harcourt A. (2005) *The European Union and the Regulation of Media Markets*, Manchester and New York: Manchester University Press.

Humphreys P., Simpson S. (2005) *Globalization, Convergence and European Telecommunications Regulation*, London: Edward Elgar.

Krebber D. (2001) *Europeanisation of Regulatory Television Policy: the Decision-making Process of the Television without Frontiers Directive from 1989 & 1997*, Baden-Baden: Nomos Verlagsgesellschaft.

Levy D.A. (1999) *Europe's Digital Revolution: Broadcasting Regulation, the EU and the Nation State*, London and New York: Routledge.

Michalis M. (2007) *Governing European Communications*, Plymouth: Lexington Books.

Sarikakis K. (2004) *Powers in Media Policy: The Challenge of the European Parliament*, Bern: Peter Lang.

Online resources

http://www...

Combined with the online resources mentioned in Chapters 6–11, it is highly recommended in the first instance to start with the following. They offer entry portals into a world of regulatory development of the highest order:

- *EUMAP* http://www.eumap.org
- *Europa* http://ec.europa.eu/information_society/policy/ecomm/todays_framework/market_access/index_en.htm
- *European Audiovisual Observatory (EAO)* http://www.obs.coe.int
- *European Commission Europa* http://europa.eu
- *European Journalism Centre (EJC)* http://www.ejc.net
- *Hans-Bredow-Institut* http://www.hans-bredow-institute.de
- *Institute for Information, Telecommunications and Media Law (ITM)* http://www.uni-muenster.de/Jura.itm
- *Ofcom* http://www.ofcom.org.uk/static/archive/Oftel/ind_info/eu_directives/index.htm
- *Oxford University Programme in Comparative Media Law and Policy, including the Reuters Institute for the Study of Journalism* http://pcmlp.socleg.ox.ac.uk/archive/rl_research.html

References

BVerfG (1987) BVerfGE 57, 2951 BvL 89/783. Rundfunkurteil – *Third Broadcasting Case* (FRAG case) (1987)

EU (1989) Council Directive 89/552/EEC of 3 October 1989 on the coordination of certain provisions laid down by Law, Regulation or Administrative Action in Member States concerning the pursuit of television broadcasting activities, *OJ*, **L298**, 17.10.1989, 23–30.

EU (1997) Directive 97/36/EC of the European Parliament and of the Council 30 June 1997 amending Council Directive 89/552/EEC on the coordination of certain provisions laid down by Law, Regulation or Administrative Action in Member States concerning the pursuit of television broadcasting activities, *OJ*, **L202**, 30.7.1997, 60–70.

EU (2002a) Directive 2002/21/EC of the European Parliament and of the Council of 7 March 2002 on a common regulatory framework for electronic communications networks and services, *OJ*, **L108**, 24.04.2002, 33–50.

EU (2002b) Directive 2002/20/EC of the European Parliament and of the Council of 7 March 2002 on the authorisation of electronic communications networks and services, *OJ*, **L108**, 24.04.2002, 21–32.

EU (2002c) Directive 2002/19/EC of the European Parliament and of the Council of 7 March 2002 on access to, and interconnection of, electronic communications networks and associated facilities, *OJ*, **L108**, 24.04.2002, 7–20.

EU (2002d) Directive 2002/22/EC of the European Parliament and of the Council of 7 March 2002 on universal service and users' rights relating to electronic communications networks and services, *OJ*, **L108**, 24.04.2002, 51–77.

EU (2002e) Directive 2002/58/EC of the European Parliament and of the Council of 12 July 2002 concerning the processing of personal data and the protection of privacy in the electronic communications sector, *OJ*, **L201**, 31.07.2002, 37–47.

EU (2002f) Commission Decision 2002/676/EC on a regulatory framework for radio spectrum policy *OJ*, **L108**, 24.04.2002, 1–6.

EU (2004) Directive 2004/48/EC of the European Parliament and of the Council of 29 April 2004 on the enforcement of intellectual property rights, *OJ*, **L157**, 30.4.2004, 45–85.

EU (2006) Decision No 1718/2006/EC of the European Parliament and of the Council of 15 November 2006 concerning the implementation of a programme of support for the European audiovisual sector (MEDIA 2007), *OJ*, **L327**, 24.11.2006, 12–29.

EU (2007) Directive 2007/65/EEC of the European Parliament and of the Council of 11 December 2007 amending Council Directive 89/552/EEC of 3 October 1989 on the coordination of certain provisions laid down by Law, Regulation or Administrative Action in Member States concerning the pursuit of television broadcasting activities, *OJ*, **L332**, 18.12.2007, 27–45.

Hans-Bredow-Institut (2005) *Interim Report Study on Co-regulatory Measures in the Media Sector*, study commissioned by the European Commission DG Information Society and Media, tender DG EAC 03/04, Hamburg, 19 May.

Harcourt A. (2004) EUI Working Paper RSCAS No 2004/44, *Institution Driven Competition: The Regulation of Cross-Border Broadcasting in the EU*, Florence: European University Institute, Robert Schuman Centre for Advanced Studies http://www.iue.it/RSCAS/WP-Texts/04_44.pdy

Harcourt A. (2005) *The European Union and the Regulation of Media Markets*, Manchester and New York: Manchester University Press.

Humphreys P. (2006) Globalization, regulatory competition, and EU policy transfer in the telecoms and broadcasting sectors, *International Journal of Public Administration*, **29**(4–6): 305–334.

Humphreys P., Simpson S. (2005) *Globalization, Convergence and European Telecommunication Regulation*, London: Edward Elgar.

Lange A. (2001) *Impact of the Directive Television without Frontier's on the circulation of audiovisual works in the European Union*, European Audiovisual Observatory contribution, workshop organised in Brussels (29 May 2001) by the Cab.

Pelkmans J. (2001) Making EU networks competitive, *Oxford Review of Economic Policy*, **17**(3): 432–456.

Pira International (2003) *The EU Publishing* Industry*: an Assessment of Competitiveness*, Luxembourg: European Communities.

Prosser T. (2006) *Co-Regulation Measures in the Media Sector* Seminar 2, Brussels, 19 January 2006 Study commissioned by the European Commission, Directorate General Information Society and Media, Unit A1(Tender DG EAC 03/04).

Prosser T. (2008) Self-regulation, co-regulation and the Audio-visual Media Services Directive, *Journal of Consumer Policy*, **31**(1): 99–113.

Reding V. (2007) Speech at 10th General Assembly of Belgian Platform Telecom Operators and Service Providers, Brussels, 21 March.

UK Ofcom (2006) *The Communications Market 2006*, London, Ofcom.

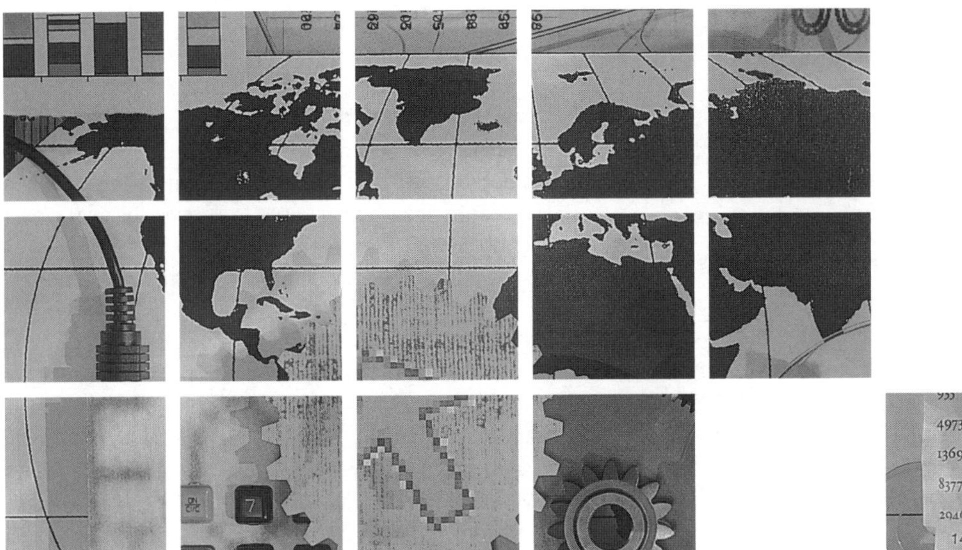

Chapter 5

Media theory in the European context

Structure of the chapter

Introduction: using theory

Media theory and European integration

Context: the theories of European integration and media development – some concepts

- *New institutionalism*
- *Consociationalism*
- *Federalism*
- *Functionalism*
- *'Neofunctionalism'*
- *Liberal intergovernmentalism*

Debates on the EU theories of integration

- *Uncertainties and questions for the future media architecture in Europe*
- *Market size and economies of scale*
- *New regional and global corporate players*
- *A bundle of counter criticisms*
- *Theorising and the media*

Media and communication theory

- *Approaches 1: Politics and policy: power, discourse and control*
- *Approaches 2: Economic liberal materialism*
- *Approaches 3: Social and political spheres: democracy*
- *Approaches 4: Time, culture, history*

Using theory with research methods

Critical review

Media theory milestones and contemporary debates

1. *Media theory vs communication theory*
2. *Modernism vs post-modernism*
3. *Dominance vs pluralism theories*
4. *Complexity (chaos) theory, choice and the internet*
5. *The information society*
6. *The digital age or the digital society*

Learning objectives

When you have completed this chapter you will be able to:

- Reflect upon various theories about the European media which combine media and European integration.
- Understand why theories and models are used to analyse the media.
- Recognise that media theories are hotly debated by academics and are important for development of media policy-making because they relate to political judgements embedded in policy.
- Identify a range of competing theories within a changing media landscape.

Themes

Below you will find a simple statement or series of statements around the six themes. They should *not* be read as a given fact. They are more like hypotheses (see Chapter 2) which need to be proved, discussed, debated and then used in your own analysis of the subject. The ideas and approaches in this book are always to be considered with an open mind, this is important in university study and is what makes it distinct from pre-university study.

Diversity of media

There are a variety of theories to explore the media *in situ* including the European context. Inside the EU the 'media' is associated with a diverse technology which is in the process of converging, but its diversity remains predominant even during a period of transition. The media too is a collection of organisations, both public and private, changing over time, and often functioning differently in different countries. These factors need debate and modelling to understand their importance.

Internal/external forces for change

In our analysis of the media we need to be aware of the internal media dynamic within the national industries but also mindful of the global, international, EU and even sub-national, local pressures that are pressing for change. This theme alerts us to this question and points to the internal, national dynamic and the external pressures driving change and the theoretical questions it creates. We need to consider this 'new' model in our theories of how media adapt.

Complexity of the media

In Europe, the distinction between public and private sector broadcasting is being blurred, with a mix of public and private finance being used to develop the 'old' media and the 'new'. These ideas impact upon our theoretical as well as practical understanding of the media in Europe.

Multi-levels

Across the EU, media business and public broadcasting are reforming at global, national and local levels and at a quickening pace. No longer is the nation state the only level at which the media interacts. The levels are generally subsumed into the 'globalisation' debate, whereas on the ground it is local and global as well as European levels which are in play. This means we need to rethink our theoretical approaches in a multi-level way more than perhaps we did in the past.

European integrative environment

In the context of this book's investigation, one theme has been of major interest: the Europeanisation of the media market. Europeanisation is both a private and a public sector concern and is political and economic and, in the long term, cultural. This theme alerts us to some of the ideas expressed by European integration theory and how they may impact upon EU policy concerns.

Cultural values

The media for most us is not just a technology or a business but a content-laden communicator of cultural and social values: in a word 'content'. This theme reminds us throughout that the question of culture is ever-present in our analysis of the market place.

Essentials

- Understanding the contemporary European media scene is complicated not only by the diverse nature of its performance and organisation but also by the many theories that surround the discipline. There are notable commentators, such as Siebert, Hallin and Mancini, McLuhan, Habermaas and Albert, and many more, who focus their attention directly on the media as a subject unto itself. Many other views spring from older more deeply held philosophical positions from Marx to Chomsky to Lyotard.

➤ Equally, there is much to reflect on across the borders. There are the academic communities of the non-English-speaking nations of Europe let alone the new members of the EU in Central and Eastern Europe, plus the Anglo-Saxons, where differing political, social and cultural traditions of thought dominate. Equally, non-EU countries may well have different views on how communities and communication systems work in society.

➤ Important too are the more scientific methods of data analysis which include the use of referred research methods such as audience sampling, comparative variables and consumer demand and economics. These are the lifeblood of market analysis and are used extensively by governments and media corporations alike.

Introduction: using theory

To explore the media in Europe means to understand that theory as well as practice and market analysis is subject to debate. Commentators debate the role of the media in all its forms using different models of appreciation and philosophy. Debate and explanation are the backbone of analysis and we cannot avoid their use or relative importance.

The media has a set of well-established theories dedicated to understanding its place in the modern world. These theories are often used in the arguments about the future direction of the media. Notwithstanding this, the EU is a 'unique' market and perhaps we need to start by understanding some of the debate about the EU as a body politic in which the media operates. To do this, the chapter divides our enquiry into three steps: EU integration theory and the media; media theory and Europe, which sounds the same as the first but is not; and lastly a review of contemporary debates coming out of what might be considered as major media milestones. Combining these three strands of media reflection of course is not simple, but it is both creative and useful.

To help us explore, we may start with the European context. In the EU this means understanding some of the theories explaining why integration of markets and politics and media is occurring, over and above the economics (Chapter 3) or the changes in the regulatory world (Chapter 4). For this we can refer to a range of theories on European integration built up over many decades.

Media theory and European integration

In what might be called the 'digital age' in Europe, we find that there are considerable signs not just of 'globalisation' but an argument about 'convergence' of media technologies (see Chapter 4 and Chapter 6 onwards). Despite the fact that they are subject to similar pressures, societies have organised themselves differently, and this is often reflected in the different media across Europe: in programming, ownership, politics, organisation and rules and regulations surrounding the media, some of which have already been discussed elsewhere (Chapters 1 and 4).

On the surface, it appears logical to assume that with such convergence there would be some similar convergence of European or even global societies. In policy terms there is much evidence that this is beginning to happen inside the EU. However, in media terms, so far, diversity of content is as much the case as convergence, which asks us to answer the question, both practically and theoretically, why? This is where commentators start to debate and argue.

Many of the differences of view will come from our different conceptions of the relationship that media has to its society and how society views its media: a two-way dialogue one could say. Available to us are a wide range of theories which underpin the view of media analysts. The origins of these theories are to be found in philosophy and historical tradition. This chapter does not attempt to repeat them in detail, but they are dealt with as 'approaches' and 'milestones' as the chapter proceeds (see also the suggested books and articles in the further reading and references sections that are of considerable use and include McQuail, Watson, Crowley and Mitchell, Collins and so on).

There are also some pitfalls to avoid whilst using theory, especially in dealing with the EU.

- Many theories of the media depict the media as occupying an easily understood political and geographical space. This is an over-simplification. For example, to talk about the 'American', 'European' or even 'global' media is to ignore local and regional differences, let alone the role of finance and capital differently applied in different places.
- To add to the complexity, many theories describe the media as if it works in tune, almost exclusively, with deeper more socio-economic forces that are beyond the national or cultural. This might be seen as a classical 'materialist' position: 'Marxist', for example (and apologies to the purists for some simplification), which argues that global capitalism creates a superstructure of owners (the bourgeoisie) who impose their values on mass audiences (the proletariat and worker). This is achieved through media ownership which then governs the values and ideas emanating from this dominating and vested interest group. This is opposed by some who argue the opposite: 'capitalism' is described as a way to liberate individual and collective innovation and provide value and effective use of resources across all societies, potentially for the 'good' of all people. These are often seen as the 'big picture' views.
- However, if we compare the media in different societies, such as the case in Europe, we may find more diversity than many theories assume. In this case we may need to start questioning the 'big picture' views because, at base, they may imply that the producers and audiences (societies) are similarly economically driven and passive to national identity, when in Europe, as an example, plainly, they are not.
- In a similar fashion, it is tempting to see the media generically because the technology crosses so easily the accepted sociopolitical, geographical borders: a television set or an MP3 player is the same, in broad terms, everywhere it could be argued. Even so, the content of media or how it is interpreted will be different depending on where the technology is used. We may switch on the same type of television set, but it may well be different soap operas we will view when we do so. The media is often described as if it is easily transplanted from one space to another when, more accurately of course, media provision is nationally, culturally or even linguistically determined: or so the European case seems, once again, to illustrate.

Context: the theories of European integration and media development – some concepts

Political scientists let alone media theorists have been grappling with our understanding of the EU. It is unique in the sense that its member states have joined together over a period of time in a more or less definable geographical space to create common policies. Over a half century, if not longer, theories of how or why or in what form the states are integrating have been examined, altered, debated and added to in academic and political circles.

There is no consensus and the debate is constant. Present-day thinking leads to two major approaches, both of which are in a way measurable and therefore perhaps substantial. Both rely on the inter-relationship between **supra-nationalism** and **intergovernmentalism** and both may be connected to the role, theory and practice of the media.

New institutionalism

In this description states become entangled in the development of new trans-national policies, forming committees, constitutions and courts. In effect, they create new institutions for new challenges. New institutions mean new ways of organising the pursuit of common political policies which benefit most, if not all.

In this approach we can measure the extent of integration and inter-relationship between states by their political policy-making, the number of legislative acts and the range of common policies (Peterson and Sharp, 1998; Peterson and Bomberg, 1999), which can include the media. We can even measure their effectiveness from inputs to measurable outcomes. We measure, for example, how many trans-national telecommunication projects there are and how much the courts are used for resolving corporate conflict and creating media case law. In the EU case this latter means referring to case law from the European Court of Justice as well as national courts.

Consociationalism

This integrative theory (Chryssochoou, 2001) argues that despite the important institutional relationship between say the EU institutions and the member states, it is the coalescence of the societies at a functional level, below government, that characterises how societies inter-relate with one another.

In this approach we can measure how mobile people are within a territory, what media they share, how often they interact by mobile phone, the extent of broadband usage and online gaming and the degree to which there are trans-national corporations operating in an area, to take notable examples. Even at the level of distribution and production, we can evaluate how much effort goes into the development of cross-national media programmes and resources; for example the 'ARTE' television collaboration between France and Germany (see Chapters 4 and 9).

Two other theories will enhance our understanding of the present-day architecture of the European media: federalism and functionalism, both of which were absorbed later into an amalgam often called the 'Brussels Method' or what might be considered an additional theory 'neofunctionalism'.

Federalism

Federalism is an old and accepted practice of integrating communities, and there are many varieties in the world. At its heart, 'Western' federalism (as opposed to 'Eastern' European, communist command-economy states of the past) accepts that people within societies are different and will remain on the whole different. Even so, for the sake of peace and harmony and security they can set up constitutions in which all can engage and follow.

The degree of integration depends on the cohesion and acceptance of common aims by the various communities: examples around the world show the varieties that are to be found – Germany, Switzerland, the USA, Canada and the Russian Federation. In media terms, we may well find diversity being enhanced as the media should reflect the diversities of the communities that make up the federal state.

Stop and consider 5.1

Whether these societies will have a common 'broadcasting' system again will depend on the technology available and a political, community will to create it. The weaker the will to create a common market, the greater the tendency for more local, national production. This applies to newspaper production as well as the audio-visual. Some societies have greater regional presence in newspaper production than national newspaper titles: this is the case in Germany and France and elsewhere in Europe. Is it possible to create a common cultural area called 'Europe'? Or is it 'naturally' always going to be some kind of federation?

Functionalism

Functionalism is more materialistic, even economic in form, and sees society made up, more or less, of individuals and communities whose prime 'function' is to work the 'material' of their labour. The more efficient the organisation or society, the more it uses the earth's resources to better humankind. Therefore, functionalism sees national territories as an anomaly, even a dangerous hindrance, to the correct function of human society which should be seen as 'global' in nature. Its aim too is harmony and peace but providing for material efficiency.

Stop and consider 5.2

Broadcasting or newspapers which are national or even 'trans-national', functionalist theorists may argue, can be a misunderstanding of human activity, diverting energies into differences which can lead to conflict. In broadcasting or reporting terms, the 'globe' demands universal principles, they would claim, on which we all must agree. Functionalism demands global governance, even a global media.

In contemporary times, this can be seen in the arguments over media products at the World Trade Organisation (WTO). Within functionalism then, the materialism and the relationship between people allows for individuality but also an integration of purpose which makes us all inter-dependent. We live in one world, they would say: we are of one humanity. Yet, does this view describe accurately enough the world we occupy? Is it too utopian? Human history is made of difference rather than unity, it seems. Is this right? What are the arguments for and against this kind of view?

'Neofunctionalism'

1. This theory is both federalist and functionalist in form – political and constitutional and materialist, using economic betterment (and capitalist economic theory) for the majority as the motor for political change.

Stop and consider 5.3

This means the media has to respond to economic forces which are transactional (based on product transfer and communication) and trans-national, but also to markets that are more nationalistic. But clearly, some of the commentators argue, the media is based on the same technology everywhere and 'national' characteristics are not important. Or there are commentators who argue that the media is part of a 'national' cultural characteristic of a very deep nature and 'trans-nationalism' cannot include cultural products like the media. Can the theory of neofunctionalism be useful to understand the 'real' mechanisms that create the media? Or is it contradictory as a theory?

2. As a political and policy mechanism, it uses what it calls 'the exclusive logic of expansion' – 'spillover', creating a movement of integrative change based on merging policies across boundaries, drawing communities together but in an evolutionary manner. For example, this could be the view one takes of the EU Television without Frontiers Directive (EU, 1989, 1997) which has led to the Audiovisual Media Services Directive (EU, 2007).
3. It relies on enticing the elite, be that in politics or business (trade) or the media, and their self-interests to a point where their management and leadership core role would be pro-European and less nationalistic and therefore inclined to be more integrative. In Europe this means being pro the EU and its aims and objectives as agreed by a set of integrating international treaties (see Chapter 1).

Stop and consider 5.4

It is argued for the purposes of integration in the EU that this means that private media organisations are encouraged to maximise their markets and look out beyond their nations. Even so, the EU also lays down that national public broadcasters have to keep an eye on trans-national and national competitors and be *administered by their national regulators. Is there not a contradiction in the policy arrangements if this is the case? What do you think?*

4. It uses one policy and then another (step-by-step) to create an integrated approach and greater harmonisation between states. For example, inside the EU, starting from iron, steel and coal and moving to agriculture in the 1950s, the priorities became commercial policy and later media and telecommunications policies in the 1980s and 1990s. Parallel to this came monetary policy leading to a single currency (2003) for the 21st century.
5. It uses the acceptance of the principles of community and consumers and citizens' law as the cohesive element for individuals, communities, societies and states. In the EU, the European Union Court of Justice legal decisions and judgments take precedence over national interpretations, for example.

Not everyone accepts the inevitability of 'transnationalism' or 'globalisation' or 'Europeanisation'. Some political scientists have come to the conclusion that evolutionary processes of integration in Europe have not only preserved the nation states but in fact strengthened them.

Liberal intergovernmentalism

Unlike the more integrative theories mentioned above, this description (Moravcsik, 1993) of international relations in Europe argued that common integration was not likely. Nation states would use trans-national organisations to defend their existence, not fundamentally alter their foundations.

> **Stop and consider 5.5**
>
> *This means that perhaps nation states will work together on media policies, but only in general terms. Mainly they work together, either in the private or public sectors, for means of protective defence against outside 'foreign' competition. The evidence available to us on this is contradictory. Does this theory seem feasible?*

1. Nation states were drawing some of their national policies together, but on the basis not of the greater common European good but national self-interest. It was useful, it was argued, even practical, to work toward cooperation on immigration, drug trafficking, cross-border policing and even, in a limited way, some forms of defence, but this did not mean surrendering national sovereignty. Some liberal intergovernmentalists may argue that the media in particular, because of language and culture, is steeped in the question of sovereignty and that is why so much media control remains at a national level inside the EU.

> **Stop and consider 5.6**
>
> *This means that if we really want to understand the media in Europe we need to look at the different positions of the member states and not necessarily just EU commentaries. How do we do this?*

2. The supra-national institutions like the European Commission and the European Parliament were not that important in setting the agenda for policy-making. More correctly it was the work surrounding the Council, including the European summits where the representatives of the nation states came together, that was most important.
3. In particular, both in the public mind and professional commentaries, the national bias in European Union Intergovernmental Conferences (IGCs), see Chapter 1, is a display of national, government bargaining.

> **Stop and consider 5.7**
>
> *The consequence of such a view leads us to believe that each national media public service broadcaster (PSB) responds nationalistically to European policies and will tend to be inherently critical of them.*
>
> *This theory can often be used to illustrate the bargaining position of states when it comes to media policy. It may also explain why the European model has still maintained a core interest in public broadcasting, because core national political interests are so entwined in public broadcasting systems. They have continually defended their position. But is the media world changing because of 'globalisation' and 'convergence': are we in a different age? Perhaps not?*

Debates on the EU: theories of integration

Uncertainties and questions for the future media architecture in Europe

So how has this situation affected the media provision in Europe and why are these political theories of integration important? Because, as we can see from one area to another around the world, for the media, context and politics matter. In the normal day-to-day announcements of changes in the press or media we can often miss this. Let us take a TV channel example *Euronews* which has recently relaunched itself into the market place (see Case Study 5.1).

The full answers to the questions raised in the case study are of course open to debate. What is probably not so questionable is our understanding that without a context much of what is being announced would not be comprehensible. *Euronews* in particular

Case Study 5.1

EuroNews

The following extract from a recent newspaper report raises lots of different questions. In this box we will not answer all of them, but we can use this chapter and its ideas to come back to this case study and ask:

- Why was *EuroNews* created and who finances it and why? This leads to the bigger question as who creates the media, when was it created and why?
- Why is *EuroNews* rebranding and who are its main competitors? This leads to a bigger question on what is competition and why is it important? Who creates competition? Who benefits? What is the media for?
- Who does *EuroNews* target as an audience and why? Is it changing and why?

TV channel EuroNews is undertaking the biggest overhaul of its on-air branding since its launch 15 years ago to create a brand to better compete with rival services CNN, BBC World and al-Jazeera. The new channel branding, which is being rolled out from today, has been two years in the making. It includes scrapping its EU blue colour scheme in favour of 'pure' news positioning, introducing a 'Pure' strapline and a white circle motif. EuroNews' new on-screen branding, created by French advertising agency Fred Farid Lambert, will extend from the look and feel on-air to promotional idents for the channel. The blue-and-white 'block' lettering of the EuroNews brand name is also being rejigged. 'The problem was first of all increasing competition, when we launched there was maybe five news channels, now there are more than 100,' said, the EuroNews managing director, Michael Peters. 'The sector is dominated by big brands such as BBC [World], CNN and even al-Jazeera and although we are the most watched international news channel in Europe no one knows this.' . . . Peters said the new look aimed to tackle perceptions of EuroNews being a 'low cost' channel and too European focused, with it often being wrongly perceived as the 'TV of the European Commission'. . . . EuroNews' rebrand and ad campaign, involving an investment of in excess of €5m (£3.95m), aims to make a virtue of the fact that the rolling news channel has no presenters . . . Peters said. 'It works perfectly for running on the internet, or mobile phones, we are like a video on demand channel on TV.' EuroNews, which launched in 1993, is backed by €50m of funding a year from the European Broadcasting Union, a group of government-owned public service broadcasters. 'Perception is weak because we don't have a big commercial group behind us, like CNN which we were set up to take on after the first Gulf war and there is a new long-term need to invest in our brand,' Peters said.

Source: EuroNews rebrands to take on rivals, *The Guardian* (Sweney, 2008). Copyright Guardian News and Media Ltd, 2008.

is probably unthinkable as a product without understanding the development of the EU and the general European interest it represents.

- Notice the global competitive stakes at play with the mention of BBC World, CNN and al-Jazeera, and the need to reach out to audiences.
- Note who is a substantial investor – the European Broadcasting Union – an organisation created in 1950 to support the development of PSBs (in the main) across Europe but one which is not an official part of the EU institutions.
- Note when *Euronews* was created – at a time of major conflict. Is this significant, and if not why was it mentioned?
- Note how the managing director now speaks of 'new long-term need to invest' in the 'brand', but of whom is he thinking: more state taxes? The public? But which public – national or European? Investors from the private sector? Advertisers? Subscriptions from users? Commentators may well disagree with each other on the answers to any of these questions.

This kind of contextual enquiry is not new. Trying to explain how the media works in its context has always been a part of academic tradition. The seminal work undertaken by Siebert *et al.* (1956) suggested that the press (and by implication today's media and that includes the newly branded *Euronews*) is shaped by a nation's and by implication EU politics and ideologies. Writing from the 1950s Siebert argued that we can locate different types of media by the type of **political regime** under which they operate. He, with his colleagues, created four models:

- authoritarianism (monarchical early presses);
- libertarian (USA);
- social responsibility (Europe),
- communism (the 'Soviet').

This type of work has been carried on more recently by Hallin and Mancini (2004), where they have argued that there are not just four models of analysis for contemporary media (including the press) operating in Europe but what might be considered to be **geo-political sub-divisions** which they call:

- the 'Mediterranean or Polarised Pluralist Model';
- the 'North/Central European or Democratic Corporatist Model';
- the 'The North Atlantic or Liberal Model'.

The work is intriguing although, as we shall see later, it is often the case that more 'national' comparisons are made in the first instance rather than political typologies such as these.

They are not alone in trying to formulate comparative models. Across Europe there are many commentaries worth pursuing. Pierre Albert (Professeur Emérite de l'Université Panthéon Assas) in French academic circles carefully balances the **historical and cultural factors** impacting upon the press (Albert, 1985, 1990):

- Societies are formed by their history in political, economic, social and then cultural ways. This shapes and provides for empirical differences in readership behaviour based on these socio-cultural factors. These are useful parameters for market analysis. His work, for example, on the history of the French press is a model for many. He rightly, even from the early days, draws a further distinction between presses (and in that sense the media in general), and in particular he reflected upon what he termed:
  - the European Press, by which he meant in the main 'continental Europe';
  - the Anglo-Saxon – the 'English Press' and the 'American Press';
  - The non-Western, by which he meant Russia (or the Soviet Union as it was called in another age) and Japan.

In each case he implies that there are distinct **national characteristics** to the way in which the publishing industry, and especially the press and by implication all media, produces its products. However, Albert's work, and the others mentioned, are only a small part of an increasing amount of academic effort and market analysis to understand the changes taking place in the press and publishing worlds and in the wider media. They are all symptomatic of the perceived need in the modern world to describe the media in its different settings; at the same time, exploring the level of convergence between the different contexts.

National and then comparative national studies have been a tradition in much academic and business analysis but, as the media market opens up in our own age in a global or even an EU manner, new questions on trade and on new communication technology are occurring. Increasingly, the make-up and form of media in Europe is being framed by the general principles of the market and the politics of the EU as well as national and even global pressures. The question might be asked by whom, for what and why. Does the work of Siebert *et al.*, Hallin and Mancini and Albert provide answers or clues to what *Euronews* is doing for example?

Certainly, we could argue that following on from the end of the Cold War, and mixed with greater media connectivity such as cable, satellite and digital platforms, the global market and our knowledge of each other is changing, fast. The local has become more global and the global more regional. Producers of media look beyond their national audiences for larger markets. The new technology allows this to happen and is hastening change.

Market size and economies of scale

Nation states can try to protect themselves from the global market but, if economic growth remains one of the driving forces for any society, few will choose to stand aside. Few have. The growth of the EU since 1958 although politically driven is economically attractive for many, as proven by six substantive enlargements, and there are more in the offing.

Case Study 5.2

BBC and Google, 2007: reaching out to new markets

The BBC, seen as a prime example of an independent charter status media organisation in Europe, has always been an important part of national UK broadcasting. Even so, in the global reach of the present era, it has just contracted (2007) to show clips on YouTube, a recently acquired part of the Google Corporation. In part the BBC will receive funding from advertising on the web site. Even in this market where the BBC is so powerful, reaching out to new markets is important: size matters, it seems.

Source: BBC strikes Google-YouTube deal, *BBC News* (Weber, 2007), http://news.bbc.co.uk/1/hi/business/6411017.stm.

The EU is a large market for goods including the media. Market size, economies of scale and financial investments are all-important aspects of the media industry. Investment capital and new streams of financing may be found anywhere across the globe trans-nationally (see Case Study 5.2 for the BBC and Google link up as an example) even if markets are regulated by existing national political systems (see Chapter 4) or economic blocs like the EU. In the EU the media industry has to work at EU as well as other levels for financing because the banking and other financial sectors are regulated at this regional level.

New regional and global corporate players

New regional and global corporate players are beginning to emerge in this new EU market, such as Bertelsmann and Pearson, Vivendi, Hachette Livre (Lagardère) as well as Time Warner AOL, International News Corporation, Disney and many more, including global media Internet players such as Microsoft, Yahoo and Google Inc., all influential, powerful and rich. Even so, nation states in the EU are trying to sustain their sovereign powers. At the same time they are trying to pool their resources in an enlarging economic market which poses both risks and opportunities for corporations and nation states alike.

A bundle of counter criticisms

- Some commentators say the EU is so diverse, so much a mishmash of political structures, that it is not useful in our understanding of media policy and development. Often those who argue this way, either philosophically or theoretically, are opposed to European integration itself, or the way the EU has been developing in recent years. Nonetheless, it is important that we think through this criticism and take the EU to account, and in so doing judge how it conducts its affairs. Certainly, there are serious debates that surround the effectiveness of, for example, its media policy.
- The fact that the EU increasingly discusses and implements policies in the media arena means it can be heavily criticised for 'meddling' in media policy which should be the business of nation states. In the modern world of global media reach, this argument seems untenable and is certainly not the majority view. Although at the heart of EU policies there is an acceptance that the media should be handled at nation-state level, in practice the collective decisions made by the EU do have a bearing on national media organisations, be they private or public.
- Another criticism might be that 'Europe' is wider than merely those belonging to the political club called the EU, although there are strong and precise legal responsibilities which define the members of the EU and make them different from nations that belong to 'Europe'. (See Chapters 1 and 4.)

Theorising and the media

To get to the roots of media analysis all notable media researchers and academics will use philosophy or theory in one way or another. Some commentators

Case Study 5.3

Advertising and public broadcasting

Within the EU it is generally accepted that there should be a private–public mix of broadcasting content. New and proposed future regulations in the EU underline the importance of providing a 'core' of public communication which is normally interpreted as some form of 'public sector broadcasting'.

The BBC has always argued a case, and so has the UK government, that to maintain independence means avoiding taking revenue from advertisers. This is not a generally accepted European view where most public broadcasters allow controlled and regulated advertising on public channels. Moreover, if you see the BBC–Google case study above, and look at the funding of international BBC World (TV), advertising funding is actually increasingly used within the BBC. This has not stopped the recent French initiative under President Sarkozy to create a French public TV channel without advertising (2008–2009).

question, for example, whether there really is any discernible content difference between public broadcasting and private broadcasting (see Case Study 5.3). This is an important contemporary debate.

Theoretically, we may need to define what is meant by the 'public' and what is meant by the 'private'. If we cannot make a distinction between the two, we may not need to have different rules for the different types of broadcasting. In the EU there are many different notions of what the public broadcaster should represent and what its role should be. The regulations in each country show this (see Chapter 4), for example in the rules on advertising and public service broadcasters. Another example could be the newspapers, mainly a private sector media. Being in private hands, it is often argued, biasses them toward their owner's views, though once again hard evidence is often missing. Even if it was the case, we rely upon them enormously for the political debate they generate and they are primary in the public sphere (see Point of View 5.1).

This view has to be tempered somewhat across the EU. Because of their history and culture, some societies will be more sceptical about their newspapers or their media in general than others. Whatever the view, there is no serious argument for public spending to support newspapers, although in Europe there are instances where this happens. This does not stop

Point of View 5.1

Newspaper titles in France: an argument from *Le Monde diplomatique*

Across the EU one of the major trends has been the reduction of newspaper titles and this has been seen as worrying. In France (*Le Monde diplomatique*, 2006) this has been argued especially acutely. The claim is that the range of ideas contained in newspapers is being reduced and this is not good for 1) ideas themselves because it is leading toward populism and is an attack on in-depth journalism and 2) the democratic purpose cannot be well served by a concentration of newspaper owners.

This is particularly important in France where national newspapers have been in decline since the First World War let alone the Second, and more so than in many other EU nations. Moreover, there appears to be a greater interest in regional French newspapers than in the national. The Paris-based national papers are extremely sensitive to their position within French society, caught as they are between global, national and regional competition. It could be argued that this worry is beyond the normal national public–private debate.

Source: Le crise de medias, *Le Monde diplomatique* (Ramonet, 2005).

some newspapers worrying about their status in a highly competitive market.

Therefore, what we often debate is not whether change is happening but rather which of all the forces for change is predominant. Debate often hangs on such established mainstream concepts as we have already seen (Chapter 1): globalisation, Europeanisation, technologism, capitalism, Americanisation, trans-nationalism, 'glocalisation', 'cultural capital', and so on. These and even more new *isms*, theories and ideas will continue to be formed as the 21st century unfolds. History and events will judge their effectiveness as tools of analysis.

There is so much change at present that some ask whether a 'new' model, a new paradigm, of the media in present-day societies is being born. In some quarters this is strongly argued (Van Cuilenburg and McQuail, 2003; and see McQuail *et al.*, 2005). This is not just about the EU; it may be applied to other regional blocs. As such, the EU is representative of how relatively rich, culturally intricate and politically diverse forms of society are coming to grips with new technological media developments in their own trans-national way.

Being what it is, the media in the EU is changing at many levels: international, trans-national, private, public, regulatory models, national, regional and even local media. Change also varies according to medium – film, TV and radio, print, Internet – both convergence and divergence running in parallel. The forces on change are direct (new technology) and indirect (European regulation), internal (within states) and external (global competition).

Media and communication theory

Some theorists like to talk about the 'mediating' role of the media as an information filter. The media is the mediator (McQuail, 2005). How powerful the mediator is may be contentious, but we do know it depicts the world round us; it paints a picture for us, by word, by audio, by the visual or by the image, by old or even new technology. It touches our imagination. That is why so much time is often given in media theory to the idea of 'meaning': how we make sense of what is being depicted: the 'content' (see Point of View 5.2). To explore the media is to explore meaning through its dialectic and rhetoric, its grammar and depiction. To understand it is to interpret it.

Moreover, social and political scientists and media theorists disagree with one another on how to interpret the evidence, and that is why the debates are so interesting and intriguing (see Point of View 5.3).

At its most glib, and like the media industries themselves, theory is prone to fashions and predominant assumptions. If these assumptions become used by those in power, it has been argued, it can change our perceptions. For example, those in charge of a nation state or any political system may encourage the media to lead us into decisions and policy-making which can radically change not only how we see the world but how we depict it. And the media if anything is a world of depiction.

So how can we unpick the European media to make some philosophical or social theoretical judgements about it? One way is to start with the primary

Point of View 5.2

Dialectics

Like the media industries, philosophy and theory do not work in a social or intellectual vacuum but, it is argued, in what is often called the 'dialectic', a world of argument, propositions and counter propositions, thesis and antithesis, synthesis. It is also a world of *rhetoric*; the power, some would say the seduction, and influence of an argument. The *dialectic* and the rhetoric are all held together in some form of *grammar*; the rules of the game and how to make assertions intelligible. Drop the italicised words into any good encyclopaedia and you will see what is meant.

Point of View 5.3

Differences of view: social scientists in action – the 'radical' left

Professor Stuart Hall's depiction of the press and the mass media is well known in UK circles. He argued that the media was biased against the lives of the black population within the UK community. This was founded on questions of class and race. This was also a cultural question as much as it was economic. In the USA, and popular in the EU, Noam Chomsky's fervent criticism of capitalism is equally well known and his recent arguments stress how the media, especially the mass media, are a diversionary exercise to occupy the population with news stories or entertainment, while those in power continue to organise society in their own interests. For Chomsky this is not just cultural, but a direct criticism of the corporations who own and direct American capitalism.

See Hall (1997) and Chomsky (2002).

arguments that have been set out in Chapter 1 and then go on to consider how to philosophise or theorise around the subjects that arise.

It was argued in Chapter 1 that within the EU powerful forces are at work. They are political, economic, social and cultural. They embrace the history of the nation states, and the way in which they adapt to new trade rules and new technology of which the media is a part.

- The EU is remodelling its communication system, at the level of telecommunications and media provision.
- Corporate mergers and takeovers within the media industry are frequent, in relative terms.
- The PSBs, an accepted part of our media world in the EU, are being thrown into new patterns of development.
- Delivery systems of the media are having major economic as well as communicative effects on us all.
- Newspapers, for example, are adapting to a world of Internet-change, online journalism and a changing advertising landscape.

While these statements are in the main accurate they are debatable, and what they mean to our analysis of the media will depend upon our theoretical approach.

Before we can test the theories and their views we need to make some simple working definitions and try to develop a working diagram. When we have done this we can look again at the theories to deepen our use of them. The categories are in the main taken from accepted and previously developed ideas by others. They have been simplified as much as possible so that we may connect ideas and various approaches.

Approaches 1: Politics and policy: power, discourse and control

In any society there are individuals or groups who wield power. The communication system embraces them; for example, government-led agendas and statements and press releases through to newspaper editorials. In other words, it can be argued that how we talk to each other and how we are governed is controlled by those who hold power over the communication system. In the media we find values and meanings and views which serve the interests of those in power. The degree to which this impacts on us depends on the different political systems in which we live. So, we need more than just media theories. We need to get to know how power works within different societies. This seems to be especially important in the European context (see Case Study 5.4).

As indicated above, from Siebert *et al.* (*Four Theories of the Press*) in 1956 to Hallin and Mancini (*Comparing Media Systems*) in 2004, there have been compelling arguments that the media is controlled by political forces. It is argued that capitalism, or the economics of society, plays second fiddle to the power hierarchy laid down by constitutions. Either by law or by naked manipulation, the media bends to the will of those in power. The media's 'discourse', its depiction of the world, will depend not on media values or inherent meaning but on political expediency and control.

Approaches 2: Economic liberal materialism

A more materialist theory relies heavily not just on power networks but on economics. This could also be linked to the theories of functionalism and neo-functionalism (see above). In modern Western countries this means the use and development of capital and the way in which we organise our working lives. This theory draws on our material well-being and the use of resources. The media will be subsumed into the economic system; driven by global, international or local finance. It may take up an active critical position of capitalism but more likely it will tend not to bite the hand that feeds it.

For EU countries there is an accepted liberal market capitalism which underpins all of those who have joined the EU. In fact, the EU as a club of nation states insists that member societies are 1) democracies and 2) regulated but reasonably free markets for labour and capital. The media within the EU is considered to be a part of the market economy and the political values that go with it: freedom of speech and right of reply are included but just as valid are profit and investment (see Case Study 5.5). These are driving forces, it is said, pulling the EU together.

Those who believe in a more materialist position argue that power never comes down to constitutional niceties or 'politics', not even the rule of law, but is based on material 'wealth'. They go on to argue that those who own or control the capital accrued by material activity hold a dominant position in society and will distort the media for their own ends. Some argue that we have good examples of such 'media barons' in the contemporary period such as Murdoch and Berlusconi, or the 'Hersant' and even the 'Bertelsmann' groups.

There are often conflicting arguments over the underlying 'message' of the media (see Point of View 5.4). There are the other 'liberal' materialists who argue that, counter to the arguments above, wealth creation, always expansive and inclusive, is a 'good' for society. It represents an efficient use of the material resources for the betterment of humanity and means that cultures will mix and develop as they brush up against one another. We learn and culturally interact through trade (Adam Smith) and this forms the basis of a moral society.

The other left-orientated 'materialist' argument is that wealth creation, based on a driving economic and capitalist system, creates opposing classes, separating and alienating people. There are those who own and those who work and this can lead to a conflict of interest. The media, they might argue, is a part of the dominant ideological order.

Case Study 5.4

Poland, Germany and UK models

When we look at the various media across Europe they appear to have similar characteristics. But this is not necessarily the case. German media has changed alongside its society and politics. We can 'periodise' these changes from the Nazi to post-war periods and later unification between East and West Germany. All have legacies that shape the German media of today. The strict censorship of the East German system for all media – print and audio-visual – has been dismantled and replaced since 1991 with the new unified German system. Newspapers, radio and television have all altered.

In Poland the media system changed considerably at the end of the Cold War. The previous government, relying on its ties to Russian communism, was replaced by more liberal capitalist ideas leading later to Poland joining the EU. Through both major events the media has adapted.

Meanwhile the UK system has remained more stable over this period but nonetheless, compared with Germany and Poland, it is much more centralised – for example with newspapers and TV broadcasting primarily located in London – and this is directly linked to British history over a long period. In Poland and Germany the media systems nowadays are much more regional in form than the UK model.

Case Study 5.5

Money makes the world go round

Reports on the fortunes of media companies are published frequently. The following feature on Mecom, a Dutch media group, is typical. It shows the amount of money at play in such ventures, even in publishing. It equally shows the complexity of the media industry:

> Mecom, the European newspaper business led by David Montgomery (chief executive), has predicted a breakthrough in underlying profits next year as cuts in the costs of its operations feed through to the bottom line. . . . Mr. Montgomery said he was making progress in consolidating 40 separate divisions at Limburg Media, the Dutch newspaper group Mecom bought last June, into five divisions. Together with restructuring at Orkla Media, 750 administrative jobs were being cut. . . . His comments came as Mecom reported a loss before tax of £24.3m for the 17 months to December 31 on revenues of £213.3m. . . . The group reported exceptional items of £23.9m comprising of foreign currency losses, redundancy costs and the launch of a free newspaper in Denmark. Operating profits before exceptional items totalled £6.4 . . . Earlier this year, Mecom raised £570m in equity funding in order to buy 75 per cent of the equity in Berliner Verlag, the owner of Berliner Zeitung, from Veronis Suhler Stevenson. It also bought 24 per cent of Wegener, a Dutch newspaper . . . Considering these acquisitions, annual revenue at Mecom was now running at about £1bn, said Mr Montgomery. Mecom, planning a full listing on the London Stock Exchange, has circulation of about 25m newspapers a week in five countries. It is on the lookout for further acquisitions and may buy the rest of Wegener.

Source: Mecom predicts surge into black on cost cuts, *FT Report* (Terazono, 2007).

Point of View 5.4

Marxist class-based critiques: Glasgow University Media group

The Glasgow University Media group developed an intriguing critique of modern media. They argued that the media was dominated at many levels and in many genres by biased reporting which has distorted the 'reality' of contemporary society (see *Bad News*, *More Bad News* and *Really Bad News*, Glasgow University Media Group, 1981, 1982). Their general comment that the media distorts and that we should use every form of critical thinking to judge the media's accuracy has been well put in the past 20 years: see also *Message Received* (1998).

The comment by Lord Annan, famous for his reports on UK broadcasting, that this group of academics were 'a shadowy guerrilla force on the fringe of broadcasting . . .' does not stand the test of time but shows the degree of debate that media theory provokes.

See: http://www.variant.randomstate.org/7texts/Media_Group.html.

Stop and consider 5.9

Some analysts from the radical left argue that economics being so important, the predominant foundation for trade relations, the media only serves the purpose of the economic system. But there is a counter argument. If this is the case, why is the structure of the media across Europe so different when capitalism has been the underlying system used for most countries in the West since 1945?

The media in materialist terms, as a part of the economic system, can be described in 'optimistic' or 'pessimistic' terms (McQuail, 2005). Either it is a part of the free movement of ideas like normal trade and is in itself benign or, in more pessimistic terms, it represents one economic class or group dominating another by its control of the media and its content.

Approaches 3: Social and political spheres: democracy

Democracy is based on a broad principle of one person one vote, but of course there are variations.

Within the EU there are constitutional monarchies and republics. Some societies have lived under the principles of democracy and the rule of law for hundreds of years (for example, the UK and Scandinavia). Other societies are new to the values of democratic government (for example, the Baltic states and former and Central Eastern Europe).

The powers invested by democracy in the individual, it is argued, will be reflected in the type of media organisation created. First, it underpins the value system of individual choice whether economically or politically. Second, it will start grouping individuals into effective public communities, social groups that have rights and concerns and an influence both as citizens and consumers. Taken collectively, the individuals and the communities will represent the democratic values in any given society. This is not a new idea (see Point of View 5.5). The stories and the headlines of daily life in the media will highlight and reinforce these beliefs.

Human activity, including how people communicate with one another, is neither just about laws and rules, nor the powerful in society. There is a need to preserve a balance between ourselves as 'individuals' and our need to combine with others in 'communities'. Our communities are at work, in leisure, in families and in social networks. Social networks are at the core, it could be argued, of how people connect with one another: My Space, Bebo and YouTube are new areas of community. However, there are older communities based on national or regional identities, and these form the bedrock of Europe's nation states. We engage with the media because it promotes our individual pleasures but also because it supports our community needs. The media is a natural form of communication between people and their interests, at all levels and in all its diversity.

There is a relationship between the producers and the consumers, between individual choices and community compromises. In dealing with and responding to the market, communities react to the media they are given. Equally, the producers of the media will be sensitive to the communities that they serve. It is a two-way process. For example, a newspaper could be jingoistic in times of war (the Boer War and the *Times* in the 19th century, or the Falklands conflict and the *Sun* newspaper in the UK in the 20th), but it will not resonate unless there is a vestige of nationalism underpinning it.

Not everyone agrees with this view of course, and there are those commentators who prefer to see 'class' values, for example, as more important than national cultures (see Point of View 5.6).

Even in societies which are authoritarian as opposed to being democracies, it is argued, diverse communication will exist even if driven 'underground'. The new technology of the Internet and the web (Web 2.0) is a living example, some would say, of how difficult it is to repress the diversity of communication and that creative mix of individual expression

Point of View 5.5

From politics, democracy to media

As early as 1831 de Tocqueville wrote:

> The effect of a newspaper is not only to suggest the same purpose to a great number of persons, but to furnish means for executing in common the designs which they may have singly conceived. The principal citizens who inhabit an aristocratic country discern each other from afar; and if they wish to unite their forces, they move towards each other, drawing a multitude of men after them. In democratic countries, on the contrary, it frequently happens that a great number of men who wish or who want to combine

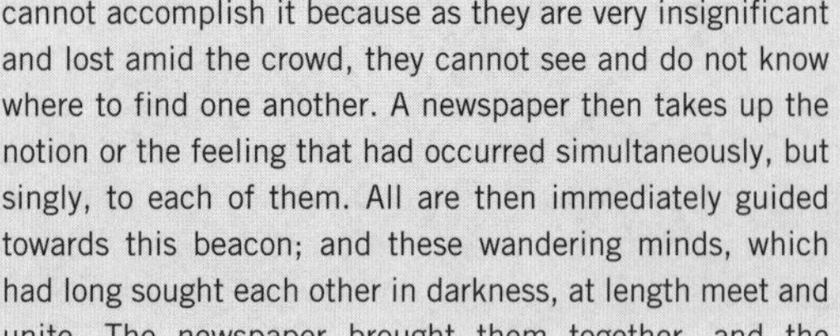

> cannot accomplish it because as they are very insignificant and lost amid the crowd, they cannot see and do not know where to find one another. A newspaper then takes up the notion or the feeling that had occurred simultaneously, but singly, to each of them. All are then immediately guided towards this beacon; and these wandering minds, which had long sought each other in darkness, at length meet and unite. The newspaper brought them together, and the newspaper is still necessary to keep them united.

Source: *Democracy in America*, Part 2, Ch. 6 (de Tocqueville, 1831).

Point of View 5.6

The work of Jorgen Habermaas

Famously, the work of the German philosopher Habermaas tried to illustrate how a public community or 'public space' was created. He located this in history: linking it with public political movements such as the French Revolution where both class and public values emerged. Still today, the meaning we give to both the 'private' and the 'public', he might argue, derives from these types of 'historical' events.

In one of his later powerful books he links this to the phenomenon of the mass media and the mass communication system. He is rightly respected for his insightful philosophical thinking, though post-modernists have often criticised his work for being too 'rational' and 'enlightenment'-based.

See (Habermaas, 1981).

and community belonging. This suggests that there is a careful balance between individual diversity (differences of opinion) and community bonding. These may be private communities or public authorities, but both are inextricably linked to the communication network and reflected in the media.

Approaches 4: Time, culture, history

Time and history have shaped different societies in different ways and their media will reflect this. For example, there is an important timeline (1945 to the present, but especially since the 1990s) in which the EU and its nation states began developing anew their media. What is reported in the news or talked about in a soap opera will reflect these differences and is a part of the local, national and even trans-national culture (see Case Study 5.6).

There are arguments about how history and time work upon us. They can fit with our language use, our way of life, our history as taught to us, both individually and socially, and even morally through religious beliefs and value systems. All are brought together into a way of behaving, a way of social interaction, that makes society what it is.

The relationship between our media behaviour and culture is important. We often copy those around us, to mimic them: when we are children in a family or with peer groups when we are growing up,

Case Study 5.6

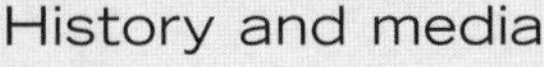

History and media

BBC TV series: *'Allo Allo'* (1982–1992)
The highly successful BBC *Allo, Allo* comedy was set in the Second World War in France. Its characters played with national stereotypes in a historical setting which was in reality one of extreme violence and Nazi occupation. Its audience would need to be aware of this tragic episode in European history and the underlying tensions between the peoples of Europe to understand its setting, especially its comedy.

Film: *Borat, Cultural Learnings of America for Make Benefit of Glorious Nation of Kazakhstan* (2006)
The end of the Cold War, the migration of Eastern and Central European people across Europe and across the world is the backdrop for the satire in the film *Borat*. Offensive, full of stereotyping, sexism, even massive historical and cultural inaccuracy, it has been a box office success.

or even with colleagues at work. Later we express ourselves through fashion or trying to break the mould; some say this could be seen as the adolescent phase. There are generational differences and even social groupings such as class, or what we think of as class, defining who we are.

The films we watch, the programmes we view, the newspapers we read and the mobile we carry are a part of this cultural, social identity: rooted in the past but changing in the present, evolving into fashion. The media in this sense is the communicator of what is normal and the latest fashion. The media establishes values and then sets out to change our attitudes to them.

A quick look at the gamut of magazine choices shows how the media industry bends to these pressures and demands. The power of the magazine content lies in mimicry by its readership of the fashions to be found on its pages. This is often associated nowadays with what is known as the 'celebrity age'. It enchants the audiences and leads to competition for the new. It also reveals to us our individual choices and communally accepted descriptions of what we imagine to be 'new' and 'old'.

Moving in and out of the given 'social identity' was more difficult in the past in Western societies than it is now. Nowadays social mobility is seen as a norm and even a politically acceptable 'good'. The media reflects these changing norms and encourages this. It does so by allowing for this new social mobility to be discussed by promoting new and pluralistic ideas and creativity. Our 'identity' will often be rooted in the past and the new cultural references that the media content provides for us.

Using theory with research methods

Applying different theories (or approaches) is one of the most intriguing aspects of media analysis, especially if we combine this with the more specific research methods. Using both qualitative and quantitative approaches in the present scene is almost obligatory. It is what distinguishes the media student from the burgeoning media analyst. To become a media analyst requires a new set of skills or competences. For example, the ability to use research methods: creating categories and variables, making measurements and using empirical data – see Fig. 5.1 and Chapter 2. Also, we need to understand the media in practice in matters such as broadcasting regulations and organisational behaviour (see Fig. 5.2). These are governed by law and regulation (see Chapter 4). They are also related to the organised working practices of media institutions and corporations and to the distribution network.

Lastly, we must never forget the consumer – the audiences, the readership, often linked to 'ratings' (see Fig. 5.3 and Chapters 8 and 11). These will be defined by social theory within the perimeters of the society in question. They are also a part of social and individual consumption. The latter is sometimes used to show how individuals and communities may respond to the choices available to them and is linked to their psychology as well as other factors.

To understand media consumption we use a large number of variables (categories) to define the consumer group (see Chapters 8 and 11). In Europe you will find many variations. For example, European

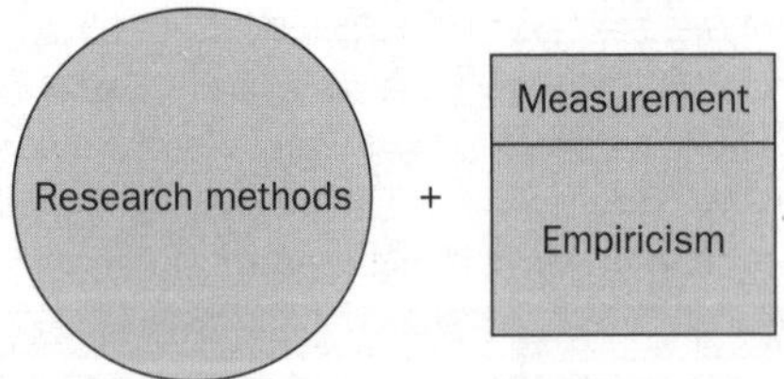

Figure 5.1 Research methods and measurement

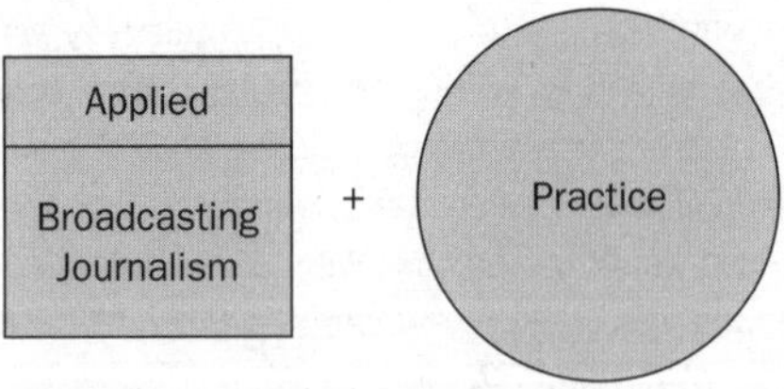

Figure 5.2 Applications and practice

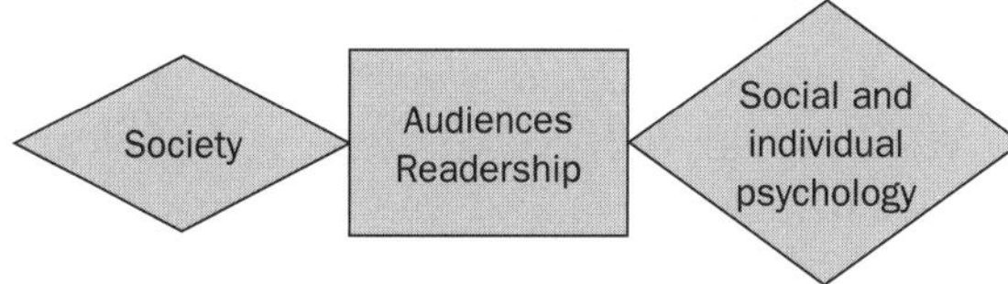

Figure 5.3 Audience readership

data shows many national variations in age, educational background, household spend, access to the Internet and consumption preferences. This is what makes the European market intriguing.

Critical review

Having established the broad approaches we can use, we need to marshal our ideas in a critical way. This means not only thinking about the media in context but also reflecting on what others have said about the subject. This is known as the 'literature review' or 'critical review': a means of bringing together contemporary commentaries into themes to explore a research question. It is an essential tool of analysis, demanding that we review work through its strengths and its weaknesses, by argument and by criticism (see Point of View 5.6).

Media theory milestones and contemporary debates

Media and communication theory come out of a broad sweep of philosophical and theoretical thinking, and there have been notable milestones along the way. All of us as students of the media need to grasp the essentials so that we can find the present debates and judge their value and their use. We can also use them to think anew about the media in Europe as a whole.

The following pointers have been used to locate some of the major modern debates: those who have influenced media and communication theories and are still current in academic and media circles and especially in Europe. Again the list is not exhaustive but indicative. We can look up some of these concepts using reliable and proven sources to deepen our knowledge.

1. Media theory vs communication theory

It may seem obvious that media and communication theories are bound together, and they are. However, there has always been a divide between what many commentators from the Anglo-Saxon tradition argue and those from what may be called 'continental' Europe.

The former have favoured the view that the media is an industry and should be studied as such. The

Point of View 5.6

The work of Marshall McLuhan: the argument and a criticism

The argument: The work of Marshall McLuhan is rightly still quoted and much used throughout many media studies programmes. His ideas are actually much more complex than often the mere headlines might suggest but, right or wrong, he is famous for his view that we are heading for a kind of 'global village' as new technology spreads through the world. In his era he was thinking mostly of television, but his general critique of new technology remains. In his view, we are marching off in the direction of globalisation where the technology and our ideas will converge.

The criticism: The trouble with this idea is that it does not explain the apparently infinite forms of diversity actually associated not just with technology but also with the societies and the communities in which they operate.

See McLuhan, 1964, 1967.

continental tradition has seen the media more as a part of a wider communication network. The media, they argue, cannot be separated from the social and political discourses that surround it. In the latter tradition, it is more valuable to see the media as a part of the social communication system.

Of course there has been a cross-over between the two traditions; and the semiotics of the post-modernists has travelled well across the divide. However, in practical terms, even today in educational institutions, the Anglo-Saxons, especially in the UK, highlight programmes within the discipline of Media Studies whereas the normal European approach has been toward Communication Studies in continental Europe.

Why is this important? Many debates about the media, the agenda setting, its role in society, hinge on how it is defined. If the media is defined as a function of society, one separated from other functions, its role is defined through what it does as an institution. Consider editors, journalists, owners, readers, audiences, for example – categories of people's jobs and their abilities. In this way we can research the media through these functional, what statisticians call, 'variables'.

Communication theory tends to argue differently. The media must be defined by its discourse, its channels of communication, its meanings and its semiotics; the world of language, meaning and depiction. This again is the world of the rhetoric, the dialectic and its grammar.

The 'new' theories about the media and its communication effects which dominate contemporary thinking are frequently hybrids; often mixing their ideas in valuable ways but often mixing the differences in approaches between them too. It is intriguing to work out where a writer's, academic's or commentator's argument is coming from.

2. Modernism vs post-modernism

One of the great divides in contemporary media thinking is the debate about modernism and post-modernism. Some would argue that they are one and the same thing, one built upon the other. Others say that they are different. Across Europe in reviews and educational establishments this debate continues and few students will be able to avoid it.

From the late 19th century to the early 20th the dominant idea was one of 'modern progress': an optimism that human beings could improve their lot through science and organisation. This has been termed 'modernism.' Man's progress was made possible by divining and understanding value and using objectivity to find scientific and even political 'truths'.

'Post-modernism', established from the mid-20th century but especially in the 1970s and 1980s in media and communication studies, argues that progress is more circumspect. As a theory and philosophy it is less optimistic, perhaps even pessimistic, and less enthusiastic about the notions of rational behaviour and progress based on technology and scientific development and objectivity. It stresses the importance of putting the 'self' into a narrative or 'meta-narrative' rather than an organised rational community of truths; a relative view that we are all different, that there are no fixed human truths, but interpretations and dialogues between us. In simple terms, for many post-modernists, and again to simplify, the world is not necessarily a rational place moving in the direction of almost inevitable progress, but more irrational. This is the human truth if there is one (reflect on this by reviewing Case Study 5.7).

3. Dominance vs pluralism theories

In one view, the media is described as being influential in placing before us an 'agenda': 'agenda setting'. It is accused of being powerful, of distorting the world, whether in fictional or non-fictional terms. By its relationship to power it is a controlling factor in the way in which we think. The audience, the readers, the listeners and even the gamers are caught in a trap where what entertains them is given to them in a form offering little control over content and editorship. Moreover, it combines to inculcate ideas and thinking dominated by those who create it, or own it or manipulate it. This argument is powerful and is used by both the 'left' and the 'right' politically. It is often referred to as the 'top-down' approach to the

Case Study 5.7

Post modern worlds – tourism: *Tomb Raider* and Angkor; *Sherlock Holmes* and London; and the *'Da Vinci Code'* and Paris

An intriguing recent research article explored how the UNESCO world heritage site at Angkor in Cambodia was having to cope with a large increase in tourists, mainly due to the success of the computer game *Tomb Raider*. This later became a box-office 'blockbuster' in the film *Tomb Raider – the movie*. The increase in tourism was based not on a 'truth' about a scientific discovery of the past, but on an imaginary 'narrative' in a movie. The 'fiction' in that sense though had a consequence and was causing conservation problems for the authorities. This raised issues on how the cinema depicts the world and how it impacts upon audiences. See Winter (2002).

This is not new of course. Nor do we have to go beyond the European shores to find examples. There is a large tourist industry in London still surrounding the supposed workplace of that famous detective Sherlock Holmes in 21B Baker Street, created by Sir Arthur Conan Doyle (1887). Of course the character is fictional and never lived anywhere other than in the writer's imagination. This does not stop the tourists travelling to the 'real' Baker Street found in central London.

In Paris, following the popularity and financial success both in book form (2004), with over 60 million sales worldwide, and a film (2006) 'blockbuster', *The Da Vinci Code*, written by Dan Brown (2004), is the basis for guided tours of the city (*Paris Vision's Da Vinci Tour*, 2007).

media and is related to 'dominance theories'. Critics of the media often use this approach as a foundation for their commentary on media provision.

There is as you might suspect an alternative view, a bottom-up approach, sometimes called or related to 'pluralistic theories'. It is argued that no matter what type of regime or society one lives in, values taken up by individuals and communities will be based on a range of ideas and sources and not those necessarily provided by the dominant group. People are different it is argued; people have choices, even the simple one of not buying or not taking part in the given media around them. In this case the consumer will make a judgement on the alteration of a news photograph such as that in the Reuters case (see Case Study 5.8). They will choose finally whether to believe and use the agency material or not. They may know that a heritage site or a fictitious detective is not 'real' but will use the entertainment value of the product to experience another world by visiting sites which stimulate their imagination: having 'fun' and – in a word – entertainment.

Case Study 5.8

Trusting the informers – the case of a Reuters photograph

Reuters, one of the largest media agencies in the world and the largest in the EU, was heavily criticised for publishing an adulterated news photograph of the Israeli–Lebanon conflict in 2006. It was alleged that the freelance journalist used by Reuters had doctored, even if marginally, a photograph to make the plight of the people in the Lebanese capital Beirut more dramatic. Or at least this is how it was interpreted. In the sensitive backdrop of war or conflict such accusations are frequent and can be damaging: damaging for the individual and the corporation. In the 'news' business we need to have trust in what we see as being accurate. Depending on your point of view the changes in the Reuters' photograph may appear small. Politically and journalistically they were dynamite. In this case Reuters reacted quickly to complaints and corrected almost instantly.

Source: See 7 August 2006, National Press Photographers Association, http://www.nppa.org/news_and_events/news/2006/08/reuters.html.

In other words, the 'consumer' – the individuals and the groups that make up the consumption of the media – have final control, especially if there are choices of media product available. It is argued that those who see the consumer as being fundamentally manipulated may misunderstand how supply and demand works. The choices that are made are acceptable to those who make them. Eventually, at least in democratic pluralistic societies, this means that the producers and distributors of the media do not finally control their consumers. In fact, they need to have a constant eye on the consumer if they are to have their products repeatedly used.

4. Complexity (chaos) theory, choice and the internet

The new media and its technology are beginning to create new debates. Some commentators are even talking about not only a new 'paradigm' (a new 'model' – see above) of the media but a new understanding of society bound to what might be called 'complexity (chaos) theory' and in which the media plays its part.

The term 'chaos theory' is taken from the disciplines of mathematics and physics and describes how systems, the predictions of how the media reacts for example, are seemingly chaotic and certainly difficult to make. However, there are patterns that can be observed in the 'chaos', although there is an inherent arbitrariness in how these might form themselves. Within organisational theory, something similar is used to analyse how organisations adapt to their environments (context), and this is known as 'complexity theory'. This theory has also been used within biological systems, where patterns emerge, but predicting exactly in which direction the organism will evolve is difficult.

Nowadays, and in similar fashion, as the consumer takes greater control of the increasing number of choices available through the media, the control of market by the producers is being challenged. As people connect beyond the previous social proximities into the new networks the Internet can provide, new groups and social communities are being formed, albeit virtual ones. Predicting how they react appears more complex than in the past.

As the distribution network becomes more complex, the choices wider, predicting behaviour by consumers will become more difficult: chaos theory seems to naturally fit this new phenomenon. There may be traceable patterns of behaviour, but actual linear predictions (how things connect directly to one another like the old analogue TV – from broadcaster to television set in a direct manner) are more difficult to compute.

Trying to predict how consumers will react is now becoming big business (see Chapter 11) as seen by web browser search competition (e.g. Google, Microsoft Live Search (Kumo) and Yahoo Search) and much of the spyware on the Internet is not just fraudulent and a nuisance but also a serious attempt to analyse what is happening to consumer choice.

The growth of the Internet and its effects on the media (and societies) are for the present more unpredictable, even chaotic (see Point of View 5.7) than many thought. The long-term shape and construction of the media in the future is still difficult to predict.

Point of View 5.7

Chaos theory and Web 2.0

The growth of what is known as Web 2.0 is often used to explain the new, more chaotic era. Moving way from media content provided by corporations, private and public, the internet has seen a rapid growth of consumer-created content, including downloads and video, arts, all forms of creativity, even games. The parallel development of open source technology also provides the individual and the consumer with the means to further control or focus on their own content need and interests rather than that provided by the major players of the old broadcasting or publishing world. This leads to endless innovation which is inherently chaotic.

Of course this needs to be seen alongside the way in which the new companies are moving into using Web 2.0-type activities to increase their own advertising revenue streams.

5. The information society

The media and the new technology interact nowadays, and this is encouraging a new model of present-day economies which is changing how society organises itself. How new this is, is debatable, but is it important. This new approach is economic but deeply involved with new technology: the 'information society'.

As we have seen in Chapters 1 and 3, this is an essential ingredient in EU thinking about the media market and its development. Moreover, it lies at the heart of the 'new economy'. In both developed and developing nations, information-led economic growth is seen as enormously important for the future.

6. The digital age or the digital society

The new models of the media are linked to digitisation. Computing and new technology are not new, but since the 1980s the impact of computing and digitisation on economies, ways of working and how we communicate with one another has transformed our working lives. The most dramatic impact of digitisation is the capacity to mix, merge and express the text, the graphics and the audio-visual in one medium. Increasingly, individuals and small communities have the means to use this new technology. It is no longer in the hands just of 'big business' but is part of our everyday lives. This trend will continue. Its impact cannot be fully predicted, but it does seem that we have entered a new digital age bringing with it a new digital form of social inter-relation with a multitude of networks.

Our knowledge of how groups and even the individuals within them are going to react to media provision is more fragmentary than it was in the past, while at the same time future trends are more difficult to predict. Regulatory models of the past which try to control the phenomenon are challenged by the internet in particular and digitisation in general. In regulatory terms digitisation means new models have to be considered, as Case Study 5.9 shows.

Case Study 5.9

The European Commission at the turn of the century: the digital network compared with analogue control

The following diagrams are taken from a turn-of-the-century European Commission presentation (2001) on the options for regulation of the media in the future. The presentation neatly encapsulates the shift from analogue to digital, and its conclusions were that the digital age is one which, by its very nature, leads to less regulation not more. Whether this is strictly going to be the case in the future remains debateable.

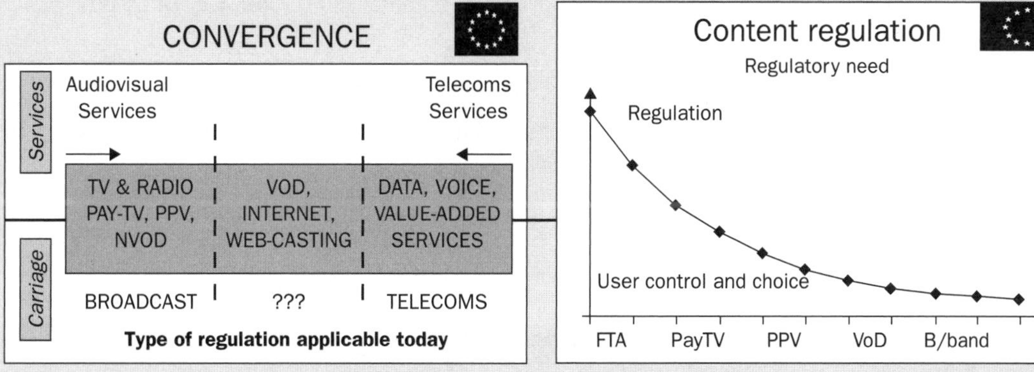

Source: European Commission, Directorate General for Education and Culture, *Audiovisual Policy, 2001*, http://europa.eu.int/comm/avpolicy/index_en.

Chapter summary

- The European media operates in a context, but if we are to explore that context we need to use both theories of European integration and media theory to unlock some of the driving forces that are operating in the contemporary age.
- Both quantitative and qualitative debates are the backbone of the media analyst's world. From debate we can explore.
- In creating an argument it is good practice to engage with creating research methods which match with the critical reviews of others we have used to ground our work.
- There are major theoreticians and commentators on the scene: our task is often to explore their ideas while at the same time remaining intellectually critical of them.

Key terms

Geo-political sub-divisions: in referring to the media in this way there is an emphasis on the sense of a geographically defined space developed through a definable political structure: in Europe this can be national or local but all specified by legal boundaries and specified territories.

Historical and cultural factors: often combined, it is a good idea to define these terms by using good dictionaries and encyclopaedias.

Intergovernmentalism: this process underlines the importance of how nation states maintain their sovereignty even if at times they may agree to cooperate with other nations with common policies.

Supra-nationalism: as opposed to intergovernmentalism, this political process underlines the importance of decision-making over and above the sovereignty of nation states, where polices are made at a collective level for the good of all.

Discussion questions

1. Why is theory useful in understanding the media developments taking place in the EU?
2. Are there pitfalls in using theory when we look at the diversity of provision across the EU and of so, what are they?
3. How do the theories of new institutionalism and consociationalism differ and how can they be used to understand the media in Europe?
4. Does the theory of neofunctionalism explain how the media has developed across Europe since 1958?
5. Siebert and others argued that the European model of media was defined as 'social responsibility': using a good encyclopaedia look up this definition and assess its importance.
6. Hallin and Mancini argue that Europe can be divided into geopolitical zones: is this a useful way to theorise about the media?
7. Assess the strengths and weakness of Approaches 1–4 mentioned in this chapter.
8. What is the difference between media theory and communication theory?
9. Does the debate about modernism and post-modernism add to or detract from our understanding of the contemporary media?
10. What is meant by dominance vs pluralist theories as they are applied to the media in Europe?

Assignments

1. Referring back to the text and the case study on *Euronews* (Case Study 5.1), answer the questions posed using the various strands of commentary within this chapter. Why was *Euronews* created and who finances it and why? This leads to the bigger question of who creates the media, when was it created and why? Why is *Euronews* rebranding and who are its main competitors? This leads to a bigger question of what is competition and why is it important? Who creates competition? Who benefits? What is the media for? Who does *Euronews* target as an audience and why? Is it changing and why?

2. What distinguishes the public sector from the private sector in the media? Make a list, justify your choice and argue the strengths and weaknesses of your argument. Ensure you define what you mean by 'public' and 'private': you may find political, social, economic and policy differences.

Further reading

In order to pursue new ideas about the media it is fruitful to look at the broad sweep of philosophies and theories of the past and then evaluate them in terms of our changing society today. Constructing new ideas is often the core of research work for postgraduate studies. This is not to say they cannot be dipped into whatever our stage of research. There are two main approaches to reading around the subject: books and noted authors and new research work in academic reviews.

Among the many excellent books available to you there are those listed below which might catch your imagination for their depth and clarity. They also contain in themselves excellent bibliographies which will help you spin off into your own search for material with writers such as the following: R. Williams, D. McQuail, M. McLuhan, P. Siebert, D. Hallin and P. Mancini, S. Hall, N. Chomsky, J. Habermaas, P. Lyotard, R.K. Merton, D. Morley and R. Collins.

A good start to media theory and European integration theory can be found in the following:

Albert P. (1985) *Que sais-je? La Presse*, 7th edn, Paris: Presses Universitaires de France.

Albert P. (1990) *La Presse Française*, Paris: PUF.

Bondebjerg I., Golding P. (2004) *European Culture and the Media*, Cultural Studies, Bristol: Intellect Books.

Briggs A., Cobley P. (2002) *The Media: an Introduction*, Harlow: Pearson, Longman (see also new edition 2008).

Chryssochoou D.N. (2001) *Theorising European integration*, London: Sage.

Cobley P. (2005) *Communication Theories: Critical Concepts in Media and Cultural Studies*, London: Routledge.

Collins R. (2002) *Media and Identity in Contemporary Europe: Consequences of Global Convergence*, Bristol: Intellect.

Crowley D., Mitchell D. (1994) *Communication Theory today*, Cambridge: Polity.

Dinan D. (2005) *Ever Closer Union: an Introduction to European integration*, 3rd edn, Basingstoke: Palgrave Macmillan.

Hallin D.C., Mancini P. (2004) *Comparing Media Systems: Three Models of Media and Politics*, Cambridge: Cambridge University Press.

Hampton M. (2001) Understanding media: theories of the press in Britain, 1850–1914, *Media, Culture and Society*, **23**(2): 213–231.

Magnette P. (2005) *What is the European Union?*, Basingstoke: Palgrave Macmillan.

McGuigan J. (2004) *Rethinking Cultural Policy*, Buckinghan: Open University Press.

McLuhan M. (1964) *Understanding Media: The Extensions of Man*, New York: McGraw Hill.

McLuhan M. (1967) *The Medium is the Massage: an Inventory of Effects*, New York: McGraw Hill.

McQuail D. (2005) *Mass Communication Theory*, 5th edn, London: Sage.

McQuail D., Golding P., de Bens E. (eds) (2005) *Communication Theory and Research: an EJC Anthology*, London: Sage.

Nugent N. (2006) *The Government and Politics of the European Union*, 6th edn, Basingstoke: Palgrave Macmillan.

Peterson J., Sharp M. (1998) *Technology Policy in the European Union*, Basingstoke: Palgrave Macmillan.

Peterson J., Bomberg E. (1999) *Decision-making in the European Union*, Basingstoke: Palgrave Macmillan.

Rosamond B. (2000) *Theories of European Integration*, Basingstoke: Palgrave Macmillan.

Siebert F.S., Peterson T., Schramm W. (1956) *Four Theories of the Press*, Urbana, IL, University of Illinois.

Watson J. (2008) *Media Communication: an Introduction to Theory and Process*, 3rd edn, Basingstoke: Palgrave Macmillan.

For reviews, much will depend on the sector you want to examine. There are some fascinating journals to explore. This chapter explored many, some of which are mentioned in the references section.

Online resources

http://www...

A good starting point to create your own website list is intute: follow the instructions and the various disciplines and record the sites as you go: http://www.intute.ac.uk/.

References

Albert P. (1985) *Que sais-je? La Presse*, 7th edn, Paris: Presses Universitaires de France.

Albert P. (1990) *La Presse Française*, Paris: PUF.

Brown D. (2006) *The Da Vinci code*, New York: Anchor Books.

Chomsky N. (2002) *Media Control: the Spectacular Achievements of Propaganda*, Seven Stories Press.

Chryssochoou D.N. (2001) *Theorising European Integration*, London: Sage.

De Tocqueville A. (1831) *Democracy in America*, 2002 edn, Chicago, IL: University of Chicago Press.

EU (1989) Council Directive 89/552/EEC of 3 October 1989 on the coordination of certain provisions laid down by Law, Regulation or Administrative Action in Member States concerning the pursuit of television broadcasting activities, *OJ*, **L298**, 17.10.1989, 23–30.

EU (1997) Directive 97/36/EC of the European Parliament and of the Council 30 June 1997 amending Council Directive 89/552/EEC on the coordination of certain provisions laid down by Law, Regulation or Administrative Action in Member States concerning the pursuit of television broadcasting activities, *OJ*, **L202**, 30.7.1997, 60–70.

EU (2007) Directive 2007/65/EEC of the European Parliament and of the Council of 11 December 2007 amending Council Directive 89/552/EEC of 3 October 1989 on the coordination of certain provisions laid down by Law, Regulation or Administrative Action in Member States concerning the pursuit of television broadcasting activities, *OJ*, **L332**, 18.12.2007, 27–45.

Glasgow University Media Group (1981) *Theory of Bad News, More Bad News*, and *Really Bad News Communicative Action*, London: Polity.

Glasgow University Media Group (1982) *Really Bad News*, London: Writers' and Readers' Publishing Co-op.

Glasgow University Media Group (1998) *Message Received* G. Philo (ed.), Longman.

Habermaas J. (1981) *Communicative Action*, London: Polity.

Hall S. (1997) *Representation: Cultural Representations and Signifying Practices*, London: Sage.

Hallin D.C., Mancini P. (2004) *Comparing Media Systems: Three Models of Media and Politics*, Cambridge: Cambridge University Press.

McLuhan M. (1964) *Understanding Media: The Extensions of Man*, New York: McGraw Hill.

McLuhan M. (1967) *The Medium is the Massage: an Inventory of Effects*, New York: McGraw Hill.

McQuail D. (2005) *Mass Communication Theory*, 5th edn, London: Sage.

McQuail D., Golding P., de Bens E. (eds) (2005) *Communication Theory and Research: an EJC Anthology*, London: Sage.

Moravcsik A. (1993) Preferences and Power in the European Community: A Liberal Intergovementalist Approach, *Journal of Common Market Studies*, **31**(4): 473–524.

Peterson J., Bomberg E. (1999) *Decision-making in the European Union*, Basingstoke: Palgrave Macmillan.

Peterson J., Sharp M. (1998) *Technology Policy in the European Union*, Basingstoke: Palgrave Macmillan.

Ramonet I. (2005) Le crise de medias, *Le Monde diplomatique*, January.

Siebert F.S., Peterson T., Schramm W. (1956) *Four Theories of the Press*, Urbana, IL, University of Illinois.

Sweney M. (2008) EuroNews rebrands to take on rivals, *The Guardian*, 5 June.

Terazono E. (2007) Mecom predicts surge into black on cost cuts, *FT Report*, 31 March.

Van Cuilenburg J., McQuail D. (2003) Media policy paradigm shifts: towards a new communications policy paradigm, *European Journal of Communication*, **18**(2): 181–207.

Weber T. (2007) BBC strikes Google-YouTube deal, *BBC News*, 2 March.

Winter T. (2002) Angkor meets Tomb Raider; Setting the scene, **8**(4): 323–336.

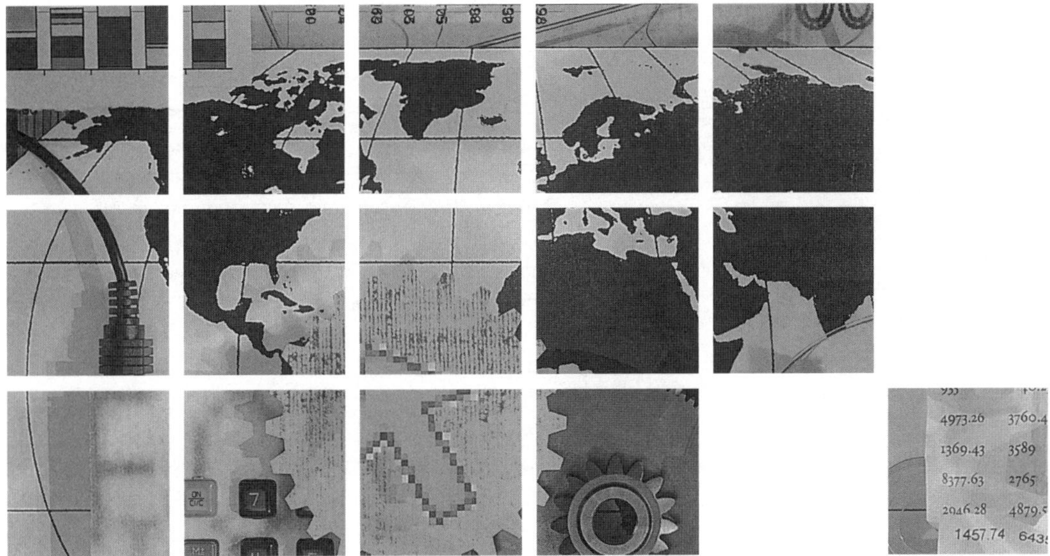

Chapter 6

Production in the EU press and publishing industry

What this chapter covers

- Introduction: the European media landscape – analysing the market
- History and precedents
- The 20th century
  - *Dramatic social and political change including war*
  - *Technology*
  - *Changing government: governments and governance*
- The contemporary era: the 21st century
  - *Globalisation, corporate growth, market concentration*
- Publishing markets and production
  - *Product development*
  - *Editorial strategy*
  - *Content creation*
  - *Brand identity and management*
  - *Marketing*
  - *Size*
  - *Pagination*
  - *Content*
  - *Layout, language and formats*
  - *Image and photography and the audio-visual crossovers*
  - *Editorials*
  - *Copyright*
- The present scene: an indication
  - *Newspapers*
  - *Periodicals, magazines and reviews*
  - *Book production and market*
- Comparative work: finding the variables (comparators)
  - *Press and publishing in general*
  - *Newspapers in national and regional settings*
  - *Books, reviews, magazines, journals, directories, databases*
  - *Regulatory framework*
  - *Ownership*
  - *Technology and the market*

Learning objectives

When you have completed this chapter you will be able to:

- Outline the growth of EU print and publishing industries in terms of its historical and, in part, technological development
- Locate some of the principal primary sources available to researchers that help us understand the changing publishing media scene.
- Describe the national, regional and local structure of press and publishing provision.
- Identify some of the principal trends over the past 20 years in the publishing and print industry across the EU.

Themes

Below you will find a simple statement or series of statements around the six themes. They should *not* be read as a given fact. They are more like hypotheses (see Chapter 2) which need to be proved, discussed, debated and then used in your own analysis of the subject. The ideas and approaches in this book are always to be considered with an open mind; this is important in higher education study and is what makes it distinct from pre-university study.

Diversity of media

The press and publishing industry in general reflects the oldest of the mass communication technologies. Its impact on European, let alone EU, history is immense, and it is a crucial part of the **European democratic dialogue**. It is also diverse in its provision and in the EU, until the very recent past, fragmented, although often nominally nationally based.

Internal/external forces for change

As the markets have become bigger, more open and more competitive, major publishing houses, even newspapers, have taken on a trans-national and even global dynamic. Equally there is in production an internal sub-national press which, depending on the country, is very important at regional and local levels. Within the EU there is also a European economic rationalisation driven by the single market whose impact is now beginning to be felt.

Complexity of the media

Unlike many aspects of audio-visual provision, there is no equal balance between private and public sector provision in the EU publishing industries. The press and publishing industry is administered and managed in the main in the private sector. Historically and today this remains the case. Being in private hands has not resulted in the industry being managed in the same way across Europe. Readerships remain different and dependent upon the different communities of consumers. Production follows this pattern even if national media concentration is the trend.

Multi-levels

Even if the private sector dominates press and publishing in ownership terms, and although similar technology has been used across the frontiers bringing forth wave upon wave of change and productivity, the market remains multi-community based. As long as the EU remains a multi-cultural consuming group of communities, its publishing and press production will remain sensitive to the different types of readership in the market. The degree to which there is consumer convergence is a matter of considerable debate. What is often correctly assumed is the growth of major global players who add to the multi-level state of the industry.

European integrative environment

The degree to which the EU press and publishing industries are being 'Europeanised' is another matter of hot debate. There are signs of considerable cross- and trans-national corporate production strategies but, at the same time, the evidence still points toward a national, language-based, multi-cultural hold on the market which makes it seem at times very fragmented and 'local'.

Cultural values

Our understanding of cultural change, and related social movements in society would do well to reflect on the changes happening in the press and in the publishing houses. Culture and the media, and especially the press and the 'textual' world, are very important historically. Change is probably slower to take place in the print industry when compared to the audio-visual sector, but change is happening. Measuring its rate is an important question as the digital age pressures the 'reading' world to adapt to the 'electronic'.

Essentials

There are fundamental contemporary assumptions about print production and especially the newspaper industry: it is in decline; journalism and reporting are decreasing in importance; it is focused on entertainment rather than public or community service; it is controlled by limited ownership (concentration); it is politically biased (toward the 'liberal' market and the 'right'); and it is threatened by digitisation.

➤ There is a sort-of-truth in all these beliefs but, taken as a whole, they paint a much-distorted view of what is happening. Only certain countries are marking out a fundamental decline in the newspaper industry (France a perfect example), and the reasons for the decline are not simple but have specific as well as universal contexts.

➤ There is still a West–East divide in Europe; some growth can be seen in the newspaper and print industries in the newly joined EU countries in Central Europe, whereas to the West there is a slight but complicated decline.

➤ In most countries there has been a growth in magazine or even **niche markets** and the print industry, although restructuring, is valued and profitable. It could even be argued that there has been an increase in journalism relative to the past. 'Entertainment-value' has always been a part of the press, but the quality end of the print industry remains in fact robust and important.

➤ Concentration of ownership is significant, but taken as a whole the EU area is still competitive and diverse. The context of political bias is better understood by national contexts in Europe than by ideological universalities. Convergence of delivery platforms is as much an opportunity as a threat, especially when combined with digitisation and translation production costs.

Introduction: the European media landscape – analysing the market

In an era of technological change, what is happening in the publishing industry has far-reaching consequences beyond the industry itself. As the influential Pira report on EU publishing said:

> It is worth stating that publishing is a very large contributor to the EU total economy both in value added and employment (as well as its vital role in providing information, developing culture and promoting plurality) . . .
>
> (Pira International, 2003).

According to one source (Datamonitor, 2007) daily newspapers account for 88.2% of the newspaper market, generating total revenues of \$24 bn (2006).

Leading players in the European market are often well known and include Bertelsmann, Axel Springer AG, News Corporation Limited and Daily Mail & General Trust plc. They are a part of what is estimated as total revenue for the publishing industry reaching \$144.1 bn (2006) with advertising revenues accounting for \$52 bn of business across Europe.

Not only is the publishing industry important, but it is also subject to a series of pressures altering its shape across the EU. Assessing these changes in the market is difficult, but separating production from distribution and consumption is helpful. All are inter-related, but each relies on different social and economic concerns. Coupled to this, press and publishing like all media does not operate in a 'perfect' market but in specific contexts which demand some level of comparison.

In EU terms, the pressures on the press are often linked to the 'spillover' effect of economic policy (see Chapter 3). In this light, the EU continues to commission work from consultancies reflecting upon the print and publishing industry from a pan-European trade and market potential point of view. Some of these we shall look at later in more detail.

Equally, the recent impetus for research study for many is the international, trans-national, global setting in which the media functions. Some of this work is excellent and underlines the importance of the **'new' media**, of which publishing is a part, as an integral element of 'globalisation' (Dicken, 2007; Flew, 2007). Even so we have not yet reached an easy 'European' definition of the publishing industry. As the European Commissioner Viviane Reding recently stated

> . . . most European media companies have not yet fully adapted their business models to leap-frog both national borders and traditional sectoral boundaries. The convergent European publisher has not been born yet!
>
> (Reding, 2007).

So seeking out sources and debates in a period of turmoil can be daunting and raises the question of where to start (see Source 6.1).

Comparative press work is a renewed area of enquiry. Later in this chapter, some preliminary comparators have been suggested that may be used to help in media market analysis. This is not to say that sources of information on the press, trans-nationally or internationally, are new, but they are becoming ever more important: the development of EU and global mergers and takeovers and the impact of trans-nationalisation are all becoming more relevant than in the immediate past. If we can establish some of the important variables, the data, the categories of comparison, we can evaluate and understand more clearly the press architecture across Europe, even if tentatively.

To do this we need to build a comparative picture on a set of accepted ideas. A standard format for example for EU newspapers is to categorise them into 'daily, national, regional, non-daily, free and sport' (EC, 2005). Yet, in an age of digital and cross-media development is this adequate?

For example, there are differences in markets between books, magazines and journals, databases and directories (both business and consumer) and online material. Moreover, the new digital age is beginning to pose fundamental questions on how the industry can evaluate consumer behaviour. This can be seen in Point of View 6.1.

Reading this 'point of view', you can see that financial matters are not far from the print industry's list of concerns. This is due to a combination of competition for readers and advertisers and the need for effective application of new technology. Market analysis of press competition in particular has

Source 6.1

Where to start?

The range of commentaries available to us is considerable but often conflicting, and many are in different languages. How then do we start? One approach which helps is to start with data. Empirical studies are not new and are a part of the press world, and especially the notable work undertaken by the World Association of Newspapers (WAN), an organisation founded in 1950. In Europe, the series dedicated under the banner of Euro-media group is informative and most interesting, as is the Datamonitor (Market Business Line) material available to most libraries. The Institute of European Media and the Hans Bredow Institute as well as the online material at the European Journalism Centre based in Maastricht are all major sources of excellent research and commentary. A new source of enlightened work and a hub of academic activity is the recently formed (in 2005) ECREA organisation (European Communication Research and Education Association), containing in its ranks many of the leading academics concerned with our understanding the European media market. There are so many more. All are available online and are good sources for material. The statistical work coming from Eurostat in these terms is also invaluable. So are the reports emanating from the joint venture between the Council of Europe and the European Institute for Comparative Cultural Research (ERICarts created in 1998).

But, as we saw also in the preceding chapters, data is often not enough. We saw that critical analysis means reviewing the limitations of the data even if we think it valid: not so easy sometimes to force the mind to look at the other point of view. We may have reasoned by now that this goes to the nub of judging statistics and data: in the end they are almost always approximations of what is being researched – useful yes, 100% accurate probably not. You might want to reflect upon this in your own research work when you are using data. Neither this chapter nor the next chapters are designed to provide us with vast quantities of data to be analysed: as recommended, use your sources elsewhere to build up data prior to analysing it and then use some of the approaches and issues that this and other chapters develop.

Point of View 6.1

Developing comparative models for the publishing industry

There is a section later on in this chapter which discusses 'comparators'. Certainly, the new technology is making analysts think anew. The following extract reveals how difficult but necessary it is to develop statistical comparative approaches that connect to readers and audiences in general. Refer back to Chapter 3 for some of the economic issues raised:

> Future analysis of the field will also need to consider the role that is played by services that cross conventional boundaries between publishing and communications. The importance of user-contributed content is increasing: many web sites now operate 'blogs' that sit within their own brands and these frequently include user feedback. However, there are also services that rely entirely on this form of content, operated either by companies, individuals all loose groupings of collaborators. These are essentially driven by the quality of the contributors, much like a conventional publication, but the format is that of a debate or dialogue. There are few forecasts for the commercial value of such services, but they are indicative of the way in which in the near future users may blend content and communication. Perhaps the most important implication of this lies in the analysis of 'media time' expenditure: time spent interacting with other people and creating content could also usefully be considered, as these will in effect, compete with conventional media for time. At the same time the frameworks in which they are carried out are creating commercial opportunities for both advertising and subscription revenue, especially in the mobile space.

Source: European Commission, *Publishing Market Watch Final Report*, p. 23 (EC, 2005).

always been very important. This is because, in the main, the industry lies in the private sector and has done so for most countries in Western Europe since 1945. Knowing what competitors are doing is the lifeblood of the press let alone its business survival. Consequently market analysis has often been locked into relatively expensive consultancy work, for example the already mentioned Pira International group is well known as are other consultancies such as Ernst & Young.

Yet, recent work for and about the EU on the press and publishing industry in Europe is now in the public domain and it sheds a fascinating light. The same can be said of reports emanating from the various European institutions such as DG Information Society and Media from the European Commission (see Chapter 1 and further reading section below) and from other consultancies, some of whom we have already considered (for example Bird & Bird, 2002; see Chapter 3). These sources of information are increasingly important in the EU market. In a hierarchy of sources, they are useful as profound, well-researched reports from primary sources which we can use to add to our secondary, more reflective commentaries in other more academic work.

Some may argue that the future debates on the direction of the industry relate not to the past but to the future of cross-over technology. Again, Point of View 6.1 could be interpreted to suggest this, but the evidence across Europe is not so clear cut. This is not least because the European context demands that we have core knowledge of the past as well as the present-day factors because 'history' appears to matter in almost any market and especially in the EU.

History and precedents

The 'heyday' for the European press was at the end of the 19th century. As for the creation of the 'modern' newspaper press, this goes back even further, to the 1620s or the 1640s depending on how you define it. Some of the latest research points to the German area around 'Strassburg' (Weber, 2006) as the first site to develop mass 'book' printing techniques associated with circulations. However, by the 19th century it was the mass media of its time, akin to putting television, radio, magazines and newspapers all into one outlet. It was the digital computer software interface of its era, but was also markedly different in style to most modern newspapers at its inception being very text-based.

On the other hand, the newspaper style of writing and expression altered quickly in the 19th century and into the 20th, just as mobile texting and RSS feeds and blogging are changing our own century: there was a move from 'objective' report-like articles to larger headlines, pictures and more sensationalism. That process of newspaper communication is still maturing today.

The press changed as soon as it was born, evolving as ever to fit its market, perhaps not at the same pace as now, but still dramatically. Newspapers came to embrace increasing industrialisation and innovation and new technology. Almost immediately, a new professionalisation of its production was evident. Its readership changed due to an increase in education and sophistication, equally becoming more political through democratisation and the growth of party politics.

There are interpretations of this change in the 19th century which paint a gloomy picture of 'alienation' and 'commercialisation', even a dumbing down of the reporting. These commentaries are not uncommon in our own age. What is evident, though, from the past is the vibrancy of the press, its widespread acceptance as a medium and its importance in the communication of political and social ideas, let alone its entertainment and news value. It was also nationally and regionally based. Although the press has become more 'visual' over time (drawings, cartoons, pictures, photography and even video-feeds now) it has relied in the main upon the written language: and language in Europe has been territorial to a large extent.

There are very few examples of trans-nationalism or, more accurately, cross-frontier ownership in the 19th and early 20th centuries. This was to come later. That is not to say that some newspapers were not read widely across frontiers, but the reasons why some newspapers were more important than others trans-nationally have more to do with indirect considerations: for example, where the Empire went, so did the press, for its general readers but equally for its 'national' civil servants and employees. The British Empire was seen as the widest and most economically successful of the 19th century, but empires were created and sustained by many European nations across Europe and in particular France, the Netherlands, Belgium, Spain, Portugal, Germany and even Italy to name but a few. Some of the oldest press witnessed the era, such as the oldest surviving British Newspaper *The Times* (created in 1788), or the earlier *Belingerske Tidende* in Denmark (1749) or later *Le Figaro* in France (1826) or *Dagens Nyheter* in Sweden (1878) and almost at the same time *The Financial Times* in the UK (1888) all of which continue today. The press did not create a 'new' Empire-based market – this was more due to national, political, social and economic policy-making – but it adapted to changing circumstances that allowed it to flourish and expand.

The 20th century

The 20th century changed the press profoundly, in terms of its production and its distribution and then its consumption. In terms of production, there are several important factors which are often seen as being pivotal: dramatic social and political change including war; the introduction of new technology; and changing **governments** and multi-levels of **governance** such as the creation of the EU.

Dramatic social and political change including war

Europe in the 20th century was dominated by war or the threat of it. Even now, Europe is emerging out of a period of 'cold war', where its boundaries are being reassessed and its peoples are looking again at their neighbours. They are renewing relations but often with one eye on the past.

There is sufficient evidence for us to say that social 'crises', including war, both hot and cold, and terror-based militancy, change the attitude of readers, journalists and owners to reporting and the press. This had started in the 19th century, if not before; for example, under the auspices of 'Empire', trade wars were reported frequently by the press, reviews and journals, at times even sensationally. They had considerable influence on the opinion of their respective readerships. Equally, and most importantly for the producers, it sales and the notoriety and even the popularity of the press and publishing in general were increased.

Yet, some would argue that the wars of the 20th century were manifestly different and global in scope. They changed people's attitude to information and press reporting because, more than ever before, they were included, involved as in no other period in history. It would be difficult to understand the development of the contemporary European press and publishing industry without understanding the scarring of two world wars emanating in part from Europe. The evidence for this seems strong (see Case Study 6.1).

If there is a general rule, it is that the newspaper industry, and publishing in general, responds well in 'free' societies. Censorship and control at times of social and political strain are poor companions to democratic discussion and debate, and this impacts upon ownership of production and readership behaviour. In Europe, the recent divide between West and East is a particularly notable example in terms of press control.

Even today it is difficult to understand modern presses without an analysis of government strategies to cope with the probing role that journalists play in the political make-up of any society. This applies not only to the wider international field of operations but also to what was and is still often called 'the Home Front': the propaganda used by society in periods of internal stress. Europe's past is dotted with examples of state control from Mussolini's Italy, to Franco's Spain and the ravages of Hitler's and Goebbels Germany.

War and in particular in our own age the fear of war or terrorism brings with it arguments for censorship. It remains a 'hot' debate within democratic societies just as it has in the past. The question of control and the press has been with us of course ever since the very first presses, but the total war machine of the 20th century was unlike any other. It has altered societies from the first major conflagrations, such as the First and Second World Wars as we have seen, to the conflicts of our own post-1945 contemporary age: Korea, Vietnam, the Congo, Cuba, the 'Yom Kippur' war, former Yugoslavia, Afghanistan, the Middle-East in general and Iraq, to name but a few.

War and terrorism change our attitude to the state and how we react to it, and newspapers and the media in general are the conduit for state and official (and unofficial) information. At times, they are also a

Case Study 6.1

The impact of war on newspapers: France and Germany

The French publishing industry in the late 19th century was an integral part of a wave of enthusiasm for the 'new' media of newspapers. It flourished as the industry did across the rest of Europe. However, during the First World War (1914–1918), and then compounded by collaboration and coercion during the Second World War (1939–1945), the French press was apparently damaged by censorship and state control. The 'reputation' of the French national press was badly broken during these periods (Kuhn, 1995). It is not the only reason, but it is usually assumed that the French 'lower than average equivalent European national newspaper readership' is a reflection of readership cynicism emanating from this past. Moreover, well-known and present-day French presses like *Le Monde* and *Libération* owe their existence to the upheavals of the war period.

Each nation has its historical roots and we have to nuance our analysis depending on context. Germany, for example, has a high readership as a proportion of 'national' population, but it is also interesting to note that German (both West Germany and now reunited Germany) newspaper readership is mainly regional and not national. This too in part reflects two world wars and in particular the post-Second World War settlement that reinforced a federal form of German governance that was a direct reaction to the propaganda-centralising authoritarian years of the Nazi period (1933–1945). It is argued that this underpins readership behaviour in Germany even today (Hickethier, 1996).

part of the democratic voice of opposition to government or specific policies. More than this, newspapers tend not just to report but to interpret; they take on a character, a view. Objectivity and authenticity are important in all media, but papers will personify their material and the reader will identify. If the newspaper distorts too much, as was the case in French newspaper history in both world wars, circulation can be damaged (see Case Study 6.1). It is for this reason that politically healthy societies try to maintain political pluralism, with a range of newspaper outlets allowing for differing views and debate. In the private sector, as we have considered in Chapter 3, the economics-based anti-monopoly measures are often used to ensure not just competition but also this political and social pluralism.

Newspapers will make mistakes, but a deliberate bending of the truth over a long period will distort and undermine the 'trust' the public has in its competence and professionalism. Competitors, if there are any, can and will take up the disenchanted. The public can even turn away, become politically apathetic – a claim for example that is being made about young readers in our own age, though the reason why this is the case needs more investigation.

Technology

Applied technology has brought not only new means of production but, most importantly, fierce competition for the newspaper industry: radio and film first and then of course the mass impact of television. To this must now be added the computer screen and the World Wide Web, both of which emerged at the end of the 20th century. Nowadays this is reflected in the increasing number of 'Screen Studies' programmes as opposed to sector media analysis in universities.

Much has been made of this technological wave of invention, not least the argument that we are all moving toward a 'global village' where, to simplify McLuhan's view, the 'medium is the message' (McLuhan, 1964). In press terms this is not as evident as perhaps in the digital audio-visual world, and certainly the technological changes within the press did not alter the fundamental architecture of its production in the early or mid-20th century.

Even so, we appear to be on the cusp of a new age which starts in the later 20th century: cross-media agencies and content are becoming ever more important; the visualisation and graphics, the formats, the cross-media selling of journalism, the techniques of information gathering and reproduction are all changing. The digital age is having a major impact on our thinking about future press production and the future of readership. Although there is strong evidence of a drop in newspaper 'paper' readership compared with the past, this has to be set against a backdrop where owing to Internet access to news we are reading more than ever before.

Nevertheless, this emphasis on contemporary globalisation can be overdone. The existence of press agencies has always been a beacon of trans-national practice, illustrating how global gatherers of the news cross frontiers. Today, for example, the 'latest' news from Reuters and Agence France-Presse (AFP), competing head to head with US rivals such as Associated Press (AP) and United Press International (UPI), passes directly into the production process, influencing the agenda across many countries and many types of media. This has been happening for a very long time and stretches back into the 19th century let alone the 20th. The gathering of information, it seems, is as important to humankind as the gathering of wheat or rice for harvest.

No matter the pressures for change, the press as an outlet in the widest corporate communication terms in Europe today overall remains vibrant, profitable in most sectors and very diverse, despite the concerns for its future. Moreover, the competition for information is not now limited to other newspapers but extends to other media outlets too: the bloggers, the mobile, the hand-held TV, let alone the MP3 player and iPod.

Changing government: governments and governance

As governments change, so do the rules of press engagement and media agendas. Across Europe, since 1945, governments have risen and fallen in the wider context of changing international relations and assumed ideologies. The innovative, some would say unique, form of the EU has been a part of this process. This is important because at the heart of government power is not only the legislative–executive role it assumes but also its direction of the economy. In the EU so many of the economic policies are to be found not only at the national but at the EU level, and this has created an inter-weaving of European (trans-national) and national interests.

Therefore, the business atmosphere in which the press operates will depend on the buoyancy, the trends and the alterations inside the market: this touches the producers, the distributors and the consumers. When governments maintain stability and growth in their markets and economies, they will often be rewarded by elected power. Even if it is in some quarters unpopular, the *raison d'être* for the very existence of the EU is based on the idea that grouping nations together serves the interests of its member states both economically and politically.

The multi-level decision-making process which is now the EU, a mix of EU collective and individual national decisions, impinges upon the market, including the publishing industries (see Chapter 1). Needless to say, there are huge debates on the EU's efficiency and effectiveness as an organisation, not least in its handling of the sensitivities of the media industry including print and publishing (see Chapter 5) in its different national settings. It is for this reason that much of the broadcasting world has been left to national and not trans-national regulation.

Moreover, the double-edged sword of press power lies not only in its role as a conduit for governments or the EU or media 'barons'; it is also a channel for the population to vent its mood and its prospective electoral power. Nowadays this electoral role includes many levels inside the EU: local, regional, national and EU levels of reaction. Catching the mood of the reader or even this wider 'European' 'electorate' is one of the arts of contemporary journalism and product development.

Few governments in modern democracies can survive unpopularity for too long. Even the more remote European institutions (see Chapter 1) centred in Brussels expend a great deal of effort trying to 'communicate' to their perceived audience: the 'citizens' of the EU. Yet, this has been slow a process. It has only really accelerated after the imposition of universal suffrage for the European Parliament in 1979, and then later the creation of citizenship following the Maastricht Treaty in 1993, all of which was linked to the powerhouse of European integration and to the on-going market changes started by the creation of the single market and the building of the euro currency in 1987 and 2001, respectively.

Of course it is often argued that the owners, reporters or editors are 'in control' of the media and thus its authority, and it is they who have the 'ear' of government. That is why so much has been written about the power of the producers in all the societies of the EU. However, the relationship between readers and press production is not simple, and in the end there is always a dialogue being arranged between both sides of values which come together in what is often called 'public opinion'. At times it is the press and publishing industry which 'represents' the voice of the people (its readership and its owners) and at other times it is describing directly the voice of the people through reporting social change or new social concerns.

Stop and consider 6.1

It could be argued that the power of 'public opinion' is the root power of all the media. Touch the public sentiment and the power structures will need to respond one way or another. In our own age, it could be argued that the more global we become, the more we are defined as European, the more information we absorb, the more our sensibilities are changed. But how true is this view? What about the argument that the 'public' has little control over the press agenda? That it is the power of the owners and those who produce the press agendas that have the real influence.

It is not surprising therefore that the target of much press reporting is the government of the day. Look across a range of good-quality daily newspapers such as *Corriere Della Serra* and *Repubblica* in Italy, *De Telegraaf* in the Netherlands or *El Pais* or *La Vanguardia* in Spain, and political commentating and reporting are not far from most headlines. Governments, and by that we can include the EU decision-making process, are the first port of call for those demanding social change, and they are also the first target for criticism if they do not respond to shifting values or fears in societies. It is not therefore surprising how much content in the quality press, especially at election times, is dedicated to political stories.

Across the press in all the societies which are now embraced by the EU and the wider Europe, the 20th century is littered with examples of media 'campaigns', some national (the fall of governments) and some trans-national (the growth in importance of the EU), and even events that can only be explained in global terms (war, environment, sustainability of markets, terrorism).

The contemporary era: the 21st century

One of the pressures upon governments and the EU will inevitably be social and political issues taken up by the press and the publishing world. This is its inherent power: the power of its readership and the societies they represent and communicate with. The power of 'public opinion' is increasing or so it seems in the new era of constant communication.

At the same time voices are being raised by important journalists expressing serious concerns for the future of the press and the media in general in the new European context:

> . . . two media surveys [The Association of European Journalists survey, *Goodbye to Freedom?* (Horsley, 2007) and survey update *Goodbye to Media Freedom?* (Horsley, 2008a) are both available on www.aej-uk.org. The European Centre for Public Affairs survey is on www.comres.co.uk] were written by active journalists in 20 countries, from Russia to France. Their conclusion is that a multitude of assaults and constraints have combined to drive press freedom into retreat in Europe. They include physical violence and even murder, intimidation, manipulation, censorship and enforced self-censorship. National governments are responsible for an array of increasingly restrictive laws that can criminalise the work of journalists and limit their rights and access to information, but the AEJ also questions the record of the EU institutions, finding that they have failed to show sufficient respect for freedom of media and freedom of expression, especially when journalists and cartoonists were threatened over the Danish Muhammad cartoons row in 2006.
>
> (Horsley, 2008b, pp. 41–42)

Counter to this argument, some may say that it is society (and its citizens and consumers), or in the EU case the different societies, who should play the prime role in changing media content by demanding acceptable standards of reporting, at least in times of peace and in liberal democratic countries. Even so, does not Horsley have a real point that society can only judge by and on what it is provided through its press and media? If society changes, so too it seems does the media that feeds and becomes a reflection of it. But even so, how do we maintain the balance between authority and freedom? How do we maintain the voice of authenticity? In judging how much society changes we need to understand in some measure how the press and media reacts to its varying social settings.

In Europe and the EU, societies and people are different, and so are the various presses across it. There are of course similarities, but the general generic assumptions about the press can be revisited by comparing the press across the European states. One has to make distinctions, as we have said, between production and consumption. Production techniques are manifestly similar, but consumer choice remains different because of various contextual factors: language, territory, politics, social fabric, local issues.

Production in Europe, and especially in the EU, has to be highly sensitive to its variable markets. For example, recently the communist daily national paper *L'Humanité* was reported as not only being in dire financial straits but hoping for an increase in subsidy from the French state including a general tax break for all newspapers (Jones, 2006). One could say this is a part of the 'ideological' nature of this kind of newspaper, but this may be too simple an approach. It may be surprising that the latter idea for greater forms of subsidy also had support from the mainstream French national press which was not communist.

Le Monde, *Le Figaro*, *Libération*, all of whom in that year saw sales drop by 5.4%, wanted to see some sort of assistance to the industry. The peculiarities of the French press system are not easily transposed across borders, and everywhere in Europe will have their own specific reasons for what is happening in press terms. Moreover, the national press in France needs to be assessed in supply and demand terms – it holds on to high point of sale prices compared to many other comparative countries. This compares too with a much lower price for the regional papers such as *Ouest-France* which far outstrips in circulation the national daily newspapers in France. In fact *Ouest-France* is in the top 100 best selling global dailies according to the WAN.

There is a North–South divide in Europe, and certainly a West–East divide, and this is linked to historical and ideological contexts. Equally we need to look more nationally, even regionally, to perceive the actual shape of press production. At another level, the major publishing houses are becoming cross-frontier, trans-national, international corporations of considerable importance (Bertelsmann, Finevest, Associated Newspapers, Pearson), not just in press production or printing but in publishing in general.

Moreover, they are often cross-media in intent and the digital age is accelerating this tendency. They target audiences, splitting out niche markets, spreading costs of production whenever possible and utilising new technology whenever they can, for both production and distribution reasons.

Much of this is to do with economics (see Chapter 3), but it also has a legal, regulatory and political side to it. Each nation has used law and regulation: the result is considerable difference across the EU, albeit converging (see Chapter 4).

Stop and consider 6.2

What makes the media tick? Time and time again we come back to this question. Why? Because there is so much debate about what is happening. Some might and do argue that rules and regulations govern little when compared to the power of capital and the financial system, others argue the opposite. What do you think? Are newspapers and the print industry so different to the audio-visual?

One could have assumed that the economics, for example, and capitalisation would have provided a similar publishing structure across Europe, but this is not quite the case. The 'devil' is in the detail, and press production is not an exception. Even so, regulatory regimes and financial standing have converged within the EU, although the process is far from over.

But a word of warning: when researching the publishing industry in the EU we need to be careful of over-generalisation as there are many differences between presses and newspapers in Europe. If you put the media architecture together you have a very good 'image' (some call this a 'reflection') of how and what a society is 'thinking', and what 'agendas' they are thinking about. In the EU this will be multi-layered, multi-cultural and multi-linguistic. This means we need to expect as many dissimilarities in the market as similarities.

Globalisation, corporate growth, market concentration

No matter the strength and importance of national developments, in newspaper terms, global, trans-national companies are also on the increase, as we have mentioned, leading toward production concentration, sometimes known as 'conglomeration'. This happens internally at national level as well as at international and global levels. However, as can be seen from Case Study 6.1, the national and the local remain particularly important in the print industry across Europe.

Even so, careful research into the background of most companies mentioned above shows the degree to which the market is becoming more open and certainly more European. There are cross-overs, although this is usually in the realm of the major and bigger players such as Hachette (Lagardère) and Associated Newspapers.

The idea that the print media is driven only by the interests of major shareholders and capital interests is often a misunderstanding. There are many types of company at work and they operate sometimes differently from one another. Not all major players, for example, have turned immediately to the stock market for capitalisation. This is evident with two major trans-national corporate players, Bertelsmann and Bonnier, who have remained 'family' non-listed companies for decades, and who functioned as and alongside other national and local production press networks. Needless to say, whether using stock exchanges or not, maintaining profit margins and controlling operating costs are crucial.

Getting the product right is dramatically linked to innovation and investment from capital and revenue returns and these remain paramount, as are all the management financial skills to be found in the corporations. This is often linked to the need to spread risks across the sector, and it applies to corporate construction but equally to content.

The media generates its own content-led genre-hopping, where stories about film, for example, occupy pages of newspaper celebrity news; or where sport on television is discussed endlessly in newspapers, magazines and web sites. In an increasingly urbanised, materialistic environment, 'readers' (who are also listeners and viewers) are confronted by similar social concerns; crime, employment and gender issues for example. The press and publishing world does not turn away from any of the other genres (soap operas, game shows and the full panorama of AV scheduling – see Chapter 9), and in many respects these shared topics drive the content of the print industry as much as its own journalistic agenda. Much of the magazine bonanza at present is linked to new forms of entertainment: the Internet, gaming, TV shopping, mobile videoing, let alone the growing interest in the new technology itself. The new technology allows too for a fast sharing of views (and stories), compounded by tight and clever press agencies which feed the media networks, including the press (see Chapter 7 on distribution), and generate and complement the content.

The trend toward similar types of content is based, it is argued, on a fundamental shift toward a more 'liberal', freer-market orientation in societies and is an apparent fact. However, it is long in its development, contextually more diverse than many believe and evolutionary not revolutionary in its impact. This is especially important in the print industry which in the main is in private rather than public hands.

Driven by the economics, and where one would assume that monopolistic tendencies would prevail, difference in press and publishing production across Europe is actually the norm. Moreover, the tight relationship between production and consumption means that the readers (or potential shoppers from an advertising point of view) remain in the ascendant.

In Europe, the readership (via language, culture and interpretation) and the rules under which journalists work (via law and regulation) are different from one area to another, and this is the force which maintains diversity and variety. This was always the case even in the national frameworks of the press: there was always competition and different sub-national markets.

Trans-nationalism has widened the game though, increased the networks and chequered the globe into different patterns, to the point that it seems to be a new architecture. And it is, but the dynamic has always been there; there was no golden age of 'stability' or what is often called 'normative certainties' (McQuail, 2000, p. 134). There may have been assumptions about the market, and in some areas limited choice, but the nation states in Europe are mainly social and community patchworks, not representatives of cohesive mono-cultural nationhood, and the press architecture in Europe, even today, reflects this.

Stop and consider 6.3

What is trans-nationalism in the EU context? A simple definition often refers to 'transnationalism' (note the two ways of spelling) as being a loosening of ties between institutions and nations, but in the EU there is giving up of sovereignty to the EU institutions for the purpose of policy-making – see Chapter 1. Is what the EU aiming for trans-national? Is not the purpose of EU policy, no matter how difficult and no matter how contentious, to harmonise production and distribution practices in the market place for the greater integration of its member states and their peoples? What role does the press have in informing its readership of such issues? Many have argued that the press reporting of EU affairs has been woeful (Andersen and Weymouth, Insulting the Public?, 1999). Is this right?

It is sometimes argued that the fear that the modern press is dismissive of diversity and pitched against notions of equality, or even that it is collectively and nationally against the EU, is to invest in the press too much political and even moral power. The real nature of power is located in the real decision-making in societies, either in government or amongst the populace.

The impact of 'globalisation' and 'Europeanisation', therefore, does vary from state to state. However, production costs are also increasing, pushing companies to concentrate their resources. The markets are widening, and the access to new markets and cross-production, cross-media and cross-frontier opportunities indicates a future where concentration or conglomeration will continue. Competition within the industry remains enormously keen, and is not based just on the technical, productive level but also on the creative effort upon which the print media thrives.

In this atmosphere, newspapers are changing their formats and their styles. The number of individual newspaper titles in countries (apart from the new Central European member states of the EU) is reducing, but pagination, content choice and the range of material available to readers are on the increase, at least in the quality press, and not in decline. This explains the increased number of those employed in the industry over the past few years. Digitisation and new technology, overall, are compounding this process.

This has always been the case in newspaper production, even when there were periods of greater and then lesser concentration. Even so, the contemporary changes in newspaper production are beginning to crystallise into a series of innovatory approaches and creative techniques that seem new. Making sense of these many changes in a large market like the EU is not easy.

Publishing markets and production

To understand an industry in the midst of change is a challenge and always has been. This is especially the case when it is occurring at the pace of the contemporary era. Categorising markets and fitting them within national regulatory frameworks on the scale of the EU is also important, as are the trans-national implications of EU initiatives. One influential report (EC, 2005) has suggested we can review the challenges ahead for the industry by looking at the following areas.

Product development

Newspapers generally across Europe are serving an ageing, but more educated and increasingly urban, population. In many respects the 'trusted' newspaper is confronted with increasing time spent by readers on the Internet. Combine this with television use and the reading habits of many Europeans, and readers are beginning to move away from the paper newspaper format. This explains in part falling circulations and, perhaps more importantly, reduced revenue from advertising. It also explains in part the launch of 'free' newspapers across Europe from the low readership levels in the south, Spain and Portugal for example, and in the north, Sweden and Denmark.

The challenge to the industry is to develop products that appeal to the new as well as the old readers. The four major countries that account for up to 70% of all publishing are Germany, the UK, France and Italy (see later). Even so, each sector of the publishing industry illustrates different levels of competitiveness, and size of production from the big four is not necessarily linked to being the most productive. Those who show higher then average newspaper competitiveness are judged in national terms to be Denmark, Ireland, Finland and Sweden. In the magazine industry, it is Austria, Latvia, the Netherlands and Poland. In books, Italy stands out, but so does Poland.

Editorial strategy

In the EU, editorial strategy therefore varies across the industry. Moreover, editors and owners need to reflect upon the impact of the digital age. New technology is accelerating changes already inherent in the market. Across Europe there are marked differences in reading habits, and producers will need to be sensitive to the differences (see Chapter 8). This is why the trade and NACE statistics are often less than useful and there is further need for exploratory, editorial, in-house review carried out sector by sector. As has been indicated elsewhere there is a strong recommendation for companies to see the readers in terms of 'media-time' rather than as individual purchasers or readers of a single product. This is as yet not widely used and not officially classified as a method. Productivity in the 'value-chain' and product development, linked closely to consumer interest and demand, are the key areas for the future.

Content creation

The four main classifications of the publishing industry, newspapers, books, magazines and works such as directories, have in the past created separate working communities that have built their own content creation. The new digital age appears to be challenging this position, and mobility of workers and creativity from paper to online format appears to be the future for successful companies. Moreover, each category of publishing has different practices: with books authors tend to be paid royalties and 'bought in' to the process, whereas newspapers have salaried staff for content creation.

Brand identity and management

However, the mixing of new practices such as online and old copy is not an easy process, and Europe is diverse and culturally and politically sensitive. For example, the increasing use of English, and the rise of English language products, is seen by some countries as threatening. This also impacts upon brand identity and management. Mixing the skills base, including language, will be a future concern.

Marketing

Marketing will always be tailored not only to the market but to the nature of the product. However, if the product, a book or a newspaper, is changing from paper to an online or even an electronic form of distribution system, this adds to the complexity of the marketing strategy and the finance and revenue streams it relies upon.

These are the areas where the classic historic corporations well-known in the field still heavily manage press and publishing production. Equally, there are new producers emerging and new electronic and publishing software techniques. The distribution network is developing, and it has the potential to fragment but coalesce into a relatively and potentially more cost-effective Internet online provision. The older publishing houses not only face competition with each other – regionally, nationally and globally – but with the specialised and newer competition from electronic-based sources.

Competition demands greater consumer appeal for both consumer and advertiser. Admittedly, we can see that the shape of the industry depends upon past developments as much as on the new, but the process of change appears to be speeding up. Creating and maintaining the right strategy in a larger and more trans-national context is essential but the reward is the potential for higher profits.

Applying technology on a grand scale, however, takes time and entails the creation of new partnerships, skills and strategy along with money and effort. This has always been the case in newspaper production even when there were periods of greater and then lesser concentration among corporations: winners and losers in a market reacting to the constant swirl of changing ideas and different public reactions to published material. Even so, put the categories together and you have an interesting approach to the publishing world. In the UK, for example, at the first audit the leading online group was the *Daily Mail* and *The Mail on Sunday*, with an estimated 12 million dedicated users. This beat the leading brand print copy of the *The Sun* that also went online at approximately the same time.

Size

In paper terms, size matters – in costs, transport needs and the demands of particular reading behaviour. Newspapers have learnt to reduce the format of their papers. Use of printed paper and pulp is not diminishing at present, and is even rising, and this is an important cost. Also, the smaller format was thought to be more appealing to daily readers than the larger broadsheet. Even so, the old distinctions between 'broadsheet' and tabloid have little meaning in current newspaper development. More important is how to develop the product online. Few newspapers taken as a whole are making profits from direct online subscription in their initial stages. However, few would deny that the future lies in this direction.

Pagination

Pagination for some newspapers is also increasing, at the same time as the number of titles across Europe is stable or in decline. This is especially the case with, for example, Sunday, weekend reading where this is particularly applicable. Note that in some countries weekend newspaper reading is not necessarily a custom, France being a notable example.

Content

Pagination is linked to content. As newspapers, for example, battle and compete with each other and other outlets, they are adding to their content in supplements, book offers and DVD 'free' films. Content needs even more than before to relate to consumer need. In broad terms, as educational levels increase across Europe the 'quality' content is also on the increase.

Layout, language and formats

Publishing products need to attract, and language, layout and formats are key areas of the 'new'. Newspapers, book covers and magazine racks are constantly changing in a world of competition which now has to embrace marketing strategies that are digital as well as paper-based. These latter are often seen as hit-and-miss when compared to the new digital strategies which now encompass such companies as Yahoo and Google.

Image and photography and the audio-visual cross-overs

We live in a 'visual' age and have done so for some time. Newspapers and general publishing have absorbed the visual into their production. Examples of one-page photo-journalism are not rare these days and are accepted by producers and consumers alike. Equally, publishing organisations are moving online, merging the 'visual' with the text.

Editorials

The standard view that the press stands for freedom and plurality is often associated with the role of the editorial. However, concerns are being raised that as mergers, acquisitions and cross-media initiatives grow and conglomerates appear, large publishing houses result. This could erode the role of the editorial and the plurality of expression it represents and now goes to the core of democratic and party politics. We can expect national and EU concerns to be voiced, as they have been already, over this matter.

Copyright

As indicated in Chapter 4, copyright and intellectual property has always been an important part of the international trade in ideas, and these impact upon the publishing and press industries. As the finance and corporations take on increasing cross-national and even trans-national positions, equally linked to regional and local markets, the importance of rights – for authors, publishers and even readers – will take on a new dimension in the new media age.

The present scene: an indication

Almost all commentators agree on the importance, the key role that the written press still plays in the communication of ideas. It informs, it entertains, it provokes, it influences and it performs at all intellectual levels. Nowadays, it is textual, visual, comic and serious, and it comes in a variety of formats. It is delivered on paper, on mobile, on PC, online at home and at work. It is passive and active and reactive. It attracts all ages, even if capturing 'youth' consumers remains a perennial problem for the written press and in particular newspapers. Across Europe all of this is dependent upon content and context.

What is not so well-known is how fragmented the market has been across Europe until the recent past. Mergers and acquisitions are bringing to the present scene a shape which is new, but it remains also categorised into dedicated types of writing activity: books are different from newspapers, which are different from magazines. However, the Internet and the new technology are changing the boundaries in the publishing industry, especially within production and distribution.

To try to be definitive about industry trends is always difficult because they are constantly evolving. For example, newspapers remain tightly related to national frameworks and markets, whereas magazines are using cross-national formats. Yet, here too even newspapers are constantly borrowing ideas from each other. Both use press agencies enormously, and these are by their nature often trans-national and even global in form.

However, whatever the dynamic, the industry as a whole is large and influential. Newspapers it is claimed are read by more than 180 million people across Europe. From a producer's point of view, it is estimated that the book publishing industry alone is worth in the region of €20–30 bn (2000), newspapers €46 bn (2001), directories at around €8.2 bn, and the total industry between €111.8 bn and €120 bn (2001), depending upon the data sources being used. Germany, France, the UK and Italy account for 70% of the total market (in an EU of 25 members). Newspapers it is estimated make up 36.8% of production (2001), with journals and periodicals at 32% and books at 24.6% in overall production value. The e-market is more difficult to estimate, but its potential is high if US figures are a guide to what may be happening in the EU in the immediate future. Certainly, digital technologies are fast changing the ways in which content is created, combined, distributed and consumed.

It is useful to look at the present EU market as a totality. When researching data, some figures will represent the 'old' EU of 15 nations and some the 'new' of 25, 27 or more in the immediate future. (Refer to Chapter 2 for how to interpret data: the usual caveats apply over statistical information and its use and misuse.)

Newspapers

At a time of considerable competition and innovation, it may be surprising to note that in terms of turnover, number of employees and economic value-added assessments, the newspaper industry is doing well. Early figures for the first five years of the 21st century (e.g. Datamonitor) indicate similar trends to those in 1995–2001. EU trends of course need to be matched with individual national figures.

Across the EU as a whole there are disparities. Bearing in mind the development of the EU, however, there are general categories of states which can be linked to their past and their economic development: (a) Western and Northern Europe – stable and relatively strong economies post, 1945, (b) Southern Europe (both of the Atlantic and the Mediterranean) linked to post, 1945 authoritarian regimes and then later EU membership from the 1980s and more stable and prosperous economic growth in the main; and (c) Central and Eastern Europe – countries emerging from the post-Soviet Union era, that in the 1990s adapted their economies (and their media) to join the EU, achieving this from 2005. In other words, when we try to compare press models across Europe, the historical context is one that often predominates. Even so, one consistent theme beyond the specific ideologies and history is finance.

Newspapers in Europe depend in the main upon advertising. Estimating revenue over the next few years is not easy; there is no strict formula and overall expectations will be linked to the general health of the economy. The general rule is that if the (global) economy is doing well, so too is the advertising business. It varies across Europe, but newspapers can rely on between 40% and 60% of their revenue from advertising with the remainder from sales, subscriptions and other sources. It is estimated that this is similar to the 19th century, where an estimation of 50% (UK) has been made (Brown, 1985).

As with the entire publishing world, its main competition for advertising is from the audio-visual sector and in particular television and, albeit in a more minor form, radio. The effects of the Internet are also beginning to make direct in-roads into advertising campaigns, but the long-term consequences of digitisation are difficult to judge.

Advertising for a newspaper is an area of major importance for two reasons: (a) it is revenue and a cash flow generator; and (b) it is an indicator of the general economy and buoyancy of the 'market'. The extent to which this plays a major part in the editorial choice of material is debatable, some seeing it as crucial, others less so. For the latter, for example, it is claimed that an average reader can absorb only about 10% of the total advertising and information in a daily paper.

In general advertising terms TV is number one in overall investment strategies, followed by the national press, but in some cases the regional outlets. There are many types of advertisers too, some of whom are in competition with each other. However, they may still have a collective influence on content and production, and if so it is on the owner and editorial management. Needless to say evidence is sketchy on how important this is. What is clearer is that both advertisers and newspaper staff want to be in step with the customer and reader: neither wishes to alienate (shock, yes sometimes; alienate, never); inflame prejudices, distort the statistics, yes but to be out of sympathy, persistently, with the majority of its readers, financially and journalistically, is suicidal.

The trend for the newspaper market is mixed across Europe. Some countries are in decline in terms of circulation and titles, others are more static. The best-guess for the industry might be that the traditional on-paper production has now peaked after a remarkable 200 years of growth. As discussed later, the future for newspapers depends upon not only readership but also the delivery systems.

However, the demise of the newspaper due to the internet is grossly over-estimated. Companies remain profitable and creative, and the general level of reader involvement, one way or another, with quality products is both good and promising (see Case Study 6.2). 'Free' newspapers, although important as an initiative, have now it seems remained in general 'flat' after a burst of activity: underlying this of course is that nothing really is 'free', and cost will always remain an issue and a limitation on growth for such circulations.

Since 1945 commentators have worried, especially in such countries as France, about declining numbers of newspaper titles. However, the late twentieth century figures seem to indicate a slowing of this overall decline.

The emergence of alternative outlets online could be said to indicate a growth of new ideas and opinions rather than a reduction. Moreover, fears for the lack of pluralism, necessary as an impetus to or a defence of freedom of speech, should be calculated in terms of the media provision as a whole rather than one form of it. However, many Europeans fearing a lack of democratic voice in the new age, are rightly concerned about the role of the press and publishing industry.

The EU trends are from a general market point of view essential in our analysis of the publishing and press industries. Equally, diversity and difference can be found in the various national contexts. Case Studies 6.3 and 6.4 concern important countries in the future development of the industry but, at the same time, using some of our comparators, we can see that as markets they are also dissimilar. This speaks volumes for the actual market within the EU. For the market analyst we need both EU analysis as well as national, which means including national and regional structures, if we are to understand the architecture of the media in its contexts. The three following introductory case studies (6.3–6.5) represent the three main areas of EU development and enlargement mentioned above.

1. Western and Northern Europe – stable and relatively strong economies post-1945.
2. Southern Europe (both of the Atlantic and the Mediterranean) – linked to post-1945 authoritarian regimes and then later EU membership from the 1980s which provided for more stable and prosperous economic growth in the main.
3. Central and Eastern Europe – countries emerging from the post-Soviet Union era, who in the 1990s adapted their economies (and their media) to join the EU from 2005.

Case Study 6.2

Looking again at the overall EU figures: newspapers at the turn of the century

Chapter 2 introduced us to some statistical inferences we can make about the industry. When investigating an industry such as this, we need to look at a range of figures if we are to increase our understanding. As the text indicates, the industry is going through many technological and even economic changes, and this can be painted in a gloomy way. Yet when we look at the productivity of the industry, often one of the most fundamental of all the indicators in the 'value-chain' (see Chapter 3), we see that newspapers across the EU are performing well with an increase rather than a decrease in employees and higher not lower productivity.

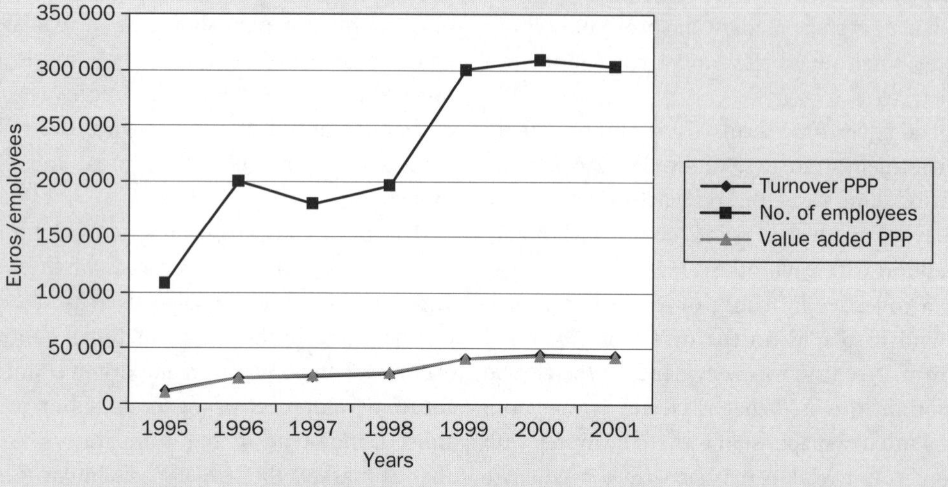

EU 25 Newspapers 1995–2001

PPP (purchasing power parity) figures created by the author using data from Eurostat.

Case Study 6.3

Press production in Germany

The creation of West Germany followed a new constitution (the Basic Law) in 1947. At the centre of much 20th century European history, the recent end of the Cold War meant a unification of West and East into the present state. The media system adapted to the political change.

With a population estimated at 82.5 million (2005) Germany is the largest state in the EU with the largest economy. It was one of the first areas to develop a press industry and remains one of the most important and active countries in terms of production and consumption. There are relatively few national newspapers when compared with some EU states like the UK, but a large and thriving regional press readership. It is estimated to have 138 independently produced outlets for newspaper production with 359 daily newspapers. If we add local editions, this rises to 1538 different newspapers. There has been some decline of readership, but penetration within the market remains over 70% (2005).

As with a great many EU states concentration of media production is the German and now the EU model, the major corporations of Axel Springer Group (*Bild*, *Welt*,

Case Study 6.3 (continued)

Hamburger Abendblatt, Berliner Morgenpost) and WAZ group (*Westdeutsche Allgemeine Zeitung, Verlagsgruppe Stuttgarter Zeitung*) being the two largest producers. The magazine industry is very buoyant and profitable with 873 general magazines and 1081 specialised periodicals (2005). There has been growth in 'weekly' newspapers, with the best known being the influential *Der Spiegel*. Press agencies include Deutsche Presseagentur (the most widely used), followed by Associated Press, German Reuters and Agence France-Presse.

Source: European Journalism Centre, http://www.ejc.net/index.php/media_landscape/article/germany/ (Kleinsteuber and Thomass, 2008).

Case Study 6.4

Press production in Spain

Since the death of Franco in 1976 and the development of parliamentary democracy, coupled to EU membership (1986), the population of Spain, estimated at 44.1 million inhabitants (2005), has seen remarkable political and economic growth. Spain is thought to be the tenth largest economy in the world.

As with many 'southern' EU states, readership of newspapers remains relatively low with a penetration of 41%, although figures for magazine readership are higher. There is both a national and a regional press. It is estimated that there are 135 daily newspapers. The market is notable for the considerable growth of 'free press' products: one estimate calculates this to reach over 7000 products. The most widely read newspaper is one of these, entitled *20 Minutos*, which is then followed by the paid edition of *El Pais*.

Concentration of media production is the trend in recent years. The press and publishing in general is supported by the Spanish press agency Agencia EFE.

Source: European Journalism Centre, http://www.ejc.net/index.php/media_landscape/article/spain/ (Salaverria, 2008).

Case Study 6.5

Press production in Poland

Following the fall in communism in 1989, Poland has recently become a member of the EU (2005). It has an estimated population of 38.5 million (2005). Privatisation of the press industry has occurred in the past ten years or so.

Poland's press is divided between national and regional readerships, with 167 daily newspapers and over 800 weeklies. There is an even larger monthly press readership. Penetration by newspapers is very high (90% written in general, 78% for daily newspapers), and is a mark of readership reaction to the 'free press' emerging from communist control and typical in most Eastern and Central European states.

Press production is concentrated but also foreign-owned with German publishers in the vanguard (H. Bauer – operating in Poland as Wydawnictwo – H. Bauer Ltd; Verlagsgruppe Passau – Polskapresse; and Axel Springer – Axel Springer Polska Ltd). They are not alone though with the presence of the Norwegian company (Presspublica) in the market. The most important press agency is the local Polish Press Agency (PAP) which is owned by the state. Important too is the Catholic Church which has its own agency: Catholic Information Agency (KAI).

Source: European Journalism Centre, http://www.ejc.net/index.php/media_landscape/article/poland/ (Lara, 2008).

Periodicals, magazines and reviews

If the newspaper industry has seen growth and some stability, even if there are signs of peaking in the beginning of the century, the figures for the magazine world show a similar picture. There has been a growth in the numbers employed (see Case Study 6.6), turnover has been maintained and the industry remains profitable. The question for all business organisations is one of 'value-added' product development – the effectiveness of the group in economic as well as creative terms. Normally this sector is classified into three: 'consumer', 'business-to-business' and 'academic'. It is estimated that the annual turnover for this industry was in the region of €37 bn (2001).

Book production and market

Like newspapers and magazines, the book sector has maintained a similarly successful profile. Its content creation tends to be based on a different relationship

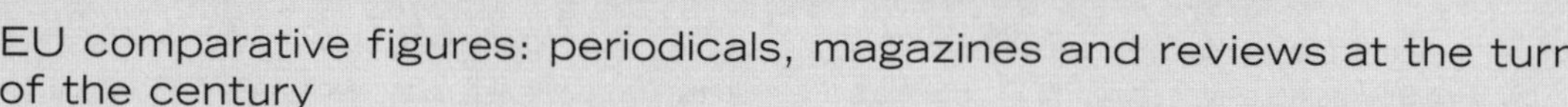

Case Study 6.6

EU comparative figures: periodicals, magazines and reviews at the turn of the century

We have seen that newspapers were productive and created employment. Comparing newspapers with periodicals and magazines, we can see below even more jobs being created although turnover and productivity had peaked by 2001. These are classic signs of growth and competition in the market place and were especially true of the late 1990s. The impact of the new technology from 2000 has yet to be truly seen over the long-term.

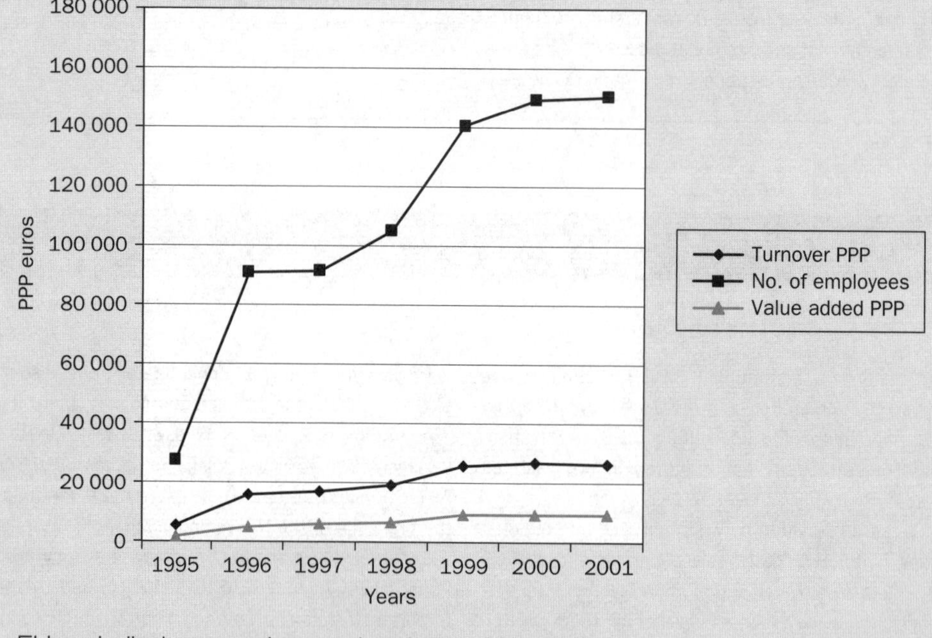

EU periodicals, magazines and reviews 1995–2001

PPP (purchasing power parity) figures created by the author using data from Eurostat.

Source: Publishing Market Watch Final Report 2005.

between author and publishing house rather than journalist and employee/employer. The book sector is also different from the other sectors and has different sets of classifications, making statistical data often difficult to compare. The industry works on 'consumer publishing', 'educational and schools', 'academic' and 'business and professional' publishing. In some countries there are also classifications for 'children's books' and those in the 'religious' field. A sub-section may also include 'directories and databases' – be that online or paper. Turnover is estimated in the region of €20–30 bn (see Case Study 6.7).

Comparative work: finding the variables (comparators)

The following series of variables is often used to compare national media models including the press and the general publishing industry. The list is not definitive. You may use the variables when you use data or commentaries in either primary or secondary sources from corporate, academic or other material. They need to be 'read' in conjunction with the other

Case Study 6.7

EU figures and comparisons: book industry at the turn of the century

As with newspapers and periodicals, the book industry has also being doing well in employment creation and productivity. Combining the three case studies together, at least in the period of study and over the sector as a whole, paints a rosy rather than a gloomy picture of the industry. This is not to say, as we shall see in the next chapters, that the industry is complacent or stagnant. In fact in distribution terms the market is beginning to shift.

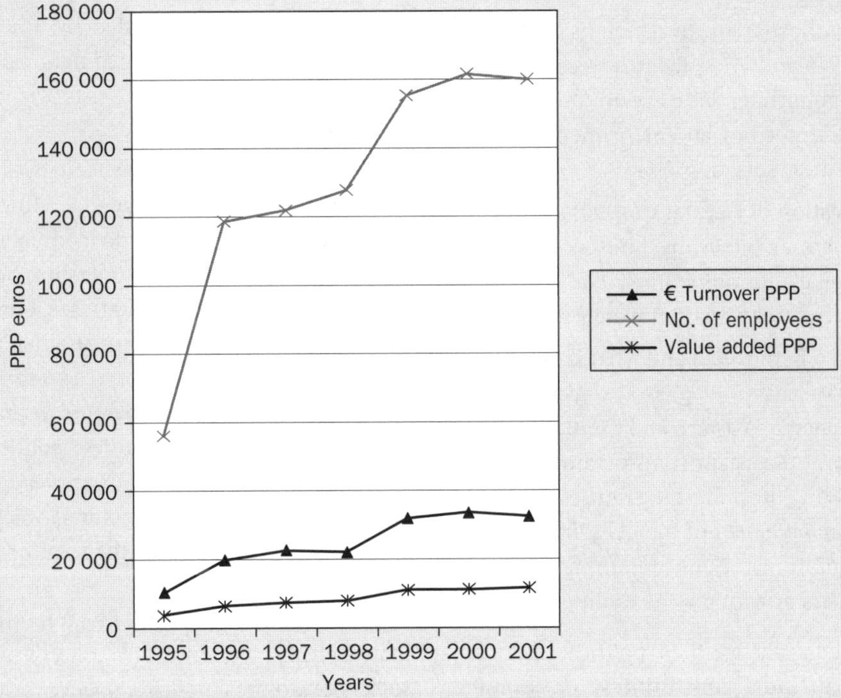

EU book industry 1995–2001

PPP (purchasing power parity) figures created by the author using data from Eurostat.

forces of change, globalisation and European transnationalisation, which have been mentioned above. They are useful for the analyst, not forgetting that academics and analysts have different views on the importance of each.

Press and publishing in general

1. The historical

European nations and their presses have their own peculiarities in terms of their history, past and even contemporary situation. They have their own constitutions and their own communities bound by territory, and they display different rhythms of change. National 'history' or historical trends are very important in media market analysis.

Across the EU since 1945 there have been major historical shifts in the individual nation states that have impacted upon the production of the press and publishing industries. The list could be long, but to name a few:

- The fall of authoritarian governments in Spain and Portugal (1976 and 1974) led to a freeing up of the press and publishing industry in these nations. This was reinforced by an enlargement of the EU to embrace these societies.
- The reunification of Germany (1990) saw the previous East German publishing houses opened up to Western capital and competition. The media of the former East Germany was completely transformed.
- The fall of the Berlin Wall and what is now known as the end of the Cold War – our present era (1991) – opened up Eastern and Central European nation states, once again transforming the entire media including the publishing houses. This led to the biggest enlargement of the EU (2005) with ten previous communist countries joining the EU and its markets and adhering to its trading rules.

Where societies change their political outlooks – creating new national constitutions or joining a major trading bloc and shifting their allegiance to a new international organisation such as the EU are good examples and significant 'events' – this changes the rules of the political and economic game. In so doing, societies will review their own social relationships both internally and externally, and that includes their elites and internal communities. The press needs to be aware of the political contexts in which it operates.

Nevertheless, in 'world-events' terms, nation states, even regional blocs such as the EU, are pushed and cajoled by the global forces of economics, politics and social interaction, and time embraces them all. Determining these global historical trends is also an important method of analysis in determining media models inside the EU.

Newspapers in national and regional settings

2. The national

Most nations consist internally of different communities with different political and social interests. The various factions or groups often club together into more or less identifiable producers tied to readerships. This can be illustrated by a combination of produced titles and supported national papers.

3. The regional

Ostensibly, newspapers are read by all and are an indicator of a collective 'agenda'. However, newspapers in societies are often divided between national, regional and even local readerships which connect to the means of production (see Case Study 6.8). Therefore, the various groups and the 'persuasion' of each newspaper bought or read are often diverse. This is an important comparator in market analysis: the 'regional' papers (often less political but, again, this is an over-simplification) are read by more local readerships, but when structured with the national framework this represents the total newspaper reading community.

Put together this can illustrate the degree of 'nationalism', 'cohesion' or collective-thinking in a society or, to use a political science term, it can be an indication of the socio-political 'cleavages' within any society. These are often associated with wealth and status and the processes of policy-making and law. Therefore, observing the architecture of newspapers

Case Study 6.8

Using sources to make comparisons – newspapers

When putting together a small vignette of each country, some invaluable sources may be used, as we have already mentioned, and the results are often intriguing: the World Association of Newspapers (WAN), the Euro-media group (often associated with the Sage press), the excellent web-based European Journalism Centre (EJC), Eurostat and Datamonitor (Market Line Business Monitor), for example. There are also local, national resources available for each EU country, e.g. Mintel in the UK. When these sources are used we will notice that the press in particular, but also linked to the publishing industry as a whole, has three types of 'national' provision inside the EU: (1) press which is very nationally orientated (the grey areas of the map below); (2) a mix of national and regional provision (striped areas); and (3) very regionally orientated nations (dotted areas). We use market analysis to try to understand why.

will show us a wider political as well as social picture of our societies, not the whole framework but an important part nevertheless.

Books, reviews, magazines, journals, directories, databases

4. Sectors

In many ways the newspaper industry is seen as the prime part of the publishing industry but, as can be seen, the book and in particular the magazine sectors, when combined, are almost as important. Book, magazine and similar productions are highly valued. Some countries are bigger producers than others – take Germany for example where production is high and where economies of scale apply.

There has also been a growth of the magazine and general publishing interests but, once again, this is complicated and represents our fourth factor. This sector assumes and connects to the wider publishing field.

Regulatory framework

5. Legal

There is also the 'legal' which is our fifth comparator: government and political involvement through regulatory choices. This is so important that we have dedicated information within Chapter 4, but this legislative power is not to be forgotten in our calculations.

Ownership

6. Owners

The sixth comparator is the private corporation or the 'owners'; this category indicates the 'private', capital-movement (investment) as well as monopolistic tendencies within a country (noting too that certain companies are trans-national and even international in size and influence); they are the major media players. Of course the question of ownership goes beyond one type of criteria and occupies all the media, in its national, regional or other forms. There is little 'public' ownership of the publishing industry in the EU.

Technology and the market

7. Technological change

Technological change is one of the most profound factors influencing production in the print, press and publishing industries. This has always been the case (see above and below). Yet in the present age, with a convergence of media occurring through digitisation, the future seems to point toward an even more dramatic reshaping of the media scene. The change may well be more evolutionary than revolutionary, but the production processes and the very nature of the print and publishing organisations will change fundamentally on almost all fronts. Even so, some societies in Europe are far ahead of others in their use of technology in the market. For example, in broadband technology and IT development the Scandinavians and especially Sweden and Finland are surging ahead of other areas and by far more than those with geographical or economic barriers to overcome such as Greece (see Chapter 11 on distribution for further details).

Measuring and comparing IT development is a key area of EU analysis and is linked to the perceived importance of 'the information economy'. The Europa web site http://europa.eu/index_en.htm (Information Society) for EU policies contains many detailed comparisons of the new technology and its market.

Merging ownership plus technical change is also making production for markets more trans-national in Europe, but it also remains simultaneously national, localised or even 'glocalised'. Moreover, to understand the industry, its technology and its market means investigating production along with the distribution and consumer network. This we have done in later chapters where we explore the new agenda more precisely.

Chapter summary

- Major social change impinges directly on the press and publishing industries at all levels of production, distribution and consumption.
- The contemporary era in Europe, and especially the EU, is going through political and social change, and this is reflected in a media market that is equally responding to exciting technological innovation.
- The European, let alone the trans-national, trends in press and publishing need to be investigated at national as well as local levels to understand fully the development that is taking place.
- Publishing production feeding into the market also needs to be understood through the different forms and types of product through which the industries function.
- The press and publishing industries are approaching a period of keen competition and continued innovation.
- Developing the right strategies to maintain their position in society will be the challenge for many companies.
- Offering the consumer what the consumer is interested in will be paramount for the producer and for product development.

Key terms

European democratic dialogue: to belong to the EU means not just to support the liberal market but also to be a proven democratic state. This does not mean that the EU has one set of rules for how democracy works. Across the EU there are many different types of democratic practice, and the word 'dialogue' used in the text tries to embrace all of them. As a word, it also suggests that the media and the press are part of the communication network and include all the players in any society not just the media.

Governance: power in society and inside the EU is related to government and state practice. The word 'governance' highlights how states operate in their own political contexts. Inside the EU there are many differences, but what holds the union together across many policies is the decision-making process that the EU represents. Governance in modern EU terms is both a multi-national and a national system and the word 'governance' in the text can be used in both contexts.

Governments: the EU is made up of different nation states and different types of government. Each of them will have their own particular means by which their government works. Most will have governments based upon two 'houses' or two 'chambers', but this is not the case for all. Denmark, for example, operates with one.

Mass media: Although not mentioned in this text the idea of a 'mass media' has been with us for some time, so a brief comment might be useful. It is a term often associated with the growth of large markets. Although it is used frequently, coming in and out of fashion, it is often difficult to define and was often associated with the growth of 'mass' populations: a reference to the 'masses' that media technology appeared to accentuate.

'New' media: Media that relies upon the digitisation of its products. This is opposed to the 'old' media which is based on separating technologies, although in fact the technologies of the 'old' media were often inter-related.

Niche markets: Specific targeted markets within a total market. This term often refers to a more focused customer-based approach to consumer behaviour, and differentiates itself, for example, from 'mass' markets.

Discussion questions

1. Why is the press and publishing industry important for society, be that in EU terms or nationally?
2. Is it possible to differentiate the press across the centuries? If yes, how?
3. To what extent does changing technology impact upon the publishing industry?
4. In the new era, what factors may we use to explore the development of the press and publishing industry in the 21st century?
5. What variables (comparators) may be used in a market analysis of European press and publishing and how useful are they?

Assignments

1. Research and find data associated with European press and publishing industry trends in production. Use the comparators in this chapter to analyse the market from (a) a European perspective and (b) EU national perspectives.
2. Choose two or three EU countries and compare and contrast the development of their press and publishing industry over the past 20 years.
3. Compare and analyse the development of the press in the different 'regions' – you can define this in many ways including East/West or North/South – of the EU.
4. Assess the importance of media concentration in publishing production throughout the EU. Does it threaten political pluralism and the operation of the market?

Further reading

The following is only indicative of the type of work available to us – from books, to chapters to reviews to reports. Nowadays you need all types for market analysis.

Albert P. (2004) *La Presse Française*, Paris: La Documentation française.

Bird & Bird (2002) *Market Definition in the Media Sector: a Comparative Analysis*, Luxembourg, European Commission, DG Competition.

Dicken P. (2007) *Global Shift: Mapping the Changing Contours of the World Economy*, 5th edn, London: Sage.

EC (2005) Commission Staff Working Paper. *Strengthening the Competitiveness of the EU Publishing Sector. The role of media policy*, Luxembourg, European Commission.

EC (2005) *Publishing Market Watch Final Report*, Luxembourg: European Commission, DG Enterprise.

EMCC (2004) *Sector Futures: in Search of a Realistic Future*, Dublin: European Foundation for the Improvement of Living and Working Conditions.

EMCC (2004) *Sector Futures: Publishing and Media: Balancing the Interests of Producers and Consumers*, Dublin: European Foundation for the Improvement of Living and Working Conditions.

Ernst and Young (2007) *Competitiveness of the European Graphic Industry*, Luxembourg: European Communities.

Europe Economics (2002) *Market Definition in the Media Sector – Economic Issues*, Luxembourg: European Commission, DG Competition.

Flew T. (2007) *Global Media*, Basingstoke: Palgrave Macmillan.

Harcourt A. (2002) Europeanization as convergence: the regulation of media markets in the European Union, in K. Featherstone and C. Radaelli (eds), *The Politics of Europeanisation*, Oxford: Oxford University Press, 179–203.

Harcourt A. (2006) *European Union Institutions and the Regulation of Media Markets*, Manchester and New York: Manchester University Press.

Pira International (2003) *The EU Publishing Industry: an Assessment of Competitiveness*, Luxembourg: European Communities.

Online resources

http://www...

Again our online resources are almost seemingly immense. The following is only an indication of major, important online organisations.

- *Council of Europe and European Institute for Comparative Cultural Research (ERICarts)* http://www.ericarts.org
- *Datamonitor (Market Business Line)* http://www.datamonitor.com
- *DG 'Information Society'* http://europa.eu/index_en.htm
- *European Communication Research and Education Association (ECREA)* http://www.ecrea.eu
- *European Institute for the Media (EIM)* http://www.eim.org
- *European Journalism Centre (EJC)* http://www.ejc.net
- *Eurostat* ec.europa.eu/eurostat/
- *Hans-Bredow-Institut* http://www.hans-bredow.institut.de
- *World Association of Newspapers (WAN)* http://www.wan-press.org/

References

Anderson P., Weymouth A. (1999) *Insulting the Public?: The British Press and the European Union*, Harlow: Addison Wesley Longman.

Bird & Bird (2002) *Market Definition in the Media Sector: a Comparative Analysis*, Luxembourg: European Commission, DG Competition. Prepared for the European Commission.

Brown L. (1985) *Victorian News and Newspapers*, Oxford: Clarendon Press.

Datamonitor (2007) *Newspapers in Europe: industry profile*, London: Datamonitor (Market Business Line).

Dicken P. (2007) *Global Shift: Mapping the Changing Contours of the World Economy*. 5th edn, London: Sage.

EC (2005) *Publishing Market Watch Final Report*, Luxembourg: European Commission, DG Enterprise.

Flew T. (2007) *Global Media*, Basingstoke: Palgrave Macmillan.

Hickethier K. (1996) The media in Germany, in T. Weymouth and B. Lamizet (eds) *Market and Myths: forces for change in the European* media, Harlow: Addison Wesley Longman.

Horsley W. (2007), *Goodbye to Freedom?*, Association of European Journalists.

Horsley W. (2008a), *Goodbye to Media Freedom?*, Association of European Journalists.

Horsley W. (2008b) 'Europe: media freedom in retreat', *British Journalism Review*: **19**(2): 39–45.

Jones A. (2006) Costly kiosk: how French dailies are struggling to retain their savoir faire, *FT.com*, 1 August.

Kleinstuber H., Thomass B. (2008) The German media landscape, in G. Terzis (ed.), *European Media Governance National and Regional Dimensions*, Bristol: Intellect, 111–124. See also http://www.ejc.net/index.php/media_landscape/article/germany/.

Lara A. (2008) The Polish media landscape, in G. Terzis (ed.), *European Media Governance National and Regional Dimensions*, Bristol: Intellect, 399–410. See also http://www.ejc.net/index.php/media_landscape/article/germany/.

McLuhan M. (1964) *Understanding the Media: the extensions of Man*, new edn, 1994, MIT Cambridge, MA: MIT Press.

McQuail D. (2000) *Mass Communication Theory*, 4th edn, London: Sage.

Pira International (2003) *The EU Publishing Industry: an Assessment of Competitiveness*, Luxembourg: European Communities.

Reding V. (2007) *The convergent publisher – Print media in the broadband economy*, speech/07/788, Publishers Forum, Brussels, 6 December.

Salaverría R. (2008) The Spanish media landscape, in G. Terzis (ed.), *European Media Governance National and Regional Dimensions*, Bristol: Intellect, 277–288. See also http://www.ejc.net/index.php/media_landscape/article/spain/.

Weber J. (2006) Strassburg, 1605: The origins of the newspaper in Europe, *German History*, **24**(3): 387–412.

Chapter 7

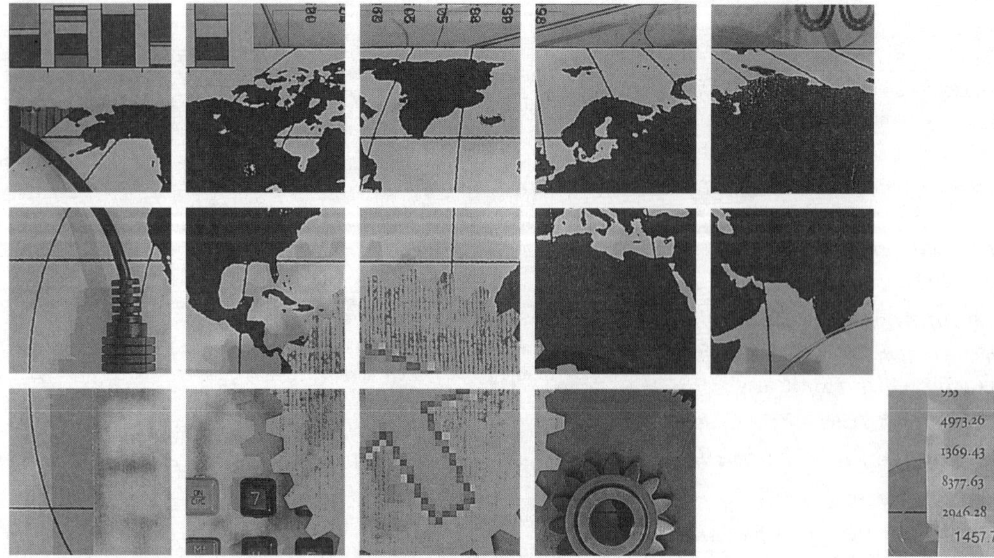

The distribution of print and published material

What this chapter covers

Learning objectives

When you have completed this chapter you will be able to:

- ➤ Reflect upon the development of new pressures changing the distribution system within the EU media environment.
- ➤ Outline new models of distribution impacting upon the press, publishing and print market.
- ➤ Link the press and print industry distribution network to other related distributive practices such as postal services and press agencies.
- ➤ Analyse press and publishing policy developments at an EU and national level.

Themes

Below you will find a simple statement or series of statements around the six themes. They should not be read as a given fact. They are more like hypotheses (see Chapter 2) which need to be proved, discussed, debated and then used in your own analysis of the subject. The ideas and approaches in this book are always to be considered with an open mind; this is important in university study and is what makes it distinct from pre-university study.

Diversity of media

Print and publishing industries around the world have been governed by technological development from the printing presses of the past to the digital age of the present. Even so, traditionally the distribution network of paper and its produce has been national and often fragmented in Europe. The result has been a diversity of media to fit the various markets and the distribution network that feeds them.

Internal/external forces for change

The digital age in the EU appears to be advancing through the twin pressures of globalisation and even Europeanisation. This is reaching a point where national distribution systems are under increasing pressure from these external forces and are altering as they adapt to cost, price and competitors. Internally, EU societies too are converging as they use the new technology for distributive purposes in an era of continued urbanisation, technology impact and increased press and other media competition.

Complexity of the media

The forces for change upon the press and print distribution systems do not mean necessarily a similarity of provision. The distribution network may be converging, but it also feeds into an already-existing complexity of consumer behaviour. As with production, the traditional distributive network is in private hands, but complexity of distributive practice in the EU remains.

Multi-levels

Whilst the press and printing industry does not have a significant public sector, its role in civil society remains very important. The levels of interest in the EU in the latter are rising as the EU investigates national and even regional levels of activity. The industry operates within a multi-level framework: collectively, a mix of global, European, national and local interests.

European integrative environment

Being in private hands, the forces of market competition in the press and print industry have been traditionally national in form. Equally there has not been a dedicated policy development at EU level within the market, but this is changing. The media industry is so important for the 'information society' that, coupled to the growth and outreach of the European Single Market, the press and publishing industry is beginning to react to 'productivity' issues, mergers and takeovers in the distribution field that are important at a EU comparative level. This will continue into the future and is proof of the pressure of 'Europeanisation' in the market.

Cultural values

Many could argue that the diversity of cultures within the EU is not fundamentally threatened by the new digital age. The EU even has a declared policy of encouraging and supporting diversity of cultural values. Yet, the development of a comprehensive framework of telecommunications and EU-wide rules on competition in the distribution system will have an impact upon our cultural assumptions.

Essentials

➤ Within the EU at present there is a vast array of differences in the distribution network and, like so much in the media industry, this is linked to a whole series of factors: the economy, relocation of production, research and innovation in product development, shopping habits, political control, transport systems, and role and speed of technical change. Even so, over the past few decades, change has been occurring apace, linked to increased competition. Driven by the EU single market, EU nations are becoming more alike in their trade and shopping practices, including the publishing industry, even though in a community sense Europe remains diverse.

➤ Along with internal EU developments, the distribution systems within Europe are being touched by corporate global competition and new forms of technology which are also impacting upon the industry.

➤ There is a divide between the past and new methods of distribution: between the classic (nostalgic) systems based on physical forms of transport and the new, that is electronic, digital systems. The former remains in the dominant position, but this is likely to change in the years to come.

➤ Convergence is therefore a result of changes within distribution as well as production and consumption. In many respects, the EU like the rest of the globe is standing at the door of a new age of distribution that could change the print industry fundamentally.

Introduction: the print industry

The European print industry is the oldest of all the media, and its distribution system is extensive and highly developed. Over the past 100 years, print distribution has evolved by adapting to new technologies that support it or, in some cases compete with it, such as telegraph, radio, film and television networks. As competition has grown, speed of reporting along with the speed, safety and reliability of delivery have become important competitive advantages to be enhanced whenever possible. Add to this, veracity, trust, relevance, interest and entertainment and you have the pillars upon which the industry has been founded in general. However, at base, it needs the distribution set-up to work to allow it to function.

Whatever happens to the print distributive system is of crucial importance to consumers, communities, nation states and governments let alone the publishing industry. Without a distribution network, the media would not function: neither producer nor consumer would be able to interact. Moreover, the new more integrated EU age has seen recent key technological and policy changes altering the environment in which it performs.

- Almost all of the communication system can now be recorded digitally and stored, not just the 'written' word ('keyboard fashioned' or 'speech recognised') but messaging, phone and e-mail, radio, television, song, film and newscast, even to the point, some might say, of over-load.
- Added to this, and quite significantly, most European governments have decided to develop online communication with all types of their constituents, transferring their printed material online and encouraging internet access. Where government goes so too does the public sector in general at all levels of civic society.
- In the EU there is a dedicated policy to encourage 'e-governance', private or public (embracing libraries, schools, local government offices, ministries, universities), throughout all the member states, not only for the sake of political, economic, social and cultural transparency, but also for cross-frontier comparisons and the communication of best practice.

Stop and consider 7.1

To what extent will the print and publishing industry change because of the digital age? If you read the hype, the world of paper and the paperback, even the newspapers, is just about to collapse and come to an end. Perhaps more important how can the impact of new technology on old industries be measured? If this is a difficult question, it is one that even the market analysts are unsure of. The next sections may help, but keep an open mind. Research methods often use something called 'grounded theory' which in essence says, let the data and as much as possible the 'objectivity' of your analysis be paramount. This is good advice.

Distribution

In classic terms, the print industry has relied on traditional transport for distribution, and this has followed the development of transportation systems: from cart to stagecoach, to motorised vehicles and especially the railway network. To this has been added since the 1950s a comprehensive national and European road system, broadly encouraged even at the EU level, in what are known as trans-European transport networks (**TEN-T**). As trade between the member states has increased, the transport system has equally integrated to support it. Although the reading of published material is often national in form, the transport of the raw material (pulp, paper and finished product) has always used a cross-frontier network and in the past few decades has been broadened and deepened. Even in an electronic age the consumption of paper has remained high and in some instances has been increasing, as can be seen in Case Study 7.1.

Transporting print is only part of the distribution network. A point of sale is needed to finally bring producer and consumer together.

- Outlets across the EU were formerly linked to specialised outlets such as 'newsagents' or licensed kiosks. These continue to be for many the prime point of sale across the EU, although this is changing. To this have been added supermarkets and other shopping outlets. Some are increasingly associated with European supply chains working across frontiers, encouraged by tourism and migration of workers and businesses. This is changing consumer patterns.
- Subscription sales remain for many EU countries very important as the means of print, newspaper and magazine delivery (e.g. Germany). These are often associated with postal services, state or private. An increasingly integrated postal system will develop over the years as postal services are privatised (**liberalised**) within the EU: the first EU member state to move to a privatised postal system was The Netherlands. New European Commission proposals for more privatisation, not of post offices *per se* but of postal services, are planned for 2009. This should lead to greater competition between postal service providers and encourage a more European and even globally a highly competitive system (see Point of View 7.1).
- New delivery techniques linked to the digital age are potentially revolutionary. Delivery online of almost all types of printed material has either

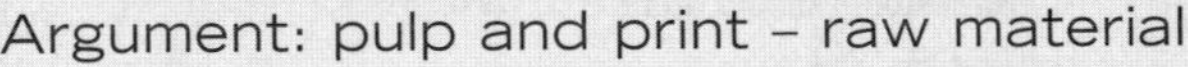

Case Study 7.1

Argument: pulp and print – raw material

7.1.2 Production

7.1.2.1 Newsprint

Despite falling circulations, newsprint consumption by the industry has either remained static or declined only slightly (magazines also consume newsprint, and the figures available do not distinguish between the two). The main reason is that the total number of pages in newspapers has increased with the use of new features and supplements. Newsprint accounts for approximately 13% of world paper consumption.

In terms of sustainability the rise in demand for pulp is increasingly coming under scrutiny.

European consumption in 1997 was 9.4 million tonnes.

European newsprint consumption and production 1990–1997

	1990	*1994*	*1997*
Production (millions tonnes)	10	11	11
Consumption (millions tonnes)	10	10	9.4
Consumption (kg per person)	12.6	15.5	13.1

Source: European Commission, *Publishing Market Watch Final Report*, Table 6, p. 73 (from UNESCO) (EC, 2005b).

happened or is happening. Some commentators and researchers predict a totally new era for the print industry, but its precise nature is difficult to judge at this stage. Future trends remain a subject of debate and a matter of interpretation.

No matter the techniques, the distribution network is profoundly important in connecting the different readerships and populations it serves. The general newspaper reach (the degree of population having contact with the delivery system) varies across Europe, but in most cases is considered to be high. Among the highest is Sweden, where it is estimated (*World Press Trends*, 2005, WAN figures for 2003) that newspaper delivery reaches almost 85% of the

Point of View 7.1

PricewaterhouseCoopers' (PwC) Report on the publishing industry 2002 – adapted by EMCC

Summary of impacts on entertainment and media sector segments

Filmed entertainment High penetration of DVDs Limited digital camera Legitimate VOD services mean little file-swapping online More local content, globally	**Television distribution** Digital upgrades Further consolidation extends convergence and product bundles Loosening of ownership regulations	**Television networks** Funding sources fragment Most content lower cost but more local New co-financing opportunities	**Recorded music** First for pervasive digital distribution New service models Increased copyright legislation
Radio and out-of-home advertising Loosening of ownership regulations Limited digital penetration Improved out-of-home alternatives	**Newspaper publishing** Loosening of ownership regulations Some digital cannibalisation Changes in classified and yellow pages	**Magazine publishing** Some digital cannibalisation Micro-niches New acquisition and distribution models	**Consumer book publishing** Translated products increase More mega-authors Publishers merge with large media companies
Internet advertising and access spending Access bundles with consumer services Increasing customer brands Broadband critical mass in industrial nations	**Business information** Continued introduction of new services Increased wireless delivery	**Educational and professional books and training** Digital learning products for corporate customers Explosion of long-distance learning	

High impact Moderate impact Lower impact

Source: Adapted from PricewaterhouseCoopers, 2002, p. 13. From *Sector Futures: in Search of a Realistic Future*, p. 13, Table 3 (EMCC, 2004)

In looking at the entertainment world through media segmentation, the influential group PwC saw IT impact that varied in intensity depending on sector. For them, the newspaper industry along with magazines may have less change to look forward to than other media. Our question is: were they right? Read the document which contains this most useful guide. In the report we may find striking comparisons and analysis being made. The work was available online through the European Commission.

Source: *Global Entertainment and media outlook: 2002–2006 – Forecasts and economic analyses of 13 industry segments* (PwC, 2002), cited in EMCC (2004), p. 13.

population; the Finns and the Danes are at just over 80%. This can be compared with some lower but significant figures; Germany at approximately 75%; France at just under 50%; and Spain with between 30% and 50%. Interestingly for France and Spain, the variations also depend on whether the newspaper is read by men or women. Most EU countries do not illustrate fundamental differences between men and women newspaper readers and the case of France and Spain is in the main exception.

There are also variations in newspaper distribution costs as a percentage of cover price (*ibid.*, 2005) depending on whether they are bought as a single copy in a retail setting or as part of home deliveries or associated subscription postal services. The average across Europe is approximately 35–45%. Sweden again shows considerable reliance on home delivery for newspapers at approximately 44%, whereas single copy purchase is closer to 21%. This can be compared to Belgium where the distribution cost for both home delivery and single copy sale is approximately 30% of the copy price. Such differences indicate the importance of geography and consumer habits in the different nations. Figures for the Czech Republic show similarities to the Belgium data, with 33% distribution cost factor for single copy sales and 40% for home and postal deliveries over the period 1999–2001 (*World Press Trends*, WAN, 2003).

Classic vs new distribution techniques

The classic distributive system is founded on the physical nature of the material used: paper. Starting from a form of pulp the paper process ends with a printed article that needs to be transported. In bulk it tends to be heavy at both the start and end of the process.

Printing is a highly specialised old skill with which generations have recorded knowledge and then communicated it by distribution. From words to graphics, from kiosk to newsagent, from post office to industry, from writer to reader, paper has been the mainstay of the print and publishing industry for centuries. The systems of transport, and therefore distribution, of the media have been built on the circulation of paper. Paper remains the foundation of the industry to this day. To understand the classic, paper-driven distribution system, we need to comprehend some of the processes involved. Case Study 7.2 gives a description used in a 'simulation' exercise to increase efficiency, which is both illuminating and useful in comparison with the digital age commentaries that follow (see Case Study 7.3, p. 150).

This leads neatly to the question, to what extent is the digital age changing the print distribution

Case Study 7.2

Simulation of product distribution – newspapers

The following description was used in an American-based exercise but it equally applies to the European case:

> . . . The paper printing operations consist of different traditions, which vary in content. These additions are different based on the geographical area where the newspaper will be distributed and on the demographics of population in those areas. In addition, each printed edition may change based on the time of the day as the news occurs.
>
> The newsroom is expected to release articles for publication at a given time of the day. However, when the news cast is following developing events, such articles cannot be generated in time; therefore the last edition printed will vary to include the latest events. For example sport events may finish after their scheduled time due to weather or to a tied game. Thus the score and the winner is not known at the time that the newsroom sends the news to press for the first edition. However by the time the latest edition is printed, the game may have finished; hence, the new article is included detailing the outcomes of the sports event.

Source: A simulation of the product distribution in the newspaper industry (Garcia *et al.*, 1999).

industry? Not only is the use of software and computing now essential in the print process, cutting costs and speeding up its manufacture and production, the distribution system can be changed into a purely digital, almost 'virtual' process, avoiding the use of paper altogether. This has not yet fully happened but it could. It all depends upon the producer and their relationship to the consumer.

Also, in distribution terms this is why the 'browser-wars' on PC and mobile, and even on digital TV, are so important. It is the browser that will be the distribution 'controller' (portal) for much of the content that now finds itself in the form of print and publishing products such as newspapers, magazines and even books. Just as we open up our newspaper or magazine and turn the pages, the browser will help do this in what is fast becoming an electronic age.

Not that the publishing industry is averse to the new age. It is perhaps false to postulate a competition of technologies when in practice across the publishing industry they often complement rather than compete with each other. There are great advantages to using the 'digital' delivery systems within the print and publishing industry:

- costs are potentially lowered;
- speed of delivery increases, and this saves 'money' and attracts consumer satisfaction;
- using e-techniques of search and marketing can enable targeted distribution;
- ease of use for both producer and consumer is improved if the software is right;
- greater creativity in the mixing of genre from word-art to animation is possible;
- greater mix of media inter-activity enables, for example, moving visual pictures in newspapers;
- an almost seamless interface between the graphic, still and moving, and the 'printed' (or 'displayed') word can be achieved – for example, serious and not so serious newspapers, national, regional and local, have complementary online editions, as well as weekly or monthly publications;
- books, textbooks, academic articles and government and even EU reports and papers can be published online increasing access and dialogue.

Ultimately, those who controlled the distribution system in the past are now faced with new forms of cross-media competition. This is perhaps the real issue – not competing technologies but competing corporations. The revolution in online newspapers is challenging older distributive systems because they are opened up to new providers and this increases competition. The older corporations are faced with online versions of newspapers with similar content, not only directly through page reporting but also through software-video equivalents (Flash, media players, shockwave, etc.), podcasting and even blogging.

This is not restricted to the large publishing houses but encompasses the whole of the distribution process. The press agencies, traditionally so important for collating and then distributing the news in all its forms, are beginning to service new IT-based companies (MSN, Yahoo, Google) as well as their traditional clients in the newspaper and broadcasting networks.

Perhaps even more important, press agencies are disturbing the established advertising structure by marketing themselves directly to the consumer (UPI, AP, Reuters, AFP, DW, etc.). As a result, newspapers will no longer be just 'edition'-driven, but will need to move to 'instant', 'breaking news' formats akin to 'live' television broadcasts (Telegraph TV and FT Video are two examples from the UK). This changes the work of the journalist, the nature of the productive process and its means of distribution as well as the method of consumption; not completely but significantly.

The new age is one where the telecommunications network is as important to the print industry as it was to the media broadcasters with the introduction of cable or satellite. Access is widening and deepening. Access through broadband, home, internet café or place of work, is becoming an increasing priority and will soon be a necessity for all: producers and consumers alike. Such a change is not cheap and demands heavy investment. The distribution models by which we understand the media in the past are changing, or so it seems.

Stop and consider 7.2

How important are models of distribution for the publishing industry and why do we create them? How do we balance out the models of the past with the models of the new? Perhaps we still need to go back and use not a judgement on the technology itself or even the connections in the distribution system but price, cost and productivity? Go back to Chapter 6 and consider the European Commission report on productivity in the publishing industry. Even better, look it up and critically review its arguments.

However, perhaps too the new age of new technology is much more fundamental than we presently assume. New technology is already a structured, crucial part of the publishing industry, impacting upon the production process, consumption and price. As for distribution, there are new technologies just on the horizon that try to replace paper with e-reading techniques. To what extent the readership will take to the new technology is still in question. However, it is probably safe to argue that e-books and e-reading will grow, perhaps becoming as much accepted as the ever-present word processing packages, now the mainstay of office and professional life. E-reading is spilling over into new initiatives like the Guttenberg project, where e-books may be downloaded for free. Increasingly, e-versions of books are downloadable at a competitive cost compared to traditional forms. This is changing the distribution system. In a recent review of the French book market, the new 'e-reading' phenomenon was listed as an important area of interest and the comments are worthy of analysis (see Point of View 7.2).

The opportunities for the digitisation of books and other products are not being missed by innovative companies. The New York based company Kirtas Technologies recently established a European branch based in the Netherlands (2008) with the expressed mission of promoting their 'page-turning' technology in Europe. Among its customers, Microsoft and the British Library stand out.

Nowhere is the new technology more visible than in the 'new journalism' of online provision, podcasting and blogging: activities within the new distributive network. This goes to the core of the communication process. Some would say that it is changing the relationship between reader and published content (see the works of Thatcher (2001), Humphreys (2002) and Christou and Simpson (2004) in the references section). The creation of an online structure is taking place within a context that is both global and European and, as we saw in Chapter 4, cross-frontier regulated or even deregulated in certain cases, but nonetheless important.

Point of View 7.2

French book market – review

There are different substitutes for books available. The scope of publishing has expanded and includes a variety of media formats and entertainment forms, such as the electronic versions of books, so-called EU books, and periodicals, as well as websites or blocks, etc. They may present significant indirect competition to established traditional channels moving forward, however at present they represent a relatively small proportion of distribution. Such substitutes have their advantages, usually it costs less to reproduce them and they are eco-friendly since they are delivered to customers in digital form and there is no need for paper, ink or other resources that are used to produce print books. Also they take less physical storage space and are easy to travel with since hundreds of them may be carried on one device and easy to read in the dark with a backlit device. Additionally readers who have problems with reading the small print books benefit from easy adjustable print size. However an e-book requires an electronic device or special software to display it and there is always concern that the book format will not be readable by future e-book devices. Also book reading devices are significantly more expensive than most paper books and the majority of the readers still prefer their regular copy in paper form. More traditional substitutes include second-hand books. Overall, the threat of substitutes is strong in this market.

Source: *Books in France: Industry Profile*, June, p. 16 (Datamonitor, 2008).

Podcasting

The use of podcasting is a symbolic shift from content-fixed channel scheduling to the new mobile media scene. It too is a part of a new distributive pattern that producers and publishers are using to increase or keep hold of their audiences and readers. Nowadays, one is as likely to see an iPod or MP3 player in use as an opened newspaper or novel. The new technology is no longer a 'music' accessory but increasingly embraces 'serious' podcasts from a variety of sources: financial news, radio programmes and television clips and spoken works such as news, business updates, educational lectures or even novels.

Of course, the controlling-content factor is an essential part of the competitive market place, and the battle for 'player' control continues with offerings from Windows Media Player to RealPlayer and iTunes, all of which are used by the publishing and print industries. Even public broadcasters such as the BBC are launching their own versions of player technology (BBC iPlayer). In Europe, the BBC has been one of the first to move quickly to embrace the 'new media' as part of its public service remit. The extent to which this develops across other EU states will depend on the different governments and the money available in the public broadcasting systems. A word of caution though: the degree of take-up within the new distribution system is probably slower at the outset than many predicted. This has been the case in the newspaper and certainly the book and magazine as well as the audio-visual sectors. As an indication from the audio-visual world, but which equally implies important concerns for publishing, a recent FT report in the UK indicated that take-up of the BBC iPlayer, and even Google's YouTube, as an alternative to commercial broadcasting, was not impacting significantly on the viewing of television, with only between 1% and 2% of programme viewing online (Bradshaw, 2008).

Blogs and blogging

In journalistic circles the advent of the 'blogger' has caused some concern. The new distribution network has allowed individuals to express their views for little cost on any matter and, perhaps more importantly, to any audience with the equipment, at any time. The professional body of journalists has been potentially threatened by 'people's journalism'.

Opinion makers have been confronted with authentic voices and opinions from the 'people'. Blogging's influence, though, can be overstated and, in response, newspaper editors and journalists have created their own working blogs, thereby complementing their traditional reporting service to readers and listeners.

Blogs and blogging are probably more important in bridging the gap between different media. They have allowed radio presenters, newspaper journalists and television reporters to set up their work in a variety of media.

Telecommunications

The new media architecture cannot operate fully without an integrated telecommunications system (see Point of View 7.3). Increasingly, commentators have noted this in their analysis, not least because of its increasing influence on the media scene but also because of its impact on the general economy.

Certainly we need to be cautious in assuming too much, but even the OECD report mentioned above went on to illustrate the many ways in which states across the globe were reacting to the new technology. The OECD has been for many years an invaluable source of information in the sector. It gave a detailed analysis of telecommunications and regulatory regimes used throughout the world in two other major reports (OECD 2006 and 2007), both of which underline the importance of the sector and its general impact on both the macro and the micro economy – see Chapter 3. These reports, taken collectively, are important in our understanding of global change, but equally in allowing us to contextualise the EU's response to the new media architecture.

Whereas media integration through the TWF (Television without Frontiers) initiative, which embraced in part media content, was and is only a limited success (see Chapter 4), the policy development of the EU in telecommunications is seen in a more successful light, even if it remains contentious. In the past EU nation states jealously guarded their

Point of View 7.3

The role of ICT in economic and social change

Not all is easy to predict, and if we look to the past we discover that we need hard data before judging the real impact of the new age. As the OECD put it in a recent report:

> The role of information and communication technologies (ICT) in economic growth and social change has received considerable attention in recent years, particularly in the debate on the 'new economy'. The production, diffusion and use of ICT vary considerably between and within countries, although they continue to spread and their economic importance has grown over the 1990s. To focus the policy debate, especially in light of the recent 'exuberance' and subsequent crash in the market value of 'dot.com' firms, reliable and comprehensive indicators are needed to track developments in new information technologies and understand their impact on our economies and societies. As ICT has only been recognised as a major source of economic and social change in recent years, official statistics on ICT are still under development.
>
> Source: *Measuring the Information Economy*, p. 3 (OECD, 2002), www.oecd.org/sti/measuring-infoeconomy.

telecommunications networks but, step by step, the telecommunications network across the EU has been, more or less, integrated (see Point of View 7.4).

In the immediate past, these changes to ICT would have affected the audio-visual world more than the publishing scene, but increasingly this is not the case. As we have seen, the publishing world has adopted the new technology; they are as involved in its development as the broadcasters before them because they have much competitively to gain. The publishing sector, as a cross-media phenomenon, can now compete in content with the older audio-visual providers,

Point of View 7.4

Telecommunications in the EU – significance

The reasons why telecommunications are so important for the EU is spelt out precisely by a European Commission paper:

> Creating a single European information space with an open and competitive internal market is one of the key challenges for Europe, within the broader strategy for growth and jobs. Electronic communications underpins the whole of the economy, and at EU level is supported by a regulatory framework that entered into force in 2003. The aims of the framework are to promote competition, consolidate the internal market for electronic communications and benefit consumers and users. It is designed to take account of convergence, in that it deals with markets and not technologies. Markets are defined according to competition law principles, based on general demand and supply side considerations, and are independent of changes in the underlying technology. The framework provides for the progressive removal of regulation as and when competition becomes effective.
>
> Source: European Commission, Communication from the commission to the council, the European parliament, the European economic and social committee and the committee of the regions on the Review of the EU Regulatory Framework for electronic communications networks and services, p. 2 (EC, 2006).

Moreover the report went on to specify:

> Electronic communications continue to be a success story for the EU. Since markets were fully opened up to competition in 1998, users and consumers have benefited from more choice, lower prices and innovative products and services. Mobile services have reached high penetration levels; broadband communications are growing rapidly. Overall growth in revenue terms in the sector continues to be strong, outpacing the growth of the EU economy. In 2005 the ICT sector was valued at €614bn, according to the Commission's 11th Implementation report which provides more information about these developments. ICT also contributes macro-economically to productivity growth and increased competitiveness of the European economy as a whole, and thus is a factor in growth and job creation.
>
> Source: *ibid* p. 4.

and it is the revolution in communication, and in particular telecommunications, that is allowing this to happen.

The European postal system: the post office

Even so, telecommunications is not the only area being changed by technology and new regulation: so also are the postal services. These too are being liberalised across the EU and will probably, in the end, become more integrated through mergers, takeovers and cross-frontier contracting. Once again, this impacts on the publishing industry. For example, where reader subscriptions pay for newspapers (a good example is Germany where subscriptions can amount to almost 70% of newspaper sales), the postal network and delivery service is an essential part of the costs to the industry.

Across the EU, postal services are altering to embrace not only a more liberalised market but also the changes that touch telecommunications because they are inter-related. Where once it was mail through the post box (see Case Study 7.3), now email often suffices; where newspapers were delivered by a 'boy or girl on a bike', they will be delivered online; where once there was a stamp there is a subscription fee to an ISP. These matters are important for the publishing industry, in all its forms, especially because of their impact on distribution.

Press agencies and distribution in the print industry

The distribution of printed and published material has been, as indicated in this chapter, a very important part of its development. Emphasis has been placed upon the effect of the new digital age on the distribution network for the 21st century. However, to fully understand the development of distribution techniques, including those for published material, we need to look at one last area. There has always been, since the creation of the press in the 16th century and, more importantly, with the growth of newspapers in the 19th century, one central focus for much of the press; the press agencies. With the gathering of information offering such a high premium in modern economies, the press agencies very quickly established themselves as the centre for data and news for journals, governments, corporations and newspapers,

Across Europe the press agencies have grown in importance and are now a very important part of the distribution network of publishing as well as broadcasting and audio-visual content. Streaming out of the 19th century, there has been a string of important agencies who have tied together into a network used by the print and publishing industry in a way which is often poorly understood. A great deal of the content in newspapers, either national or regional, will have sprung first from the agencies.

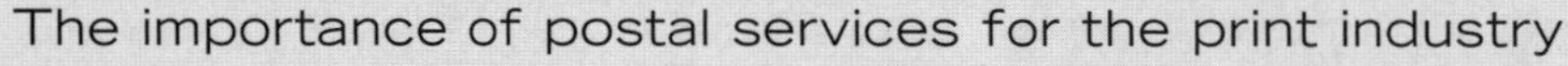

Case Study 7.3

The importance of postal services for the print industry

The postal service is crucial to the print industry and this raises the possibility of difficulties if the classic distribution network is altered. As the European Commission has written:

> For newspapers, magazines, and increasingly books, the quality and cost of postal services is of critical importance. Only 10% of consumer magazines are supplied internationally via retail outlets, with the remaining 90% relying on quality postal services. The further liberalisation of postal services in the EU may result in a reduction of distribution costs for print products. On the other hand, maintaining the obligation of universal postal services remains a matter of concern for publishers.
>
> Source: Commission staff working paper. *Strengthening the Competitiveness of the EU Publishing Sector. The role of media policy*, p. 27 (EC, 2005a).

Note the caveat at the end of the extract. The liberalisation of such a public service as that offered by the EU post offices is a delicate matter full of political consequences which go beyond the publishing industry.

The photographs, the data, the graphs, the detail of journalism will often be brought together by the agencies.

Stop and consider 7.3

Copyright often demands that we cite the sources used in books, journals and newspapers. Have you ever noticed that the 'stories' in the press are often very similar to the 'stories' on the TV? The reason may well be that the newspapers and the TV stations have used the information from press agencies. In the EU the largest press agency is Reuters: have you noticed any others? Does it matter where the information comes from? Ask yourself: who verifies our 'news'? Who makes us aware of our 'celebrities'?

The first agency in Europe was 'Agence Havas' founded in 1835 by Charles-Louis Havas. It altered its structure and recreated itself over the years and was the foundation of the present day Agence France-Press (AFP). Germany quickly followed with its own agency known as the Wolf Agency and the British created the Associated Press in 1848. Other European nations followed suit. Even so, the largest and probably most influential European press agency remains Reuters, created in 1851.

In all the discussions of new, contemporary distribution techniques associated with the digital age, it is easy to forget that these techniques have been used for a long time, and this can be seen in the development of the agencies. Press agencies such as Reuters have always used new technology to enhance their growth and power: through the 19th century this meant the telegraph, the undersea cable and the telephone. In the 20th century journalism, reporting and communicating were profoundly touched by the technology of photography, radio and film. The technology of television, often predicted to be the final nail in the coffin of paper journalism and the daily newspaper, in fact had the effect of enhancing and deepening the content of the publishing world.

What we learn about distribution technologies and communication networks with such companies as Reuters and Cable & Wireless is how the distribution network looks for and adapts to a series of factors:

- that technologies can be made to converge and be applied to consumer demand;
- that distribution networks and entrepreneurs can come together to compete and combine and even at times co-operate to provide services for the public which are profitable;
- that corporations that adapt and are flexible and in tune with their age are often successful;
- that being sensitive to the political and economic environment is very important for distribution companies so a careful eye is needed to detect politics, policy-making and changes within society.

Distribution: European policy

As we have seen in the points of view and various case study materials, the newspaper and print industry plays a key role in the dissemination of information and is a key pillar of democracy, community and social ties. Across Europe, policy decisions have controlled the distribution of published material. However, there is no harmonious European policy supporting the newspaper or the publishing industry. Practice varies across the EU and is diverse, and nation states have met the past challenges in their own ways. Even so, there are two broad approaches by governments across the EU for the print and publishing industries: support through subsidy or tax advantage for those who produce and distribute; or, alternatively, a more market-led and 'no-subsidy' pattern for publishing material.

In the new age of cross-media, however, these trends are gradually being undermined by a set of challenges which have led to a more collective, cross-policy approach. As we have seen, the publishing industry has been drawing together its communication policies at an EU level (telecommunications and postal services for example – see above), and this is having an impact, both directly and indirectly, and changing the industry in fundamental ways. To understand the future is not to explore just the distribution practices of the past, but to see how nations are responding to these new concerns.

Online and the economics of new distribution

Online publishing is often said to be on the brink of a new era. However, the new distribution techniques will be finally judged by the economics. At present, few online newspapers are making profits. Most newspapers have added an online facility to their mainstream activity. Few can challenge its future importance, but creating a working economic model has not been easy. The new model for media online business has not yet solidified. The distribution network is in place, the regulations are being developed – self, or co-regulation within the EU (see Chapter 4), but the consumer is, so far, unwilling, in most cases, to pay the full cost of online provision.

Equally, when determining the full costs of a transaction one needs to bear in mind not only producer content costs but also the consumer's investment in the technology needed to receive the new content. To this too must be added the distributive and telecommunication costs which the producer and consumer of content must pay up front.

The newspapers which are making progress have value-added content and specific niche markets which are often subscription-based. Financial Times subscriptions (Pearson plc) and other business-orientated web sites, where accuracy and continuous updating (say for stock market share prices) are paramount, are an example.

In part this resistance to paying for e-content is due to the initial wave of optimism that welcomed in the digital age where online products and internet customers became used to 'free no-cost provision'. In part it is also due to the wariness of producers when it comes to increasing prices for online products, aware as they are of the competition and tightness of profit margins in an industry faced with structural change that is now well into two decades of upheaval. Another setback is that advertising spend is shifting toward more targeted online distribution and search engines that companies such as Google, Microsoft and Yahoo can offer, let alone the huge potential of mobile advertising.

The publishing industry cannot avoid this challenge and in fact, as has been shown in Chapter 3 on economics, to survive means mergers, takeovers, new business models, reshaping of finance and capital, economies of scale, developing productivity and innovation, widening product range, planning cross-media provision, horizontal and vertical integration, and all the other instruments available to modern business management which enhance development of the 'value-chain' (Porter, 1998).

Even if the economics are yet to be fully worked out, the trend toward e-provision continues. It raises important, even profound issues (see Point of View 7.5). European civilisation is built on our communication systems. The printed word has been the essential ingredient of the past. The storage of our 'written' knowledge, our oral traditions and scientific dialogue, our libraries, education within institutions and our cultural icons are based upon the older, classic, paper-based technologies. If the new digital age potentially changes this, to what extent does it alter the core of our civilisation?

Therein lies the debate and, as far we can see ahead, we do not have a definitive answer. However, it is little in question that the digital age changes mainly the distribution system but not the production of ideas or our use of them. Although it is argued that the message is dependent upon the medium (see Chapter 5), in the end, it could also be argued that the producer and the consumer are in control of the incoming and outgoing messages. How the messages are transported is important and a matter of technology, but in the end it does not change what we communicate or our interpretation. It does, however, change how we receive messages. What changes most, perhaps, is the relationship (competition) between the producers and the distributors. This then impacts on what the consumer receives. With the creation of podcasting and blogging as examples, and connection to telecommunication networks, we can see in part how this is unfolding.

The new digital distribution networks allow the customer even more choice than before: the choice of participation and when, how and where to participate. It shifts the control of distribution from the producers of content to the distributors of content. For example, Apple iTunes is embedded in the iPod and iPhone.

Point of View 7.5

The economics of the new digital age related to newspapers

> Most national papers now publish their print newspaper online, as well as offering additional material only available online. It has been argued that the publishing of newspaper content online will damage the industry, as many readers may switch to free online formats. However, as income from advertising now forms the majority of newspaper revenues, the switch to online formats will not be as damaging to companies as some think. The Internet is a much more versatile medium for advertising than a print newspaper; companies may use ad networks and behavioural targeting to enhance advertising revenues.
>
> Source: *Newspapers in the Netherlands: industry profile*, p. 14 (Datamonitor, 2006).

This may be the case in The Netherlands but it is to be remembered that advertising revenue and support for newspapers across the EU is different in different countries. Even so, the argument made above is an interesting one. It is not the only one. Compare the following commentary with the Datamonitor view and you will note subtle but important differences:

> The industry's online business model also needs some rethinking. Too many newspaper companies have replicated their print models online, relying on display advertisements and classifieds, instead of creating new business models. A recent study showed that as few as 10% of top print advertisers are top online advertisers in newspaper websites. These new online advertisers often require different ad metrics than those traditionally used in print media. Newspapers need to ask how much money their sites make from the beat generation, consumer direct marketing, and pay per use content. If the answer is zero, then they should not be satisfied with even 50% growth rates, because they may be missing big growth opportunities.
>
> Source: Can the newspaper industry stare disruption in the face? Lessons learned from past failures can help to ensure future triumphs, *Niemen Reports* (Anthony and Gilbert, 2006), see http://www.nieman.harvard.edu/reports/.

Combined with the extended digital telecommunications (cable, satellite, wireless internet – wi-fi), the media is no longer restricted to a particular place of use. It has become a part of an 'anywhere-everyday life'. Work (Blackberry technology, for example), communication (the mobile 3G and beyond) and general as well as specific entertainment, all use new distribution techniques incorporated into the world of 'downloads' at the click of a mouse button.

Distribution: national policies – a comment

As we saw in Chapter 6 the publishing industry is Europe's oldest medium. It is wrapped in its national geography by language, frontier and regulation; even its content is, in the main, nationally formulated. This remains the case for the foreseeable future. The nation states of the EU are not coalescing into a new European super state, or a definable 'European space' with a measurable 'European' readership or audience linked to a European distribution system.

The publishing industry, including the newspapers, magazine and book markets, remains, more or less, nationally orientated but with cross-national corporations and distribution systems tying them all together. Publishing houses are becoming cross-national corporations – Bertelsmann is a notable example, but equally corporations in the UK, France, Germany as a whole, Italy and Spain are important – with cross- and trans-national strategies for sales.

All of this is reflected in distributive practice in and across the member states of the EU (see Case Study 7.4). Although its distribution system remains national, through cable, wireless, Internet, and rail, road and air transport, across the EU the network is increasingly being trans-nationally connected. The physical transport system is increasingly integrated and linked very firmly to trade, including trade in published goods, which follows the normal rules of supply and demand.

As we can see from the above, national distribution systems are both complicated and varied. The future of course will probably remain national in form, but with increasing use of national and trans-national

Case Study 7.4

Newspaper distribution inside Europe: companies and corporations by nations – a sample

The following companies within nation states are seen as major players in the EU distributive system: for further details and analysis see World Association of Newspapers (WAN) and its *World Press Trends* series – an excellent resource.

Country	*Main distributors*	*Retail outlet details*
Austria: population 5 million	MediaPrint Morawa	Up to 8000 retail outlets are involved with newspaper selling.
France: population 60 million	NNPP (Nouvelles Messageries de la Presse Parisienne). TP (Transports Presses). MLP (Messageries Lyonnaise de Presse)	Over 33 000 retail outlets for newspapers and magazines. Most press (approximately half) is sold at specialised forms of kiosks.
Germany: population 81 million	Apart from the *Bild-Zeitung* newspaper, almost all distribution systems are linked to regional newspaper production. For *Bild*, the newspaper is sold through normal retail distribution outlets from shops to petrol stations.	Subscription services using postal networks are important in Germany for distribution. It is estimated that over 110 000 retail outlets sell newspapers.
The Netherlands: population 15 million	Postal services (e.g. TPG 2002) very important for delivery of newspapers. Equally, individual newspapers such as *De Telegraaf* have their own distribution networks.	It is estimated that there are up to 9000 press retails outlets.

Source: *World Press Trends* (WAN, 2005).

e-distribution development at the forefront. The new ICT networks are also interconnected through compatible cable, satellite and general telecommunications. Translation software now means that access across frontiers to 'foreign language' newspapers, for example, is on the increase, although in the main this remains a small percentage of readers.

Even so, this is happening in an environment where the EU encourages the movement of 'national' and cross-national published material. To follow this cross-media development we must read the above comment in conjunction with the other chapters on audio-visual development (Chapters 9–11) including the views on distribution to be found therein.

Chapter summary

- The distribution network of the publishing and print industry is being changed by the new technology. At this stage, it is difficult to predict its final destination, but the digital age is already an integral part of the press and print industry and its future in the industry is probably on the increase in the long term.
- There are major debates surrounding the impact of the new technology. From an EU and even national point of view the distribution techniques of the press are linked to other more civic connections. The divide between public and private sectors, not notable in the press and print industry, is being touched by the new age, blurring the distinctions in terms of communication.
- Nonetheless, the economics of the industry looks closely at the distribution network as a part of its costs and price calculations in an age which is building increasing competition across the different sectors of the media.

Key terms

Liberalised: the use of this word needs some care – it means different things in different settings. In the EU single market it is associated with 'privatisation' or adding to the private sector. Nevertheless the level of 'liberalisation' varies from sector to sector in the EU, and it should not be treated as just one easily defined process.

TEN-T: trans-European networks. The EU has to a certain extent prioritised trans-national network improvements including the transport system see: http://ec.europa.eu/ten/transport/index_en.htm.

Discussion questions

1. To what extent has distribution of print products changed over the past few centuries?
2. Has the EU aided or hindered the new digital techniques of distribution in Europe?
3. Has newspaper print consumption increased or decreased and, in each case depending on your answer, why?
4. Using the simulation exercise case study (Case Study 7.2), describe the use of different editions in press distribution.
5. What are the advantages and disadvantages of using digital distribution for newspapers? Apply your thinking to the EU market environment.
6. Do podcasting and blogging threaten newspapers?
7. How important is the postal system in Europe for the delivery of newspaper and print products?
8. Describe in brief terms the economic consequences of digital age related newspaper distribution.
9. Describe three EU member states' methods of distributing their print products.

Assignments

1. Compare and contrast the classic and the new distribution techniques used in the print and publishing industries. Cite examples.
2. Analyse the strengths and weaknesses of the PricewaterhouseCoopers' report on the publishing industry. It would be a good idea to dip into other chapters in the book for ideas and examples.
3. Taking the long and the short views, what impact will the digital age have on the distribution of 'print' content in Europe. What will be some of the factors leading to success? Define your terms.

Further reading

Bird & Bird (2002) *Market Definition in the Media Sector: a Comparative Analysis*, Luxembourg: European Commission, DG Competition.

Datamonitor (2006) *Newspapers in the Netherlands: industry profile*, London: Datamonitor (Market Business Line).

Datamonitor (2008) *Books in France: industry profile*, London: Datamonitor (Market Business Line).

EC (2005) *Publishing Market Watch Final Report*, Luxembourg: European Commission, DG Enterprise.

EC (2005) Commission Staff Working Paper. *Strengthening the Competitiveness of the EU Publishing Sector. The role of media policy*, Luxembourg, European Commission.

EMCC (2004) *Sector Futures: in Search of a Realistic Future*, Dublin: European Foundation for the Improvement of Living and Working Conditions.

EMCC (2004) *Sector Futures: Publishing and Media: Balancing the Interests of Producers and Consumers*, Dublin: European Foundation for the Improvement of Living and Working Conditions.

Ernst & Young (2007) *Competitiveness of the European Graphic Industry*, Luxembourg: European Communities.

Europe Economics (2002) *Market Definition in the Media Sector – Economic Issues*, Luxembourg: European Commission, DG Competition.

Harcourt A. (2002) Europeanization as convergence: the regulation of media markets in the European Union, in K. Featherstone and C. Radaelli (eds), *The Politics of Europeanisation*, Oxford: Oxford University Press, 179–203.

Harcourt A. (2006) *European Union Institutions and the Regulation of Media Markets*, Manchester and New York: Manchester University Press.

Pira International (2003) *The EU Publishing Industry: an Assessment of Competitiveness*, Luxembourg: European Communities.

Online resources

http://www..

Again our online resources are almost seemingly immense and the following is only an indication of major, important online organisations:

- *Datamonitor (Market Business Line)* http://www.datamonitor.com/
- *DG Information Society* http://europa.eu/index_en.htm
- *European Communication Research and Education Association (ECREA)* http://www.ecrea.eu/
- *European Institute for the Media (EIM)* http://www.eim.org/
- *European Journalism Centre (EJC)* http://www.ejc.net/
- *Eurostat* http://ec.europa.eu/eurostat/
- *Hans-Bredow-Institut* http://www.hans-bredow-institut.de/
- *World Association of Newspapers (WAN)* http://www.wan-press.org/

References

Anthony S., Gilbert C. (2006) Can the newspaper industry stare disruption in the face? 'Lessons learned from past failures can help to ensure future triumphs,' *Niemen Reports*, Spring, http://www.nieman.harvard.edu/reports/06-1NRspring/p43-0601-anthony-gilbert.html

Bradshaw T. (2008) TV holds its ground against web video, *FT.com*, 12 August.

Christou G., Simpson S. (2004) *Emerging Patterns of E-Commerce Governance in Europe: the European Union's Directive on E-Commerce*, Draft, Paper prepared for the 32nd Telecommunications Policy Research Conference: Communication, Information and Internet Policy, George Mason University Law School, Arlington, Virginia, US, October 1–3.

Datamonitor (2006) *Newspapers in the Netherlands: industry profile*, London: Datamonitor (Market Business Line).

Datamonitor (2008) *Books in France: industry profile*, London: Datamonitor (Market Business Line).

EC (2005a) Commission Staff Working Paper. *Strengthening the Competitiveness of the EU Publishing Sector. The role of media policy*, Luxembourg, European Commission.

EC (2005b) *Publishing Market Watch Final Report*, Luxembourg: European Commission, DG Enterprise.

EC (2006) *Communication from the commission to the council, the European parliament, the European economic and social committee and the committee of the regions on the Review of the EU Regulatory Framework for electronic communications networks and services*, Brussels, 29 June.

EMCC (2004) *Sector Futures: in Search of a Realistic Future*, Dublin: European Foundation for the Improvement of Living and Working Conditions.

Garcia M., Centeno M., Penaloza G. (1999) A simulation of the product distribution in the newspaper industry, *Proceedings of the 1999 Winter Simulation Conference*, Farrington P., Nembhard H., Sturrock D., Evans G. (eds), vol. 2, 1268–1271.

Humphreys P. (2002) Europeanisation, globalisation and policy transfer in the European Union: the case of telecommunications, *Convergence: the Journal of Research into New Media Technologies*, **8**(2): 52–79.

OECD (2002) *Measuring the Information Economy*, Paris, Organisation for Economic Co-operation and Development.

OECD (2006) *Policy Considerations for Audio-visual Content Distribution in a Multiplatform Environment*, Paris: Organisation for Economic Co-operation and Development.

OECD (2007) *OECD Communications Outlook 2007*, Paris: Organisation for Economic Co-operation and Development.

Porter, M. (1998) *The Competitive Advantage of Nations*, Free Press.

PwC (2002) *Global Entertainment and media outlook: 2002–2006 – Forecasts and economic analyses of 13 industry segments*, New York: PricewaterhouseCoopers.

Thatcher M. (2001) The Commission and national governments as Partners: EC regulatory expansion in telecommunications 1979–2000, *Journal of European Public Policy*, **8**(4): 558–584.

WAN (2003) *World Press Trends*, Paris: World Association of Newspapers.

WAN (2005) *World Press Trends*, Paris: World Association of Newspapers.

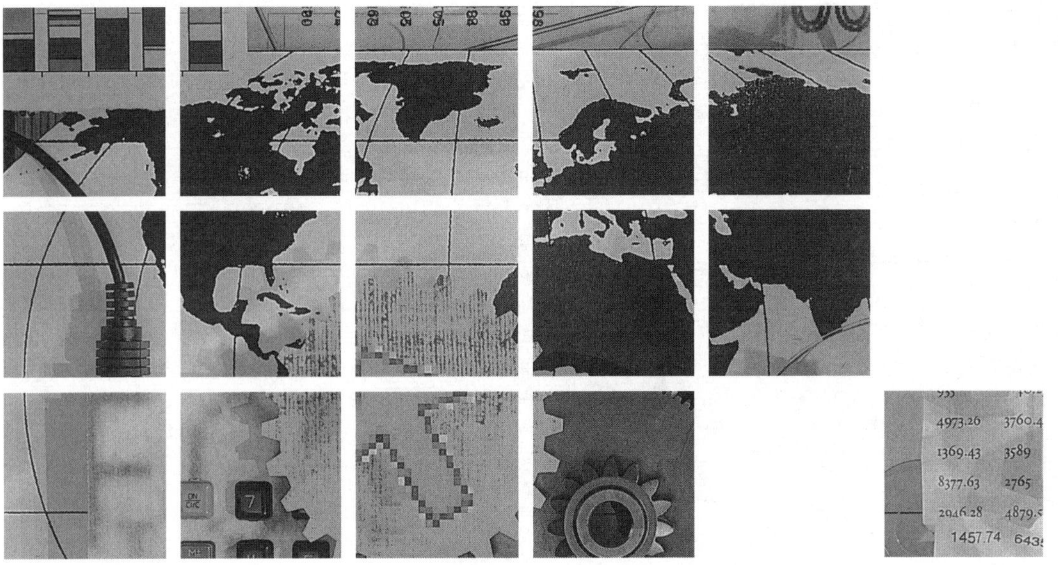

Chapter 8

The consumption of print and publishing material

What this chapter covers

Learning objectives

When you have completed this chapter you will be able to:

- Identify a variety of sources that can be used to assess the print and publishing consuming environment.
- Outline the interweaving of interests in corporate structures that impact upon consumption.
- Ascertain the major corporations operating in the EU print and publishing market.
- Discuss the relative differences between 'mass retail' and 'distance sales' and their impact on the consumption of print and publishing products.
- Compare and contrast consumption across a range of products including newspapers, periodicals, magazines, reviews, books and advertising products.
- Locate policy developments at EU and national levels.

Themes

Below you will find a simple statement or series of statements around the six themes. They should *not* be read as a given fact. They are more like hypotheses (see Chapter 2) which need to be proved, discussed, debated and then used in your own analysis of the subject. The ideas and approaches in this book are always to be considered with an open mind; this is important in university study and is what makes it distinct from pre-university study.

Diversity of media

The print, publishing and press industries have always been diverse in consumption across the European scene and in different sectors. The separation of reading habits into the three activities of newspapers, books and magazines is added to by the presence of 'advertising' print material which is significant and profitable. Change in the market and convergence are occurring across the sector, but it is a slower process than many think in some areas. So although convergence of consumer habits appears to be happening, diversity remains important in the EU.

Internal/external forces for change

The print industry has been for most EU member states in private hands. Competition is keenly felt in all forms of publication. Although often seen in national terms, competition is increasingly trans-national and even global. However, the internal dynamic of the regional press for example shows the range of pressures within the sector.

Complexity of the media

The fact that the print industry is in the main in private hands does not necessarily make the sector less complex. The historical development of the print industry and the various regulatory controls around it has been deep, wide and various. The most notable change has been the inclusion in recent years, following the downfall of the 'Iron Curtain', of Central and Eastern European states who are emerging from state control and censorship. This has allowed for a surge of consumer activity in these areas.

Multi-levels

It is intriguing to note that the press, and especially newspapers, across the EU is more likely to be regional in form than national. Trans-national newspapers do occur but, because of language and printing practice, they often remain better understood in the national sphere. Even so, convergence of production and distribution and a trend toward a concentration of ownership of the print and publishing industries across the EU is happening, and this is a major factor for their immediate future. The full impact of this upon the consumer is yet to be fully evaluated.

European integrative environment

The EU has set out through the Single European Market a framework for company and corporate practice with which the private sector needs to comply. The print and publishing industries, although often nationally described, must now be seen in terms of the EU dimension of the market as much as global or regional pressures. Policies such as 'right of reply' and citizenship rights are now a part of the consumer scene for all EU citizens.

Cultural values

Despite the increasing impact of new technology on the sector, reading remains a paper-based exercise for the great majority. Although this will change as the years unfold, as with content, the cultural dimension embedded in the industries remains in many ways beyond the medium, located in deeper social, political, historical and even ideological concerns for the communities that make up the EU. All of these inhabit the world of the EU consumer.

Essentials

➤ The print industry from a consumer's point of view across Europe is healthy and vibrant, but it faces competitive challenges which are bombarding the consumer: television, internet information, new delivery platforms, larger and more complex markets, all of which are working and being financed on a global as well as a national scale. These are adding to the existing and long-standing range of competitors in newspapers and magazines which operate more at local and national levels.

➤ All of this brings together a range of issues, not only in terms of competitivity and innovation, but also more fundamental questions: what is, for example, a newspaper in the digital age, what is it for, and for whom it is written? Are we heading for a new world where 'news' (or information) is apparently 'free' and always online? Moreover, and to complicate matters, in the various parts of the European scene, consumer choice is located in different interests which are often local as much as they are trans-national. The answers are not easy.

➤ However, there are signs that the market is changing, but how much and why has encouraged new areas of investigation into consumer behaviour. This occupies owners, editors and journalists and also the financial backers. The list of interested parties does not stop there: advertisers, stock markets, and owners with their own capital, including multi-national, national, regional and local corporations as well as private individuals, infamously called the 'press barons' (Curran and Seaton, 2003) in the past or 'media moguls' in the present. They are all part of the production, distribution and consumption equation.

➤ In the end, the market will be driven by consumer choice or, more accurately, consumer purchase practice. To date the consumer in the European market while keen on new products is also slower to change than many producers and distributers often portray. In Europe this is due to the persistent national, linguistic and even historical tendencies that underpin the various communities.

Introduction: assessing the material available to researchers for the publishing industry – the data

Before looking at the various publishing consumer-linked sectors we need to reflect on the data available to us as researchers. In some cases data will be partial, and it is often defined differently across the EU countries making comparisons an inexact science. There is a lot of data available, especially if we use national and retail sources, but making sense of the figures is another matter.

Data as we have seen is always linked to the purpose of the research (Chapter 2). So in reflecting on the choice of data, it is good to link our material to the question which we are seeking to answer. Drawing full data across the EU in the publishing industry is therefore fraught with complications. As researchers it is often a good practice to refer to the methodology and the difficulties of the statistics used in your analysis.

One of the best data sources is Eurostat, and we shall use some of its data in this chapter. One of its primary functions as a database is the study of trade, and it is very useful in looking at overall consumption in an EU context. Another good source is the European Journalism Centre (see Source 8.1), and without doubt one of the best and most reliable resources is the World Association of Newspapers (WAN) (see also Source 8.1). The published and freely available resources of the Organisation for Economic Co-operation and Development (OECD) are invaluable, although the publishing sector is not covered as fully as the new technologies of the audio-visual. Since 1998 the Compendium series of 'Cultural policies and trends in Europe' under a Council of Europe and the European Institute initiative for comparative cultural research is excellent. There are so many more.

Despite the difficulties of finding and using consumer-based material, there are many very worthy data-based sources open to us, each with their own strengths and perhaps weaknesses. For example,

Source 8.1

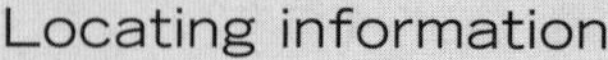

Locating information

Locating data and commentary on the print and publishing industry on the World Wide Web is not always straightforward. The following list is an extract from the listed sites on the European Audiovisual Observatory website. Care is needed to ensure we are using up-to-date material of a reliable nature. All sites should be used with some caution. In this case, and even with an excellent resource such as the European Audiovisual Observatory, many of the sites indicated could not be used and have been excluded from our list below because of updating issues or changes in web addresses. Nonetheless, the list below is indicative of one small part of the material available to us as researchers.

Press and Journalism: Institutes and Professional Organisations: Association of European Journalists; European Journalism Centre; European Newspaper Publishers' Association; Federation of European Magazine Publishers; International Press Institute; World Association of Newspapers.

Directories of Newspapers, Magazines and Websites of Newspapers: Benn's Media (Hollis Publishing), Media Guardian.

Book Publishing: World Wide Library: publishers; *The Bookseller*.

Datamonitor (Market Business Line) uses data for 'Europe' based on a sample rather than the full complement of EU member states and refers to non-EU (e.g. Norway) as well as EU countries in its assessment of sector development (e.g. publishing and/or the newspaper industry). Even one of the most definitive reports on EU publishing (EC, 2005) uses a sample as a base for the analysis and not the full EU membership which in 2008 comprised 27 member states.

Most trade data is recorded (e.g. Eurostat) through NACE categories which have recently been updated. To complicate matters, within the industry you will find detailed analysis of the market which is beyond the standard classifications of NACE (see Chapter 4) or trading categories. A typical example is indicated in Case Study 8.1. It illustrates how important factors such as content, market segment and different editions are taken into consideration for sales advice in the book industry (in this case in the UK). In reviewing the actual development of the market it is good to refer to both the standard categories of trade *and* the industry's own analysis.

Moreover consumption involves not just products but also how they are delivered to us. In the present era, the industry is coming to grips with a new impetus in technology which is directing some of the changing pattern of consumer behaviour (Chapter 7). This is not new: from block press to rolling cylinder, from scribe to microprocessor, from radio to television, from cable to analogue to digital, the industry has adapted to technological change, and so too has the consumer. As a prime source of 'news' and

Case Study 8.1

How to categorise the various aspects of the industry: beyond NACE classifications

Trade categories are very useful in our understanding of the industry. But often inside the industry more detailed analysis occurs beyond NACE classifications. As an example, notice the importance in the book industry of hardback and paperback editions. Why is this important? Cost and profit are dominant of course, but it also depends on where a book is read and what kind of reader and outlet is being targeted. The USA uses slightly different categories – in the USA version known as NAICS.

Point of View 8.1

Hans-Bredow-Institut, Germany

Recent work from the Hans-Bredow-Institut, for example, points towards factors which include new technology of course; but this is only a part of the changing EU-based cross-national consumer behaviour.

- Greater cross-language audiences/readers are dependent upon level of education and competence.
- Technical change is providing for easier access, e.g. internet, cable, and this is potentially important for larger cross-national audiences/readership.
- More trans-national products are being created e.g. *Euronews* and *Eurosport*, although many remain founded on the audio-visual.
- Greater mobility (integration) in Europe means wider 'audiences'.
- Interpreting the multi-layered reasons for choice is leading to continuing debate on how to evaluate the data.

Source: http://www.hans-bredow-institut.de/english/index.html.

Note: the *Working papers* section is excellent and so is the Institute's published handbook: *Internationales Handbuch Medien* 2004/2005 (International Media Handbook, 2004/2005).

information, the publishing industry has spread its range to embrace a cohesive, more entertainment-led market; hence the growth in magazine and similar consumption.

Assessing the impact of the new technology is a constant question within the industry; this should not come as any surprise as the industry has always been fundamentally technologically-driven. A recent report from the Hans-Bredow-Institut (see Point of View 8.1) reminds us that, for example, trans-national consumption is not just about technology but is as much to do with consumer choice *in situ*.

Certainly, the consumer will react to the 'availability' of e-resources; the internet and 'blogging', for example, are seen as real challenges to newspaper professional reporting and standard entertainment magazines. Ultimately, some commentators seem to envisage that we are moving toward the demise of the paper newspaper, although the present consumption figures do not necessarily indicate this.

Interpretation and judgement

Interpretation and judgement of the comparative research data material is also important but is complicated by language differences across Europe. However, it does appear that content is converging in a world of easier access to international and even European formats. Take a quick look at the front page of many of the newspapers across the EU and we will note similar types of format in use. In certain instances some newspapers have even experimented in the joint sharing of material, e.g. *The Guardian* in the UK worked for a while with the newspaper *Libération* in France. Editorials and cartoons (humour) may stubbornly remain local in their approach, but it is perhaps surprising to see how much is similar across the EU, especially in the newspaper market, although nominally it remains nationally defined by consumer tastes.

What is equally powerful to note is how the consumption of the media, including many publishing products, has, until very recently, been structurally tied to the territorial and political constitutions of the nation states. There is great diversity across Europe in how newspapers, for example, are consumed, even if they look similar. This varies from the much centralised, national structures such as the constitutional monarchy of the UK, to the much more regional–national balances you find in Federal Germany and even Republican France. This mimics not only the formal political construction but also the fundamental societies and communities that form the nation states of the EU.

Stop and consider 8.1

When we consider consumer behaviour in a comparative way, how useful is it to measure the influence of 'nationality'? It is true that much of the data available to us is put in national form, in one way or another, such as that used by Eurostat. But in a world that is moving into trans-national media, where translation of material into many languages is not only culturally and technologically possible but often driven by the need for large readerships and hence profits, are national figures useful? Ask yourself this question as the chapter unfolds. There is perhaps no one definitive answer.

Mobility and cross-national consumption in general within the EU is on the increase as noted by the latest migration figures, albeit a minority affair to date. Yet, the data on consumption often looks contradictory from a pan-European point of view. In the main newspapers and publishing houses are doing well, but overall readership is declining even if the decline is marginal in some sectors; newspaper readership in some countries is declining, but newspapers overall have seen a trend towards increasing pagination, especially in the quality press. Magazine readership is increasing, but the sharing of cross-frontier material means you may see the same photograph of a celebrity in a variety of formats and languages across the EU, emanating from an ever smaller band of successful press and photo agencies.

In the final analysis, though, it is the major structural changes happening in production and distribution techniques across the EU which are impacting on all consumers in all or most communities of the EU (see Case Study 8.2). The industry is a significant

Case Study 8.2

Newspapers and publishing in Germany and France – news reports

Keeping a weather eye on newspaper reports concerning the publishing industry is worthwhile. They often indicate corporate and policy movements of importance. For example:

Guardian Media; Flora Wisdorff, 9 December 2004, reported under the banner 'Germans turn to tabloids – but not as we know them', that the broadsheet *Die Welt* had absorbed a new sister paper a tabloid *Welt Kompakt*, beginning an experiment in using smaller size formats, a forerunner of what is now called the 'Berliner' format. It was it seems a success and the format has rapidly spread across many European newspapers including the quality press in the UK. The old separation between broadsheets and tabloids, based on what was seen as different reading consumer groups, has increasingly become meaningless across the EU.

Financial Times; Adam Jones, 31 July 2006 reported under the banner 'Costly kiosk: how French dailies are struggling to retain their savoir faire', that most French newspapers were under severe financial strain with representatives of the left-leading newspapers in particular trouble. He reported that the long-lasting editor of the newspaper *Libération* had been sacked as the paper had been absorbed into the Rothschild family of companies. Representative of the movement of 1968, the newspaper *Libération* had finally been absorbed into the mainstream 'capitalistic' system: it was a poignant and significant moment in recent French press history.

Financial Times; Odile Eposito, Ross Tieman and Lutz Meier, 5 July 2007, under the banner 'Axel Springer shelves French tabloid plans' reported that one of the major publishing groups in the EU was holding back on launching a French version of its successful German *Der Bild* newspaper even though it had targeted over 120 000 outlets for sales. The publishing chief said the proposed €12 million project held 'more risks than opportunities'. Indicative of the problems of creating trans-national operated newspapers, the report also pointed out that the publishing group Axel Springer was retaining control of its four successful magazines sold in the French market: *Tele Magazine, Vie Pratique Gourmand, Vie Pratique Madam* and *Vie Pratique Santé* – all lifestyle publications. This is exemplary of the type of cross-national, trans-national activity which is underpinning EU corporate developments in the sector.

part of any economy, worth billions. The competition for this market, and its consumers, is no longer local, regional or national but European and global, and that competition is keen and becoming keener, whether in times of economic growth or downturn.

The figures and reports, so difficult to collate accurately across the EU, alter depending on the source. For example, in one report, newspapers are put at 37% of the total sector (Ernst & Young, 2007) in another, less than 30% (Datamonitor, 2007 – see Case Study 8.3). Even so, the broad trend remains: newspapers are important, but it is the book and the magazine market which, when combined with newspapers, makes the sector so vibrant. If you add in the advertising sector as a part of the publishing industry – and Datamonitor do in its recent reports (see Case Study 8.3) – we find that this sector of the publishing industry is the most 'lucrative'. It is equally the sector which normally suffers the most when economic downturn hits.

In this mix of competing categories and market analysis, the publishing corporations play a key role. It is convenient in our analysis to separate the print industry per se from its combination with publishing corporations, and other publishing groups. By so doing we will be able to understand more clearly how the print and publishing industry works and how it relates to its consumers.

However, before we look at the top companies who serve EU consumers, we need also to investigate how major corporations are organised into many sub-groups – the horizontal and vertical integration

Case Study 8.3

Newspaper, magazine and book market by segmentation share and including the advertising publishing sector, at the start of the 21st century

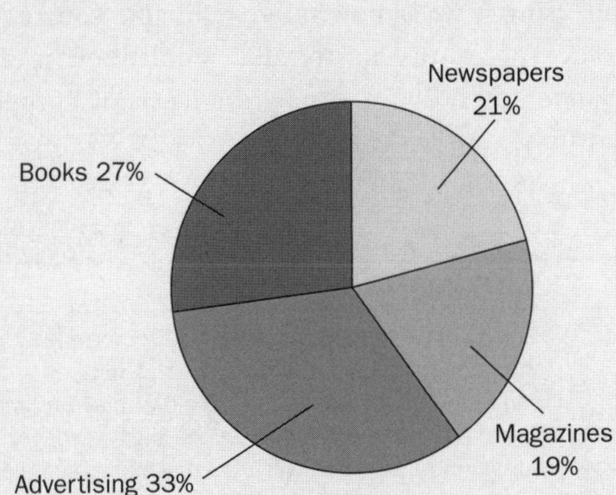

Europe publishing market segmentation: percentage share, by value (2007)

Source: Based on Datamonitor (2006, 2007)

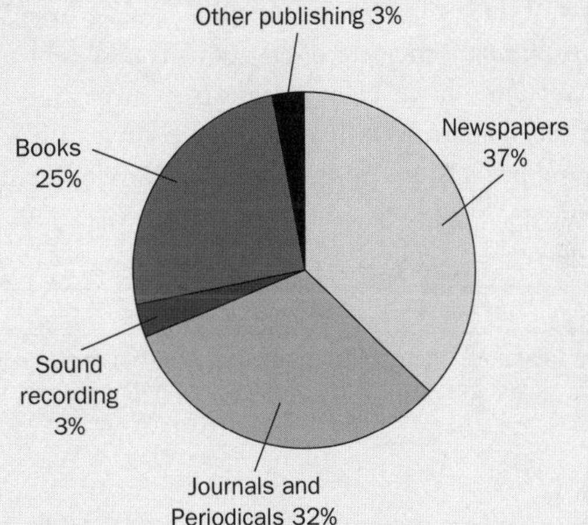

Publishing sub-sectors (in production value) (2001)

Source: Based on Eurostat, *New Cronos Database* (2004), see http://www.esds.ac.uk/international/support/user_guides/eurostat/cronos.asp.

Over the past few years the figures for 2001–2007 have indicated small movements in share. There are different ways of expressing this, but the ratios are very similar even if we compare different years. Datamonitor uses segmentation share by value (on the left) for 2007 using a sample of European countries, whilst Eurostat (on the right) uses production value for a recent report (*New Cronos*, 2004) based on the EU-15 figures for 2001.

Case Study 8.4

Vertical and horizontal integration (see Chapter 3) in practice: how companies are often structured

In the Holtzbrinck group, for example, we can see that there were major and well-known publishing houses crossing the spectrum of consumer interest (MacMillan, Channel 4 books, Picador and so on). This is the case with Hachette (Lagardère) and Time Warner, both of whom competed with Holtzbrinck. Note too, the link to the entertainment industry as a whole, where film making (Warner) and television production (Channel 4) content are embraced within the publishing industries' products. This sits alongside more traditional book publishing: books for women (Virago), fiction and non-fiction (Orion) and so on.

Main company	*Sub-divisions*
Holtzbrinck (Verlagsgruppe Georg von Holtzbrinck GmbH)	MacMillan, Channel 4 Books, Picador, Pan Books and Boxtree
Hachette (Lagardère)	Orion, Cassell, Gollancz, Phoenix, Weidenfeld & Nicolson
Time Warner	Warner, Orbit, Virago, Abacus, Little, Brown

that we referred to previously (see Chapter 3 and Case Study 8.4). What the consumer buys is often linked to these different chains of providers which at the point of sale are not easily discernible.

When the consumer buys a product it may well be a part of these complex corporations. Due to branding techniques, they are often not as transparent to the consumer as we might assume. It could be argued that this matters, as it highlights the complex financial and profit motives behind product development. On the other hand, does the consumer really worry that much about the production and the distribution techniques when it is the product itself perhaps that dominates in consumer choice? There is much to debate here.

Nonetheless and according to the latest reports, and using a well-known and reputable source, the top corporations in the EU publishing market (Datamonitor, 2007) serving the needs of European consumers are as shown in Table 8.1.

Table 8.1 Leading companies (publishing)

Leading companies	*Subsidiaries*	*Publishing*
Bertelsmann AG	RTL Group; Random House, Gruner + Jahr, BMG, Arvato (printing) and Direct Group (book clubs, DVDs and stores).	Random House includes over 100 editorially independent book publishers – e.g. Knopf and Doubleday (US), Ebury (UK), Seidler and Goldmann (Germany). Gruner + Jahr are the biggest magazine publisher in Europe (over 300 magazines, in over 20 countries).
Emap PLC	Segments: B2B; UK consumer magazines; international consumers; radio and TV. Mainly operates in the UK, Australia, the USA and South Africa.	Multi-platform media group – consumer magazines, radio, music, television, websites, trade magazines, trade exhibitions.
Axel Springer	Segments: newspapers, magazines, printing (e.g. Prinovis) and services.	Main activities focused on France, Spain, Switzerland, but expanding towards Poland, Hungary, Czech Republic and Russia.
News Corporation Ltd	A diversified, international media and entertainment company.	Operates globally, but especially the USA, Europe (major player in the UK), Australia, Asia and the Pacific Basin.

European consumption and trends

European consumption of print and published products is changing. The generally agreed reason for the change is the impact of the new information and communication technologies (see Source 8.2).

Household measurement: disposable income

Note: audiovisual comparison and further detail is given in Chapter 11.

Inside the EU, Eurostat has been following the development of European spending, including household spending, since the beginning of the 1960s under the broad heading of 'Living conditions and social protection'. Eurostat normally publishes data approximately every five years in two household surveys: Household Budget Surveys (HSBs) and 'Community statistics on living conditions'. Since the 1960s the spend on the publishing industry and books and newspapers has shown growth and development inside the EU. There are of course diversities as already mentioned elsewhere (see Chapter 2 on the handling of newspaper statistics).

However, the latest figures show a marked drop overall in the purchase of these products, and from one commentary to another it seems that the new generation in the 21st century has shifted some of its major reading and viewing habits to the electronic screen. This shows itself in the figures, at least in household percentage choices where spending is being invested in new technology at the expense of traditional published products (Eurostat Pocketbooks, *Cultural Statistics*, 2007, p. 85 available at http://epp.eurostat.ec.europa.eu/cache/ITY_OFFPUB/KS-77-07-296/EN/KS-77-07-296-EN.PDF).

> Up until 2000, Europe-wide the annual production index of the newspaper publishing sector was higher than that of the consumer goods industry and boosted the growth of publishing. Since 2000–2001 the indices of each publishing sub-activity have all been showing a downward trend, whereas the consumer goods index is continuing to rise. One reason for this reversal may be changing consumer habits, notably the success of the Internet and the on-line availability of an abundance of information and publications.
>
> (*ibid.*, pp. 75–76)

Assessing the importance of individual household spend in this sector on such matters as newspaper or book purchase is interesting, but as the figures are

Source 8.2

Changes in the economy related to information and technology: European Monitoring Centre on Change

To engage with the debates we will need a means of monitoring the sector. The EU has set up some very visible monitoring centres for a range of polices including the European Monitoring Centre on Change (EMCC) created in 2001 to review major trends in the EU economy: As early as 2003, the EMCC was reflecting on IT and technological development impact in these terms for the publishing industry:

> . . . publishing and media is a very broad category embracing a wide variety of different sub-sectors, sometimes bearing little relation to one another. Definitions of the sector vary, but generally include industries as diverse as: filmed entertainment; terrestrial, cable and satellite television; music recording; newspapers and magazines; business information; educational, professional and consumer book publishing; advertising. . . . It is a complex sector: because economies of scale are important, media markets tend to be highly concentrated, and media companies frequently operate in more than one sub-sector. This broad and complex picture means it is difficult to envisage a single future that would be both complete and relevant to the sector as a whole . . .
>
> Source: *Sector Futures: Publishing and media: Balancing the Interests of Producers and Consumers*, p. 1 (EMCC, 2003).

Point of View 8.2

Pira International (for the European Commission)

Publishing has historically been linked with the manufacturing process of printing. The two activities have become increasingly decoupled in recent years, even more in the UK than in the rest of Europe, but the linkage has left a legacy of intertwined statistics. Secondly, the activities of publishing companies – especially the largest and most important ones – have increasingly come to span the whole gamut of print products, and have expanded beyond print on paper to electronic publishing, conferences and exhibitions, training and audiovisual media. But this shift is not reflected in the way that the statistics are collected, which still tends to be confined to the old divisions of books, newspapers and periodicals. This division is adhered to by official bodies, such as the Office of National Statistics and Eurostat. These bodies inevitably lag behind developments in the economy by some years because of the need to gain broad agreement on industry and trade classifications – these aren't lightly changed because of the importance of comparison over time and between countries. These problems are exacerbated in a sector like publishing where the speed and extent of change has been significant in recent years. However, the industry itself has also largely collected statistics on the basis of the traditional divisions. Of course, it may be argued that any system of collection must be product focused rather than company focused, since a single company can produce a wide range of products across many industries. The difficulty in publishing is that the core asset – content – can be manifested in a range of forms. It may be the identical content, but it may have added-value features – for example in its electronic form it may be searchable or it may be possible to integrate it into the customer's own computer system. It may be complementary content, for example many newspaper websites differ from the printed edition of the paper. The current data collection process does not really capture that dynamic in any way.

Source: Pira International, *Publishing in the Knowledge Economy: Competitive Analysis of the UK Publishing Industry*, Main report, p. 6 (Pira International, 2002) http://www.publishingmedia.org.uk/download/02dti_competitive_analysis.pdf.

often small, they tend in most analyses to be compounded, brought together to give overall weight to the general activity. This means that in many surveys the category in which this activity occurs is a mixed one. For example, reading a newspaper or a book, using the PC online and even going to the cinema are brought together under umbrella classifications such as 'leisure' activities or even 'free time'. Some of the data can be quite detailed. Mintel reports, on consumer activity in the UK, for example, are highly specialised, drawing down differences by age or by activity, and then collating them into trends. Most nation states and certainly consultancies across the EU perform this task for the sector.

In assessing the importance of the sector, commentators often revert to product choice rather than individual spend. In this way, the true impact of the consumption can be assessed. Yet the convergence of media is raising real issues as to how to collate and interpret the data which is valuable to us. An influential and high-standard report on the publishing industry in the UK (Point of View 8.2) made exactly this point.

On top of this complexity, change and uncertainty, the latest reports (*Competitiveness of the European Graphic Industry*, Ernst & Young, 2007) are intriguing as they point toward the creation of a new pattern of shopping and a new underlying market structure. The market trends in print and publishing are linked to these factors, and they are often beyond the immediate control of the industry.

'Mass retail' (the supermarket and the hypermarket)

It may be surprising to note the importance of the retail outlet for the print and publishing industry, but in many respects it is the key space where consumers choose their print and media products. During the period 1980–2000 in Western Europe and since 1990 in the EU as a whole, there has been, as recently reported:

> . . . a massive phase of concentration . . . that has led to the disappearance of almost all small retail shops. . . . The concentration of the sector is particularly significant in three main European markets, France, Germany and the UK, where the majors hold more than 60% of the market shares. . . . The consequence for the printing industry is that printers will be faced with the increased negotiation power of the retail groups, weakening the revenues of the printers . . .
> (Ernst & Young, 2007, p. 73)

The shift to what might be called the 'supermarket–hypermarket' society cannot be under-estimated. As we have seen in previous chapters, any producer within the print industry will need to know the space and the channels by which their products can be provided to their public. The distribution outlet will be very important if the point of sale space shifts. This alters many of the production processes, let alone the distribution mechanisms used by the industry and therefore the consumer, touching upon advertising, marketing and even in a wider sense the type of shopper, the consumer, of their products. The above citation from an important and influential report illustrates that the former classic outlets of the newsagent, the bookshop, the record shop, the video and DVD outlet, are threatened by the economies of scale that the supermarket and the hypermarket offer.

Stop and consider 8.2

To what extent is consumer behaviour changed by the point of sale? Think where you bought your last print or published product. Did it matter if it was a web site like Amazon, or a bookshop or specialist agency or a supermarket? What made you make the choice: the advertising, the price, the ease of ordering, or the reviews or write-ups on the product, whether in another outlet or by a reviewer you trust? What about the different products – does this alter where you buy: newspaper, magazine, book or even advertising material? When you see data on consumption do they include where the product was bought and does this point-of-sale environment come into the equation?

The extent to which the point-of-sale environment plays a part in consumption comes down to the wider question of choice and economic competition. As we previously indicated, the fear of monopolies encourages the EU to enhance competition at levels of production and distribution so the consumer has a choice. The extent to which this is happening is where the debate lies, and not least about the print industry, upon which of course newspapers, magazines and even books and advertising material rely.

The traditional printing process has often been located geographically close to its market, in small and medium-sized companies. The revenues that the local printers have relied upon have often been associated equally with a fragmented book, magazine, brochure and even newspaper market, if you include regional presses as well as national ones. Although traditionally fragmented, it should be emphasised that newspapers have been merging, buying across sectors (vertical and horizontal integration) for many decades in many European countries and that the same process is beginning to take place in their respective printing presses.

The advent and power of the new supermarkets within the distribution chain will impact upon the revenues of such companies. As we have seen in Chapter 3 on economics, where competitive advantage and economies of scale are key areas of market and product development, the growth of mass retailing will encourage the coalescence of interests and company mergers for the producers and a rationalisation of the distribution network. This will not be a revolution overnight but an evolutionary process which touches all aspects of the print and publishing industries, including consumption patterns.

Couple this to technological change, in a word the 'digital' age, and we are seeing a new publishing landscape being created in the 21st century. Printed and published products alike will be touched by this movement. The trends are already there to see, and the consumer and consumption will be indicative of the changes.

'Distance sales' (online sales)

If consumer behaviour is being altered by the changes in producers, distributors and the retail industry, the impact of online sales, sometimes known as 'distance sales', is as important if not more so.

The indications are that over the past 15 years the growth of online sales has been accelerating. This has touched the print and publishing industry in two ways. First, advertisers and advertising revenue, are increasingly being placed using analysis of consumer behaviour linked to use of the web. Second, many of the print and publishing industries are responding and placing their products directly either on the web itself or on the online sales sites which individual consumers can log on to.

Moreover, like the retail industry itself, distance sales or online sales are becoming an increasingly concentrated sector. The growth of corporations such as Amazon.com or eBay, or even direct online web sites for individual retail stores is a phenomenon which is relatively new and growing.

Although traditional sales through retail outlets, supermarket or specialist, remain for the time being the most important consumer practice, increasingly consumers are going online to order their products. The reasons behind this are often complex: price, availability and ease of use are all factors that the consumer will now reflect upon before purchase.

The EU distance sales market, it has been reported, has grown by 47% between 2000 and 2005. Whilst retail outlets linked to the print and publishing industry have been dropping in some areas, internet sales have been increasing. In the EU the impact varies from country to country, but in broad terms it is happening everywhere: the trend is likely to continue. In 2003 it was reported that the UK had become the largest e-commerce market inside the EU, but equally France, Italy and Germany have seen increased consumer activity in this area. Datamonitor's Marketline (see online resources) under 'Online retail', 'Publishing', 'Books' and 'Newspapers' is an excellent source of sales data within the industry.

Newspapers

As we have seen from our study of data in economics and statistics, trying to gauge exactly how the newspaper industry is faring in the present age is not easy, although on the surface there is a plethora of data from a variety of sources. Data is often contradictory and sometimes only partial as companies react to the new digital age. The detail it illustrates depends on the parameters (variables) being used and the research questions being posed, so work needs to be done to untangle its meaning.

Even so, the trends which we have seen developing over the past few years across the industry are the bedrock upon which change in the industry is based. It is useful then to at least review the 'old' categories of the publishing industry, bearing in mind that the classifications and the age we are entering will alter our perceptions of the industry in the very near future.

In broad productive terms, the newspaper industry from a corporate point of view is still very powerful, economically successful and, with an increasingly literate, educated and mobile public, potentially profit-laden (see Case Study 8.5). Rising costs indicate a paper industry still full of demand for its raw pulp material: paper and newsprint.

At the same time, the number of newspapers, as opposed to publishing in general, has reached either a point of saturation or a peak in the EU, in paper form, with a decrease in titles and increasing concentration of ownership. Some countries in the EU are showing a rapid decline in readership; others are more stable. In general Eastern Europe (the former communist influenced countries) has seen rising readership figures but, after the first ten years of integration with the West, this is now stabilising (see Case Studies 8.6, 8.7 and 8.8).

Moreover, from a consumption point of view, there appears to be a shift occurring in the readership, with a marked age difference, although there are some contradictions along the way: readers of newspapers in print form are ageing, it is argued. The new generation appears to be less interested in newspapers, or newspaper content, in its present form. Needless to say, we need to be careful and not too definitive in the multi-media multi-platform world of the present day: 'reading' is a wide-ranging activity and just because some elements among younger readers are not purchasing 'news' does not mean that they are refusing to read similar information elsewhere albeit in different forms.

The reasons underlying this are probably complex, and it should not be seen only as a response to the

Case Study 8.5

EU national newspaper circulation 1995–2001 (sample)

The predominant position of the UK and Germany followed by a second tier of France, Italy, The Netherlands and Spain is to be noted.

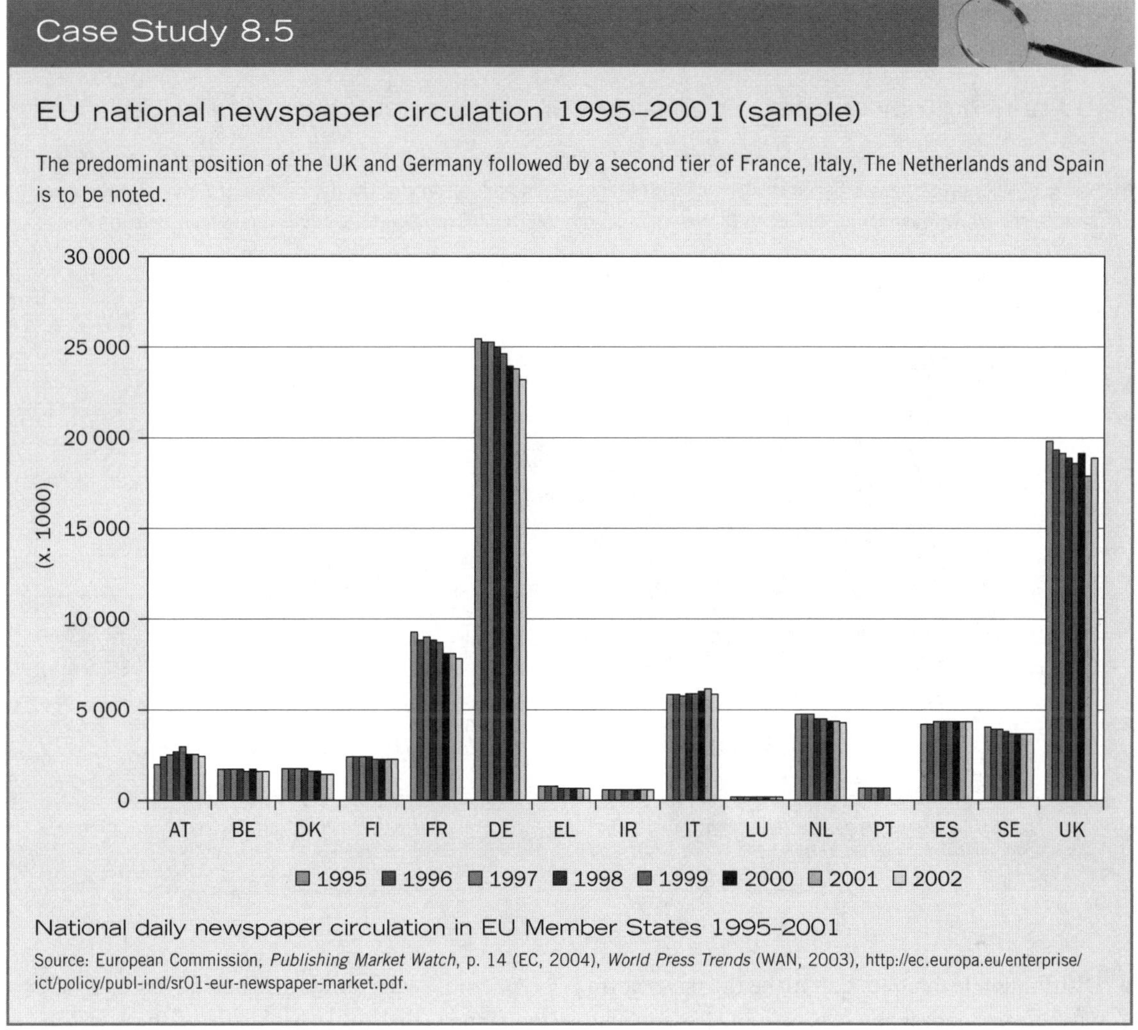

National daily newspaper circulation in EU Member States 1995–2001

Source: European Commission, *Publishing Market Watch*, p. 14 (EC, 2004), *World Press Trends* (WAN, 2003), http://ec.europa.eu/enterprise/ict/policy/publ-ind/sr01-eur-newspaper-market.pdf.

new digitally-based distributive technologies. As we have seen (Chapter 5), there are many theories to explain the development of any media system, and these will include social, cultural and political as well as economic forces, impacting on the consumer. Not least of course is the way in which non-daily newspapers are treated and consumed differently across Europe.

The various factors altering the younger generation in particular, but perhaps all generations eventually, include:

- IT access – meaning that information and entertainment are often freely available from a range of sources: headlines on mobiles, bulletins in news clips, television services as well as e-print.
- Increasing levels of participation in education within the EU (and it varies with the economic development of each nation state), from primary to tertiary to continuous professional training. This means that access to high-grade news and analysis is widely available to increasing numbers from a variety of high-class sources, and in particular is linked to the growth of non-daily sales, especially the weeklies and monthlies, with such products as *The Economist* or *Le Monde diplomatique*, *Les Echos*, etc.

Case Study 8.6

EU national newspaper circulation per 1000 population 1995–2002

The previous figure (Case Study 8.5) showed the 'big' national figures, but if we review the newspapers through this 'variable' setting the figures become different with Finland standing out in the EU as the one of national newspaper readers, though Sweden is not far behind. There is a strong tradition of newspaper reading throughout Scandinavia.

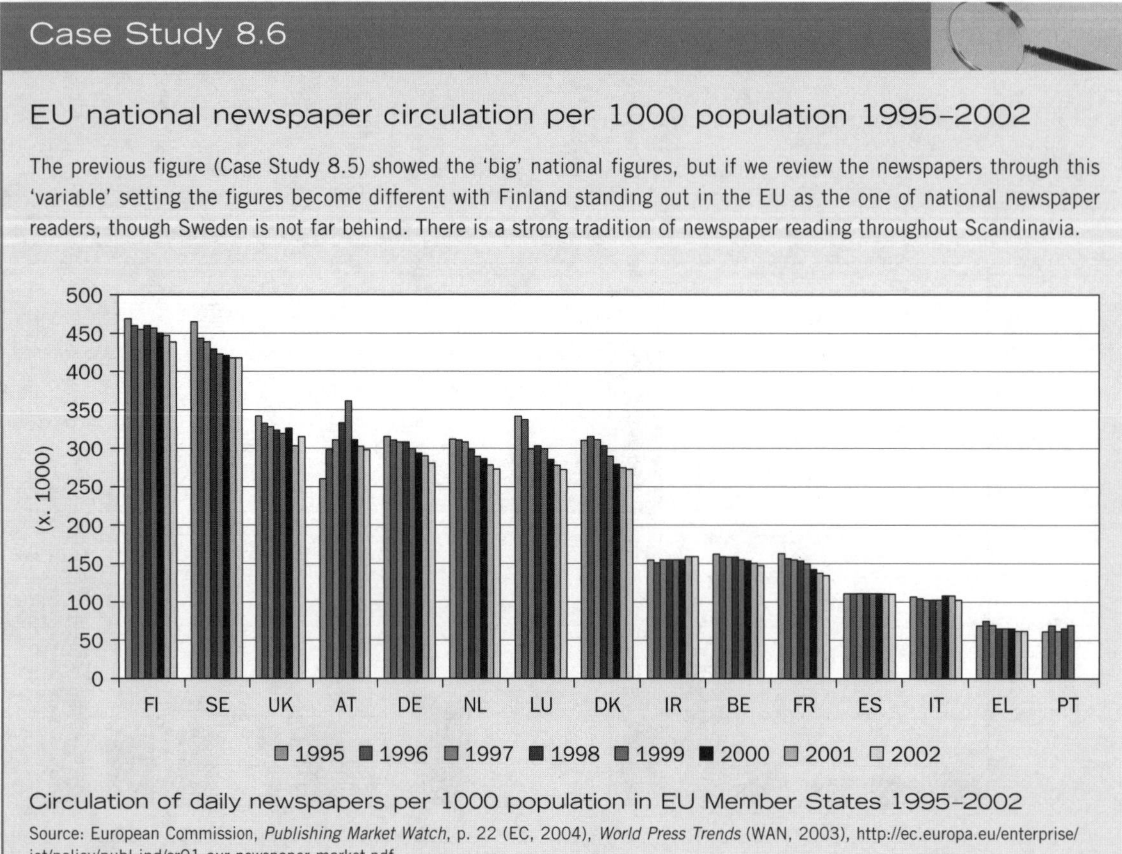

Circulation of daily newspapers per 1000 population in EU Member States 1995–2002

Source: European Commission, *Publishing Market Watch*, p. 22 (EC, 2004), *World Press Trends* (WAN, 2003), http://ec.europa.eu/enterprise/ict/policy/publ-ind/sr01-eur-newspaper-market.pdf.

- Distribution techniques that make the paper form of newspaper appear obsolete, slow and less enticing.
- The advent of 'free' (based purely on 100% advertising revenue) 'light' newspapers, which some readers find sufficient for 'news', compared to the deeper coverage in conventional newspapers, based on a 'subscription or sale plus advertising' revenue model (see Chapter 5).
- Other media absorbing the young (in the main), pulling them away from traditional reading-related pursuits (Sony's Playstation and Microsoft's Xbox and general PC games, home video and DVD, and online entertainment in the round).
- New forms of communication that circumvent normal writing and journalism such as blogging and podcasting, Facebook, MySpace, Bebo, and other similar sources.

As can be seen above, the new IT-based distribution system, that underlies many of these factors, is having the biggest impact on the forecasting of consumer choice. Most commentators see this as an immediate concern, but equally an issue for the print industry's foreseeable future, which also impacts upon consumption (see Source 8.3).

Moreover new evidence seems to suggest that this is not just a generational concern but is much more structural:

> The decline in newspaper circulation in Europe has been ongoing for two decades, with little sign of recovery. Evidence from research suggests that the decline is general across all age groups. Taking into account that circulation has also been falling in the US and Japan, it seems reasonable to assume that this decline is of a structural nature.
>
> (EC, 2005, p. 23)

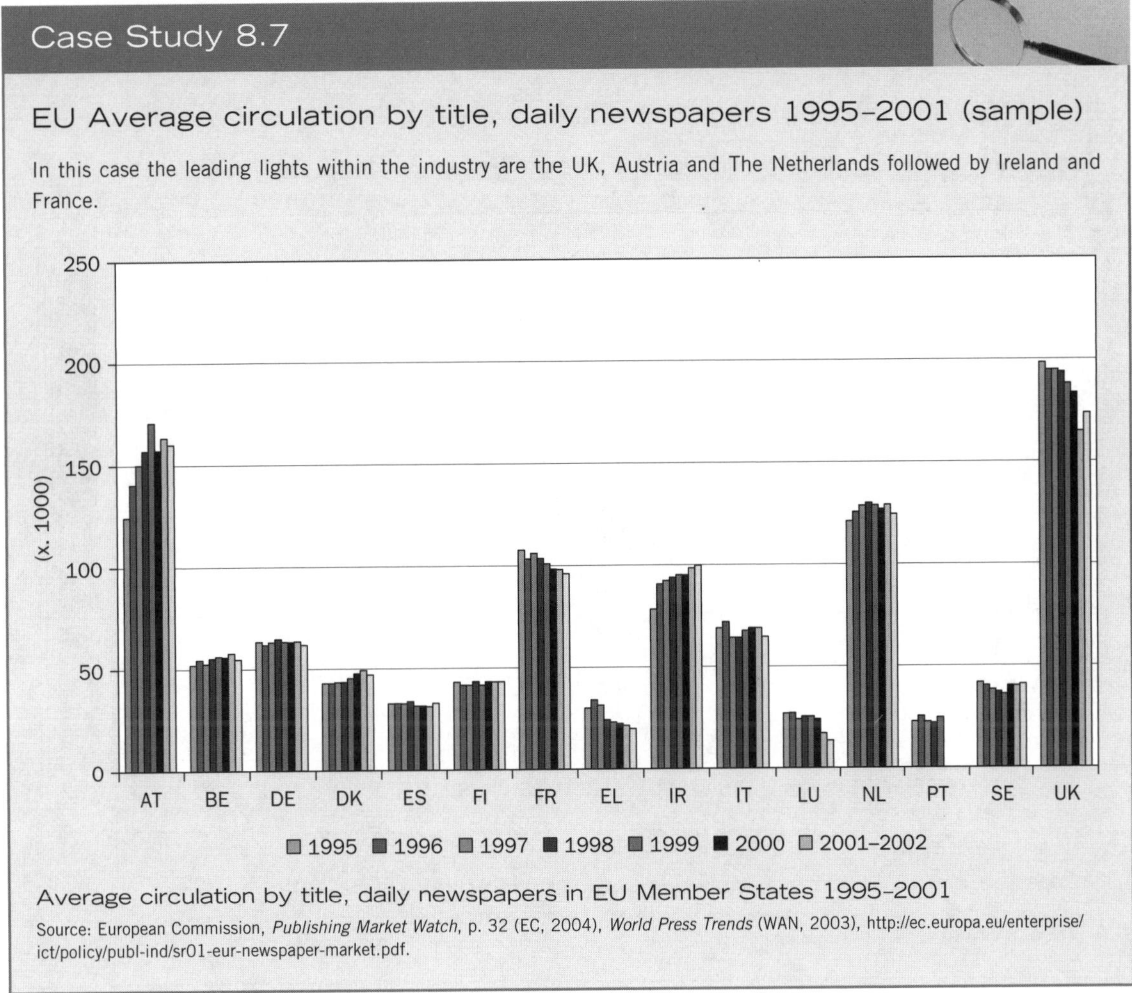

Case Study 8.7

EU Average circulation by title, daily newspapers 1995–2001 (sample)

In this case the leading lights within the industry are the UK, Austria and The Netherlands followed by Ireland and France.

Average circulation by title, daily newspapers in EU Member States 1995–2001

Source: European Commission, *Publishing Market Watch*, p. 32 (EC, 2004), *World Press Trends* (WAN, 2003), http://ec.europa.eu/enterprise/ict/policy/publ-ind/sr01-eur-newspaper-market.pdf.

Even so, as we have seen in previous chapters, the EU publishing industry as a whole remains buoyant when all the sectors are brought together, and these sweeping statements need to be put into a closer context if we are to understand the changes taking place.

'Free newspapers'

The advent of the 'free' newspaper has been a marketing and distribution success (see Case Studies 8.4, 8.7 and 8.9). It is also a sign of the times where new means of attracting advertising revenue have led to innovation in distribution practice. The first major 'free' newspaper in the EU was introduced in Sweden, *Metro*, quickly followed by papers from many of the large publishing houses aimed at targeted audiences in London (*Metro*, *London Lite*), Paris (*Metro*) and so on.

Most free newspapers are associated with larger publishing houses where economies of scale and competitive advantage can be used to best purpose (see Chapter 3). They are a part of a wider movement which includes the Internet and the web where advertising can be more targeted than before. Readerships are different for different newspapers, and the latter can be structured to appeal to different markets. Broadening the content to take in a wider audience but with less depth has obvious advantages, especially if papers are 'free' to the reader in

Case Study 8.8

EU non-daily newspapers 1995–2002 (sample)

Note here that the leading players were the UK, by far the biggest, followed by France and Finland.

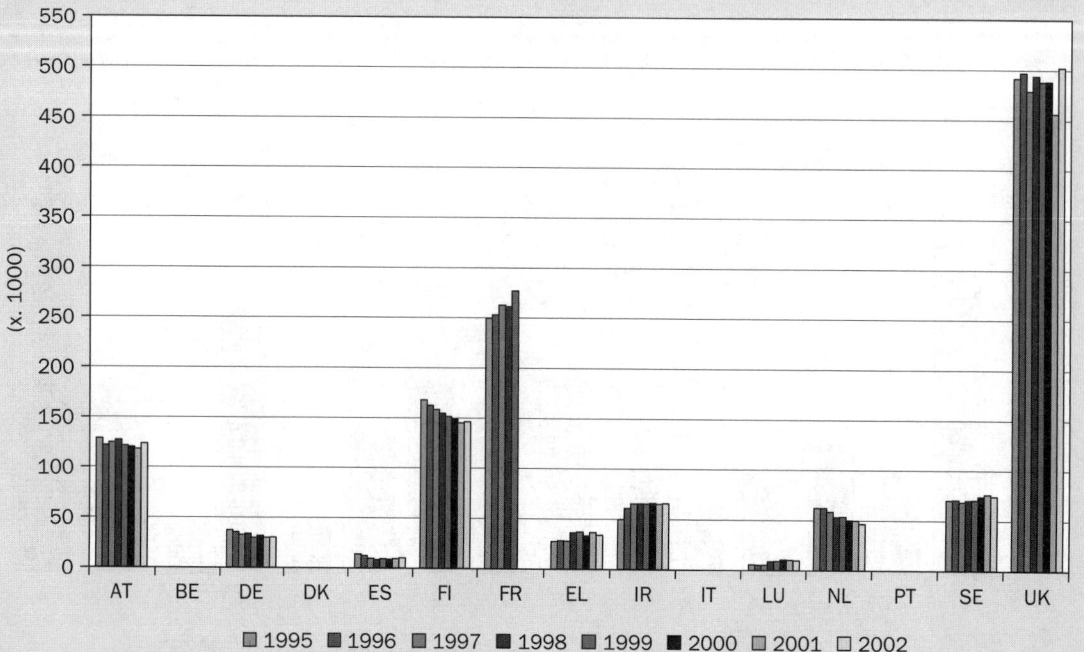

Number of non-daily papers published in EU Member States 1995–2002

Source: European Commission, *Publishing Market Watch*, p. 27 (EC, 2004), *World Press Trends* (WAN, 2003), http://ec.europa.eu/enterprise/ict/policy/publ-ind/sr01-eur-newspaper-market.pdf.

Source 8.3

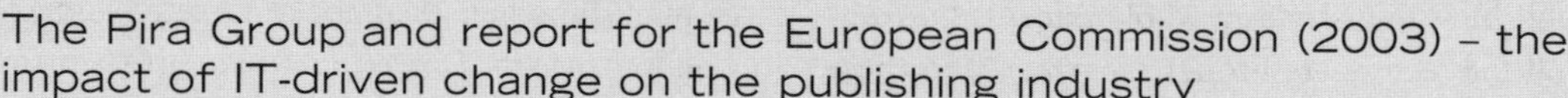

The Pira Group and report for the European Commission (2003) – the impact of IT-driven change on the publishing industry

The Pira-based European Commission report (2003) was designed to develop a greater understanding of the competitiveness of the EU publishing scene, investigating the possible impact on production and consumption: it included a commentary on the development of IT that is very telling. Note the keywords again below:

> **Gatekeepers** still exist and **closed networks** continue to be operated and therefore must be considered as an element within the sectoral value network. However, the multiplication of potential domestic and international **secondary markets** and the emergence of technologies and open networks allowing direct access to the consumer have fundamentally changed the nature of the relationship between content creators and gate keeping organisations. Operators of closed networks and providers of exclusive content may be challenged by disruptive technologies which may – legally or illegally – circumvent or challenge their position within the **value network**, shifting power to new forms of intermediary. One such example is the role played during the last few years by peer-to-peer file-sharing services such as Napster, KaZaa and Groove. (p. 35) '. . . The Internet has had the greatest impact on breaking down the boundaries between the publishing subsectors and between the publishing and audiovisual sectors, creating opportunities for both cooperation and competition . . .'
>
> Source: Pira International, UK, *The EU Publishing Industry: an Assessment of Competitiveness*, pp. 35–36 (Pira International, 2003), http://ec.europa.eu/enterprise/ict/policy/doc/pira_2003_1046_en.pdf.

Case Study 8.9

EU free newspapers

Germany, the UK, France, Spain and The Netherlands lead in this initiative for the time being.
The first set of figures shows EU member states 1995–2002 (sample).

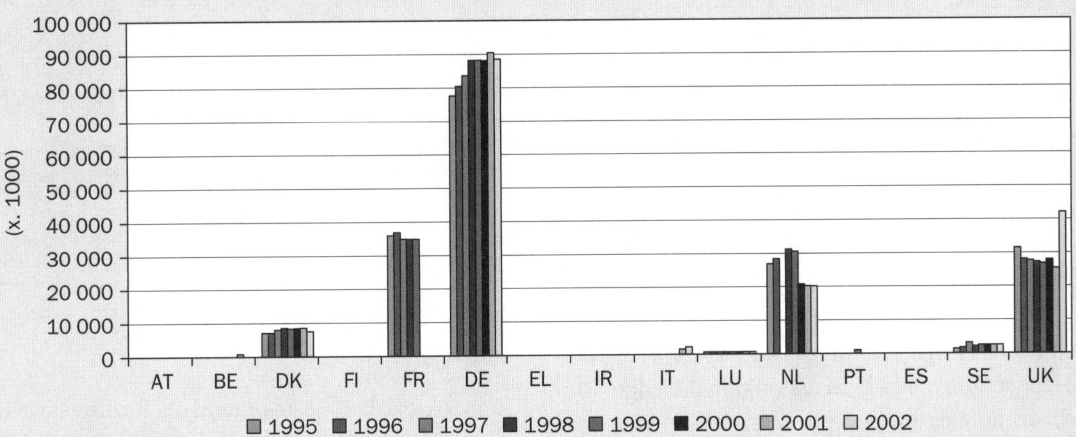

Freesheet newspaper circulation in EU Member States 1995–2001

Source: European Commission, *Publishing Market Watch*, p. 17 (EC, 2004), *World Press Trends* (WAN, 2003), http://ec.europa.eu/enterprise/ict/policy/publ-ind/sr01-eur-newspaper-market.pdf.

The second set shows the impact of this type of newspaper in the new EU accession countries 1999–2002 (sample). The Czech Republic was by far the biggest player among the new countries of the EU at the start of the 21st century.

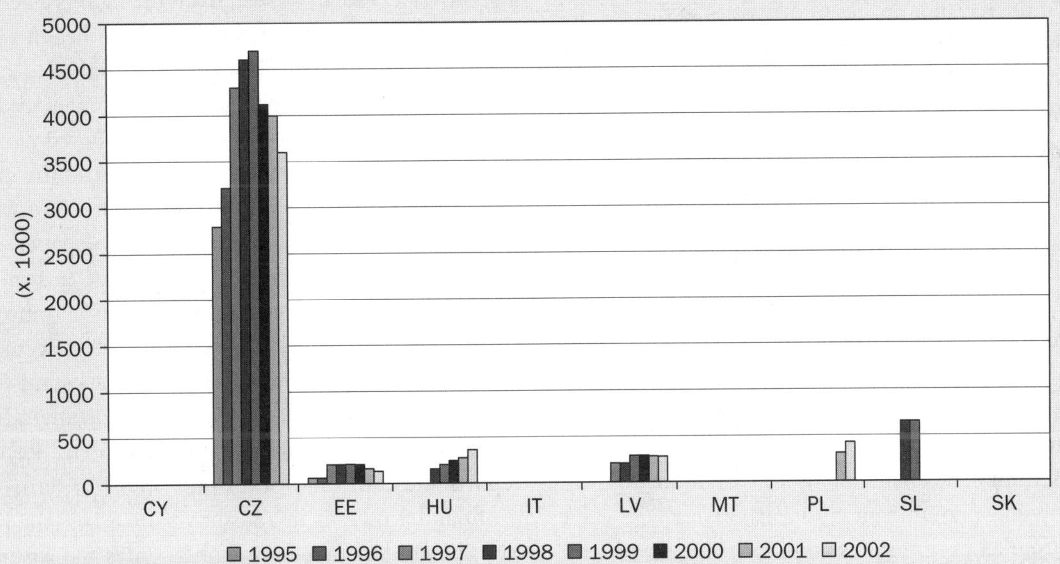

Freesheet newspaper circulation in new EU accession states 1995–2001

Source: European Commission, *Publishing Market Watch*, p. 18 (EC, 2004), *World Press Trends* (WAN, 2003), http://ec.europa.eu/enterprise/ict/policy/publ-ind/sr01-eur-newspaper-market.pdf.

Source 8.4

World Association of Newspapers, *World Press Trends* (WAN, 2008)

The growth of free newspapers is a global phenomenon but with Europe well advanced. The following is an extract from the recent 2008 report:

Free Dailies

- A total of 312 free daily newspapers (*across the globe*) had a combined circulation of 41.04 million daily, a circulation increase of 20 percent over one year and 173.2 percent over five years.
- When free and paid-for circulations are combined, free dailies account for 7 percent of the total world-wide, 23 percent in Europe, 8 percent in the US and 2 percent in Asia.
- The six largest free dailies are *Leggo* in Italy (1.95 million copies), *Metro* in the United Kingdom (1.37 million copies), *20 Minutos* in Spain (1 million copies), *Metro* in Canada (990,000 copies), and *Que!* and *ADN* in Spain (959,000 copies each).

See online release: http://www.wan-press.org/article17377.html, 2 June, 2008.

circumstances that encourage fast reading (e.g. train and bus stations) and local and regional readers who may not indulge in in-depth material on their area but are willing to look through 'free' and advertising-based content, either as readers or shoppers, or more likely as both. They are also more attractive to urban rather than rural areas because of the transport system and the daily movement of workers in often set, predictable patterns.

Of the recent launches of new titles in the EU, it is in the realm of the 'free' newspaper that most activity is occurring (see Source 8.4). Although there are new payment-based titles, this is the exception not the rule. As we have seen, the overall number of pay-for titles is diminishing not increasing.

Periodicals, magazines and reviews

Compared to newspapers, the periodical, magazine and review market across Europe is expanding, in certain markets but not all. As we have seen in Chapter 6, the sector has many participants but with dominant, national or cross-national groups occupying pre-eminent positions, at least in value. The market prognostic is good for some of the leading players in consumption terms. Underlying the optimism, though, there are figures that point to a worrisome future for some in the industry, even if profits remain high for those who may remain.

Books

The book market has maintained a healthy development across the EU, although some markets are more profitable and extensive than others. For the time being, it could be argued that book publishers have been assisted rather than hindered by technology. Advertising revenue is less important in the book industry, where sales and marketing play a full part in a book's sale. As can be seen from the figures given in Source 8.5, the book industry remains a healthy element across the sector. The new e-sales linked to such e-services as Amazon plc, have complemented and increased the sale of books. This has worked alongside the efforts of the major publishers and the sales outlets from specialist shops to supermarkets.

The book sector is different to the newspaper and magazine sectors in so far as its revenue income is based upon the book itself and not on extraneous advertising revenue. This is not completely accurate if you consider placement sales and marketing (see later), but the general view is that consumers buy books for their written or graphical content. Recent reports illustrate that book publishing in terms of profit and growth is in a healthy state across the EU. The integration of new member states has given a recent boost to book publishing as these areas have the most publishing activity.

The sector is normally divided into the various types of books: the largest sector is often specified as

Source 8.5

Datamonitor, *EU publishing*, 2006 estimate for 2008

EU – relative value of the book industry compared to other publishing sectors – in figures. Compare these figures with other sources and there will be differences. Reflect on the many types of data sources at work – see opening sections of this chapter.

Category	*% share*
Advertising	33.20
Book sales	26.40
Newspaper sales	20.50
Magazine sales	19.90

Source: *Publishing in Europe: industry profile* (Datamonitor, 2006).

being consumer books (51%); the next two areas, educational (15%) and higher educational books (26%), include dictionaries and professional manuals. The smallest sector (8%), and in an era of Harry Potter not to be under-estimated, is the sector for children's books which has seen a considerable recent growth in titles (up 47%) in 2002–2004.

Once again, precise and accurate statistics are still difficult to gauge and often contradictory. The variables used are often associated with NACE categorisation, but across the spectrum of data analysis many other variables and categories are often used within the industry.

As with newspapers and magazines, the book sector is showing trends towards corporate concentration and, although there are increasing numbers of titles, there appears to be a corresponding decrease in employment in the sector. This may be due to economies of scale, new technology or both. It may also be due to a change in consumer behaviour. Productivity is the key to development within the sector and is the buzzword for most sectoral and management attention as the competition for publishing looms, not just from the traditional competitors such as the USA but from Asia, and in particular China.

The four major countries for book consumption in the EU, linked to production, are the UK, Germany, France and Spain. The five publishing leaders by sales, estimated at 53% of the total market share, are British (Pearson), French (Hachette), German (Random House and Macmillan) or American (HarperCollins).

What is most interesting about book selling (e.g. UK book publishing) is how important the book chains are: for example Waterstones in the UK and FNAC in France. The entry of the supermarket and hypermarket into book selling has not yet had the major impact some predicted. However, the latest reports from the industry note the disquiet that increased competition is creating within this sector of the market, not least because of varying rates of tax applied across the EU (see Case Study 8.10).

Advertising sector

Advertising can be seen as an industry apart from the mainstream publishing of printed material. This is not the view of those within the industry, and the material collected by Datamonitor for example is fully aware of the importance of the advertising industry and its links to published material. In many respects, in both traditional paper form and e-commerce, advertising is a part of the publishing world (see Source 8.6).

This goes to the heart of the dilemma for the sector: to what extent should the sector rely on advertising and to what extent on direct subscriptions and payments from the consumer (see Source 8.6 and Case Studies 8.9 and 8.11)?

Although there are many factors influencing advertising revenue, it is the new distribution techniques that highlight the areas of growth. For both newspapers and periodicals, the digital age is the market challenge that must be mastered.

Case Study 8.10

Varying tax rates (2004)

Tax rates (VAT/TVA) vary across the EU and are one of the diverse factors borne in mind by the industry.

VAT rates for publications in EU Member States

Country	*Books*	*Periodicals*	*Newspapers*	*CD-ROM/online*	*Standard VAT Rate*
Austria	10.0%	10.0%	10.0%	20.0%	20.0%
Belgium	6.0%	6.0%	0.0%	21.0%	21.0%
Denmark	25.0%	25.0%	0.0%	25.0%	25.0%
Finland	12.0%	22.0%	0.0%–22.0%*	22.0%	22.0%
France	5.5%	2.1%	2.1%	20.6%	20.6%
Germany	7.0%	7.0%	7.0%	15.0%	15.0%
Greece	4.0%	4.0%	4.0%	18.0%	36.0%/16.0%
Ireland	0.0%	12.5%	12.5%	12.5%	21.0%
Italy	4.0%	4.0%	4.0%	19.0%	19.0%
Luxembourg	3.0%	3.0%	3.0%	15.0%	15.0%
Netherlands	6.0%	6.0%	6.0%	17.5%	17.5%
Portugal	5.0%	5.0%	5.0%	17.0%	17.0%
Spain	4.0%	4.0%	4.0%	16.0%	16.0%
Sweden	6.0%	6.0%	6.0%	25.0%	25.0%
United Kingdom	0.0%	0.0%	0.0%	17.5%	17.5%

* Rate in Finland varies according to distribution channel: subscription purchase is 0%; single-copy 22%.

Note: rates may have changed since 2004.

Source: European Commission, *Publishing Market Watch*, p. 100 (EC, 2004), European Publishers Council (http://www.epceurope.org/), http://ec.europa.eu/enterprise/ict/policy/publ-ind/sr01-eur-newspaper-market.pdf

Source 8.6

Publishing in Europe – contrasting views

As one leading consultancy points out:

> Advertising sales proved the most lucrative for the European publishing market in 2006, generating total revenues of $51.6 billion, and equivalent to 33.2% of the market's overall value. In comparison, sales of books generated revenues of $41 billion in 2006, equating to 26.4% of the market's aggregate revenues. The performance of the market is forecast to accelerate, with an anticipated CAGR of 2.6% for the five-year period 2006–2011 expected to drive the market to a value of $176.5 billion by the end of 2011. Comparatively, the US and Asia-Pacific markets will grow with CAGRs of 1.9% and 4.4% respectively over the same period, to reach respective values of $126.4 billion and $110.1 billion in 2011.
>
> Source: *Publishing in Europe: industry profile* (Datamonitor, 2006).

This can be compared with the European Commission view.

> The revenues of some sub-sectors of publishing are heavily dependent on advertising. In most EU countries newspapers depend on advertising for between 50% and 60% of their revenues, in the case of Luxembourg it is even 80%. For directories, 67.5% of revenues resulted from advertising in 2003 . . . Only for book publishing is advertising of relatively low importance. As a result, the decline of advertising revenue in recent years has affected the profitability of many publishing companies. The strong dependency on advertising revenue makes the publishing sector very sensitive to advertising restrictions. These may have a considerable impact on the revenue base of the sector and this should therefore be carefully assessed before any restrictions are imposed.
>
> Source: Commission staff working paper. *Strengthening the Competitiveness of the EU Publishing Sector. The role of media policy*, p. 21 (EC, 2005).

Case Study 8.11

EU advertising: changes in the market – 2002

This presentation neatly displays the 'volatility' in advertising revenue for a sample of EU member states. The cluster arrangement between 25% and 40% appears to be the strongest message from this data.

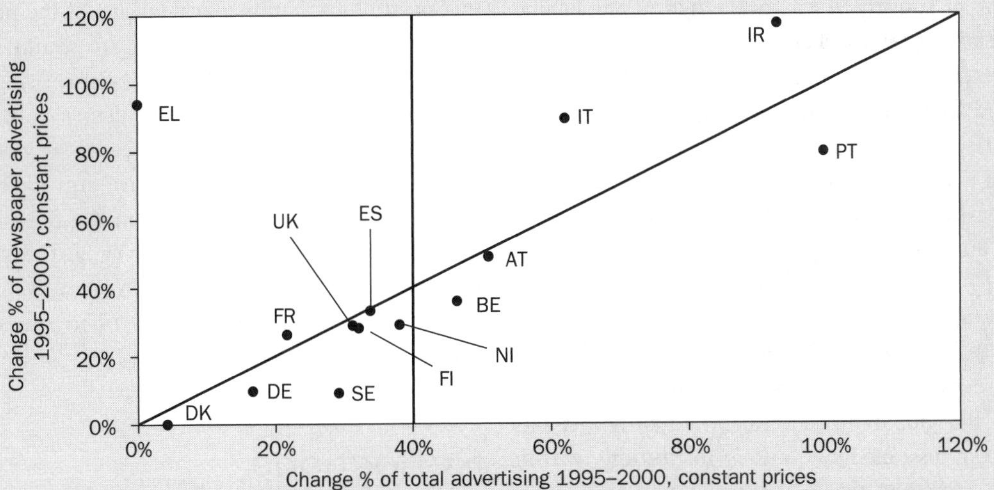

Change in the newspaper share of total advertising in EU Member States (1995–2000 at constant prices)

Source: European Commission, *Publishing Market Watch*, p. 38 (EC, 2004), *World Advertising Trends 2002* (WARC, 2002), http://ec.europa.eu/enterprise/ict/policy/publ-ind/sr01-eur-newspaper-market.pdf.

If there is one aspect or factor that binds together production, distribution and consumption it is finance. It is the advertising which is so important within private sector and corporate thinking about publishing. Advertising revenue is very important in the print industry: for newspapers and magazines in particular but also more generally.

Books, often seen as unconnected to advertising, are very closely linked to marketing strategies which of course embrace advertising. The importance of being a 'best seller' is a very important part of the marketing of a book and its distribution through the book chains. Not yet fully developed but on the horizon, we should not be surprised to see a dedicated supermarket advertising campaign on television, radio and in the newspapers for published material as profound as we currently see for the promotion of quality food or other household goods. It may be an electronic hypermarket that sells us our printed material in the future, but the principle will remain. Advertising revenue cannot be taken out of the equation, when looking at the consumption of printed and published products.

Consumption: European policy

Note: See audiovisual comparisons in Chapter 11 for the latest developments such as 'Marketwatch'; see also Chapter 5 on European integration theory and especially neo-functionalism.

Is there an over-riding EU policy to promote and encourage print and published products across the member states? The simple answer is no but, as with most policy drivers in Europe, the policy practice is a little more subtle. The fundamental drivers to European integration in the 21st century are in many ways being left to market forces. Traditionally the products and consumption of published material have been in the hands of the private sector across Europe. This is not quite the case historically in some member states, for example those of Central and Eastern Europe who until recently came under the strict control of communist regimes. Moreover, the amount of subsidy given to a range of publishing products has been excellently reported in the already-mentioned 'Compendium' series on 'Cultural policies and trends in Europe' (Council of Europe and ERICarts).

This is not to say that the EU and its institutions are unaware of the importance of the publishing sector and its consumption within the EU, as this chapter has indicated all along. There has been some considerable policy movement recently to collect data on the publishing industry across the EU in order to measure its importance and its economic potential within the global market. Report after report has been commissioned by various institutions within the EU including the European Commission itself. The reason: entertainment and cultural products are increasingly profitable for those who are able to produce or distribute effectively to a readership which in the main is becoming more affluent. This applies to the entire EU, its member states and its peoples.

Consumption: national policies

Traditionally the printing and publishing industries have been regulated and measured in national terms. Most of the measurements, the collection of data about consumption, are nationally led and consequently it is difficult, at times, to compare performance across nations because the data is collected in different ways. The link between cultures, language and consumer behaviour has been equally nationally framed. The wider market and the cross-frontier opportunities for sales and product development have impacted upon the corporations but not necessarily the national, political or social institutions that surround them.

There are deep-rooted national links to book, newspaper and magazine publishing, at least in terms of its content, through language and cultural traditions that remain important for national consumption. Yet, as the corporations become increasingly transnational with both global and local strategies, and where distribution systems are converging either technologically or financially, the national restraints on consumption will diminish.

The upside of the comparative vs national data is that we do have national evaluations of the publishing and printing industry which are sound and in many cases very detailed. This is not surprising bearing in mind the importance and history of the print industry not only in Europe but across the globe.

Hallin and Mancini (2004) have argued that the media industry and by implication the press can be divided into geopolitical zones. To gauge the national positions it is therefore illuminating to evaluate at least one nation in the three described zones – see Chapter 5.

Reflections

As we have seen in previous chapters, the principal driver of any media is the capability of the consumer to choose a product within a competitive environment and of the producers to satisfy the demand created. In the economics of supply and demand, competition is essential. In consumption terms, the purchase by individuals of a book here and a newspaper there may seem trivial in comparison with the many billions of euros involved in the finance and capital aspects, so important at the production and distribution level. While household spend may be small as an individual choice, added together it is the bedrock upon which production and distribution depend.

The aesthetics of consumption – the appeal of the 'printed product' (textual, graphics and image, journalistic engagement) – is related to the investment both in financial and human terms. However, in the end and in so many ways in the EU, the consumer is a final arbiter of the production and distribution processes, and this is expressed as a matter of choice which we can see in overall consumption.

Satisfying demand with suitable products – whether text or graphic – is always a mix of science, technique, good management, innovation, research and, sometimes, taste. The heady mix of publishing professionalism, that is aware of these factors, and the creativity needed to link it to demand, are important elements for enticing and then retaining consumers. The link shows itself in continued and 'loyal' consumption.

Equally, publishing products serve many needs. They may embrace the nostalgic past, the new, the fashionable, the changing interests within the societies in which we all live. In the publishing industry this will include the social, political, cultural and economic preoccupations which are constantly shifting around us in world and local affairs.

Consumers and their consumption are part of the chain of 'interests' which are not merely an exercise of the 'imagination' but also one of behaviour: where and how we work, with whom we meet, live and communicate, what interests us and what does not, what constrains us, and what freedoms are normally socially permitted. In the EU this may well be very diverse.

Content and the reasons why someone consumes information or entertainment depend ultimately on the consumer, and the consumer is a multi-faceted 'player' – age, sex and gender, race and ethnicity, citizen or subject, rich or poor, educated, national and multi-national identities, even geographical locality and mobility, all combine into a concoction which the so-called (mass retail) media has to enmesh, entice and work with. The result is our consumption.

Chapter summary

- The press and publishing industries are an important part of the EU economy.
- The industry as a whole has seen its influence grow rather than decrease in an age that perceives the value of 'information', not just in social and political terms but as a driving economic factor for wealth creation.
- The sector is divided into four: newspapers, magazines, books and advertising material.
- The market is highly competitive and increasingly so in a global and trans-national environment.
- At the same time the industry is often judged and measured in its national and sub-national settings.
- The major players in the field tend to be seen as Germany, the UK and France, but in consumption terms the Scandinavians tend to lead the group.
- Although mainly in the hands of the private sector, the EU institutions are increasingly concerned with encouraging productivity across the member states in order to face the global challenges and what are perceived as opportunities.

Key terms

Closed networks: media networks that are controlled by licence, copyright or other means.

'Gatekeepers': often used as a term by media analysts underlining the power of those who control access to media content – see the work of Negrine (1996).

Secondary markets: referring to the resale and reuse of media content often in other formats or contexts.

Value network: a term used to indicate that revenue, and therefore income, is part of a complex economic cycle of value enhancement, with various stages of production, often called a 'value chain' (see Chapter 3).

Discussion questions

1. Note at least two difficulties in handling data about the consumer across Europe. Discuss how to overcome the issues.
2. Name five good sources for consumer material concerning the print and publishing industry.

3. What is NACE (refer to Chapter 4) and why is it important in understanding the print industry? What is the US equivalent (refer to Chapter 4 again).
4. Refer back to the Hans-Bredow-Institut findings and discuss the merits and demerits of each hypothesis.
5. From the news reports case study (Case Study 8.2) which of the three reports is most important and revelatory and why?
6. Which part of the publishing sector is the most valuable in terms of segmentation share across Europe?
7. Taking Holtzbrinck Gmbh as an example, how does vertical and horizontal integration link to consumption patterns and consumer awareness of the market?
8. Which four leading companies provide for the most consumption of publishing material in Europe? It may be useful to look at company reports to broaden the material in the chapter.
9. What are the strengths and weaknesses in 'household spend measurement' in the European publishing market, bearing mind changes in the industry due to new technology?
10. In your judgement how important are mass retail and distance sales (including online) for the publishing industry now and in the immediate future?
11. Evaluate in broad terms the newspaper market using the samples provided in the chapter and elsewhere.
12. Evaluate in broad terms the 'free' newspaper market using the samples provided in the chapter and elsewhere.

Assignments

1. Using one of the recommended sources for data on publishing in Europe evaluate the next ten years of development in the market, bearing in mind the lessons to be learnt from the past. Use the whole book and all the chapters to help create an argument.
2. Using examples from at least two EU countries draw out the data on the print and publishing industry of each one and assess the relative strengths and weaknesses of the national print and publishing industries. A good comparison may be the UK and German industries.

Further reading

In most national libraries it is reasonably easy to find established works on national presses. With so many nation-states involved this section is not able to list them all. However, start by dealing with primary as well as secondary material and in line with the aims and objectives of the chapter it is recommended that you read:

Boczkowski P.J. (1999) Understanding the development of online newspapers: Using computer-mediated communication theorizing to study Internet publishing, *New Media & Society*, **1**: 101–126.

Datamonitor (2008) *Books in France: industry profile*, London: Datamonitor (Market Business Line).

Dobrev S.D. (1999) The dynamics of the Bulgarian newspaper industry in a period of transition: organisational adaptation, structural inertia and political change, *Industrial and Corporate Change*, **8**(3): 573–605.

EC (2005) Commission Staff Working Paper. *Strengthening the Competitiveness of the EU Publishing Sector. The role of media policy*, Luxembourg, European Commission.

Edegcliffe-Johnson A., Weismann G. (2007) Bertelsmann teams up with private equity, *Financial Times*, 21 March.

Ernst & Young (2007) *Competitiveness of the European Graphic Industry*, Luxembourg: European Communities.

Eurostat (2001) *Special feature on Publishing and Printing*, Luxembourg: European Commission.

Gulyas A. (2003) Print media in post-communist East Central Europe, *European Journal of Communication*, **18**(1): 81–106.

Law A. (2001) Near and far: banal national identity and the press in Scotland, *Media, Culture & Society*, **23**(3): 299–317.

Mintel (2005) *European Retail Handbook – October 2005*, London: Mintel Group.

Mintel (2005) *Regional Newspapers – UK*, London: Mintel Group.

Neuberger C., Tonnemacher J., Biebel M., Duck A. (1998) Online – the future of newspapers? Germany's dailies on the world wide web, *Journal of Computer-Mediated Communication*, **4**(1), available at: http://jcmc.indiana.edu/vol4/issue1/neuberger.html.

Pira International (2003) *Publishing in the knowledge economy: Competitive analysis of the UK publishing industry*, London: Department of Trade and Industry.

Rosie M., MacInnes J., Petersoo P., Condor S., Kennedy J. (2004) Nation speaking unto nation? Newspapers and national identity in the devolved UK, *The Sociological Review*, **52**(4): 437–458.

Wadbring I., Weibull L. (2000) Metro on the Swedish newspaper market, *Mediatique No 20*, www.comu.ucl.ac.be/ORM/Mediatique/metro.htm.

WAN (1999) *Strength in Numbers: the Challenges for Newspaper Advertising*, Paris, World Association of Newspapers.

WAN (2001) *The Newspaper*, **1**(1), December, Paris: World Association of Newspapers.

WAN (2005) *World Press Trends*, Paris: World Association of Newspapers.

WAN (2008) *World Press Trends*, Paris: World Association of Newspapers.

Whitaker BookTrack (2004) *Book sales yearbook*, London: The Bookseller.

Wilcox L. (2005) Metro info! Fierce reactions to regime competition in the French newspaper industry, *Media, Culture and Society*, **27**(3): 353–369.

Online resources

http://www...

As a sign of the times, all the recommended reading above is available free and online. Equally look up the various recommended sources mentioned at the beginning of the chapter.

- *CultureObservatory (Culture Statistics Observatory)* http://www.culturestatistics.net
- *Datamonitor Marketline* http://www.datamonitor.com

References

Curran J. and Seaton J. (2003) Power Without Responsibility: The Press and Broadcasting in Britain, 6th edn, New York and London, Routledge.

Datamonitor (2006) *Publishing in Europe: industry profile*, London: Datamonitor (Market Business Line).

Datamonitor (2007) *Publishing in Europe: industry profile*, London: Datamonitor (Market Business Line).

EC (2004) *Publishing Market Watch*, Luxembourg: European Commission, DG Enterprise.

EC (2005) Commission Staff Working Paper. *Strengthening the Competitiveness of the EU Publishing Sector. The role of media policy*, Luxembourg, European Commission.

EMCC (2003) *Sector Futures: Publishing and media: Balancing the Interests of Producers and Consumers*, Dublin: European Foundation for the Improvement of Living and Working Conditions.

Ernst & Young (2002) *Mergers and Acquisitions: Trends in the European Publishing Industry*, London: Ernst & Young.

Ernst & Young (2007) *Competitiveness of the European Graphic Industry*, Luxembourg: European Communities.

Eurostat Pocketbooks (2007) *Cultural Statistics*. Luxembourg, European Commission.

Eurostat (2004) *New Cronos Database*, http://www.esds.ac.uk/international/support/user_guides/eurostat/cronos.asp.

Hallin D.C., Mancini P. (2004) *Comparing Media Systems: Three Models of Media and Politics*, Cambridge: Polity Press.

Negrine R. (1996) *The Communication of Politics*, London: Sage.

Pira International (2002) *Publishing in the Knowledge Economy: Competitive Analysis of the UK Publishing Industry*, London: Department of Trade and Industry.

Pira International (2003) *The EU Publishing* Industry*: an Assessment of Competitiveness*, Luxembourg: European Communities.

WAN (2003) *World Press Trends*, Paris: World Association of Newspapers.

WAN (2008) *World Press Trends*, Paris: World Association of Newspapers.

WARC (2002) *World Advertising Trends 2002*.

Chapter 9

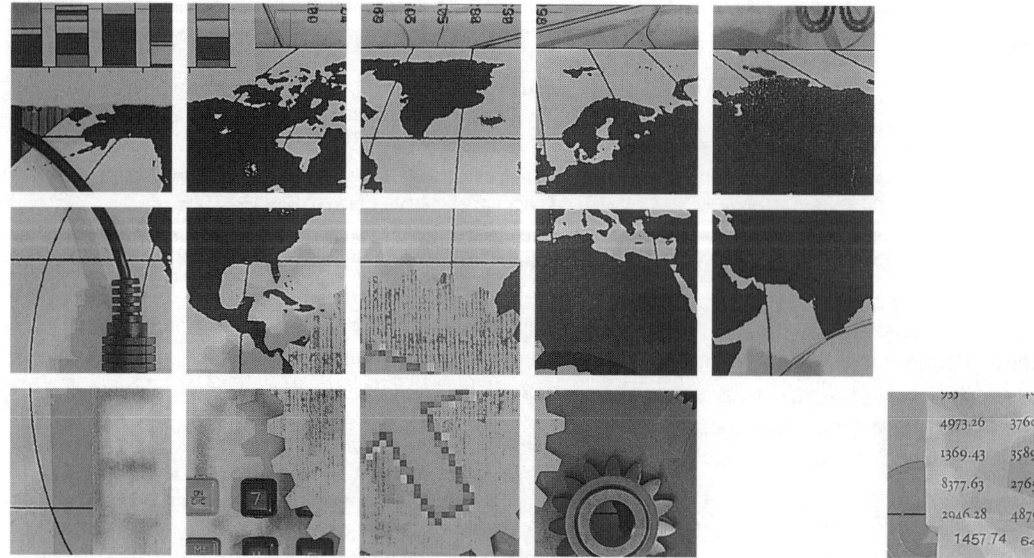

Audio-visual content in the EU: production and scheduling

By Andrea Esser

What this chapter covers

Learning objectives

When you have completed this chapter you will be able to:

- Outline the development of audio-visual production in the EU and the principal economic, political and technological factors determining it.
- Locate some of the primary sources available to researchers of the changing audio-visual production scene.
- Identify differences amongst EU countries as regards the production of audio-visual content and understand the reasons for the diversity to be found.
- Understand the factors that impact on the production and scheduling of fiction programming and that determine the relationship between (national) domestic, EU and US fiction.
- Describe some of the principal debates over the past 30 years in audio-visual programming across the EU.
- Identify and understand current and future trends of audio-visual content.

Themes

Below you will find a simple statement or series of statements around the six themes. They should *not* be read as a given fact. They are more like hypotheses (see Chapter 2) which need to be proved, discussed, debated and then used in your own analysis of the subject. The ideas and approaches in this book are always to be considered with an open mind; this is important in university study and is what makes it distinct from pre-university study.

Diversity of media

To some extent audio-visual programming in the EU is converging. National differences in the production and scheduling of audio-visual content are becoming eroded in many ways. Even so, the traditionally grown diversity is still visible and strong: different countries produce, buy and schedule in different ways. Varying economic, sociocultural and legislatory frameworks mean diversity will continue to exist.

Internal/external forces for change

Changes in audio-visual production are not just a result of new (digital) technologies and sociocultural developments. Economics and media policy have a major impact on what is being produced and scheduled. Moreover, there are pressures at the local, national, EU and international levels. Forces for change are manifold and together build an intricate web of influences shaping audio-visual content. When analysing the market we need to be aware of the many different forces for change.

Complexity of the media

The production and scheduling of audio-visual content is a complex process, raising many interesting questions. After the introduction of private commercial television the debate centred on the provision of programming, public versus private, and the perceived threat of the Americanisation and commercialisation of content. In more recent years, the internationalisation of production and other new ways of funding have come to be of interest. Moreover, the digitisation and convergence of the media is introducing new types of television content, with added-value and interactive features.

Multi-levels

Audio-visual production is changing rapidly at the global, trans-national, national and local level. National markets are becoming ever more commercial and with it more international. Policy concerning production and trade is implemented at the national, EU and global (GATS) level. Production groups are expanding globally, and programming is increasingly characterised by internationalisation. Many genre trends these days are international; expensive productions are increasingly financed at the international market; and television formats, a huge and growing trend since the late 1990s, are truly global.

European integrative environment

Through the 'Television without Frontiers' Directive (EU, 1989, 1997) and the Audio-visual Media Services Directive (EU, 2007), the EU has set out a legislative framework which the audio-visual sector needs to comply with. The audio-visual industries, although still nationally regulated, must be seen as a part of the EU market. EU policies, such as quotas for European productions and independent productions or funds to support production and distribution of European content (MEDIA programme – EU, 2006), all impact on national television production and scheduling within the EU's borders.

Cultural values

Cultural values and traditions are reflected in the production and scheduling of audio-visual content. National governments as well as the EU support audio-visual production for cultural reasons. Production quotas, subsidies and tax incentives are policies implemented to foster expressions of national culture and to retain cultural diversity across Europe. Even so, we must be careful not to ascribe everything to culture. Audio-visual policy at the national, EU and international level often also has an economic objective, and many production and scheduling decisions result from financial and economic considerations.

Essentials

➤ From the 1980s onwards television experienced significant architectural changes that affected the production, sale and scheduling of audio-visual content. In the 1980s it was US programming, production values and scheduling practices that influenced the changing European market(s) in hitherto unknown and, to some, threatening ways.

➤ In the 1990s, it was much highlighted that a localisation trend came to define television programming. While this was true in parts, the assessment proved to be simplistic. The empirical analysis of programme production, trade and scheduling discloses complex and uneven patterns. Moreover, it reveals that important differences continue between European countries at the same time that a process of convergence is taking place – much of it attributable to international formats, production values and scheduling practices.

➤ With the major growth in channels, the issue of funding has become more significant. With increasing commercialisation and competitiveness, it is a much greater determinant for programme production today than it was in the days of public service broadcasting (PSB), or even in the early days of the public service–private commercial duopoly.

➤ The new millennium, moreover, is characterised by the introduction of new television genres and of television content expanding into other media – both a result of digitisation. Television content is refashioning fast, and the continuing trends for market concentration, convergence and internationalisation mean the market will keep spinning for some time to come.

Introduction: analysing audio-visual programming in the EU

The analysis of programme production, trade and scheduling reveals not only diversity across Europe but also enormous complexity within each national market and across the various market levels – the local, the regional, the national, the trans-national and the global. When tracing the development of content production, we need to take into account economic, legislatory and sociocultural factors. To fully understand past, current and future changes, we need to be aware of the historical context, the framework of the single European audio-visual market and international programming trade and programming trends.

Sources

Data sources for a market analysis are multitudinous (see Source 9.1). At the national level we have trade journals such as *Broadcast* or *Televisual* in the UK or *Media Perspektiven* and *epd Medien* in Germany. However, today there are also many trade journals dealing with the production, financing and trade of audio-visual content that are international in outlook. Examples are *Cable & Satellite* or *Television Business International* (TBI). *Screen Digest* is a great source for in-depth reports on audio-visual programming and monthly sector updates. Unfortunately, *Screen Digest* is for subscribers only and very expensive, but there are many interesting free excerpts on its website and it is worth checking. The most important data source for the EU market is the European Audio-visual Observatory (EAO), based in Strasbourg.

The difficulty when researching audio-visual production and scheduling is in finding comparable data. That is why the data collection of the EAO, established in 1992 to gather and circulate information on the audio-visual industry in Europe, is so valuable. Another problem for a market analysis in this field is that producers are not keen to reveal

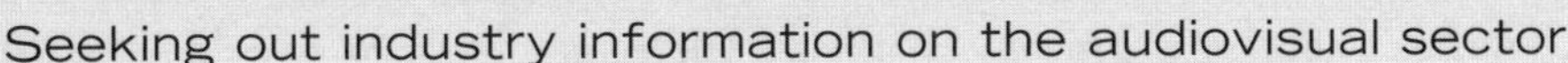

Source 9.1

Seeking out industry information on the audiovisual sector

Television trade journals (English language with an international outlook):

- *Broadcast* (www.broadcastnow.co.uk/index.html) covers television production and distribution and gives free online access to its archived articles. Its main focus is the UK.
- *C21Media.net* (www.c21media.net) offers information on new programmes from around the world, in-depth profiles and features. Free access to archive.
- *Cable & Satellite* (www.cable-satellite.com) covers cable, satellite, terrestrial, IPTV and Mobile TV development.
- *DOX Magazine* (http://www.dox.dk) published by the European Documentary Network, is a bi-monthly subscription magazine dedicated to the production and distribution of documentaries.
- *Kidscreen* (www.kidscreen.com) provides free information on the production and licensing business in the audiovisual children's sector.
- *Screen Digest* (www.screendigest.com) offers subscription based monthly publications and special in-depth reports, free excerpts of which can be found on the website.
- *Screen Finance* (www.biz-lib.com) monitors UK productions and co-productions, national and international regulation.
- *Television Business International* (TBI) (www.tbivision.com) is a subscription-based but very useful source when researching television production and programme trade.
- *TV World* is a subscription based magazine focusing on television programming from around the world.
- *Variety* (www.variety.com) offers a wealth of archived information on audiovisual production and distribution for free.
- *World Screen* (www.worldscreen.com) covers international television production and trade and gives free online access to its archived articles.

Statistical yearbooks and other valuable sources:

- *Statistical Yearbook* of the European Audiovisual Observatory (www.obs.coe.int). The website offers legal and statistical information about audio-visual production but much less than the wealth of data to be found in the printed annual publications.
- European Broadcasting Union (www.ebu.ch/en/index.php). The association of Europe's public-service broadcasters provides access to all its position papers on EU audio-visual policy online as well as information on the Eurovision programme exchange.

their turnover. Often the figures we get are hence no more than estimates. To get around this problem, the EAO collates data on audio-visual content as programme hours scheduled by broadcasters across Europe.

Before we start looking at some statistical data outlining the production landscape and programming trends across the EU, a quick overview of the internal and external forces for change is needed to help us understand why television programming has developed in the way it has. This will also allow us to make predictions about the future.

History and precedents

Like the press, television developed in a context of national regulation, even more so, one could argue, since this medium has been much more heavily regulated than the press. Like all the world's nations, European governments shape their broadcasting systems in line with their political nature, and Siebert *et al's* (1963) models of the press (advanced by Hallin and Mancini, 2004) were not just valid for print but also for television. Tracking its early history, we can see certain shared elements, but we need to distinguish between the paternalistic or social responsibility, Western European model and the communist Central and Eastern European model.

In Western Europe, it was the public-service ideology that determined the development of television. The media, it is believed, have a social responsibility, and public-service broadcasting – defined by its quasi-independence from the state and freedom from market forces – was thought to fulfil this role best. Besides these two organisational determinants, the PSB was also given basic principles to adhere to: diversity of content, objectivity and plurality of opinion, universal access and quality programming. These principles sought to help PSBs achieve their perceived mission of serving the nation and its democratic system.

The social responsibility objective, coupled with a desire for control, led to a triple monopoly: the PTTs (telecommunication operators) were responsible for the transmission, and the PSBs first for the programming and second for its production. Programme production was not only determined by the monopoly, however, but also by the definition of audiences as citizens rather than consumers. Television programming was a result of what the authorities believed audiences should watch. It was a top-down approach and can be contrasted with the bottom-up approach of the liberal US broadcasting system, where audiences decide what is being scheduled and often produced in the first place.

Europe's prolonged belief in PSB, as compared to the USA, is a result of the Second World War, during which the media was used as a means of propaganda by the Fascist regimes. To avoid this ever happening again, the Fascist media of Italy and Germany were remodelled in 1945 along lines approved by the Western allies. The BBC, which had gained admiration during the war for its independent reporting, became the role model for the structuring of the PSBs of many European countries. The PSB was to be the guarantor for responsible and worthwhile media use. It was expected to play a significant role in setting up democracies across Europe and reinforcing agitated national identities.

Television in Central and Eastern Europe, in contrast, developed to support the communist ideology. Although similar to the western European PSB model in its objective to serve the aims and the needs of the state, both the relationship between broadcaster and state and television's assumed roles differed from those in the West. Television, like all media, was to belong to the state, defined as the working-class – effectively the Communist Party. Control therefore lay directly in the hands of the government. Based on Lenin's theory of the press, broadcasting was to support revolution, not democracy.

What the two European systems shared were the objectives to socialise, educate and inform – something that affected content production and that resulted in a much lesser focus on entertainment compared with the USA. Also, the degree to which Western European broadcasters are independent of their respective governments is debatable. Some are more so than others, and we should in fact think of individual European countries as being on a scale of independence, with the 'Western' and 'Communist' models as no more than two symbolic poles. Today this problematic is less relevant. With the collapse of communism, broadcasting in these countries changed as well. It came to share many of the developments that Western European countries had begun to experience in the 1980s, only in a much more radical way.

The 1980s

By 1980, no Western European country except for the UK, Luxembourg and Monaco had yet broken its PSB monopoly. Luxembourg and Monaco were too small to finance a public-service broadcaster, and the UK had set up ITV to break the BBC's monopoly. ITV was heavily regulated, though, and subjected to various public-service broadcasting objectives. Then in the early 1980s a new phase in Western European broadcasting began. Technological developments and a shift in ideology towards neoliberal policies across Europe affected a restructuring of the broadcasting model. The PSB monopoly was replaced by a public service–commercial duopoly. Private commercial television with its objective of making money rather than serve the nation made its inroad into Europe and this affected programming in major ways.

Technological development: satellite and cable

The old PSB monopoly had not only been justified on grounds of the belief in the media's social responsibility, but in part also on the scarcity of terrestrial frequencies and technological interference. This changed when it became obvious in the late 1970s that satellite technology would allow for communication to be transmitted by satellites. In 1977 1000 satellite transponders were assigned at the WARC conference to countries in Europe, Africa, Asia and Australia. Suddenly the scarcity argument was enervated. Moreover, while it had been easy to control the limited reach of terrestrial signals, stopping satellite signals at national borders was impossible. The traditionally national character of broadcasting policy was affected. A raft of negotiations and agreements at European Commission level was set in motion and national media legislation began to consider the new environment (see Chapter 4).

Developing cable technology added to this. While the problem of border control did not exist with cable transmission, it helped render the scarcity argument invalid. Also, cable operators were naturally eager to add channels to their portfolio. However, they could only make money by offering something that added to what audiences were getting free over the air and, ideally, something that was more attractive to them. With the number of channels growing, demand for content grew manifold; and the competition for particularly attractive content led to an increase in prices.

Sociopolitical context: ideological shift to neoliberalism

Media and non-media groups with commercial interests were increasing their pressure on national governments to change legislation in favour of introducing private commercial television. A general ideological shift in society helped their cause. Socialist governments were being replaced in several countries by conservative governments in the early 1980s, and the belief in free market forces took over. Also, it was becoming clear that some of the old major industries, like coal and steel, were no longer financially viable, and governments needed to find new industries to create jobs and sustain the wealth of the nation. Across Europe the information sector was identified as this future saviour, and broadcasting, so heavily protected until the 1980s, was set free (see Case Study 9.1) to contribute to the economic growth of Europe's nation states.

The reasons why there are such considerable time differences in regulating for private commercial television and launching private commercial channels are many and too complex to discuss in detail. A few interesting examples, though, should help explain the most vital, economic factor. Germany, the first country to legislate for private commercial television, was hastened to do so by great pressure from local media owners who were rightly expecting that their large and wealthy country had huge potential to generate profits from television advertising. Even more important, though, in speeding up legislation was pressure from across the border. With the help of the new satellite technology, Luxembourg's commercial broadcaster CLT was developing a channel to target the German market. This meant that jobs and money that could be created in Germany would be lost to Luxembourg. Naturally, the German government set out to counter this threat. France was under the same pressure.

Austria, on the other hand, did not legislate for private commercial television before 1997 and did not launch a channel before 2003. This was because with its 8.2 million inhabitants it is not only a small country with an accordingly much smaller advertising income potential but, in addition, it has a large neighbour with the same language. Austrian investors have to compete with the much bigger German broadcasters – a difficult undertaking. The same is true for Ireland.

Commercialisation and its effects on programming

The extension and growth of private commercial television in the mid-1980s and 1990s across Europe led to a growing reliance on US fiction imports. Apart from the new channels' limited financial resources

Case Study 9.1

Introduction of private commercial television in Western Europe

The following demonstrates that in Western Europe alone, and discounting the UK, Luxembourg and Monaco, it took 16 years before all countries had implemented regulation allowing for private commercial television. The speed with which this happened varied between countries, depending above all on the position of the individual governments, the pressure they had from local companies eager to invest in television and the pressure from investors across borders.

Country	*Regulation allowing for private commercial*		*Launch of 1st national private commercial TV-channel in the country*
	Regional TV-channels	*National TV-channels*	
Austria	–	1997	2003
Belgium	–	1987	1989 1985 pay-TV/Film net (licensed in 1986)
Denmark	1981	1988	1997
Finland	–	1993 (but: priv. MTV since 1958 on YLE)	1993 (MTV receives its own licence)
France	–	1982	1984 pay-TV/C+ 1987 privatisation of TF 1
Germany	–	1981 (84–89 put into Länder-regulation)	1984
Ireland	–	1988	1998
Italy	1974	1984	1977 (net of local channels)
Luxembourg	–	1929 (31)	1954
Monaco		1954	1954
Netherlands	–	1990	1995
Norway	1981	1990	1992
Portugal	–	1991	1992
Spain	–	1988	1990
Sweden	–	1991	1992
Switzerland	–	1984 (but only in 1992 firmly established)	regional language offerings since 1994
UK	1954	1954 1955	

Source: Author compiled table.

for production, lack of an independent production sector meant that the heightened need for programming could not be met domestically in the early phase of market commercialisation. The large US market in contrast could support large volumes of high-cost fiction and had already developed long-running series. For the new European commercial broadcasters buying US series meant an inexpensive way to fill large amounts of transmission time and to bind audiences to the channel.

Not only programmes, though, were imported from the US. Production values or styles, such as the personalisation of news, were also copied. Studying five EU countries in the mid-80s, Silj and Alvarado (1988) contended that, in France and Germany, the enormous success of *Dallas* and *Dynasty* had an impact on the production of indigenous series. Elements of the US serials, such as basic dramatic situations, cinematic and dramatic stylistic devices and production methods, they claimed, were absorbed. Moreover, **stripped scheduling** and the scheme of **lead-in** were imported from the USA.

Searching for popular ideas for new **entertainment** programmes, the new commercial broadcasters invariably turned to the experienced US market. Copying from the USA was not new, but the extent of borrowing was. The infotainment style, for example, was exported from the USA and taken on by all European countries. It was cheap and popular. Italy was one of those countries that experienced a vast increase in informational material. As far as fiction is concerned, programmes of unknown genres were usually imported first, and later local adaptations were produced. By 1997, soaps and sitcoms were copied locally in European countries. Fiction about the supernatural (*The X-files*, *Profilers*, *Pretenders*, *Nowhere-Men*, *Enemies*, *Millennium*) followed.

Stop and consider 9.1

The public service television model that has characterised television across Western Europe for the first 40 years of its existence has been replaced with a public service–private commercial duopoly. What were the factors that pressured governments to introduce private commercial television? And what were the effects of the commercialisation of television on programming?

Changes in content production

With the audio-visual industry identified as an important growth sector, European governments, and this is true especially for the large countries of France, Germany and the UK, have shown much interest in supporting that growth in the hope of creating jobs, attracting investment and increasing export revenues. On the other hand, European governments still subscribe to the traditional cultural objective of promoting a distinctive national broadcasting landscape, serving audiences as a point of cultural identification and allegiance. Both objectives mean support for the production industry, showing above all in financial aid. We will turn to the issue of financing after a quick overview of the production sector.

The producers

Before the 1980s, across Europe most television programmes had been produced by the PSBs of each country. A few European PSBs, foremost among them Britain's ITV companies and Germany's ZDF, commissioned a few programmes from the independent sector, but the sector did not amount to much until the expansion of commercial television and, in the UK, the founding of Channel 4. This changed, with **independent production companies** gradually increasing in number and strength.

At the European level, listings from the EAO of the leading production groups can be used to illustrate the changes (see Source 9.2). By 2003 only five of the ten leading production groups were owned by leading broadcasters: the RTL Group and PSB ARD in Germany, private commercial Mediaset in Italy, Canal+ in France and ITV in Britain.

By 2006, only one of the top seven production groups in the EU was linked to a traditional broadcaster: the RTL Group content division (now in second place), owned and built up by German media giant Bertelsmann. Production group Lagardère (No. 5) is owned by French media giant Groupe Lagardère, which like Bertelsmann started out in publishing, but only moved into television production and distribution in 2000, when it entered an alliance with French pay-TV operator Canal+. Endemol, an originally small Dutch independent production company, now topped the list of EU production groups. It was bought by Spanish Telefonica in 2000 and sold again in 2007 to a consortium involving Italian media giant Mediaset. Overall, the development of the list of leading television production groups in the EU reveals that purely national broadcasters such as British ITV or German ARD no longer play in the league of leading producers. It is groups driven by an international strategy, and in particular the huge horizontally, vertically and diagonally integrated media groups, that now head audio-visual production.

If we take a look at the national level and the standing of independent producers in relation to producers belonging to a broadcasting group, we find interesting differences between countries (see Point of View 9.1). Depending on which data we

Source 9.2

Leading production groups in the EU

The following table can be used to demonstrate that in 2003 amongst the Top 10 television production groups in the EU there was an equal share between production groups belonging to traditional European broadcasters and production groups set up as independents. It also begins to indicate the concentration that is happening in the production sector in the first decade of the new millennium, with financially strong groups, such as RTL, buying up small independent production companies on the way.

Ten leading TV production groups in the European Union (2003)

Rank	*Group*		*Ownership*	*Country*	*2003 operating revenues in € million*
1	RTL Group (Content Division)(1)(2)		RTL Group/Bertelsmann	DE	1294
	Sportfive (cons.) (46.4%)(2)			FR	595
	Thames Television			GB	102
	Grundy UFA	e		DE	75
	Talkback Productions Ltd			GB	49
	Pearson Television (Italy)			IT	43
	Grundy Light Entertainment	e		DE	
	Gyula Trebitsch (64%)	e		DE	40
	Delux Productions			LU	
	Grundy Productions Ltd			GB	
	Grundy France			FR	18
	Fremantle France Productions			FR	13
	Be Happy Productions			FR	7
	Alomo Productions			GB	
2	Endemol Holding N.V.		Telefonica	NL/ES	914
	Endemol UK Plc			GB	127
	Endemol Italia			IT	103
	Endemol France	e		FR	
	Zeppelin Television			ES	
	Gestmusic Endemol			ES	
	Endemol Belgie			BE	14
3	Mediatrade (2)		Mediaset	IT	
4	Groupe Canal+		Groupe Canal+	FR	
	Nulle Part Ailleurs SNC			FR	31
	Expand Drama			FR	21
	Starling			FR	28
5	Bavaria Film (cons.)(1)		ARD	DE	240 (2002)
6	HIT Entertainment PLC			GB	240
7	Tele-Muenchen (2)	e		DE	180 (2002)
8	Carrere Group			FR	149
9	ITN		ITV	GB	137
10	Arbol Producciones S.A.			ES	114 (2002)

e = estimated
(1) Includes feature film production.
(2) Includes rights trade.
Note that Lagardère Active is not ranked because of lack of information.

Source: Based on data from *EAO Yearbook 2004* (EAO, 2004).

look at we get a different impression, though, of the relative strength of independent producers in various European countries. Drawing on a variety of sources and perspectives thus helps us better understand data.

The high market share of independent production in Spain, France and Italy, displayed in the first graph, is reflected in the leading ranks of independent film producers only in the case of France, the country with the highest government support for the audio-visual sector in Europe. Germany ranks No. 3 because of its combination of market size, wealth and generous government support. The UK, despite having the lowest level of independent production, ranks No. 1

Point of View 9.1

A comparative assessment of Europe's independent producers

The following demonstrates how different our impression of the standing of a production segment can be depending on the statistics we look at. For instance, if we compare the share independent producers have in Europe's five largest television production markets, we can see that there are significant differences between countries. These differences result from institutional, historical and cultural features specific to each country, and regulatory variation that acts more or less in favour of independent production. In Germany and the UK, the independent production sector seems relatively weak when compared to the share of producers belonging to a broadcasting group. However, if we compare the added up strength of the 50 leading individual independent producers as measured by revenue and country, we get a different picture. Independent producers in the UK and Germany now appear (in the second graph) in a much better position than in the first graph.

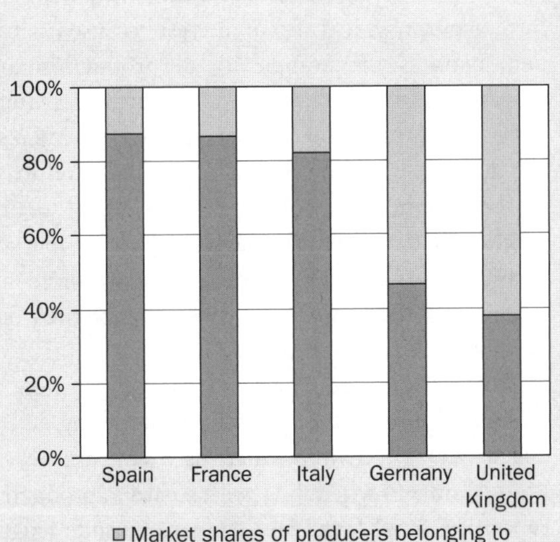

Breakdown of broadcast national TV fiction: TV fiction from independent producers and producers belonging to broadcasting group

Source: Based on data by Jezequel and Lange (2000).

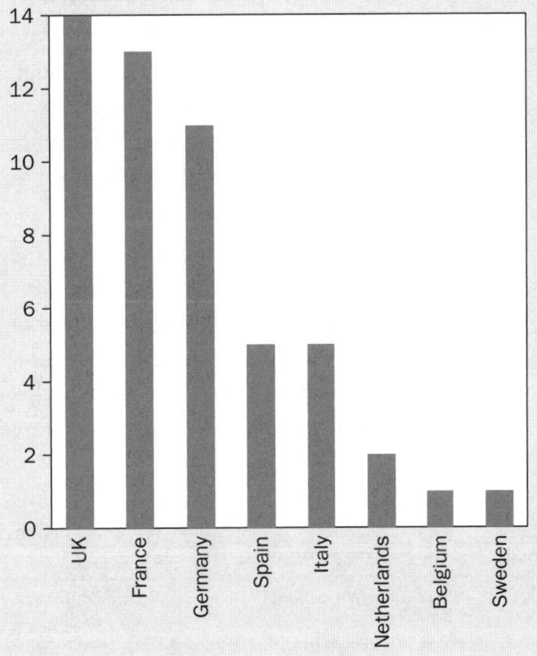

Number of independent film production companies filling the 50 leading ranks, based on revenues and country of origin

Source: Based on data from the *EAO Yearbook 2004* (EAO, 2004).

with 14 leading independent production companies. Its prominent position is also reflected in the fact that ten of these 14 companies rank among the first 25. Its advantages when it comes to international distribution, it seems, are not easily outrun.

It is not just the UK's independent production companies, though, which are disproportionately successful. Overall, the UK is by far Europe's most successful content producer and distributor. In terms of international programme sales it ranks No. 2 globally, far behind the USA but with a significant lead before Germany, France and Canada (see Table 9.1).

For the international market British producers have several major advantages.

1. *Comparative advantage of English*: while countries like Germany and France do much to support their audio-visual industries, the UK's potential for foreign sales is much higher. Most important, programmes can be sold in the original version to many countries and, even in those countries where every programme is dubbed, the infrastructure and expertise to translate from English exceed by far those existing for any other language.
2. *Creative talent*: historically the BBC has set high standards and is known worldwide for quality programming. Today London is the largest media hub in the Western world providing an abundance of creative talent and television expertise.
3. *Lead in digital television*: for the future too, the UK's competitive position looks good. UK producers today are operating in an environment that is providing them with a lead in digital television and thus a head start in experience with multimedia and interactive content, leading even before the US.

Table 9.1 AV programme sales

2007	*Country ranking*	*% international programme sales*
1	USA	75.9
2	**UK**	**7.2**
3	Germany	3.7
4	France	2.9
5	Canada	2.7

Source: *Rights of Passage 2007*, p. 20 (TRP, 2008).

Changes in television production: convergence, diversity, complexity

If we look at the changes in what is being produced, how much is being produced overall and in which categories, we find both convergence and diversity at the European level. Simply saying programming is still very much nationally determined would be too simplistic. At the same time, saying production now is the same in all markets is not true. Making general claims about production is impossible as patterns are very uneven and changes frequent. Also, it is different for each genre.

News and sports programmes are usually still produced nationally. They may be influenced by successful programmes and programming trends from abroad, usually the commercially experienced US market, but all in all they have remained a more insular business. In fiction, though, the picture is different. Here we have a strong trans-national and international aspect. Fiction, moreover, is an interesting area of study because prime-time fiction traditionally gets the biggest slice of the financial cake, and for our purposes it is also of interest because it nicely demonstrates the complexity of production and scheduling. In the following we will focus on fiction.

Fiction production is characterised by interesting and noteworthy differences between countries. If for instance we compare the kind of fiction formats that Europe's five largest television markets invest in, we get the impression that there are strong national, historically grown preferences (see Case Study 9.2).

However, the EAO also attests an 'erosion of national differences' in fiction programming (EAO, 2001a, 2002a), claiming there is a convergence in production and scheduling, with regard to productive capacities, serial formulae, standard episode length, genre breakdown and patterns of exploitation of domestic and foreign products. Interestingly, investment in fiction, too, showed common trends for Europe's big production markets, as Case Study 9.3 on the development of fiction demonstrates.

Case Study 9.3 also shows that many of the factors impacting on what is being produced are not

Case Study 9.2

National differences in investment terms in the case of fiction formats

The graph shows the diversity to be found with regard to preferences for the various fiction formats amongst Europe's five largest television markets. While TV movies and their offshoots, anthology and mini-series, occupy an important place in German, French and Italian production, Spain and Britain prefer series-based TV fiction (series and serials), investing almost nothing in the production of the closely cinema film-related TV movie.

Format definitions:

- The anthology or collection format 'involves different types of TV fiction, with different characters and production team, but which come under the same generic title'.
- Mini-series 'involves 2 to 6 episodes of a single TV fiction series';
- Serials include 'open serials' and 'closed serials', the latter involve at least 7 episodes; this category is only significant in the United Kingdom';
- Series 'involves open and shut episodes with the same central characters recurring in each episode'. (Jezequel and Lange, 2000, p. 5).

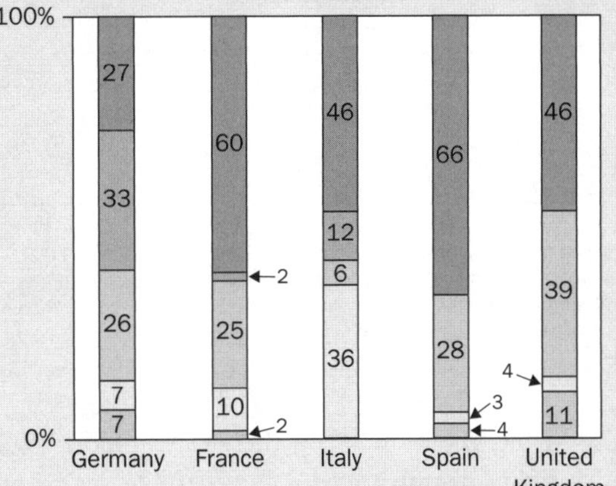

Financial value of each format as a percentage of total national productions

Source: Based on INA data, Jezequel and Lange (2000), p. 5.

Case Study 9.3

Shared trends in fiction production

Television markets can display significant similarities as far as production patterns are concerned. For all five major television markets 1996–2000 was a positive period, with average fiction production going up by more than 43%. This was because:

- most private commercial broadcasters were well-established by that time and could fall back on bigger programme budgets;
- competition within markets was strong and called for investment in local productions;
- prices for US fare had risen and made acquisitions from the USA less attractive.

Likewise, after 2000, conditions for fiction production worsened in all countries because of:

- a new priority for game and reality shows;
- the weak position of independent television producers;
- a prudent reliance on tried and tested formulas.

TV movies were particularly badly affected. Series fared better. They are popular with broadcasters because they create loyalty, are an easy way to fill schedules, can be used for prime-time and daytime scheduling, and have proven to be successful for audience ratings. In 2000, the series format was more widespread than ever before in European television schedules. Series had gone up from a 29% share of the format range in 1996 to 37%.

Source: EAO press releases and statistical yearbooks.

Table 9.2 AV production (EU)

Rank	*Country*
1	Iceland
2	Luxembourg
3	Switzerland
4	Denmark
5	Norway
6	France
9	Britain
⋮	⋮
22	Germany

Source: Based on Screen Digest calculations relating the number of films produced per million head of population in 31 European states in 2003. It has to be noted though that, given the low levels of production in the small territories and the small population, the ratio can vary widely from year to year (Screen Digest, 2005a, p. 7).

cultural but economic. Together, Case Studies 9.2 and 9.3 have demonstrated a considerable degree of both diversity and complexity. This is heightened if we include in our analysis fiction production in small countries. Producing fiction is cost-intensive, and small countries hence fall far behind in terms of volume and revenue. Yet again, if film output is related to population, we get an altogether different and interesting picture, as shown in Table 9.2.

The small Nordic countries and Luxembourg perform strongly because of stable government support. While cultural reasons are more prevalent for the Scandinavian countries, though, the Luxembourg government's support is traditionally and exclusively rooted in economic interests. Production here is not bound to Luxembourg culture and identity but to foreign investors who are attracted by Luxembourg's tax incentives. The 6th and 9th places for France and the UK, respectively, confirm their status as the lead production territories. Germany, on the other hand, under-performs markedly when it comes to relating production to the size of the national market.

Financing

The production of content cannot be studied without knowledge and understanding of financing mechanisms. Historically, television programmes have been financed by broadcasters, and this is still true to a great extent today.

In the case of PSBs, across Europe most are financed through a mix of income sources: licence fees, state grants, advertising and other commercial revenues. For most Western European broadcasters, the share of public funding is higher than that of commercial funding. An exception is Spanish RTVE, which is quite heavily dependent on advertising revenue. Also, it receives its public money from grants rather than a licence fee – a somewhat less secure income source. The BBC in the UK, Sweden's SVT and Norway's NRK are exceptions in that they take no advertising at all. Amongst Central and Eastern European broadcasters there are also vast differences. Polish TVP relies heavily on advertising, whilst Ceska Telvizie receives more than half its income from public funding (see Case Study 9.4). Regardless of the source, though, the size of the nation is vital in terms of what can be produced and to what standard.

The vast differences in the annual total income of PSBs range from €292 m in Portugal to nearly €6.9 bn in Germany, Europe's largest television market. It is also interesting to note large differences in annual revenue *per capita*, as demonstrated in an EAO table with data from 2000, which range from €12.4 in Poland and €20.9 in Greece to €156.3 in Switzerland and €115.2 in Denmark.

In general *per capita* differences reflect the wealth of the nation. International comparisons of advertising expenditure and economic wealth have revealed a strong and positive correlation, which is only rarely interrupted – in cases where legislation restricts advertising. In case of the licence fee, it is a combination of wealth and necessity, created by the number of inhabitants. Switzerland (7.6 million inhabitants, divided amongst three language areas) and the Scandinavian countries, for example, are rich and can afford to pay a high licence fee. In comparison to wealthy Germany (82 million inhabitants) or France (64 million) this is also necessary because the former countries' populations are small and there are substantially fewer people to finance production.

Case Study 9.4 hopefully makes clear how, because of the high production costs of television, small countries have a huge disadvantage in producing appealing content and building up an efficient and productive audio-visual industry. Small countries

Case Study 9.4

Differences in financing public service broadcasting across Europe

The following table shows the differences in regards to the sources of revenues between Europe's PSBs. It also reveals the vast differences in total revenue. The advantages of both size and a nation's wealth, to offset production costs, become obvious when comparing some of Europe's PSBs, who theoretically should offer similar services.

Income of PSBs in 2006

Country	*AT*	*CH*	*CZ*	*DE*	*ES*	*FR*	*BG*	*NO*	*PL*	*PT*
Channel	*ORF*	*SRG*	*Ceska Televizie*	*ARD, ZDF*	*Grupo RTVE*	*France 2*	*BBC*	*NRK*	*TVP*	*RIP*
Total Public Income, %	**49.9**	**63.2**	**52.8**	**85.5**	**43.9**	**53.5**	**75.7**	**95.0**	**28.2**	**76.8**
Aids/Grants, %	–	0.5	–	–	43.9	–	5.7	–	0.2	–
Licence Fee, %	49.9	62.7	52.8	85.5	–	53.5	69.5	94.7	28.0	–
Other public income, %	–	–	–	–	–	–	–	–	–	76.8
Total commercial income, %	**32.6**	**36.8**	**23.3**	**13.5**	**55.2**	**41.9**	**24.3**	**0.9**	**60.1**	**23.2**
Advertising & Sponsorship, %	32.6	30.3	23.3	6.1	52.8	37.8	–	0.9	61.1	16.5
Programme sales, %	–	3.8	–	–	1.2	–	4.7	–	–	–
Other commercial revenue, %	–	2.8	–	7.5	1.1	4.2	12.4	–	–	6.7
Other income, %	**17.5**	**–**	**15.6**	**1.1**	**0.9**	**4.6**	**–**	**4.1**	**11.7**	**–**
Total income in € million	927	1,108	183	6,852	1,320	1,751	5,740	462	487	292

'–' means no income or not accounted for.
Figures for CZ, DE, NO and PL are from 2005.
Source: based on country by country data in EAO's 2007 yearbook (EAO, 2007).

are disadvantaged not only because there are fewer people in the home market to finance local programming, but also because of their inherent structural scarcity in terms of social differentiation, economic net product and available resources such as capital, know-how, creativity, talent, competence and a professionally trained workforce. In the 1980s and 1990s, there was a common understanding that small states in Europe will almost inevitably lose the commercialisation and internationalisation game. Interestingly, the format boom, which we will discuss later on in this chapter, has enabled some small countries to compete successfully with larger markets.

Stop and consider 9.2

The differences in the ways that PSBs across Europe are funded are substantial, but even more substantial are the differences in the total of annual revenues and hence programme budgets. Why is it important to acknowledge this? What might the consequences be?

Financing private commercial television

The introduction of private commercial television and the increasing competition it brought with it did not alleviate the financial problems of small countries; on the contrary, it seems to have exacerbated them. Regardless of how many viewers are watching, costs of transmitting a channel and producing each programme screened are more or less fixed. Hence, private commercial broadcasters, who pay for their productions and programme acquisitions with the money they earn from selling advertising time, have traditionally aimed for high audience figures to achieve the revenue necessary to cover these costs.

However, since the 1980s the number of general interest and niche channels has multiplied; with a high number of channels to choose from the audience for individual channels shrinks and with it the latter's advertising revenue potential. The benefit gained from being able to deliver narrowly defined groups to advertisers is diminishing. Each year the share of advertising budgets spent on internet advertising is growing and there is no medium as well-suited to niche marketing as the internet.

Declining audience figures for the major channels together with new recording technologies, such as the US model TiVo and other personal video recorders (PVRs) that allow for ads to be skipped, are perceived as a great threat by the advertising and broadcasting industries. As a result there seems to be a slow shift from buying airtime for commercials to sponsorship, enabled by a relaxation in sponsorship laws at the national and EU level. Moreover, advertisers are increasingly becoming directly involved in creating and producing television content, a trend we will discuss at the end of this chapter.

A fairly recent and growing form of generating revenues is subscription. Whilst pay-TV was introduced in the USA already as early as the 1970s, European countries only started launching pay-TV services in the 1980s, and it was not until the 1990s that they took off. In most countries, most viewers were content with the extended terrestrial free-to-air offer that the introduction of advertising-financed broadcasters had brought. Their desire for more choice was limited, and a demand-push by broadcasters was necessary to convince them to pay extra.

By putting premium content, blockbusters and big sporting events as well as programmes addressing niche interests, on to subscription channels, bit by bit audiences were convinced to spend some additional money on television consumption. Premium content is a result of the gradually changing strategy of windowing, the economically sensible attempt to exploit content to the maximum by making it available on different platforms at different times and at differing prices, depending on the viewers' willingness and ability to pay.

The differentiated pricing model not only maximises the overall revenue but has been shown to be successful because programmes can be profitable even though no window they sell through is profitable on its own. Whereas in the past some programmes would not have been produced because they were financially unattractive for a free-to-air broadcaster, today's intricate exploitation of consumer spending strengthens possibilities for audio-visual content to become economically viable. This also implies that total resources for producing and acquiring audio-visual content have expanded.

Today income from direct viewer payments already represents a substantial share of broadcasting revenue in some European countries, notably the UK, Ireland, France and Sweden. How much of this income stays with the cable or satellite operator and how much is passed on to the broadcaster depends on various factors, the most important being:

- the attractiveness of a television channel, i.e. does the platform operator judge it necessary to offer this particular channel to its customers;
- the strength of the free-to-air market.

With a large attractive free-to-air market for competition, cable operators have little leeway to set premium prices and as a result limited means to pay premium channels. The latter will still aim for cable transmission, but their income will depend to a much greater degree on advertising.

Because Europe, in contrast to the USA, has produced some fairly strong free-to-air markets and has a population that grew up with free television (licence fee discounted), we can expect the mixed model to continue in the foreseeable future. The expectation of many that pay-TV in its current form will inevitably come to dominate European markets, following the US model, has to be viewed with caution. The experience of Europe's largest television market, Germany, speaks against this, and so too does the recent success of the UK's digital platform FreeView. However, for markets with a much smaller advertising potential, pay-TV is more likely to be the way forward. Also, we can expect a constant growth in pay-per-view spending in all markets. In the long-term the latter is the most likely form of pay-TV.

Funding high-cost productions

Financing becomes an issue of particular interest where cost-intensive productions are concerned. Here researchers will find a wide range of industry sources available, enabling them to identify current trends. As these trends have economic as well as potential cultural implications, it is also interesting to study policy in this area. In the past few decades, policy was aimed at supporting both culture and the audio-visual economy. An interesting and difficult question is whether these two objectives can be jointly supported.

We will look at the funding of films, abolishing the traditional distinction between films intended for screen release and films produced for the television market. Television is not only feature films' secondary market, but in Europe it is broadcasters who, next to public funding, play the most important role in financing feature films. The following thus will use the term film regardless of where the production was first screened.

If we compare European to US productions, it is worth highlighting that the former are characterised by public funding. The reasons for funding are economic as well as cultural in nature. Supporting regional/national culture and identity has always been a vital aspect of broadcasting, and it is still reflected in both national and EU communication and regulation today (see Chapter 4). The economic reasons are more recent. Both objectives result in support for the production industry, but there is a conflict when it comes to deciding which types of programmes to endorse. Funding bodies are torn between giving money to local and 'culturally worthy' productions and giving it to commercially promising fare, which implies targeting the international market with something that is more universal in content and that adopts certain international standards.

European film production is supported at the regional, national and local levels by various schemes, offering loans or subsidies for script development, distribution and exhibition. Nationally, most countries have at least one if not more of such funds, and often they are complemented by fiscal schemes such as tax shelters. The degree of support is partly reflected in the national rankings of European production companies, given above.

France is the most noticeable example of national public funding. Its key production subsidy is CSIPA (Compte de soutien à l'industrie des programmes audiovisuels), a fund made up of levies on pay-TV subscriptions, videos and television advertising. CSIPA accounts for roughly 15% of production budgets. Broadcasters provide around 52% of funding – due to production quotas that demand investment in programming of domestic origin and content quotas stipulating a minimum of 40% French-originated content. Foreign sales provide around 13% of production budgets. As well as CSIPA, France has a tax-based financing system, Sofica, under which companies and individuals can invest money into film productions and are offered tax write-offs if at least 90% of one year's investment is invested again in the next year.

Germany, too, is a European country with generous systems of film financing. Interest-free loans are provided by the Ministry of the Interior and by the national film Industry Support Agency (Filmförderungsanstalt). In addition, each region has a film support scheme, providing grants in return for economic effects. Local public and private broadcasters are partners in several of these schemes. Spain, like France and the UK, offers tax breaks next to subsidies for box office successes and funds for script development, distribution and exhibition. Italy stands out among the large Western European countries for having no specific support scheme for film production. However, film-makers can access public sector finance through the Banca Nazionale del Lavoro for national projects and co-productions involving other EU states and a few other countries with which Italy has co-production agreements (Westcott, 2002, pp. 27–37).

At the supra-national level, the EU launched the **MEDIA programme** in 1991(–1995). It was continued by MEDIAII, running from 1996–2000, MEDIA Plus (2001–2006) and MEDIA 2007 (2007–2013) with a budget of €755 m. The programme's general objectives are:

- 'to preserve and enhance European cultural diversity and its cinematographic and audiovisual heritage, guarantee accessibility to this for Europeans and promote intercultural dialogue;
- to increase the circulation of European audiovisual works inside and outside the European Union;
- to strengthen the competitiveness of the European audiovisual sector in the framework of an open and competitive market'.

(EC, 2006a)

The programme demonstrates the impact the integration attempts of the EU have on the audio-visual sector. The third bullet point of the quote about the programme's objectives also mirrors the media policy especially of the EU's larger member states, the UK, France and Germany, who are all trying to achieve cultural as well as economic benefits through financial aid.

Public funding is limited of course, and broadcasters find it increasingly difficult to finance a range of films, or even fiction series, of high production value at the national level. First, the competitive broadcasting environment means that more attractive programmes need to be financed with a stalled or even decreasing budget. Second, according to German industry executives, US fiction series of high production value mean that expectations of audiences are being raised in this genre. German audiences, they report, have got used to 'the visual allure and the dramaturgy of series such as CSI and seem to demand it with increasing insistence' (Schawinski, 2007, p. 94). To match the production budget of US fiction, which on average is about five times that of a European production, though, is difficult with a much smaller home market.

Financing through the international market

To be able to produce high-cost fiction, and also documentaries, European broadcasters hence turned to funding these at the international market. During the 1980s and early 1990s the number of co-produced and co-financed programmes was growing substantially. Because of the bundling of financial means, topics can be produced in high quality. Moreover, distribution is safeguarded in several countries whilst the risk is split. Reports in trade journals at the time testify how European as well as transatlantic co-productions and co-financed programmes were gaining in popularity (see Point of View 9.2).

However, co-productions lost some of their attractiveness from the mid-1990s onwards. Within the overall local production budgets, the period 1996–2002 saw no further significant growth in co-productions, and 2003 even saw their share falling. The drive to secure large audiences on a consistent basis, the difficulty of scheduling single 'event programmes' and the continuing popularity of light entertainment made co-productions a less attractive choice. We will turn to light entertainment towards the end of the chapter.

Point of View 9.2

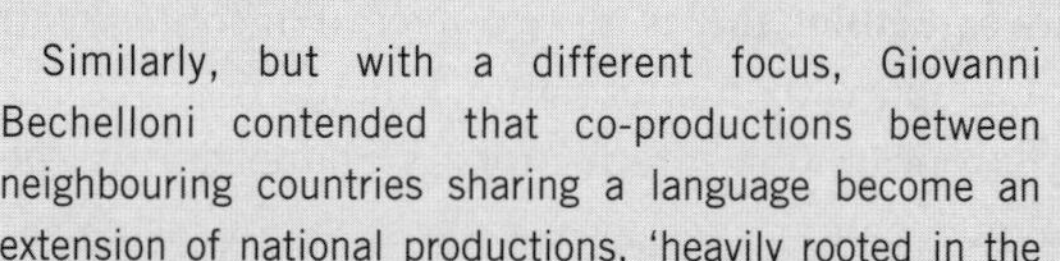

The assessment of co-productions

For our market analysis we have to keep in mind that the data we find influences our assessment of certain categories or trends, such as co-productions here; but also that our own research interests and assumptions influence our interpretation of the data we find.

Thus, from a cultural point of view, trans-national co-productions have been much criticised. German researcher Miriam Meckel argues that most co-productions fulfil certain format claims that the US market requires and are more a form of co-financing than of co-production (1994, pp. 121–124). This echoes George-Michael Luyken (1989, p. 92), who also stressed that co-productions with US partners implied not only a standardisation of English as film language, but also of narrative forms, plot patterns and image formats, thus running contrary to cultural autonomy and variety.

Similarly, but with a different focus, Giovanni Bechelloni contended that co-productions between neighbouring countries sharing a language become an extension of national productions, 'heavily rooted in the culture of the dominant country' (Bechelloni, 1998, p. xvi).

Both these arguments are interesting from a cultural point of view and certainly worth studying. But we can also take an economic perspective, which would lead us to conclude that co-productions allow all, including small and financially weak nations, to participate in producing costly programmes for the home market, and open foreign markets that otherwise would remain closed. Maybe this is better than leaving all the costly productions to the world's handful of large television markets?

An alternative route to co-production for the financing of high-cost fiction was selling local productions internationally. Efforts to do so increased significantly from the late 1980s onwards, as reports in trade journals attest (see Source 9.3).

Advertiser-funded programming

Finally, it is interesting to note that broadcasters are currently looking into new ways of funding their audio-visual content. Because ad-skipping technologies, such as TiVo and PVRs, are expected to reduce the power of advertising, brand owners display a growing interest in the idea of financing audio-visual content. Increased investment in sponsorship is one alternative to advertising, but advertisers in addition now seek to have direct input into content with which they can associate themselves.

The latest trend thus is advertiser-funded programming (AFP). The term of course is still also used to refer to the traditionally indirect funding of programmes and commercial channels through advertising, but in commercial circles it is used today to describe programming directly funded by brand owners, who are also involved in its creation. Examples of such 'branded content' are globally franchised shows, such as *Gillette World of Sport*, the *Orange Playlist* (see Case Study 9.5), *The Real DIY Show* (B&Q) or *Fashion House* (Nokia) – programmes in which emotions and desires are strategically linked to brands.

Many advertisers have come to see entertainment content as a valuable, even if rather indirect, way of communicating their brand values. The effectiveness of the traditional advertising paradigm – built on attracting hundreds of thousands of readers and viewers – is waning, they believe, and new ways of disseminating advertising messages are hence desperately searched for. AFP is one such way. Steve Heyer, president of the Coca-Cola Company, envisages a new

Source 9.3

Voices from trade journals

The following indirect quotes, taken from a variety of trade journals, show how producers were increasing their efforts to recoup their costs in the international market.

In 1988, media journalist Colin Brown wrote that Europe was increasingly 'customising' or 'Americanising' its product either to suit US partners or to recoup costs through international sales; and in 1996 his colleague Patrick Frater reported that more European companies than ever before were producing films in English.

Source: Big bang fires the great debate on TV quality, *Screen International*, p. 15 (Brown, 1988); Language lessons, *Screen International*, pp. 14–16 (Frater, 1996).

Olivier-René Veillon, CEO of distributor TV France International, noted that in Europe the times were over when production companies concentrated on the growth of the indigenous market. From around 1995 onwards, the style of management, he said, fundamentally altered. All big and small enterprises as well as most television channels were developing international strategies. The French production industry, for example, by 1996 achieved 20% of its turnover abroad, selling rights to or co-producing with foreign companies.

Source: quoted in: Mit Deutschland in die Offensive gehen, *Blinkpunkt Film*, 35/98.

In a similar vein, Jan Mojto, one of the CEOs of the German Kirch Group, claimed that what was happening elsewhere mattered very much. Respecting international standards and public expectations was seen as vital in this. In 1997 the Kirch Group sold 3200 hours of German-language programming, compared to just 1000 hours five years earlier. Its competitor RTL presented itself at the 1998 **Mipcom** in Cannes with 104 home-produced programmes, all synchronised into English for the international market.

Source: Jan Mojito quoted in Hansen and Roxborough (1998); Mipcom '98: Kirch wieder im Mittelpunkt, *Medien Aktuell*, 28 September.

Case Study 9.5

Orange Playlist

Produced by Endemol's subsidiary Initial, sponsored by Orange and broadcast on the UK's ITV, the 30-minute *Orange Playlist* show gives viewers a rundown of the top five MP3 downloads as well as the top five ringtones of the week (the top 20 of each chart are listed on the official website, http://www1.orange.co.uk/playlist/). Each episode features celebrity guests and competitions, as well as a discussion of current hot topics on which viewers are invited to comment using premium rate SMS and interactive voice response (IVR).

According to Morgan Holt, former Executive Producer Interactive at Initial, the *Orange Playlist* was developed to reflect changing patterns in music sales. The ringtone market was expected to account for 12% of total music sales by 2008. More important though seems the benfit gained from the brand awareness built for both Orange and Endemol through the show. As Holt says: '*By integrating mobile technology into the programming, we are able to interact with our viewers – helping them to get more from their mobile and building our own brand awareness*' (in Springer, 2007, p. 117).

era of 'co-creation', in which the 'killer application' is 'the convergence of the marketing trinity: entertainment content, media and brands' (Thinkbox, 2008).

For broadcasters and producers, on the other hand, AFP is an attractive added source of financing content in an ever tougher market place. Production companies such as Celador International, Endemol and All3Media have set up divisions to work with advertising clients on new ways of marketing brands and financing content. Elisabeth Murdoch's Shine: M was set up as a joint venture with advertising giant the WPP Group to provide branded content. Advertising and media agencies have created commercial arms especially devoted to the branded content sector (e.g. Mindshare's 'The Wow Factory', Starcom's 'Starcom+), and broadcasters, too, have set up or assigned existing departments to look into new partnerships with advertising clients (e.g. Discovery Networks Europe).

The following quote, taken from the website of the Branded Content Marketing Association (www.thebcma.info) nicely explains what the advertising industry is hoping to gain from getting involved in the production of entertainment.

> By enabling these new entertainment experiences, brands gain significant fame and goodwill. By creating more value for the consumer, more value for businesses is created.
>
> It means taking the philosophy and message of a brand and translating that into entertainment properties that consumers want to engage with, e.g. films, TV programmes, music, events, digital, sponsorship, and merchandising. Creating brand entertainment based on the things that really matter, consumers volunteer their attention. It is the move from interruption to attraction.

Also note that the TV marketing body Thinkbox has published a guide that 'brings together opinion and insights from the key stakeholders (producers, brand owners, content specialists and broadcasters) with the aim to review what has been learned to date and to explore how the process of broadcast AFP can be made easier' (www.thinkbox.tv). Moreover, it describes the legal requirements in the UK, as outlined by Ofcom in 2005. A further site of interest is http://adage.com/madisonandvine/, a website 'where commerce meets content' hosted by trade journal *Advertising Age*.

Stop and consider 9.3

The last few pages have revealed major changes in the financing of audio-visual production. Think about possible implications the various trends might have. Are they positive, negative or a mix of both? What could you as a policy-maker do to avoid negative implications?

Entertainment on our television screens: production, acquisition, scheduling

The last section has explored above all the economic forces that affect both change and diversity and that also require the researcher to look beyond the national level when researching television programming. It is this trans-national and international aspect of programming that the following will explore a bit further. The question of domestic versus US fiction is an interesting one. With the onslaught of private commercial television, many politicians and academics came to fear the 'Americanisation' of television, but trends in the 1990s suggested that home-produced programmes were the way forward.

Moreover, the question of whether and how European integration is reflected in programming schedules across Europe is intriguing. EU policy documents from the early 1980s reveal the belief in the need of a common European audio-visual service or space for creating a European identity. But does the scheduling of fiction suggest European integration?

Finally, the rise of formatted programming in the late 1990s is a fascinating area of study. What are **television formats**? Where do they come from? How are they produced? And why are they so popular with broadcasters and audiences alike?

Data on all these three areas will be provided, and cultural, legislatory and economic factors will be explored to help us read the empirical data.

US fiction on Europe's television screens

US content has a long history in Western Europe's broadcasting schedules, and studies before the mid-1980s prove that the noted flood of US fictional material was nothing new in most countries (see Source 9.4). Undeniably, though, its overall share increased with the onset of commercial television.

An update of this graph (Source 9.4), unfortunately, is impossible as the EAO has changed the number of countries included in its scheduled fiction statistics. The *2007 Yearbook* only provides comparison between 2005 and 2006 data. Overall though this data can be used for a rough assessment of how fiction imports are developing.

The comparison of 2006 figures with those of 2005 shows that (a) the share of imported fiction from other European countries had decreased; (b) European co-productions had slightly decreased; (c) co-productions with non-European countries had increased; and (d) imports from third countries had also decreased (EAO, 2007, Vol. 2, p. 152). This allows us to conclude that as in the years before it is the share in co-productions with non-European countries that continues to grow, whilst European co-productions are slightly decreasing and imports from European and third countries (including the USA), too, are falling (since 2004).

Domestic vs US fiction

While some continue to lament the Americanisation of our television, many academics, alongside industry professionals, came to highlight audiences' preference for local productions in the 1990s. Source 9.4 proves that, when it comes to imported fiction, reliance on US fare has not decreased. The little decrease there is has been made up for with co-productions with the USA. But what about the claim that local programmes came to replace US content, in particular in peak-time schedules?

EAO statistics show that the 1990s saw an increase in domestically produced content and that there was a tendency for prime-time to become increasingly domestic while US content was filling off-prime schedules. Also, various television yearbooks and trade journals reported in the 1990s that most television stations had come to view indigenous productions as their flagship programming and were thus scheduling it in prime-time. Many drew the simplified and presumably desired conclusion that this proved viewers wanted a homogenous, indigenous product.

If we read trade journals carefully, though, we note that imported movies featured prominently in many broadcasters' prime-time schedules; and there was plenty of evidence of the unabated popularity of US programmes. In the mid-1990s, the Top 10 single

Source 9.4

Where does non-domestic fiction broadcast on European television screens come from?

The following graph can be used to demonstrate the overwhelming dominance of US fiction amongst fiction imports on Western European television screens. It also shows that the reliance on US fiction rose continuously after 1996 (the year when the EAO started collating comparable data). The slight decrease of US imports after 1999 is partly the result of inter-European co-productions increasing slightly, but more due to a growth in US co-productions with Europe. The loss for the USA was much slighter than it appears.

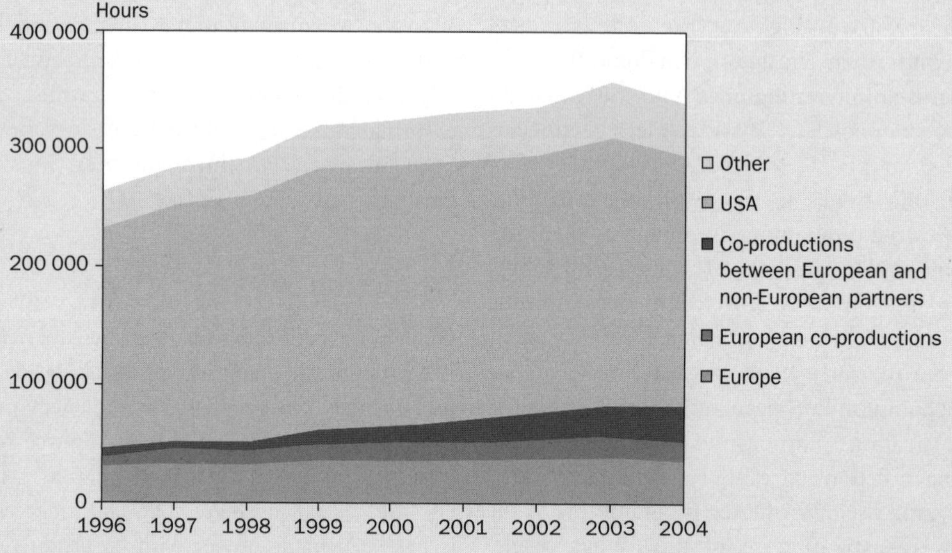

Origin of imported fiction broadcast by TV channels in Western Europe in hours broadcast, 1996–2004

Source: Based on ETS/EAO data, EAO Yearbooks (EAO, 2002b, 2005).

programmes of several of France's television channels included many American movies, and the same was true for Greece, Italy, Norway and Sweden. In Germany, the Top 10 single programmes were either sporting events or American movies. The unabated enthusiasm for US products in this country is remarkable considering that Germany is Europe's largest television market with huge programming budgets at its disposal. Also, competition among free-to-air broadcasters is stronger than in any other European market. Even so, local productions only seemed to be part of the ordinance.

Both scheduling and the balance between home-produced programmes and acquisitions are more complex than usually accounted for. There are annual ups and downs in each country, at different times. For example, while between 1996 and 2000 an expansion in domestic fiction and a contraction in US fiction was observed on *average* (Britain being an exception because Channel 5 had reversed this trend), the period 1999–2000 already revealed a reverse trend for prime-time in three of the five countries noted. In the UK, Germany and Italy, US imports were on the increase, making a significant leap from 30% to 44% in Germany, and from 38% to 49% in the UK. Also, by 2003, the share of US fiction in weekly schedules had risen from below 50 to 52% (EAO, 2004, Vol. 5, pp. 64–67).

While the much-stressed popularity of indigenous content during the 1990s led many to believe that increased competition coupled with customer demand cannot but lead to a continuing growth in local productions, most commentators ignored the fact that investment in either indigenous productions or imported programming is a result of a complex combination of various factors (see Table 9.3).

It does not all depend on audience preferences, as many academics and industry professionals would have us believe. It may be more relevant to view home-produced fiction and foreign imports, especially US ones, as complementary programmes (see Case Study 9.6).

Television fiction and European integration

The trade in fiction does not suggest a 'Europeanisation' of television markets. Whilst such a process is clearly manifested in EU regulation and policy – above all in the Television without Frontiers Directive's 'minimum rules' and the requirement that broadcasters reserve a 'majority proportion' of

Table 9.3 AV investment factors

1. Competition within the broadcast market	Increased competition in a market means that broadcasters need to deliver what is most popular with audiences. Local programming is more popular than foreign programming if the home-grown content delivers quality similar to that of foreign acquisitions.
2. Budgeting constraints	1. Start-up channels usually have a small budget and therefore tend to import heavily in the beginning. (This has led, for example, to the trend in the UK running counter to that of the other big European markets after the launch of Channel 5 – see above.) 2. When advertising income declines (as for example in 2001), broadcasters have less money to spend on programming and thus invest less in production. 3. Where fragmentation shrinks audience figures and with it advertising and subscription revenues, programming budgets are cut. If prices for acquisitions are cheaper this results in a decrease in local productions.
3. Prices for foreign fare	Prices for foreign off-the-shelf fare are not stable but depend on many factors. In the 1980s, for example, US imports proved a cheap and popular source of programming. But with the steadily rising programme demand, competition for US acquisitions rose and with it the prices for popular US fare. As a result producing popular domestic fare gained in attractiveness. Prices, moreover, fluctuate depending on exchange rates, the strength of trade unions and changes in policy, in particular tax incentives.
4. Support of local production through quotas and subsidies	The example of France (see Case Study 9.6) shows that the high share of imported fiction from other European countries is a result of the 60% quota for European content. The high production volume, on the other hand, is undeniably the result of government support.
5. Scheduling practices	Successful import and export is dependent on programmes fitting into the standard slots of local broadcasters. This concerns the length of a programme, the number of episodes and whether new, unfamiliar genres can find a suitable slot in local schedules.
6. Shift in the share of genres broadcast	The 1990s and the first years of the new millennium have shown that a big shift to the less costly light entertainment genre has enabled a growth in local productions. Should the audience tire of light entertainment and shift its preference to high-cost productions, most countries would have to increase their share of imports and co-productions again.
7. Popularity of individual foreign shows	Big local hits will always attract the interest of foreign buyers. They are seen as less risky than content that has not yet been tested.
8. Availability of production talent and facilities	Small countries are usually disadvantaged here. The government support in Luxembourg, though, has managed to turn the tables, and the Scandinavian countries, too, are making headway thanks to state support and the chances that the popularity of the less costly light entertainment formats has opened up for producers (see below).

Case Study 9.6

Domestic vs US vs European fiction

Graph 1 demonstrates that in 2000, with the exception of France and Spain, even during prime-time domestic fiction did not feature much more prominently than US fiction. In Italy it was even lower.

Figures for the whole day (Graph 2) reveal the undisputed dominance of US programmes. Particularly interesting here is France, with the relation between US and domestic fiction being nearly reversed.

The graphs also demonstrate that there is little interest for European programmes in Europe. France broadcasts by far the largest amount of European programming, Spain is in second place. UK broadcasters show next to no fiction programmes from Europe; Australian imports have a large share in the 'other' category here. Italy and Spain (and the same is true for Portugal) prefer the linguistically and culturally more proximate Latin American programmes (usually telenovelas) to European fiction.

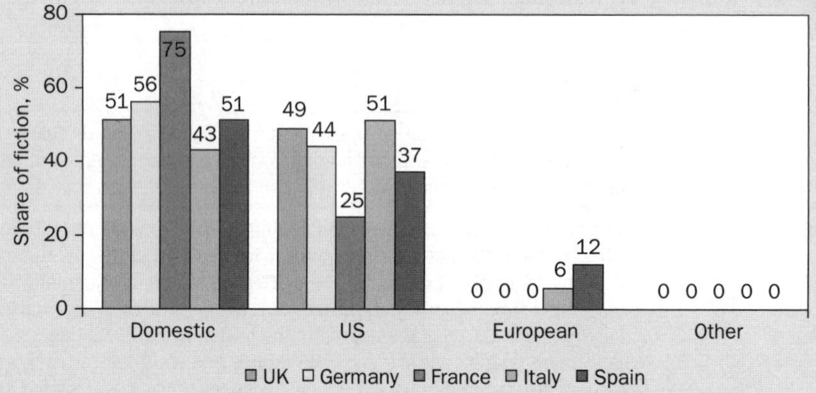

Graph 1 Geographical origin of TV fiction during *prime-time* in Europe's five largest television markets.

Source: The graph is based on *Eurofiction* data, which measured TV fiction programmed by major networks in the sample week 12–18 March 2000 (EAO, 2001b).

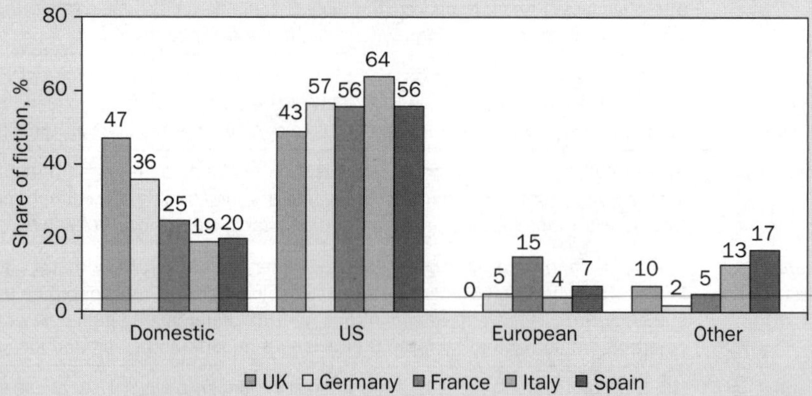

Graph 2 Geographical origin of TV fiction *throughout the day* in Europe's five largest television markets

Source: The graph is based on *Eurofiction* data, which measured TV fiction programmed by major networks in the sample week 12–18 March 2000 (EAO, 2001b).

their total transmission time for European works – the development of inter-European programme trade is sobering. But what about this quota for European works? Does it have no effect at all?

A few broadcasters ignore the quota completely (notably BSkyB in the UK and all cable and satellite channels in Italy); new channels have to adhere to the rule only 'progressively' and 'where practicable' (1997 revision); and the majority of broadcasters across Europe who comply (i.e. schedule at least 51% of content with European origin) achieve this with overwhelmingly domestic productions (EC, 2006b). As the graphs on scheduled TV fiction above have demonstrated, the percentage of non-domestic European programmes is minimal. Notable exceptions are those small European countries that share a language with a bigger neighbour (see Case Study 9.7).

The share of fiction Austrian public service broadcaster ORF and Swiss German-language public service broadcaster DRS import from Germany is recognisably larger than those from other European countries. ORF2's and DRS's import share from Germany even exceeds by far that of the USA. The Swiss French-language public service channel TSR imports a large share from France, and so too do the two French-language Belgian broadcasters. Public service broadcaster RTBF1 (now La Une) imports a much higher share from France than private commercial channel RTL-Tvi, which has a higher US share. Interestingly, it also has a higher share of fiction imports from Germany, the biggest market of the RTL Group. It should be pointed out, however, that German fiction did well in other European markets, too, in 2004. Finally, we should note that a large proportion of the substantial shares of co-productions are collaborations between these small countries and their bigger same-language neighbours.

The low interest in programmes from other European countries may suggest there is no such thing as a European identity yet. Even so, common arguments about language problems and differing cultural mentalities are no sufficient explanation for Europe's export failure in general. It is only part of the problem. All European countries are well accustomed to and happy with either dubbed or subtitled programmes from the USA, but Canada, the UK and

Case Study 9.7

Fiction imported by TV-channels in Austria, Belgium and Switzerland

The 2004 data from Austrian, Belgian and Swiss broadcasters reveals how these countries' broadcasters import noteworthy to substantial amounts from their European neighbours.

Origin of fiction imported by TV-channels in Austria, Belgium and Switzerland in 2004

	DE %	*ES %*	*FR %*	*GB %*	*IT %*	*Other EUR %*	*US %*	*European co-production*
AT								
ORF 1	**5.76**	1	0.59	2.08	0.15	0.87	67.64	9.99
ORF 2	**52.06**	0	0	0.29	0.32	0.03	21.29	**25.54**
BE								
RTBF1 (FR)	**6.94**	0	**18.58**	1.34	0.37	0.14	47.12	**18.37**
RTL-Tvi (FR)	**12.64**	0	**10.69**	2.83	0	0	59.25	6.89
CH								
DRS (DE)	**34.39**	0	1.21	2	0	1.57	8.63	**35.77**
TSI (IT)	4.22	0	0.38	2.35	**7.28**	0	55.47	13.90
TSR (FR)	3.34	0.23	**15.82**	0.93	0.30	0.28	60.93	10.33

Source: Calculated by the author based on information provided in EAO (2005, Vol. 5, p. 96).

Australia, too, fall way behind the USA in the export statistics. Moreover, nobody would deny that the USA, too, has a distinct culture. It is different, though, from European countries in that people all over the world have been familiarised with it through its television content. As early as 1914, 85% of the world film audience was watching US films. A much more convincing explanation for the US's trade success compared to Europe's is its combination of:

- high lead in production expertise;
- much larger production budgets;
- advanced experience with the demands of a commercial TV market;
- sophisticated and powerful distribution network;
- high marketing expenditure;
- high familiarity across the world.

As has been shown above, the increased commercialisation of Europe's television markets has led to the production of more internationally saleable programmes. What Europe is lacking is not just the production budgets to match those of the USA, but also a comparable distribution infrastructure and the marketing budgets available to US distributors – admittedly a difficult, if not impossible, undertaking given the much smaller size of European distributors with therefore lower budgets and the difficult and risky task of promoting films from countries without much of a reputation (compared with Hollywood) and possibly languages for which there is no translation infrastructure.

There is one area though, where European producers have been very successful in the past ten years, surpassing US producers: television **formats**, the new prime-time staple. Programme formats are developed in one market and then sold internationally, usually for local adaptation. Creating and selling formats, rather than finished programmes, has allowed European producers from both large and small countries to grow. The factors that have brought about this change are economic as well as cultural. The interesting question that arises for the researcher interested in culture is whether a daily dose of television formats leads to a convergence of television and with it maybe even a convergence of cultures.

The rise of formats

The format boom started in the early 1990s, when talk shows and game shows proved very popular with viewers. In the late 1990s this success was followed by formats for reality shows, and in the new millennium by hybrids, such as *Faking It*, *Wife Swap* or *Changing Rooms*, creating variations of the old genres of observational documentary, game shows and soap drama. Since the mid-2000s, there have been reports about the 'return of the game show to prime-time schedules', either in the form of the revival of classic studio-based variety and quiz shows (e.g. *Deal or No Deal*, broadcast in the UK, Austria and Poland, or the return of *Family Feud* to Germany, Portugal and Switzerland); or in the form of new game show formats, giving contestants the chance to change the course of their lives (e.g. *For the Rest of Your Life*).

Formats, a kind of indirect programme import, have not only come to constitute a major share of the overall programme offer of some channels, but have come to determine primetime schedules and even national Top 10/20 programme lists. Table 9.4 can be used not only to prove top audience ratings for these shows but also to prove that they work exceptionally well in various countries.

To give an example of their trans-national pulling power: to date, one of the most successful examples is *Who Wants to Be a Millionaire?*, created by British producer Celador in 1998. By 2006 the show had been sold to 105 countries, 67 of which had produced local adaptations. In Europe it has ranked among the Top 10 programmes in Sweden, Holland, Germany, Britain, France, Italy, Hungary, Estonia, Slovakia and Slovenia.

For broadcasters formats are attractive for various reasons:

- offer a proven track record of success in other countries;
- enable the creation of popular 'domestic' programming;
- fuel local and in-house production and contribute to domestic production quotas;
- provide high-volume titles;
- can be produced relatively cheaply.

Table 9.4 2004 top rated formats in a selection of European countries

Belgium (North)	*A Farmer Wants a Wife* *(Pop) Idol* *Wife Swap* *Under Construction*	Slovakia	*(Pop) Idol* *Girl in a Million* *Who Wants to be a Millionaire?* *Wife Swap*
France	*That'll Teach Them* *(Pop) Idol* *The Bachelor* *Wife Swap*	Hungary	*Who Wants to be a Millionaire?* *Megastar (Pop Idol)* *The Bachelor*
UK	*I'm a Celebrity Get Me Out of Here* *Strictly Come Dancing* *Big Brother* *Wife Swap* *You Are What You Eat* *Brat Camp*	Germany	*Who Wants to be a Millionaire?* *I'm a Celebrity Get Me Out of Here* *Pop Stars* *The Swan*

Source: Collated by the author based on information provided in *Television Yearbooks – European Key Facts* (IP Groupe, 2005). All listed programmes made it into various national Top 10 or 20 hit lists, as measured by audience ratings.

According to trade publisher Screen Digest the number of formatted shows broadcast between 2002 and 2004 rose by over a third (Screen Digest, 2005b). By 2004, the popularity was such that the global format business was worth €2.4 bn, and the trend showed no sign of letting up. Even formats for comedy shows were now crossing borders. Germany's prime-time and prize winning improvisation comedy *Schillerstrasse*, screened first in autumn 2004, had been sold to 16 territories on four different continents, including the USA, two years later. In Europe it had been bought by broadcasters in Belgium, the Czech Republic, Denmark, Finland, France, Italy, the Netherlands, Romania, Spain and the UK.

The UK is the biggest exporter of formats worldwide, with a global market share somewhere between 33% (Freemantle research) and 53% (TRP, 2008). Its most successful programme, Celador's *Who Wants to be a Millionaire*? (1998), followed by the success of *Survivor* (2000) led British producers to plunge into developing formats for the international and US market. The second most important format export nations are The Netherlands and the US.

Interesting to note is the chance that format development opened up to small countries. Sweden, Norway and Denmark all embarked on the profitable business of inventing and distributing inexpensive formats. Moreover, where all other genres had failed, the huge prime-time success of big-money game shows and reality shows across Europe opened the way into the US market. According to an industry source, US networks were turning to Europe because it was more advanced when it came to reality programming.

Another interesting aspect, highlighted by Iosifides *et al.* (2005, pp. 152–153), is that a change in economics seems to reflect the growing importance of the format business. Format fees based on a percentage of the production budget (5–15% per episode) and limited amounts of consultancy are no longer their lynchpin. For increasingly complex reality formats involving ordinary people and prime-time entertainment formats, the value of a format rests on selling production expertise, incorporating casting, filming and editing skills to make a successful show. For hit shows like *Who Wants to be a Millionaire?* or *The Weakest Link*, broadcasters are sold complex packages and computer software. This practice not only increases returns but also ensures that in the interests of preserving creative control over what are perceived as global brands there is little opportunity for deviation.

To grow revenues further format-owners have moreover been getting increasingly involved as co-producers and producers, setting up production subsidiaries abroad. British RDF, for example, produced *Wife Swap* and *Faking It* for US channels in the USA itself, reaping production revenues as well as format fees. BBC Worldwide co-produced *The Weakest Link* with local partners. In 2007 and 2008 the trade press was full of reports of producers setting up business and expanding further abroad. To name but a few interesting examples, Endemol was reported to be increasing its presence in Korea; Telemundo International to be looking to co-produce in Central Europe; FremantleMedia to entering a strategic alliance with a Japanese independent producer; and the BBC to be taking up production offices worldwide.

To conclude on a cultural note, the above has shown that even though many have been stressing the importance of local flair and local production since the 1990s, production trends in the new millennium ensure that a substantial amount of trans-nationalisation of television content is taking place. Formats, a kind of indirect programme import, came to take a major share of the overall programme offer of some channels and a major share of prime-time schedules. In the statistics they are labelled as indigenous production; regulatory agencies are prepared to look at them as domestic; and with audiences, too, the finished programme registers as home-grown.

Programme formats, as well as programme length, newly introduced genres and production practice, should no doubt be viewed as examples of programming undergoing a process of trans-nationalisation. If adapted versions of game shows and series alone are taken into account in prime-time surveys, the amount of 'national' programming is decreased to quite an extent. Even so, evaluating such internationalisation is a matter of interpretation. Albert Moran (1998), for example, argues that national adaptations are less evidence for a factual globalisation trend, but rather express the strength of national identities. German researcher Hans J. Kleinsteuber (1992), on the other hand, looking at various localisation strategies, has decided that much of the claimed localism is camouflage for a system of local distribution of centrally produced material; the outcome not more but 'pseudo-localism'. We leave it up to the reader to decide what camp he or she is in.

Other programming trends in the new millennium: added-value, textual convergence and interactivity

Added-value programming

In recent years there has been a significant rise in 'added-value programming', where extra revenue is created by television programmes being accompanied by phone-ins, spin-offs and merchandising products. Many children's programmes, cookery shows or game shows can be used as examples of this, including *Who Wants to be a Millionaire?* (Case Study 9.8).

The growth in added-value programming has been much supported by digitisation and new communications technologies, allowing for a whole new range of ways in which content can be exploited. Numerous shows have demonstrated the ability to create new revenue streams from online applications, SMS text messaging, premium phone lines and sponsorship across different platforms on television and the web. As far as content being distributed across a variety of media platforms is concerned, with income from television only being one revenue stream among others, Endemol's *Big Brother* is exemplary (Case Study 9.9).

Added-value is not just about revenues, though; it is also about building strong brands – something of ever-growing importance in today's world of information overload. Moreover, many added-value features have another benefit: offering a more interactive approach to television, they engage the viewer, creating feelings of both empowerment and loyalty. As Rob Clarke, senior executive vice president of FremantleMedia, says: 'Interactivity is not just there as a revenue source. It's there to build in loyalty to the series. Websites are more than just an add-on to a production. Now it's part of the whole process. I can't overemphasise that. It will become more and more driven that way' (cited in Esposito, 2006, p. 58). In the following we will look a bit more closely at the aspects of interactivity and branding. The latter

Case Study 9.8

Added-value programming: *Who Wants to be a Millionaire?*

Who Wants to be a Millionaire? is a good example of a television programme being exploited to the full via television spin-offs and merchandising products.

Who Wants to be a Millionaire?

On TV:

Themed editions

- Celebrity
- Parent & Child
- Couples
- Olympic
- Valentines

Interactive → In the UK BSkyB's Gamestar portal offers 24h play

Retail products

- Board games → Sold more than 1m units in the UK; 1.5m in Germany; top selling board game in France in 2001+2002
- Play stations
- Quiz books → Nearly 2m sold in the UK
- Christmas crackers
- Chocolate games
- Mobile games → Launched in 30 countries, with over 400m subscribers
- Interactive DVDs

Source: based on *Rights of Passage. British Television in the Global Market*, p. 26 (Colwell and Price, 2005).

Case Study 9.9

Big Brother

Big Brother constitutes the first major success of television programming being distributed on various platforms to reach maximum audience potential. In Germany, for example, besides watching the daily broadcast on terrestrial channel RTLII, and a weekly summary on its larger sister channel RTL, viewers could also subscribe to a channel on the pay-TV platform Premiere, which would let them watch the action in the Big Brother house 24 hours a day. There was a *Big Brother* magazine, mobile updates and, for €0.99 Internet users with T-Online, Germany's largest Internet service provider (ISP), could watch a three-minute video with highlights of the day. Moreover, RTL's *Big Brother* web site offered a 24-hour streaming video, which in 2004 pulled in 100 million page impressions a month.

Ruud Hendriks, responsible for overseeing all on-line activities at Endemol Entertainment, explained that building up the television station's Internet site with hugely popular shows such as *Big Brother* did not just allow them to sell advertising online, but also added income generated from the ISPs, who profit from attracting new subscribers. In Spain, for example, as much as 25% of the Internet traffic during the peak of the show's run was generated by visitors to the *Big Brother* site.

Stephan Zingg, senior interactive project consultant at Endemol International, argued that using various media not only boosts potential revenues but for some shows, ancillary revenues are as important as the TV licence fee they get from the broadcaster. Following the *Big Brother* success, Endemol today aggressively pursues potential revenues from telephones, mobile phones, the Internet, SMS, iTV applications and other technologies for every single format it is developing.

Sources: Fast forward to the future, *World Screen.com* (Winslow, 2004); The Rights Stuff?, *World Screen News*, October, pp. 184–87 (Tasca, 2000).

will be dealt with in the final section on textual convergence.

Interactive television content

Interactive television (iTV) is still poorly defined. A tentative attempt at providing an academic definition of iTV has been made by Jens Jensen:

> iTV can be considered a new form of television that makes it possible for the viewer to interact with the medium in such a way that he gains control over what to watch, when to watch, and how to watch, or directly opens up for active participation in a programme.
>
> (Jensen, 2005, p. 105)

This definition is still sketchy. It fails to overcome the difficult fact that people, in a way, have always interacted with the television, or any other medium. Audiences have always been able to decide over 'what to watch' (or maybe not to watch), 'when to watch' (and when not to watch), or 'how to watch', in the sense that they may have been doing other things at the same time or that their viewing attitude may have varied between programmes. Were they watching for escapist reasons, to learn something, or were they reflecting on and analysing what they were seeing? Or maybe all of those things at once? Of course, the interactive possibilities Jensen has in mind are more enhanced.

Thus, it may be helpful to keep in mind the concept of interactivity as outlined by Lister *et al.* (2003) in relation to new media. The authors distinguish between the instrumental and the ideological level. The instumental level describes users' ability to directly intervene in and change texts they access. Audiences become 'users' rather than 'viewers', exploring, playing and experimenting with the material at hand. At the ideological level, interactivity provides a more powerful sense of user engagement with media texts. Users have a more independent relationship to sources of knowledge, greater choice and a more individualised media use.

While the Internet of course allows for even more user intervention at the textual level and an even more individualised media use than iTV, most of the following examples are a huge step in the 'viewer becoming a user' direction. Also, taken together with Jensen's quote, they reveal what can be considered as iTV today:

- alternative story lines;
- electronic programme guide (EPG);
- intelligent agent/personalised TV (TiVo);
- home shopping;
- home banking;
- selecting camera angles for sporting events ('enhanced TV');
- interactive news;
- real-time voting;
- interactive games;
- interactive advertising;
- access to database and online information;
- internet access;
- video-on-demand (VOD) and near-VOD.

A useful programme typology has been developed by Interactive Television International (iTVi), an industry lobby group. It divides iTV into four categories:

1. Television programmes that are not modified by the interactivity, the interactivity runs parallel to the show (e.g. web site with additional information; e.g. *LOST*).
2. Television programmes that are modified by the interactivity (usually through phone-ins; e.g. *Big Brother*).
3. Television programmes assembled by the viewer from several broadcast signals (e.g. camera angle in sports events).
4. Interactive services that can eventually become television shows. They do not appear as 'show' to viewers at the moment but may become accepted as normal TV content (e.g. interactive weather reports; traffic information; stock quotes; betting).

Interestingly, but not unexpected by the industry, the 'killer application' of iTV thus far has been gambling. In the world's most advanced iTV markets, France and the UK, gambling has been Canal+'s and

BSkyB's by far best iTV revenue producer. The consulting and research firm Forrester expect iTV betting in Europe to grow from about €400 m in 2004 to €3 bn in 2009. Total iTV revenue, they estimate, will grow from under €1.6 bn in 2004 to about €13 bn in 2009. A substantial amount of the latter is expected to come from interactive advertising (Winslow, 2004).

As pointed out by entertainment specialist Rob Clarke (cited in Esposito, 2006), interactivity is not just beneficial in terms of generating direct revenues, though. It also has an indirect monetary value in that it creates loyalty, which in turn binds viewers to a particular text. By offering viewers running engagement, producers and broadcasters aim to prevent them from switching over to content provided by competitors. The case study of *Lost* below (Case Study 9.10), embedded in the trend for textual convergence, nicely demonstrates how audiences can be retained with textual extensions and the interactive engagement they create with a show.

Textual convergence

Like interactivity, textual convergence is a trend with enormous implications for the production of audio-visual content. At the simplest level, textual convergence means that texts from different sources come together. More clearly, whereas different media all used to have their own, unique content, now we find the same, or related, content across a variety of media. Of course it has to be noted that the practice of using successful content from one medium and reworking it for another is nothing new. Taking novels and adapting them for the screen is an old and well-established practice. But the extent of using the same content for adaptation across a range of media is new.

A popular combination these days is blockbusters and games. Films turned into computer games include *Star Wars*, *Blade Runner*, *Goldeneye* and *Mission Impossible*. However, increasingly it also happens the other way round. *Mortal Combat*, *Tomb Raider* and *Streetfighter* started as games and were then made into movies. The significance of this convergence does not just show in numbers but also in the fact that even Oscar-winning directors engage in the cross-over. For instance, Steven Spielberg has developed at least three original games for the world's largest games developer, Electronic Arts (EA), and Peter Jackson worked on the movie version of sci-fi shooter *Halo* and has been closely involved in the game version of *King Kong*.

A second growth factor is the number of platforms across which content is spread and exploited. *Men in Black*, for example, has been sold as a movie, a video, a TV series, a game and a magazine. The *Big Brother* case study above has shown that TV shows, too, are now being exploited across multiple platforms. As with interactivity, textual convergence is not only about optimising the financial exploitation, though, but also about branding and about binding audiences. Why, owners of audio-visual content ask themselves, should we let the audience go just because they switch off the television? This thinking is heightened by the fact that research increasingly reveals young people are switching to other media and/or are relegating the television to a background medium while they surf the Net, instant message, text or play online games.

Case Study 9.10 illustrates how broadcasters attempt to retain audiences of *Lost* by offering them textual extensions online. It also demonstrates how other objectives are achieved with the textual extensions.

The resulting convergence of 'original' and promotional content is something David Marshall has illuminated (Marshall, 2002). It has long been an aspect of children's marketing, with comic heroes being made into television programmes, their characters used on cereals and sold as toys, he says. However, today adult entertainment, too, sees promotional material being commodified. Documentaries about 'the making of', interviews with stars or dedicated web sites launched before the release of a film, are examples of this. A whole new converged product package is created – something for which Marshall has coined the term 'intertextual commodity'. The *Blair Witch Project*'s promotional development, for example, he argues convincingly, was an integral part of the experience of the film and contributed much to its success.

Case Study 9.10

Brand building and binding viewers – *Lost*

To bind viewers and strengthen its brand as a premium-content channel with top fiction programmes, SkyOne, for instance, offers the following textual extensions for *Lost* on its web site:

- information about the show and individual episodes;
- news about *Lost* and its production;
- a photo gallery with stills;
- video clips from the current season and interviews with the actors;
- information about each of the main characters;
- cast wallpapers for downloading;
- exclusive and behind-the-scene features;
- podcasts, which 'dissect every episode in full';
- a discussion forum, which featured 1847 topics by August 2008, with viewings in the hundreds, thousands and sometimes even tens of thousands.

The website also advertises

- the *Lost* magazine;
- the *Lost* video game;
- the opportunity to watch missed episodes on Sky Player.

Print and outdoor advertising, trailers and stories placed in television listings magazines and other media, all of which display the Sky logo, remind the viewer of the 'must-see' character of the show, completing the marketing of both the *Lost* and the *Sky* brands.

Source: www.skyone.co.uk/lost/.

To give another of Marshall's examples of an intertextual commodity: *Tomb Raider* originated in 1996 as a PlayStation adventure game and was then turned into a movie. Its heroine, Lara Croft, achieved celebrity status. A soundtrack was published, an official web site and fan web sites were created, and Lara started endorsing products (boots, diveware, mobile technology, Land Rover, fast food restaurant Taco Bell, Pepsi) and made guest appearances in other comics. Today almost all stars, Marshall concludes, sell not only their own image and the products they are directly involved in (films, TV shows), but also the products they endorse as well as the media reporting about them.

On a concluding note it should be pointed out that all this textual convergence must be seen in the context of a larger convergence trend in the media industry. Textual convergence is rising rapidly not least because of technological convergence (e.g. the Internet providing voice telephony, audio and webcasting) and market convergence, where traditionally distinct media and communications players are entering each other's business. Cross-media expansion has a long history; but the process has accelerated in the past few decades, with large trans-national media corporations (TNCs), such as Bertelsmann, Time Warner or News Corporation, massively spreading their business in book, magazine and newspaper publishing, radio and television broadcasting, and film and television production. Moreover, convergence does not stop here. Due to technological convergence the latest wave of market convergence involves broadcasters, ISPs and telecommunications firms. Thus, BSkyB, originally a satellite broadcaster, now offers free broadband access and telephony; and BT, a traditional telecommunications operator, offers broadband and television. Both market and technological convergence will be illuminated in the next chapter. For the future production of audio-visual content, convergence no doubt has major implications.

Chapter summary

➤ The introduction of private commercial television in Europe in the 1980s had a significant impact on the production of audio-visual content. Economic considerations have become the foremost defining factor of production; content has been commoditised.

➤ There is an argument about the extent to which audio-visual content in Europe is influenced by the USA. We can attest that the demand for US fiction is consistently high. The large home market and the well-established international trade network enable US producers to offer fiction of unrivalled high production value.

➤ Other influences coming from the USA, such as scheduling practices, new genres or production values, all result from the commercialisation of television, something the US market is most experienced in.

➤ Television formats, though, have changed this structural imbalance to some degree. Formats come from many different countries these days.

➤ At present, we can experience fundamental changes in the financing of audio-visual production. Producing for the international market, cheap (formatted) light entertainment and AFP are the most prominent.

➤ Finally, the digitisation of content opens up intriguing research areas, with interactivity and convergence being the key concepts here.

Key terms

Entertainment: programme category which usually includes all programmes that have a primary entertaining function. This is for one, light entertainment, such as game shows, and the sub-category 'fiction'. Movies originally made for cinemas, television films, series and serials all belong into this sub-category.

Format: There are various (confusing) uses of the term, two of which are important here. In a broad sense, it expresses the formal structures and patterns of programmes, with the concrete content playing no role (see Case Study 9.2). In a narrow and much more recent usage (see pp. 206–8), it expresses the sum of all elements that are characteristic of a TV programme, whereby tradeability is a vital aspect. Formats are sold in the form of a 'bible', a compilation of information about the original pitch, the casting, technical requirements, lessons learned, a shooting schedule, music and graphics, a crew list, a budget sample, and anything else of value to the production team. There is no accepted definition, however, and laws to protect formats vary from country to country.

Independent production companies: defined by Jezequel and Lange as 'any production company that does not have any equity link with any of the broadcasters on the list of the [sampled] 41 channels that have ordered and broadcast TV fiction programmes. A producer belonging to a group operating theme channels will be considered here as independent. The criterion is significantly different to the regulatory criteria in force in some countries, especially France' (Jezequel and Lange, 2000, p. 12).

Lead-in: means of tying a viewer to the channel by continuing to broadcast the same type of programme – a practice also known as creating audience flow.

MEDIA programme: an EU European Commission based initiative to encourage European audio-visual production and distribution.

Mipcom and **MipTV** (Marché International Des Programmes De Télévision): Europe's most important trade fairs for audio-visual programmes taking place in Cannes, France.

Stripped scheduling: meaning the same programme formats are broadcast at the same time every day, starting on the full or the half-hour where possible. It provides the channel with clearly defined long-running programming slots. The viewer becomes familiar with a certain type of programme, knows what to expect and thus, it is hoped, remains loyal to the channel.

Discussion questions

1. What are the principal trends in audio-visual production in the late 1990s and the new millennium?
2. Considering in particular the case of small countries, do you believe audio-visual production should be viewed as an important cultural entity that needs to be protected by regulation?
3. In which ways has US programming had an impact on the European audio-visual sector? How would you go about proving your claims?
4. Would you consider local adaptations of international formats as 'true' local programming? Why, or why not?
5. What are the advantages and what are the disadvantages of interactive television?
6. Why is there a trend for content to be exploited across as many platforms as possible?
7. What are the new forms of financing television and why are they necessary?

Assignments

1. Using the annual statistical yearbook of the EAO, compare the origin of fiction in both large and small European countries.
2. Locate three sources that help you research AFP and reflect on why they may be similar or different in outlook.
3. Find five web sites representing lobby groups in the area of audio-visual production.

Further reading

Bens de E., Kelly M., Bakke M. (1992) Television content: dallasification of culture? in K. Siune, W. Truetzschler (eds) *Dynamics of Media Politics*, London: Sage, 75–100.

Biltereyst, D. (2001) Reappraising European politics to protect local television content against US imports, in L. D'Haenes, F. Saeys (eds), *Western Broadcasting at the Dawn of the 21st Century*, New York: Mouton de Gruyter, 83–108

Brown A. and Picard R.G. (eds) (2004) *Digital Terrestrial Television in Europe*, London: Lawrence Erlbaum.

Doyle G. (2002) *Understanding Media Economics*, London: Sage.

EAO (2007) *Yearbook 2007 Film, Television and Video in Europe*, three volumes, Strasbourg: European Audiovisual Observatory.

Humphreys P.J. (1996) *Mass Media and Media Policy in Western Europe*, Manchester and New York: Manchester University Press.

Iosifidis P., Steemers J., Wheeler M. (2005) *European Television Industries*, London: BFI.

Meier W.A., Trappel J. (1992) Small states in the shadow of giants, in K. Siune, W. Truetzschler (eds), *Dynamics of Media Politics*, 129–142.

Weymouth T., Lamizet B. (eds) (1996) *Markets & Myths. Forces for Change in the European Media*, New York: Longman.

Online resources

http://www...

- *Branded Content Marketing Association* http://www.thebcma.info
- *EU* http://europa.eu.int/comm/avpolicy/media/index_en.html
- *European Audiovisual Observatory (EAO)* http://www.obs.coe.int
- *Media Programme* http://ec.europa.eu/information_society/media/index_en.htm
- *Thinkbox* http://www.thinkbox.tv
- *Screen Digest* http://www.screendigest.com

References

Bechelloni G. (1998) Introduction, in M. Buonanno (ed.) *Imaginary Dreamscapes: Television Fiction in Europe*, Luton: University of Luton Press, xiii–xviii.

Blickpunkt Film (1998) Mit Deutschland in die Offensive gehen, *Blinckpunkt Film*, 35/98.

Brown C. (1988) Big bang fires the great debate on TV quality, *Screen International*, no. 674, 15 October.

Colwell T., Price D. (2005) *Rights of Passage. British Television in the Global Market*, Report commissioned by the British Television Distributors' Association and UK Trade & Investment, February.

EAO (2001a) *European TV Fiction Production in Decline*, Press Release, 9 October, Cannes.

EAO (2001b) *TV Fiction Programming: Prime Time is Domestic, Off-Prime Time is American*, Press Release, 9 October, Cannes, http://www.obs.coe.int/about/oea/pr/pr_eurofiction_bis.html.

EAO (2002a) *European TV Fiction: Highest production level in a turbulent environment*, Press Release, 7 October, Cannes.

EAO (2002b) *EAO Yearbook 2002*, Strasbourg: European Audiovisual Observatory.

EAO (2004, 2005, 2007) *EAO Yearbook 2004, 2005, 2007*, Strasbourg: European Audiovisual Observatory.

EC (2006a) Media 2007, Online overview, http://ec.europa.eu/information_society/media/overview/2007/index_en.htm.

EC (2006b) *Seventh communication on the application of Articles 4 and 5 of Directive 89/552/EEC 'Television without Frontiers', as amended by Directive 97/36/EC, for the period 2003–2004*, SEC (2006) 1073, Brussels, 14 August.

Esposito M. (2006) All singing, all dancing, *TBI*, Oct/Nov, 55–58.

EU (1989) Council Directive 89/552/EEC of 3 October 1989 on the coordination of certain provisions laid down by Law, Regulation or Administrative Action in Member States concerning the pursuit of television broadcasting activities, *OJ*, **L298**, 17.10.1989, 23–30.

EU (1997) Directive 97/36/EC of the European Parliament and of the Council 30 June 1997 amending Council Directive 89/552/EEC on the coordination of certain provisions laid down by Law, Regulation or Administrative Action in Member States concerning the pursuit of television broadcasting activities, *OJ*, **L202**, 30.7.1997, 60–70.

EU (2006) Decision No 1718/2006/EC of the European Parliament and of the Council of 15 November 2006 concerning the implementation of a programme of support for the European audiovisual sector (MEDIA 2007), *OJ*, **L327**, 24.11.2006, 12–29.

EU (2007) Directive 2007/65/EEC of the European Parliament and of the Council of 11 December 2007 amending Council Directive 89/552/EEC of 3 October 1989 on the coordination of certain provisions laid down by Law, Regulation or Administrative Action in Member States concerning the pursuit of television broadcasting activities, *OJ*, **L332**, 18.12.2007, 27–45.

Frater P. (1996) Language lessons, *Screen International*, no. 1045, 16 February.

Hallin D.C., Mancini P. (2004) *Comparing Media Systems. Three Models of Media and Politics*, Cambridge: Cambridge University Press.

Hansen E., Roxborough S. (1998) Television in focus, *The Hollywood Reporter*, German television special issue, 9 June.

Iosifidis P., Steemers J., Wheeler M. (2005) *European Television Industries*, London: BFI.

IP Groupe (2005) *Television Yearbook – European Key Facts*, Neuilly: IP Groupe.

Jensen J.F. Interactive content, applications and services, in A. Brown, Picard R.G. (eds) (2005) *Digital Terrestrial Television in Europe*, London: Lawrence Erlbaum, 101–132.

Jezequel J-P., Lange A. (2000) *Economy of European TV Fiction*, Executive Summary, Strasbourg: European Audiovisual Observatory, http://www.obs.coe.int/oea_publ/eurofic/tv_eco_summary.pdf.en.

Kleinsteuber H.J. (1992) The global village stays local, in K. Siune, W. Truetzschler (eds) *Dynamics of Media Politics*, London: Sage, 143–153.

Lister M., Dovrey J., Giddings S., Grant I. (2003) *New Media: A Critical Introduction*. London: Routledge.

Luyken G.M. (1989) Strukturen und Perspektiven der Europäischen Film- und Fernsehprogrammindustrie, in W. Gellner (ed.), *Europäisches Fernsehen – American-Blend? Fernsehmedien zwischen Amerikanisierung und Europäisierung*, Berlin, Vistas, 87–94.

Marshall P.D. (2002) The new intertextual commodity, in D. Harries (ed.), *The New Media Book*, London: BFI, 69–81.

Meckel M. (1994) *Fernsehen ohne Grenzen? Europas Fernsehen zwischen Integration und Segmentierung*, Opladen: Westdeutscher Verlag.

Moran A. (1998) *Copycat TV: Globalization, Program Formats and Cultural Identity*, Luton: Luton Press.

Schawinski R. (2007) Die TV-Falle. Vom Sendungsbewusstsein zum Fernsehgeschäft. Zürich: Kein & Aber.

Screen Digest (2005a) Europe leads USA on films per head, *Screen Digest Newsletter*, January.

Screen Digest (2005b) World trade in television formats, *Screen Digest Newsletter*, April, 100–101.

Siebert F., Peterson T., Schramm W. (1963) *Four Theories of the Press*, Urbana, IL, University of Illinois Press.

Silj A., Alvarado M. (1988) (eds) *East of Dallas: The European Challenge to American Television*. London: BFI.

Springer P. (2007) *Ads to Icons. How Advertising Suceeds in a Multimedia Age*. London: Kogan Page.

Tasca E. (2000) The Rights Stuff?, *World Screen News*, October, 184–87.

Thinkbox (2008) *The Thinkbox Guide to Advertiser Funded Programming (AFP)*, http://www.thinkbox.tv/upload/pdf/Thinkbox_Guide_to_Advertiser_Funded_Programming.pdf.

TRP (2008) *Rights of Passage 2007*, Taunton: Television Research Partnership, http://www.pact.co.uk/uploads/file_bank/rightsofpassage2.pdf.

Westcott, Tim (2002) European feature animation: report, Brussels: Cartoon.

Winslow, George (2004) Fast-forward to the future, *WorldScreen.com*, Oct. www.worldscreen.com/featuresarchive.php?filename=1004cover.

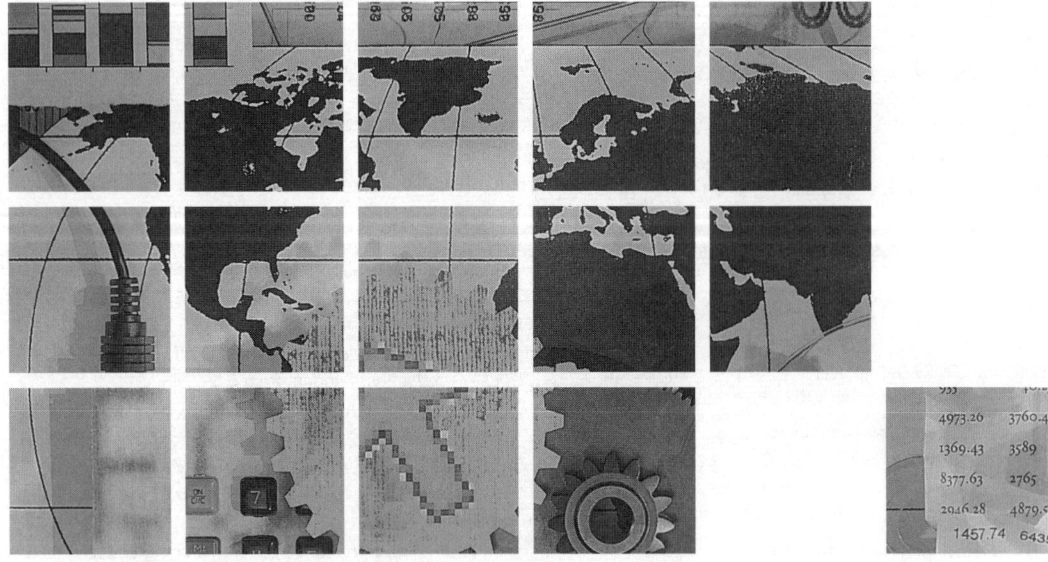

Chapter 10

The distribution network of the audio-visual in the EU

What this chapter covers

- Introduction: a period of change
- Television and radio
- Film
- Classic vs new distribution techniques
    - *Models of distribution, AV and the regulatory debate*
    - *EU television and radio on the digital distribution age*
    - *The cable industry, telecommunications and the AV industry (broadband and Internet)*
    - *Video formats from DVD to related film*
- Distribution: European policy
- Distribution: national policies
- The impact on public sector broadcasting

Learning objectives

When you have completed this chapter you will be able to:

- Reflect upon the development of new pressures changing the audio-visual distribution system within the EU media environment.
- Outline some of the new models of distribution impacting upon the various audio-visual industries such as television broadcasting, film, video-on-demand and multi-media.
- Link the audio-visual industry distribution network to other related distributive practices such as broadband communications.
- Analyse audio-visual policy developments at an EU and national level.

Themes

Below you will find a simple statement or series of statements around the six themes. They should *not* be read as a given fact. They are more like hypotheses (see Chapter 2) which need to be proved, discussed, debated and then used in your own analysis of the subject. The ideas and approaches in this book are always to be considered with an open mind; this is important in university study and is what makes it distinct from pre-university study.

Diversity of media

At a moment of considerable change, Europe is both diverse in its audio-visual provision but, at the same time, as with the rest of the world, technologically converging. Because the audio-visual industries are often displayed upon similar-looking screens (television, film and even computer), we often assume that the industries are held together in one cohesive form. This is not the case, and diversity of technology has until the recent past meant considerable diversity of audio-visual delivery across Europe.

Internal/external forces for change

The forces for change in the audio-visual distribution system are driven fundamentally by new technology and questions of finance. At the same time, the new technologies are being harnessed by both internal and external forces, often at a regulatory level; the digital age is being drawn at a national, European and global level. In a world which is already networked, the connections created by telecommunications, satellite, cable, television delivery systems and multimedia packages are drawing us closer together nationally, in a European form and globally.

Complexity of the media

The variety of industries that have created the audio-visual world, television and film, video, DVD and multi-media packages, has meant that its organisation is complex. This has been compounded across the EU with regulatory regimes that have separated public and private provision. The new digital age is raising issues on the future of public and private provision, especially in television provision, that go to the heart of the relationship between producer and consumer. The role of the distribution system will be a key factor in the immediate and long-term future of all the audio-visual industries.

Multi-levels

To analyse the audio-visual industries we need to frame them inside the EU as well as in their national settings. Even so, all of the audio-visual industries, in one form or another, are altered by the multi-level distribution system emanating from the producers and the technical innovators. This applies to television, film, video and multimedia products.

European integrative environment

It is probably insufficiently understood that the audio-visual distribution network inside the EU has been a major policy agenda item for some time. This is linked to the political and economic integrative environment that encourages the member states to work together. There have been considerable shifts in policy-making at the EU level which have allowed the audio-visual industries to operate at a trans-national, European and even trans-frontier level. Although there has been some resistance to proposed changes around national public sector broadcasting, the gradual opening up of the industry to private sector dynamics is very much a part of EU integration, albeit contested by many (see Chapter 5). This has enhanced the opportunities for the various industries to compete in a global and trans-national market.

Cultural values

Many could argue that the diversity of cultures within the EU is not fundamentally threatened by the new digital age. Moreover, the EU has a declared policy of encouraging and supporting diversity of cultural values. Yet, the development of a comprehensive framework of communications and EU-wide rules on competition in the distribution system will have an impact upon our cultural assumptions. This has meant that some sensitive cultural issues inside the EU have had to be addressed.

Essentials

➤ Technology has, in part, and in the immediate past, separated the various elements of the audio-visual industries. Television was different from film, which was different from video cassettes and multi-media gaming for example, and in part this was accentuated by different distribution systems. To simplify, this meant that television was found through analogue systems of delivery, film at cinemas, video (VHS) on separate boxes and multi-media on computers. In many respects this world still persists, but we have reached a moment of considerable change. The digital age is converging all of these technologies into packages of multi-platform delivery systems.

➤ As was said in Chapter 7 on distribution in the print industry, audio-visual convergence is equally a result of changes within distribution as well as production and consumption, even if the impact of the technological changes is emanating from different sets of questions and concerns. In many respects, the EU like the rest of the globe is standing at the door of a new age of distribution that could change the audio-visual industry fundamentally.

Introduction: a period of change

The catch-all category of the **'audio-visual'**, or even the word **'video'**, is often applied to the industry. In the modern age this is useful because of the nature of the products being brought together through digital convergence. At the same time, the audio-visual industry is a mixed bag of products that need to be seen in their own light. The convergence of various technologies in film, television and radio, for example, does not mean that we can treat all the different aspects of the industry in exactly the same way: perhaps in the future and by 2020, but not quite yet.

Even so, the audio-visual industry is in a period of change. Nowhere is this more important than in the distribution of its products and, in particular, the transmission mechanisms used by the different industries to reach out to their customers. Inside the EU this is being expressed, some might say 'directed', through telecommunications policy and audio-visual directives (see Chapter 1). As with the press and publishing (Chapter 7), the changes brought about are imposing themselves upon the various audio-visual products in ways not foreseen even a few years ago.

Sometimes we describe provision in terms of linear and non-linear media. In the former there was an assumption with any media provision that an audience or a listener would start at the beginning of the show and follow through to the end with no interactivity. Non-linear behaviour, associated with the new technology, assumes that the consumer, or participant, will use the product with a level of interactivity starting and taking up the product as and when the consumer wants. This latter idea is more akin to computer behaviour than the former which is often equated to cinema and film watching.

More than this, competition in the market place is creating waves of activity which touch the heart of the industry. This has been accelerated not only by new technology but by the impact of a growing European Single Market and the political decisions associated with the Lisbon Agenda (2000 onward – see Chapter 1), let alone the growing global corporate presence of new business players in the established national broadcasting systems (see Chapter 9).

In this context the EU market is beginning to show signs of turmoil. It is easy to find comments and analysis such as the following:

> In the context of the global broadcasting and cable TV market, Europe showed the worst performance of the regional markets . . .
>
> (Europe being described in this case as one of the major audio-visual 'regions' of the globe, compared for example with other regions such as the USA or Asia)
>
> . . . over the period 1999–2003. During the next five years, the market is expected to experience steadily accelerating growth rates. The escalating popularity of subscription TV and the rollout of digital networks

> across Europe will inevitably serve to alter the competitive landscape of the broadcasting & cable TV market in Europe.
>
> (Datamonitor, 2004)

Such comments need to be carefully analysed for the developments taking place are not just about finance or only about the new technology, but encompass also changes in the regulatory context in which the industries operate. This means understanding, again, the way in which the EU works (see Chapter 1) at both EU and national levels.

The type of new technology being applied to the distribution of audio-visual products is the same everywhere, but the control and the regulation of the market is held traditionally, inside the EU, by the member states. Thus, when we analyse the market and the fundamental changes which are occurring, we will find movement toward convergence but also diversity of media control in different states and in different ways. Examples of this will be given later.

Stop and consider 10.1

Since 1945 Europe has seen a great deal of technological innovation developed and planted in the various societies – mass media television, cable and satellite, the change from black and white screens to colour and so on. No matter the similarity of the technology, how it was used across Europe was often different, from content to programme timing and even regulation. Although there has been some convergence because of the EU, states still remain very different from one another. Is this going to be the same in the 'digital age'? Is there something different about digital convergence compared to technologies of the past?

It is important therefore to understand the debate about convergence, and the classic versus new distribution techniques in the audio-visual world. Equally, we need to understand the debate in terms of the different industries that traditionally, at least in part, kept themselves technologically divided. This is what this chapter is designed to do in an introductory manner. The sources available to us to do this are manifold, but where do we start (see Source 10.1)?

The digital age, as we have seen previously, impacts upon all forms of the media. In the press and publishing industries we are seeing a paper industry change into an electronic one (Chapter 7), even if, so far, partially. Equally, the digital age transforms the technology of the audio-visual into electronic form: not from paper in this case but from radio waves into various forms of digital distributive technology. This

Source 10.1

Where to start?

As indicated previously (Chapter 6), the range of commentaries available to us is considerable but often technically complicated, and many are in different languages. How then do we start? One approach which helps is to start with data. Empirical studies are not new and are very much a part of the audio-visual scene. In this light, the notable work undertaken by the Audio-visual Observatory, set up in 1992, and the work led by André Lange are exemplary. In Europe, the series dedicated under the banner of Euro-media group is informative and most interesting, as is the Datamonitor (Market Business Line) material available to most libraries. The Institute of European Media and the Hans Bredow Institute, as well as the online material at the European Journalism Centre based in Maastricht, are all major sources of excellent research and commentary. The latter is especially good in indicating national sources of comment which are essential in this field, e.g. agencies such as Ofcom in the UK are replicated across the EU member states. There are so many more. All are available online and are good sources for material. The statistical work coming from Eurostat in these terms is also invaluable.

Also, each nation state inside the EU will carry a wealth of information from their communication agencies, some governmental and some working on a consultancy basis. Seeking out the national figures pays enormous dividends even if we need comparative skills to interpret them across the EU.

makes for a distinction between the world of print and publishing and the audio-visual world. At the same time, it provides for a link between them as they both converge into the electronic platforms that can be shared.

As we have seen (Chapter 9), producers of the audio-visual are reliant on the means by which their content is delivered. This is where the 'new' age is having its greatest impact. Gone are the days of a single network service based on broad analogue systems. These have been overtaken by a digital distributive technology that allows the delivery of content in many different forms and in many different ways. One of the more dramatic ways of seeing this is through the social networks now created on the web. Here we will find mail, chat-rooms, photos, video clips and games, let alone music and radio-based and linked television clips. A cursory look at sites such as Digg, Facebook, Flickr, Photobucket, Truveo and YouTube, which the makers of the new social network orientated browser Flock call, brightly, 'media streams', could surprise more traditional media consumers.

From a consumer's point of view, the digitally-created product will not necessarily look 'content' different. We do not change our view of a film or a television programme or listen differently to a radio broadcast just because the distribution technique has moved into digital technology. Moreover, from a consumer point of view, whether we are watching a screen, a film, a television show or an advertising clip at the cinema, this does not fundamentally alter our interpretation or enjoyment of the product.

This is not to say that there are no enhancement issues in using the digital technology. The opposite is the case. Producers in a multi-media world can put to use the power of the digital tools now available to them to improve sound quality and add supplementary messages to a radio programme; create amazing graphics used in films and multi-media products; and transmit to **high-definition** screens. All of these are attractive ways in which digital products enhance the consumer experience. Moreover, the creative power of the producers is also in the hands of the consumer with software image programmes such as *Picasa* (Google), *Photoshop Elements* (Adobe) and *Windows Photo Gallery* (Microsoft), plus many more.

Yet, from a distribution point of view the movement from radio and analogue technology to digital technology is really even more profound and goes beyond the immediate enhancement of a product. In the very recent past, the producers and organisers of the communication, distributive network isolated themselves from each other by design, by technology or by regulatory control (for the last see Chapter 4). The future will look different.

Television and radio

For example, as we have seen in previous chapters (see Chapter 9 for many examples and cases), the producers and broadcasters of European radio and television were primarily set up by state broadcasting systems. Across Europe the public sector was added to by private sector channels into a 'duopoly': the private and public sector mix. The technology available in the early days restricted the number of channels, and most nations did not go beyond six national TV channels using the old aerial radio wave techniques of analogue broadcasting (Noam, 1991, 1992). This was the fundamental model used by nation states inside the EU. Tied to this, the distribution network, television (and previously radio) was also often state-controlled and regulated in most cases either by licence or even ownership through public service broadcasting.

Stop and consider 10.2

To what extent does the 'ownership' question impinge upon the distribution network? There are fierce critics of the increasing deregulation of the markets within EU nation states and overall in the EU. They argue that the new distribution networks, linked to an almost quasi-monopoly of US production (see Chapter 9), is leading to a simple mix of content that is national and USA dominated and not opening up the markets to alternative material. Reading from here onwards, perhaps we need to keep this in mind: how important is control and ownership of the media in what we see and listen to, no matter how much the development of new technology allows new ways to deliver it to us?

Even radio transmission and the necessary radio spectrum needed control if the technology was to work across the geographical space in Europe. The analogue world even for radio (short-wave, **AM** and **FM**) had technical restrictions applied to it just as television did. These are the areas that are changing. The digital age means that the capacity of transmission is increasing. The digital signal can be squeezed into a narrower, transmissible signal by a series of new technologies (IPTV, VOD, digital TV, Sat-TV) often drawn together into what are termed collectively as the 'pipes': the network that connects one part of the system to another using technologies which are dissimilar but which are able to communicate with one another (again refer back to Chapter 9 for more detail and cases). No longer is there such a restriction, as in the past, on the number of radio and television channels inside the digital transmission: be it delivered by cable, satellite or mobile telephony. A proliferation of channels has resulted, of which most consumers are now increasingly aware. Even so, the financial background to the new innovation and products is being questioned (see Point of View 10.1). Are we on the verge of a crisis? The question is being debated.

To illustrate this it maybe useful to look at two case studies across the EU from different but neighbouring countries: Belgium (see Case Study 10.1) and The Netherlands (see Case Study 10.2).

Point of View 10.1

Proliferation of audio-visual channels across the EU – a crisis?

The following extract from an interview with the Director of the Audiovisual Observatory on 17 January 2003 illustrates some of the present-day dilemmas.

André Lange: Audiovisual is experiencing an unprecedented crisis.

Question: Ten years on, what have been the major changes in Europe's audiovisual media?

André Lange: In television, the emergence of digitisation has vastly increased the number of channels. We have now reached almost 1,200 channels with national coverage. When we first made a census in 1994, there were 261! Together with the local and regional channels in the Observatory's 35 member countries, this amounts to a total of more than 4,700. The second striking fact is the upsurge in cinema-going, which has returned to the levels observed 20 years ago. There is also the development of DVD, which follows upon the rapid growth of video and the Internet with its new facilities for audiovisual streaming. Then there is the whole area of video games, which was in its infancy when the Observatory was set up. Video games created by European companies now account for almost 19,000 permanent jobs, in development and publication alone, not to mention jobs in distribution and retail. That means more jobs than film and TV fiction production combined. But European videogames companies are now in crisis and have started to cut jobs.

Question: In this context, why do you talk about a crisis in Europe's audiovisual industry?

André Lange: It's paradoxical. On the one hand there is an increase in consumption and company turnover, and at the same time, in spite of this growth, we have observed a decline in financial performance in all branches except video over the past two years. We have recently seen major setbacks among big groups, even bankruptcies. The most striking is the crisis affecting cinema theaters, which have heavy deficits since 2000. In 2000, in 9 of the 15 European Union countries, television – and I mean all channels – was in deficit, mainly because of digital TV packages, which called for substantial investment, and also because of the sharp increase in the cost of programme rights, especially for sports programmes. Since 2000, TV channels funded by advertising have been hit by the recession in advertising markets, and the crisis is now affecting production and distribution companies. And even the public television sector is moving into deficit. As a whole, this situation should be a matter of concern.

Source: http://www.obs.coe.int/about/oea/interview.html.

Case Study 10.1

Distribution of audio-visual: Belgium

The distribution network in Belgium has always related to the bi-lingual multi-national community that it served. The tradition and importance of the national public broadcasting system serving the Dutch and French (and smaller German) speaking communities was quite early confronted with a highly-developed cable system from the 1960s. The public service broadcasting system, though, has remained popular with audiences, although its so-called 'monopoly' position was in effect ended by law in 1987. Belgium being a country with high standards of living, it is not surprising that they have embraced the new technology. Telephone service providers have included Belgacom, Telenet, Tele2 and Euphony. Both fixed and mobile networks are extensive and mobile companies have included Proximus, Mobistar and Base. By 2007 Belgium was classified in the 'high **broadband** penetration' bracket. Bundled services are well provided for and the present market includes IPTV and VOD.

Sources: European Commission, *E-Communications Household Survey* (Eurobarometer, 2006); European Journalism Centre, Media Landscape (2008), http://www.ejc.net/media_landscape/.

Case Study 10.2

Distribution of audio-visual: The Netherlands

There are no national government-owned television or radio stations in a highly sophisticated and probably unique form of Dutch audio-visual network which is provided by private companies but regulated in the public interest. The cable network is extensive and according to one source:

> An average cable-network contains apart from the ten national Dutch-language-channels at least one regional or local channel, two Belgian Dutch language channels, Dutch MTV and one or two other Dutch music channels, Dutch spoken or Dutch subtitled special interest channels (Discovery, Eurosports, National Geographic), BBC 1 and BBC 2, German channels and a choice from TV5 (France), RAI Uno (Italy), TVE (Spain), TRT (Turley), CNN etc. – 25 to 30 channels is normal. (EJC, Media Landscape, 2008).

The distribution set-up encourages multiple channels, including up to 15% market share being taken up by international and European regional offerings. Cable penetration is estimated to be amongst the highest in Europe. Telephone service providers have included KPN Telecom and Tele2. Mobile coverage is wide and has included the following companies: KPN, Vodafone, T-mobile, Orange and Telfort. Broadband use is extensive with high-speed bandwidth.

Sources: European Commission, *E-Communications Household Survey* (Eurobarometer, 2006); European Journalism Centre, Media Landscape (2008), http://www.ejc.net/media_landscape/.

Film

As can be seen from the extract above, the digital age is impacting upon the audio-visual world in general and also upon film, even though in the immediate past the film industry was different from television or radio. The techniques of film production and equally consumption were rooted in technologies and distribution which were different to analogue technology. However, as the years passed, film techniques, camera work and working practices have seen a great deal of crossover, particularly in distribution, between the worlds of television and film. Producers and broadcasters work together in the film and television industry for economic as well as entertainment reasons. At an EU level this has meant a general statement of support for the film industry (see the **MEDIA programme**, Chapter 1, and Point of View 10.2) which

Point of View 10.2

The European Commission on film aid and the MEDIA programme

We firmly believe that whatever State aid there is for film should have the cultural aim of ensuring that Europe's national and regional cultures and creative potential are expressed in the audiovisual media of film and television. At the same time, though, it should also aim to lead to a sustainable European film sector . . .

Source: European Commissioners Neelie Kroes and Viviane Reding, State aid: future regime for cinema support, Press Release, 22 May (Kroes and Reding, 2008).

Point of View 10.3

OECD

As a recent OECD reports says:

> Even in 2007 . . . (the) . . . evolution towards more broadband applications and increased use is far from complete. Suppliers of broadband services and digital content have to reinvent their technology and services as well as the delivery of these services. In fact, compared with earlier estimations, new broadband applications such as converged digital content services (online music, film and video, etc.) took longer than expected to arrive. Digital content services, video-on-demand, video conferencing and interactive offers are still in their experimentation phase. The goal of 'broadband content anywhere, anytime and on any device' is still remote. The widespread use of advanced mobile broadband services has yet to emerge in most OECD countries.

Source: OECD, *Broadband Growth and Policies in OECD Countries* (OECD, 2008).

has been the case in the past and carries through today.

Nonetheless the full impact of the digital age upon the industry, especially in terms of distribution, continues today as it has spread first into **CD** and **DVD** and now into internet download technologies (IPTV and VOD). These stand on the threshold of mass-produced, high-definition products which are bound to influence the film industry. The classic distribution techniques of the past – a cinema showing or the film shown on television – are being disturbed by new digital techniques. The new digital products and digital delivery systems are enhancing and accelerating the convergences between the industries. Not least, this can be seen where the product is consumed, which now varies vastly when compared to the past and includes the laptop and the mobile telephone, among many other types of device.

However, from a global let alone an EU point of view the development of the new digital age takes time and money (see Point of View 10.3).

The above report (Point of View 10.3) goes on to highlight the importance of:

- speed;
- availability;
- pricing;
- the difficult impact that the new technology is having on existing business models (see Source 10.2).

Classic vs new distribution techniques

There is no easily identified moment when one technology is superseded by another. In the 20th century it was assumed that one media network would correspond to one service provided. For example, television systems were designed for one purpose, whereas telephones and telephony were designed for another. Even radio, with a technology close to that

Source 10.2

The digital age and film in the EU

Examining the relationship between the film industry and the digital age is an important area of investigation. Sources for this are varied and many. Each nation state will have its own agencies for exploring the national film industries, and at an EU level the work done by the Audio-Visual Observatory is excellent. Reports coming out of the OECD Directorate of Science, Technology and Industry are most useful in comparative work. Bear in mind, though, that in some instances nowadays this work needs to be purchased for individual subscribers, but it should also be available within academic library exchange. Europe's European Commission 'Information Society' and audio-visual and media websites are also full of the latest news and developments at an EU level.

of television, was often in organisational terms kept apart. The analogue world meant that due to the restrictions of the technology there would be limited content based on a narrow band of delivery choices. In television and even in radio terms, what this meant was 'channel scarcity': limitation to the number of channels and even the number of programmes that could be presented to the public. This also meant that the major mass media providers could have what is known as 'high social impact' upon their audiences. For the audiences and the consumer or the media products, this also meant little user control, limited choice and limited scope for inter-activity.

The digital 21st-century alters the 20th century dynamic. Nowadays it is possible, and it is increasingly the case, that a media network provider (BT Broadband, Tiscali or Virgin media broadband) can offer not one service but many: telephone communication, television programmes, radio, music downloads and all the paraphernalia that we as consumers are rapidly becoming accustomed to. The digital age also means that the restrictions on delivery capacity are considerably looser, providing for more channels and the proliferation of programme choice. This in turn provides for a wider choice of content providers. The European Commission in particular has reported on and underlined the importance of narrowcasting, VOD and recording techniques for audio-visual content. Equally, the relationship to the consumer and content is changed, with greater activity and interactivity permitted by the use of these services and with new and innovative software often associated with the new digital products.

Taken together, the changes from the 20th century to the 21st are also altering the landscape for the producers. There are new players who can now be associated with the development of new channels, new ways of delivering programmes and the provision of a wide range of services. The multi-media age is now upon us.

Models of distribution, AV and the regulatory debate

All of this means that our previous models of audio-visual distribution have to be altered. Many commentators, including the European Commission, recommend that we bring together the four major elements of the distribution network into a converging pattern. The former separation of services between the audio-visual on one side and telecommunications on the other should now be drawn together, just as the technology physically allows this to happen. Equally the 'carriage' services, the physical or technological network, which was separated into broadcasting on one side and telecommunications on the other, should be brought together into the same working, technical model.

This type of model-making is very important. The digital age does not just impose itself upon producer and consumer, nor even just on the techniques of distribution, but impacts equally on the regulatory model: the regulations that govern what we see and hear. Herein lies the debate about the future of the European audio-visual industry. To what degree do we regulate, deregulate or, to use the latest thinking, co-regulate (see Chapter 4) the audio-visual market? For European integrative purposes there was always an argument that the policing of regulation was difficult so the strong voices within the industry pointed to lower regulatory models which, in the main, the EU has embraced, but the debates continue as to how this should be fully implemented.

Of course this does not mean the end of regulation. Licensing and radio frequency, the radio spectrum, will continue to be controlled. However, broadcasting and telecommunications licences could be replaced by a general authorisation for transmission providers. The very nature of the European Single Market is designed to encourage transparency of supply and demand and, by separating carriage, the transmission network, from the services, it allows for the continuing development of what is known as 'must carry' policies. This means that the transmission network across the EU is kept to as neutral a definition as possible (the 'must carry' provisions within the EU – see Chapter 4), allowing the service providers equal rights to use the network to provide their services, be they radio, television, film, music, multimedia products, telephony or similar such products.

On the issue of content, as we have seen previously (Chapter 4), member states of the EU have already laid down fundamental objectives and principles through which the European market will operate. This includes freedom of expression, democratic pluralism, cultural and linguistic diversity, protection of minors and consumer protection. Despite the changing distributive network, in terms of policy pluralism is very important in the EU model and as such the EU is trying to lower the access barriers for citizen and consumer information (see Chapter 1 on 'policy trails' and 'frameworks').

It is not in the power of the EU itself to do this of course (see Chapter 1), but it shows the intention of the member states to corral and promote this type of policy. It is encouraging, as best it can, in the various different national settings, the use of a variety of portals for consumers, using as wide a framework of communications as possible. We must not forget, of course, the prime economic arguments (see Chapter 3) which argue that competition within the market place should be assured.

In consumer protection, the issues that the new distribution network throws up relate to advertising and editorial content not only for television or radio services but the whole range of services that the internet, broadband and cable and satellite in general provide.

The arguments about classic and new distribution techniques, when combined with new descriptions and models of distribution in the audio-visual industries, point to a converging, technologically-driven market place. However, it would be wrong to think this will happen overnight or that it will happen to all member states inside the EU at the same time. Changes of policy and technology are exciting but also in this field expensive. Nation states will react differently and in different ways to the challenges ahead (see Case Studies 10.1 and 10.2 regarding Belgium and The Netherlands above).

For the time being, the old distribution system will remain in place for many and digital changeover will come into being only from 2012 onwards for most EU countries. Accordingly, it is still pertinent, despite the new models, to talk about the older audio-visual classifications, bearing in mind that models of distribution are beginning to change most areas of audio-visual development.

EU television and radio in the digital distribution age

Some commentators (Rangone and Turconi, 2003) see the 'new' audio-visual world as nothing less than a television 'revolution'. In fact, some would argue that the very term 'television' is defunct and has to be redefined. It is argued that what is happening to the audio-visual industries, especially television and radio, is a movement towards a new form of multimedia society, built against the backdrop of the new 'information society' (see Chapter 5). Certainly, what is happening in distribution terms is a convergence of many different aspects of the industry which is changing the pattern and processes associated with the delivery of products. These factors include:

- digitalisation of the TV signal (DTV);
- development of alternative access technologies (wireless cable, coaxial cable);

- broadband and streaming video technologies (IPTV);
- introduction of WebTV (internet services on TV);
- introduction of interactive and personal television solutions (e.g. set top boxes that allow for recording or control of timing, or even replay of content) (*ibid*, 2003, p. 48).

All of these technological innovations are very important. Many technical articles, reviews or books on the subject are littered with acronyms like those above and clever product developments founded on the digital world. For those interested in the technical side of these developments, it is fruitful to delve into the background and development of a new wave of large, medium-sized and even small companies missing from the new distribution techniques and applications.

Important as these are, in the end, the content producers, the programmers, the broadcasting organisations, the internet providers and the software providers will make judgements based not just on technical innovation but on economics: competition and financial judgement. For those who are responsible for exercising some control over content and those interested in maintaining as free a market as is possible, the new innovations in distribution give rise to political and social as well as economic policy decisions.

So far in the EU the trend since the mid-1980s if not before has been for greater liberalisation and to some extent harmonisation of the market. In the days of analogue broadcasting, state control remained easier. The new era throws up not only new opportunities but, equally, profound political decisions on the nature of the new broadcasting scene.

Nowhere is this more relevant for the television and radio industry than in its relationship to a telecommunications network which has not only been privatised across the EU but now holds the keys to a technological network for the delivery of many of the new and combined audio-visual services. As mentioned above, this includes audio-visual set boxes with providers from a range of new companies outside the normally accepted national public broadcasting systems, and where cable services companies offer many services, including television programmes, music, radio and much more.

Although the dawn of a new technological era was somewhat darkened at the end of the 20th century, with many new technological companies threatened by a lack of investment or, more importantly, a lack of profit, this did not stop the growth of broadband. Across the globe, using new and old cables, the broadband technology is in the vanguard of the new; creating mass, distributed, technological innovation with possibly considerable social consequences and potentially high earning for those who provide customers with packages of entertainment they want at an affordable price. This is the key to understanding the move from analogue to digital delivery.

For the customer the broadband revolution is still rooted in the audio-visual world of the screen. The screen can be either the television, the personal computer (PC) or the mobile. The fact that broadband offers companies and corporations, and many new players on the scene, an opportunity to gain access to customers is only now beginning to have a real impact.

The cable industry, telecommunications and the AV industry (broadband and Internet)

The classic delivery system for television and radio was through radio waves to an aerial. The television set needed a cable from the aerial to the box or, in the case of the radio, through an inbuilt aerial usually inside the radio. The telephone cables to the house were not linked to audio and visual entertainment, and certainly not to the television set unless by specialised cable networks. They were normally provided for telephony.

The new technology of digital delivery was initially encouraged by cable companies who would lay their own cabling systems alongside the cables of telephone and telephony. At the same time, the telephone cables could be used to transmit digital signals, but most were held in Europe by state nationalised telecommunications organisations (Deutsche Telekom or

France Telecom, for example). Under EU initiatives they were of course to be privatised, facilitating the development of a wider, more European, network. Equally, across Europe telephony and telecommunications were usually organised through national systems. The creation of a privatised industry would also accelerate cross-national mergers of companies, once again enhancing the trans-national development of the European telecommunications network. Even so, in the early days there were considerable differences in how states organised their cable industries, be that for telephone or later television cables. More than this, some countries were early starters in building cable networks and others slower. For example, Belgium had laid an extensive cable network in the 1960s and had encouraged its consumers and citizens to engage with an international world of international channels much earlier than many other states inside Europe. Most other EU states followed later, typically from the 1980s.

The new distributive system across Europe now uses all means, all the different types of technology and ancillary equipment, to bring together the delivery of audio and visual services. Across Europe there has been a diversity of provision: from areas of relatively minimum investment in some southern states, for example, to northern and western Europe which has built extensive cable networks and provided for many services using telephone cables, satellite and aerial to digital boxes, founded on a variety of software that assists the delivery of the audio-visual form from film to television, VOD and other similar products.

The initial enthusiasm for the provision of alternative cables to existing connections was very much an idea of the 1980s and 1990s. However, the entrenched markets, the expense involved and some consumer reticence slowed the process of extending new competition-based cable operators in many states, and by the 1990s and across Europe the process had slowed. Across Europe and in different ways in different countries the cable companies tried to make a profit, but many of these corporations and companies would fail, particularly by the end of the 1990s in the era known as the 'dot.com bubble'. Since then cable has seen increasing **concentration of ownership**. This is happening across all EU states. Moreover, the nation states throughout the EU extended the single market into the field of telecommunications and their cable industries. The result has been an acceleration of the audio-visual network based upon the cable industry and existing telecommunications lines. As an indication, some of this has been discussed in previous chapters (see Chapter 4).

Even if the initial impetus for creating a digital, cable network across Europe faltered in the 1990s, we can still see that the groundwork which is now beginning to bear fruit in the 21st century was being laid. By the year 2008 it was estimated (see Fig. 10.1) that Europe could boast 66 million cable television subscribers; in digital cable it was estimated that there were 10.9 million TV subscribers. Moreover, cable telephony subscribers, often established in competition to the two previous public service and later privatised national telephone systems, have reached 10 million subscribers. Over 13 million cable Internet homes have now been provided for. The revenue associated with the cable industry is now estimated to be in the region of over €17 bn. Cable revenues generated by Internet and phone, often with some of the fastest growing profit areas, now account for 40%.

Concentration of ownership has seen the following companies taking leading national positions: in Britain NTL/Telewest (now Virgin Media), in France Noos SA, Numericable and FTC (France Télécom Câble), in Spain ONO/Auya, and in Germany KDG+Unity. Encouraged by the member states of the EU, national telecommunication systems have now been privatised, and across Europe the intention is to encourage competition which in the end could well be trans-national. This obviously fits with EU integrative aims and objectives, but underlying the push are the economic benefits for both consumer and producer which the new digital delivery provides.

Technologically this mix of delivery systems allows for a series of services but, in particular, it brings together television, radio, music, VOD and telephony. The old classic business models for all the organisations that provided and delivered these types of services are now of course challenged. New cable technology and new software have accelerated the quality of the broadband network. This is true across the EU in general, bearing in mind the usual caveat

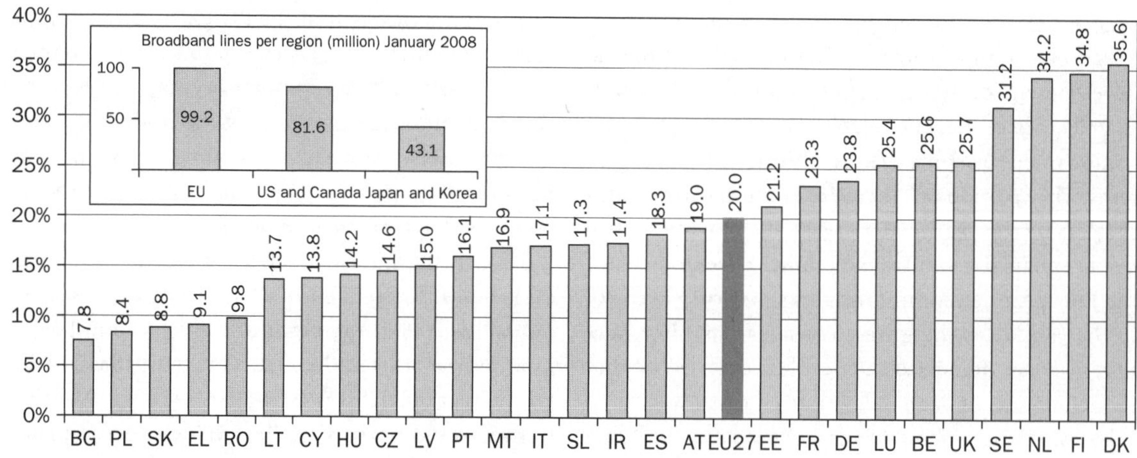

Figure 10.1 EU broadband (by country).

Source: *Preparing Europe's Digital Future: i2010 Mid-term Review*, Graph 1 (EC, 2008).

that across the EU there are very large differences in the range of services provided by the new digital broadband network to the different states.

Moreover, new technology does not come cheap, at least from the producer and distribution sectors. Even so, this has not stopped investment, despite the earlier difficulties in the 1990s in the 'dot.com bubble' era. Considerable innovation is occurring within the market and is linking all the technologies into an almost fully integrated working system including satellite, digital television and Internet television models: the resulting new distribution techniques are a challenging and heady mix for all the corporations and the companies that serve it.

Video formats from DVD to related film

Nowhere is this more important than in the film industry and its relationship to video formats, CD, DVD, **MPEG** (versions from MPEG2 to the recent MEPG4) or analogue videotapes (VHS and Betamax), and its ever-important association with television networks. According to many across the EU, especially in the more sophisticated markets, the cinema, the theatre of the film, is not the important revenue maker it was, although the film industry, in certain sectors, is booming. The reason for this is the selling on of film products through the distributive chain to a variety of outlets, increasing as it goes the profit levels which popular and large audiences generate. A film is no longer made purely with cinema in mind but for television and on-going retail sales in as many formats as possible: from video cassettes to CD; from CD to DVD; and now Mp3 or downloadable sources through digital or digitable transmission systems. Put together this means a changing, adapting industry.

Distribution: European policy

The development of EU policy on the new technology and its distribution system alongside the existing public sector broadcasting has an intriguing history. However, despite the complicated path, the different policy trails (see Chapter 1), the different agendas and national or private sector lobbying for example, the steady growth of decisions in this field and at an EU level is highly significant. The general European integrative movement has at long last now embraced the European communications system. From the Television without Frontiers Directive to the directives associated with telecommunications, there has been a general movement to frame EU governments and their citizens into a network which will enhance communication between members. The debates that surround the role of the EU institutions in doing this are hotly contested.

The degree to which the EU policy-makers are developing a European distribution system based on agreed technological standards may come as a surprise to many. The number and variety of decisions that are being made in the field are considerable. They go beyond the television and audio-visual industries into the very specifics of how we communicate with each other, in some cases down to the smallest detail, for example: the latest European Commission decision on broadband wireless access (EU, 2008a); a decision on harmonised conditions of spectrum use for the operation of mobile communication services on aircraft (EU, 2008b); decisions on the use of the radio spectrum for the implementation of systems providing mobile satellite services (EU, 2008c); or even decisions on the harmonised use of the radio spectrum which includes radio local area networks (EU, 2005).

On the surface, such technical details seem far away from the fundamentals of the television, film or general video industries. Yet, the development of technological capacity throughout the EU in the area of telecommunications which allows the television, film and other industries to bring together their services into a carriage network is now accepted as an inevitable future by all members of the EU. These new innovations, specific in intent, are still a part of a wider framework of communication integration across the EU and even beyond. This capacity represents a striking, multi-layered connectivity between the producer on one side and the consumer on the other, and is of considerable importance for the future.

This can be seen already in the development of European VOD service by delivery format. In original material from the European Commission drafting of the 'audiovisual media services draft directive' (EU, 2007) it was estimated that European VOD services through the Internet had now reached over 59%. The second largest category, just under 30%, was through IPTV, followed by cable at 7%. The number of paying and VOD services in 24 European countries, between 2002 and 2006, had risen from 1 in 2002 to over 140 in 2006. In the lead amongst the EU countries were France and The Netherlands, followed by the UK and Germany, with the least engaged being the Czech Republic and Slovakia. Yet the overall trends for all countries are upward (EAO, 2007, 2008).

As for the operators of the new VOD services in Europe, by the end of 2006 it was the telecom operators who led in delivering the services, followed by broadcasters, and then by what are known as 'aggregators', those who provide packaged services across a range of services, and then the cable operators followed by the retailers. Those who were not in the vanguard of service providers, and this may come as some surprise, were the DVD renters, archive holders, copyright agencies or even film groups or video publishers.

As we shall see in Chapter 11 on consumption, the building of a network with technological standards which harmonises the EU need not mean that the market is easy to follow. There remains linguistic and cultural segmentation; there are problems in creating economies of scale at an EU level for both film distributors and film distribution, let alone problems of branding European films as being different within a market which is both national and global in form.

Distribution: national policies

The shift from an analogue world to a digital one can be symbolised by the parallel distributive development of analogue systems on one side and the new cable industry as it emerged in the 1980s, and more profoundly in the 1990s, on the other. Governments across the European Community and now the EU responded differently. However, the trend over the past decades has been intriguingly researched with some interesting results.

Wherever you look inside the EU, there has been a gradual consensus that national governments and states should play a less direct regulatory role in a distributed network and the new technologies that feed it. However, this does not mean that states are avoiding their responsibilities for consumers with regard to such matters as content or abuses of the system. The nation state still plays, and will continue to play, a very important part in the policing of audio-visual products in all the forms in which they are produced.

Equally, this does not mean that all the nations are responding to the development of new technologies and its relationship to the cable industry at the same time and in the same way: the truth is far from this. In detail there are many differences.

The larger countries such as Germany, France and the UK all reacted differently to the new cable industry which they initially believed to be secondary to and less important than the older and more established broadcasting and analogue systems. Yet in their different ways the nation states were forced or encouraged to reconsider and to embrace the new technology in one fashion or another. The result has been, at least in terms of delivery systems, acceptance of the EU position that the system should be as neutral as possible. This allows for an open access policy for as many producers as possible to as many of the consumers as possible. In terms of timeframes, this might mean some disparities across the many member states, but in the end the trend is one direction for the EU.

The impact on public sector broadcasting

The development of a technologically converging market in the audio-visual field raises important questions on the future of European public service and public sector broadcasting. This situation is complicated because across the EU and the individual member states, public television providers vary from one country to another. For example, in Denmark it was estimated that five public channels accounted for just under 70% of the market in 2004, whilst in the neighbouring Baltic states and to the south in Greece the public service sector held less than 20% of the market. What impact digital delivery will have on this varied and complicated media scene is not yet fully clear.

There is a broad view, accepted by most EU member states, that public service broadcasting must be protected and has a place in the broad European media architecture of the future. The dilemma comes from translating this agreed policy into a world where the consumer complies. If the digital delivery systems provide greater choice for the European consumer, will they adhere to the public sector broadcasting and associated telecommunications networks and use the services provided by public sector provision? This is a real question with important ramifications depending upon the answer. Questions such as these are being discussed at many levels of debate about the industry: by nations, the EU and even informed and important organisations such as the European Broadcasting Union (EBU). Point of View 10.4 indicates the language of debate in a recent discussion of European Commission proposals for changing aspects of telecommunications provision.

Of course, in the end, public-sector provision in the new digital delivery age depends on finance and investment and on content: not only the finance to produce and to deliver, but also the content that relates to the public space or public area in which the consumer or citizen can be identified. It appears from a EU ruling (2001) that the detail on how individual member states define public service provision, and therefore collectively respond to the digital age, will be left to the member states. The arguments continue. There will be no specific European-level directed definition of what constitutes a public service remit, at least not in the near future: more likely, as is now the case, a fine tuning of the principles by which the member states agree to step forward into the future in audio-visual policy will be the agenda. This also applies to public service financing: there will be no strict rulings on the detail of how public service broadcasting is financed in the individual states and a variety of financial models is likely.

Even so, the full impact of the European Single Market demands a competitive, level playing field. Depending on which state in the EU we analyse, the 'public sector' may well diminish in size, whilst the EU private sector and the distribution system widens. Equally, regulation will be used at an EU level to ensure that the telecommunications and delivery systems are as 'neutral' as possible, and provide for what is called, as we have seen, 'must carry' services for all.

How public service broadcasters fit within these political and economic parameters is yet again another interesting question which needs to be resolved. Inside the EU, therefore, not only will we

Point of View 10.4

European Broadcasting Union positions on the future of public broadcasting and telecommunications

In a recent (2007) debate on the future of telecommunications and its impact upon the audio-visual, the EBU (representing in the main the public service broadcasters) proposed amendments to European Commission proposals. In them you can see the EU vs nation state arguments being fought through. In this area of transformation, such matters are often highly charged and sensitive, not least because of the role of the public service broadcasters and their various, national remits:

> Spectrum policy and spectrum management have traditionally been a means whereby Member States have pursued cultural and media policy objectives in the broadcasting field.
>
> The 2007 Reform Proposals introduce significant changes to spectrum management. Unlike the traditional planning (allocation) of spectrum and Member States' administrative systems of assigning frequencies to particular users and uses, the Commission suggests the introduction of a flexible market-based approach, including spectrum trading and the possibility of auctioning spectrum. At the same time the Commission aims to harmonize spectrum use at the European level. There is no general audiovisual exclusion from the new spectrum management approach. However, Member States have the power to make certain limited exceptions/restrictions with a view to promoting cultural diversity and media pluralism.
>
> Recital 23 [the rationale for a recommendation] in particular, confirms the competence of the Member States to define the scope and nature of any exception regarding the promotion of cultural and linguistic diversity and media pluralism. In this way, the 2007 Reform Proposals of the European Commission confirm to a certain extent the 'conciliatory' approach taken in 2002. However, such a clarification in a Recital is not sufficient and, unfortunately, the same approach is not carried through, in a coherent manner, in other parts of the Reform Proposals.
>
> It is therefore necessary to introduce a number of amendments to safeguard audiovisual media policy objectives. While some of the EBU amendments are more of a clarifying nature, others are essential to prevent the cultural and media policies of the Member States from being undermined, and especially as regards the proposed new provisions on implementing powers, spectrum trading, spectrum pricing and the granting of individual rights of use.

Source: EBU proposal for Amendments to the draft Amending Directive regarding the Framework, Access and Authorisation Directives ('Better Regulation'), pp. 1–2 (EBU, 2008).

find considerable variety in public-sector provision but also often a fragmenting market because of new delivery systems. Equally, a tension will remain between on the one side those who are associated with public sector provision, and on the other the private sector, anxious to determine the profit return on its considerable private sector investment. The shift to the new Internet-based network is now very obvious in the 21st century: that phrase 'watch this space' could not be more apposite.

Chapter summary

- There is an argument about the extent and pace of the new digital age as it impacts upon the various industries inside Europe. What is not in question is that it is changing the delivery patterns and hence producer and consumer behaviour.
- Whether it involves the industries associated with television, radio, film or even multi-media programmes, change is occurring in all EU states. Even so, there remains considerable diversity of provision and differences in take-up of the new technologies.
- Fundamental questions are being raised as to the economic and business models that the new age appears to be creating for the audio-visual industries.
- The question of the role of the public service broadcaster in a new multi-platform age is an intriguing one. The EU has set its mind on protecting the public service remit but, as yet, it is difficult to be absolutely clear what the new EU public service broadcasting system will finally look like.

Key terms

AM: widely used frequency bands, usually divided into short-wave, medium-wave and long-wave depending on size of the modulation.

Audio-visual: (sometime spelt audiovisual) a term used to bring together all products that fall into the categories of audio (e.g. radio) and visual (screen products including television).

Broadband: a signalling method used in telecommunication technology – often associated with the cable industry and the growth of the Internet.

CD: compact disc – a storage device for recording and keeping digital material.

Concentration of ownership: usually a phrase implying both mergers and acquisitions within an industry, reducing the level of competition at least in terms of the number of potential producers.

DVD: digital versatile disc – a storage device for recording and keeping digital material with greater capacity than a CD.

FM: a frequency band used to deliver high-quality radio broadcasting.

High-definition: higher definition is a reference to an increased number of lines on a television screen, usually 720 horizontal lines or more of video format resolution.

MEDIA programme: an EU European Commission based initiative to encourage trans-national European audio-visual.

MPEG: Moving Pictures Expert Group – standards applied to digital coding.

Video: similar as a word to above mentioned 'audio-visual' and is used in different settings in different ways. Sometimes it refers to the technology of video cassettes but it is more likely nowadays to refer to the general audio-visual products with an emphasis on the visual.

Discussion questions

1. When did the digital age start for the audio-visual industries?
2. What is the fundamental difference between the analogue system and the digital? Why is this significant?
3. Take the extract from André Lange (Point of View 10.1) and discuss the strengths and weakness of the arguments put forward.
4. To what extent will audio-visual regulation need to change to fit the new digital age?
5. How is broadband technology changing the distribution system in the EU?
6. What is the future of EU policy on audio-visual matters? Create three points and discuss their merits.
7. Is public sector broadcasting threatened by the growth of digital delivery of audio-visual products for television, radio or film?

Assignments

1. Go to one of the mentioned data sources on audio-visual distribution and choose a recent report. Critically review it, using some of the ideas within this chapter, for example in terms of the debate about whether the change is a revolution or an evolution; or the possible impact of technological change at a global or European level compared to the national.
2. Make a list of five new technologies which are bringing about convergence in the audio-visual world and assess their relative importance.

Further reading

Core books with excellent bibliographies are as follows:

Altman E., Goyal S., Sahu S. (2006) A digital media asset ecosystem for the global film industry, *Journal of Digital Asset Management*, **2**(1): 6–16.

Braun J. (2008) *Audience measurement developments and challenges as digital TV is taking off*, Eurodata TV (Mavise) Presentation, 9 April.

Cook P. (2007) Supporting contemporary German Film: how triumphant is the free market? *Journal of Common Market Studies*, **15**(1): 35–46.

EAO (2004) *Transfrontier television in the European Union: market impact and selected legal aspects*, Background paper prepared by the EAO for a Ministerial Conference on Broadcasting organised by the Irish Presidency of the EU, Strasbourg: European Audiovisual Observatory.

EC (2008) *The Future of the Internet*, Luxembourg: European Commission.

Eik N., Nikoltchev S. (2003) New European rules for the communications sector, *Iris*, Strasbourg: European Audiovisual Observatory.

Fickinger A., Lumio M. (2008) *Telecommunications in Europe, 2006*, Eurostat Data in focus, December, Luxembourg: European Commission.

Guibault L., Nikoltchev S. (2004) The legal protection of Broadcast signals, *Iris*, Strasbourg: European Audiovisual Observatory.

Harcourt A. (2005) *The European Union and the Regulation of Media Markets*, Manchester and New York: Manchester University Press.

Harper G. (2007) Emobility and the new cinema of complexity, *Journal of Contemporary European Studies*, **15**(1): 15–22.

Hubregtse S. (2005) The digital divide within the European Union, *New Library World*, **106**(3/4): 164–172.

Katz Y. (2002) The diminishing role of governments in cable policy, *European Journal of Political Research*, **38**: 285–302.

Michalis M. (2007) *Governing European Communication*, Plymouth: Lexington Books.

Noam E. (2009) *Media Ownership and Concentration in America*, New York: Oxford University Press.

Rojanski V. (2006) The European's Audiovisual Policy, *European Issues*, No. 48, Foundation Robert Schumann.

Strothmann P., Scheurer A., Nikoltchev S. (2002) Media supervision on the threshold of the 21st century: What are the requirements of broadcasting, telecommunications and concentration regulation, *Iris*, Strasbourg: European Audiovisual Observatory.

Weissenborn N., Nikoltchev S. (2007) Broadcasters' access to broadcasting frequencies, *Iris*, Strasbourg: European Audiovisual Observatory.

Withey R. (2003) (Mis) understanding the digital media revolution, *Aslib Proceedings: New Information Perspectives*, **55**(1/2): 18–22.

Zong L., Bourrbakis N. (2001) Digital video and digital TV: a comparison and the future directions, *Real Time Imaging*, **7**, 545–556.

For a widening review-based search use contemporary journals, and there are many. See the references section for just a small part of what is available.

Online resources

Where to start because now there is so much? Some have been mentioned in the text. Use the websites of the following as a launch pad:

- *CultureObsevatory (Culture Statistics Observatory)* http://www.culturestatistics.net
- *European Audiovisual Observatory (EAO)* http://www.obs.coe.int
- *European Commission: 'Information Society' portal* http://ec.europa.en/information_society/index_en.htm
- *European Journalism Centre (EJC)* http://www.ejc.net
- *Eurostat* http://ec.europa.en/eurostat/

References

Datamonitor (2004) *Broadcasting and Cable TV in Europe*, London: Datamonitor.

EAO (2007) *Video on Demand in Europe*, Strasbourg: European Audiovisual Observatory.

EAO (2008) *Video on Demand in Europe. Second Survey of VoD Services as of January 2008*, Strasbourg: European Audiovisual Observatory.

EBU (2008) EBU proposal for Amendments to the draft Amending Directive regarding the Framework, Access and Authorisation Directives ('Better Regulation') COM(2007)697 final, Geneva: European Broadcasting Union.

EC (2008) *Preparing Europe's Digital Future: i2010 Mid-term Review*, Luxembourg: European Commission, Information Society and Media.

EU (2005) Decision No 513/2005/EC on the harmonised use of radio spectrum in the 5 GHz frequency band for the implementation of wireless access systems including radio local area networks (WAS/RLANs), *OJ*, **L187**, 19.7.2005, 22–24.

EU (2007) Directive 2007/65/EEC of the European Parliament and of the Council of 11 December 2007 amending Council Directive 89/552/EEC of 3 October 1989 on the coordination of certain provisions laid down by Law, Regulation or Administrative Action in Member States concerning the pursuit of television broadcasting activities, *OJ*, **L332**, 18.12.2007, 27–45.

EU (2008a) Commission decision on the harmonisation of / the 3400–3800 Mhz frequency band for terrestrial systems capable of providing electronic communications services in the community, *OJ*, **L144**, 4.6.2008, 77–81.

EU (2008b) Commission Decision 2008/294/EC on harmonised conditions of spectrum use for the operation of mobile communication services on aircraft (MCA services) in the Community (final text), *OJ*, **L98**, 10.4.2008, 19–21.

EU (2008c) Decision No 626/2008/EC of the European Parliament and of the Council on the selection and authorisation of systems providing mobile satellite services (MSS), *OJ*, **L172**, 2.7.2008, 15–24.

Eurobarometer (2006) *E-Communications Household Survey*, Luxembourg, European Commission.

Kroes N., Reding V. (2008) *State aid: future regime for cinema support*, press release, Brussels, 22 May.

Noam E. (1991) *Television in Europe*, Oxford University Press.

Noam E. (1992) *Telecommunications in Europe*, Oxford: Oxford University Press.

OECD (2008) *Broadband Growth and Policies in OECD countries*, Paris: Organisation for Economic Cooperation and Development.

Rangone A., Turconi A. (2003) The television (r)evolution within the multimedia convergence: a strategic reference framework, *Management Decision* **41**(1): 48–71.

Chapter 11

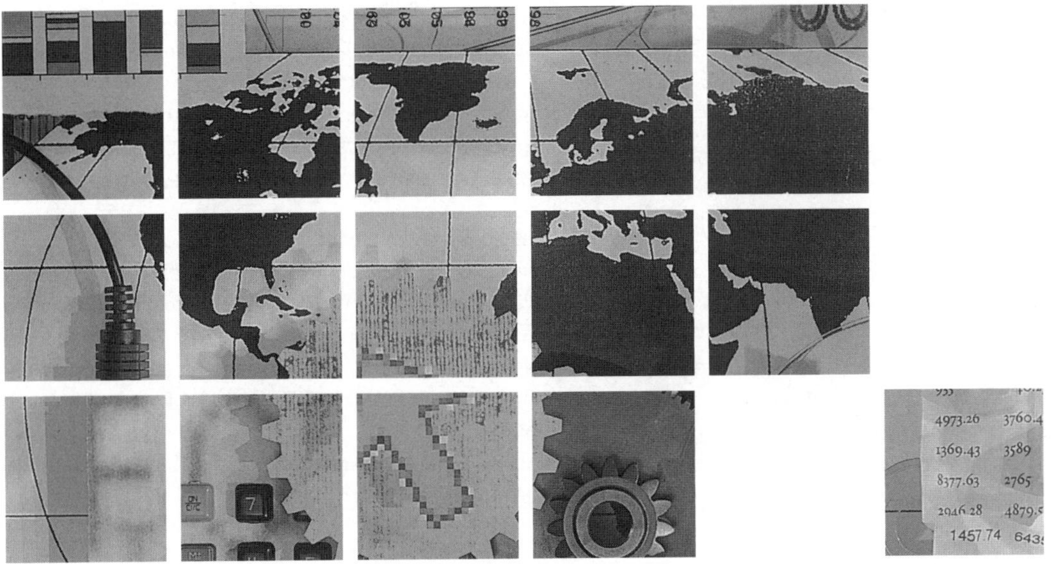

The consumption of audio-visual material in the EU: trends

What this chapter covers

Learning objectives

When you have completed this chapter you will be able to:

- Identify various sources that can be used to assess the audio-visual consumer environment.
- Outline the interweaving of interests in EU, national and corporate structures that impact on consumption.
- Compare and contrast consumption across the range of products including television, radio, film, DVD and VOD.
- Locate consumer policy developments at EU and national levels.
- Discuss, at least in part, the relative differences between public sector and private sector industries and their impact on the consumption of audio-visual products.

Themes

Below you will find a simple statement or series of statements around the six themes. They should *not* be read as a given fact. They are more like hypotheses (see Chapter 2) which need to be proved, discussed, debated and then used in your own analysis of the subject. The ideas and approaches in this book are always to be considered with an open mind; this is important in university study and is what makes it distinct from pre-university study.

Diversity of media

The audio-visual industries have always been diverse in consumption across the European scene. This was partially due to technology and partially because of a divide between public and private sector control. Separating audio-visual habits into fixed activities such as television, film watching and radio listening is beginning to change. Convergence is occurring across the sector, and this is beginning to change consumer behaviour. Although convergence of consumer habits appears to be happening, diversity remains important in the EU and will remain so in the near future.

Internal/external forces for change

The audio-visual industry has been for most EU member states first in public control and then later in a mix with private sector control. Competition is keenly felt throughout all forms of consumption, even between the public and private sectors. The increase in channels and means of access to content is making the industry even more competitive for those engaged in its production and distribution. Although often seen in national terms, competition is increasingly trans-national and even global.

Complexity of the media

The historical development of the audio-visual industry and the various regulatory controls around it has been deep, wide and various (see Chapter 9). The most noticeable is the inclusion in recent years, following the downfall of the iron curtain, of Central and Eastern European states who are emerging from state control and censorship. This has allowed for an increased surge of consumer activity in these areas.

Multi-levels

Convergence of production and distribution and a trend towards a concentration of ownership of the audio-visual industries across the EU is taking place and is a major factor in the immediate future of the industries and in the response from consumers to their products. This is showing itself especially in the debate about the future of public sector broadcasting (see Chapter 10). The full impact of this on the consumer is yet to be seen. We are at present, it appears, in a transition period between the old (analogue) and the new 'digital' era in consumer behaviour.

European integrative environment

The EU has set out through the Television without Frontiers (EU, 1989, 1997) and Audiovisual Directives (EU, 2007a) and the Single European Market (1987–1993) (EU, 1987) a framework for company and corporate practice which the audio-visual sector needs to comply with. The audio-visual industries, although often nationally described, must now be seen as being part of the EU market as much as of the global or regional scene. Policies such as 'right of reply' and citizenship rights are now a part of the consumer scene. Moreover, albeit not yet a cohesive entity, an 'EU consumer' is being framed and at least measured like never before.

Cultural values

Despite the increasing impact of new technology in the sector, especially through new delivery systems, watching and listening remains an essentially national and local cultural exercise for the great majority of Europeans, whether for information, education or entertainment.

Although this will change as the years unfold, as with content, the cultural dimension embedded in the industries remains in many ways beyond the medium, found in deeper social, political, historical and even ideological concerns for the communities that comprise the EU. All of these impinge on the EU consumer.

Essentials

➤ In the early part of the 21st century EU consumers of audio-visual products are witnessing a period of transition. The former distinctions between the many audio-visual products such as film, television, video-cassette, computer games, music CD or DVD showing through a DVD player, are becoming blurred. Across the EU the older technologies such as telephony and television, which had already reached almost saturation level – east and west – are now converging through telecommunications.

➤ There are growing signs that consumer behaviour is beginning to alter. The overall communication network is being invested in by consumers across the 490 million population of the 27 countries of the EU. In the west and in the north of the EU there is already considerable interest being shown in the Internet and new broadband technologies. To the east television and film screens are showing lively rises in audiences. The future of consuming may well be on the brink of a new digital age.

Introduction: assessing the material available to researchers for the audio-visual industry – the data

The consumption of **audio-visual** products is in the EU, as elsewhere, community-based, often nationally formed, but at the same time trans-nationally, globally connected. Nowhere is this more obvious than in the film and larger '**video**' industry. The 'blockbuster' films emanating from 'Hollywood', 'Bollywood', or even the EU through a co-production, for example, are often global, cultural products as much as they are local or national. This is not to say that 'global' film products enter the EU market on an equal footing.

The European Audiovisual Observatory has carried out recent research in this area. What we can say is that, relative to the past, there are many more points of access to trans-national products than used to be the case. Not only film but also television and video products are now part of what may be considered to be a global market, at least (and this must be emphasised) in terms of its potential. However, consumers want to see or engage with the products of distribution networks whose language, culture and control are theirs, even if historically so much of the content has been primarily American produced. This has been the case for some time with US audio-visual production dominating most markets around the world including the EU and its member states (see Chapter 9).

Stop and consider 11.1

Before we move on, perhaps we need to ponder what is a consumer? How do we define them in the 'big picture'? We have seen in other chapters how the consumer is often defined in terms of their role in economics or as part of the 'value' chain. They are often seen as the final arbiter of the process of something called 'choice'. In business terms this might seem simple, but is this view actually nothing more than a rosy picture of a real and hard-nosed, driven process of production, profit and control that has a profound cultural impact on our lives? Perhaps when we look at consumption in trans-national and international terms, we are caught in a process where choice of content and availability of products is actually rather limited? What do you think? Should we use the word 'viewer' or 'listener' or even 'reader' instead of this notion of the 'consumer'? If we change the word does it change our view of the media?

Even the radio industry, the industry which was developed at the same time as film and before television, nowadays has become, in some cases, a well-known trans-national product competing with other international radio output. Examples of this are many and in some cases historic: the UK, Germany and France, and many more European states were fairly quick to create international radio programmes for their audiences, even before the Second World War. Many were linked to the growth of Empire, a communication link for many European states to their colonies. Even after the period of decolonisation, the connections have remained. One of the most successful has been the BBC World Service which by 2008 was marking 75 years of history and the delivery of what it considers to be 'impartial news', reports and analysis in 33 languages around the world with an estimated audience of 153 million. There are, however, other notable examples across the EU such as Radio France Internationale with 45 million listeners and Deutsche Welle (65 million listeners) competing with one another and other world radio stations such as Voice of America who promote their own listings in 44 languages with over 1000 hours of material per week.

The new technology is improving and hastening the communication 'revolution', both inside established national and EU communities and beyond into a trans-national world (see Point of View 11.1). This is startlingly illustrated by an estimate (Telefonica, 2008) that in 2010 there will not only be 5 billion individual mobiles in use around the world but over 2 billion Internet users: almost a third of the global population. Count in the number of television screens and the radios and the MP3 players and you have an astonishing global level of communication. There are of course areas of the world which are less endowed than others, the African continent more than most, but the 21st century has seen an explosion of interconnectivity which previous generations and consumers would find almost impossible to grasp.

In many respects, the media market is awash with statistics about consumption, although we need to take care with their use and bear in mind that in the European environment, even on the global stage, some of the data is not fully developed. Even so, analysis of media consumption is almost an industry in itself. The audio-visual industry is so important, so all pervasive, that it interests us more than many other major industries. Some could argue the energy industry, in particular oil and energy technology, and sustainable economies are all much more important in the long-term than the audio-visual industry. However, because the audio-visual industry is an integral part of the communication system from

Point of View 11.1

World Association of Newspapers 'world digital media trends report 2008' (WAN, 2008)

The following report can be used to show (1) another estimate for the development of mobile and other audio-visual technology which can be compared with the figures above and (2) how the worlds of print and publishing (see Chapter 8) are now also thinking hard about the new audio-visual digital age:

> The second annual World Digital Media Trends report, released at a meeting of the World Association of Newspapers, said the digital platforms of newspapers are growing at a double-digit rate worldwide, as the world increasingly goes on line. The report, compiled with the help of 71 research groups, said digital and mobile advertising revenues are expected to increase 12-fold from 2002 to 2011, to about USD 150bn worldwide. The report said the number of wireless device subscriptions is expected to increase threefold to 3.4 billion from 2002 to 2011, the number of homes with broadband is likely to rise 10-fold in the same period, and the mobile telephone customer base has increased from 945 million in 2001 to 2.6 billion in 2006. The report said one study says that in some countries 'the Internet will become the primary news and information source within five years, while newspapers will lose the dominating position they have held for more than a century.' Newspapers cannot count on their print editions alone to keep them solvent, the report said. However, association President Gavin O'Reilly warned that newspapers should not rush unprepared into new mobile and Internet markets and said about 60 percent of the new revenues goes to two companies, the search engine giants Google and Yahoo.

Source: Digital media growing fast, study says, *Associated Press* (Mellgren, 2008). Used with permission of The Associated Press

which we learn about the world, it plays a central part in all societies and in all our lives. More than this, when it is successful it is also profitable. Modern information-based economies, rising educational levels and relative economic growth for most consumers have meant more time and more personal investment in audio-visual products. So corporate analysis of the consuming habits of its audience is often paramount and occupies much effort.

However, beyond the corporate there are real 'live' issues that concern the consumer and the citizen in the modern age. The work of Professor Sonia Livingstone at the London School of Economics is particularly well-known in this field and her work in the further reading section is well worth pursuing. In particular, her book entitled *Audiences and Publics: When Cultural Engagement Matters For the Public Sphere* (2005) raises important questions on the role of the new media and on our understanding of what is 'public' and what is 'private'.

In a further article, Livingstone pointedly raises pertinent questions:

> What do citizens need from the media, and how should this be regulated? Western democracies are witnessing a changing regulatory regime, from 'command-and-control' government to discursive, multi-stakeholder governance. In the United Kingdom, the Office of Communications (Ofcom) is required to further the interests of citizens and consumers, which it does in part by aligning citizen-consumer. What is meant by this term, and whether it captures the needs of citizens or subordinates them to those of consumers, has been contested by civil society groups as well as occasioning some soul-searching within the regulator.
>
> (Livingstone and Lunt, 2007, p. 51)

This type of questioning is going to the heart of contemporary debates on the issue and is being developed across Europe (see Schroder and Philips from Roskilde University, Denmark; or Walgrave, Soroka and Nuytemans from Belgium and Canada; or Jakubowicz in Poland; or Maier and Rittberger in Germany – all in the further reading section).

In this light, the audio-visual industry is also a source of cultural as well as information, education and entertainment-based knowledge. It is a key element in the political, economic and social cohesion that is embodied by communities locally and, usually, organised into nation states in the European context. In the present-day world no nation state of course is a political or cultural island even if some are geographically so described. Nation states combine with each other through trade and political allegiance. For example, this is what the EU has done since 1958 if not before (see Chapter 1). This has created a potential customer base of some 490 million inhabitants within 27 countries and growing.

The creation of the EU and of common policies for the television and audio-visual industries together with the larger policy decisions on a European Single Market are all signs of the inter-relationship that exists between its member states. It is therefore not surprising that the media, as a communication network, is intensely important for trading and state policy-making. The role of the consumer is increasingly seen as important. New technology has changed the market in terms of both production and distribution. As a reaction, policies have been created at EU and national level to safeguard the consumer and redefine the market. The question remains, to what extent have these polices been successful in creating a unified market? This is a question occupying the European Commission and the EU member states. The analysis of the EU consumer and the citizen is seen as the acid test for the future.

It is in this context that sources on audio-visual consumption have to be explored and used. The sources may be many, but understanding them and finding precisely what we might need for our analysis is crucial even if it is more complicated than we might at first think. This is true not least because of the power of competition, even between public and private sectors, which makes so much statistical material economically sensitive for producers and distributors alike.

Sources

The digital age is, as we have seen, creating greater connectivity and, by its nature, it can be global and trans-national in form. It is therefore logical to start

Source 11.1

International sources: seeking out consumer related information on the audiovisual sector

UN: the United Nations has five main areas of activity: peace and security, economic and social development, human rights, humanitarian affairs and international law. Under the economic and social development section, the UN provides considerable amounts of data on governments, population, social development, science technology and productive sectors. See also UNICEF and UNESCO Institute for Statistics – branches of the UN with information on the digital economy relating, for example, to literacy, take-up of computers, cultural product international flows, and number of radio and television sets in European countries. See also ITU, another UN branch dedicated to information and communication technologies.

OECD: Organisation for Economic Cooperation and Development. An organisation designed to encourage democracy and market economies, it gathers data on economy, governments, innovation, social trends, finance and sustainability. There are sections available on information and communications policy as well as data on measuring the information economy including data from EU member states.

EU: The two major sites for EU data are Eurostat and the Audio-visual Observatory. Both have been mentioned throughout this book as primary and important sources of information on the audio-visual industries. There are many more, but these are very good as a starting point.

with international gatherers of consumption: international organisations such as the UN, UNESCO, the OECD and the EU (see Source 11.1) draw together statistics with various purposes in mind.

These are rich and useful sources, but they may not provide us with detailed consumer attitudes. We need to look elsewhere for more detailed analysis. Therefore it is often a good idea to supplement the data with national statistical information, drawing comparisons as we develop our ideas and include the local, national within the EU, and global contexts (see below for some examples). Also, the various agencies of statistical information will include both public and private sources, some of which are publicly and freely available while others are found in specialist statistical monitoring consultancies which are often prohibitively expensive to use for many student researchers.

Drawing comparisons (assessing relationships) between one set of consumer behaviour and another is often at the heart of media statistical effort (see Chapter 2). In addition, as we have seen previously, defining the consumer is not necessarily easy. Standard practices may include age, gender, educational attainment, economic wealth, language, literacy and many other reasons, including the often used 'household spend' indicator. It is useful to start with established data from the various sources (see above and below) available to us, not forgetting to ask ourselves who created the data and for what reason.

Consumption: European trends

The consumer in the EU was not only important in developing the European Single Market (1987–1993), and before it the whole trading ethos surrounding the original Rome treaties in 1958, but is now being targeted as important in delivering services of the highest quality across the EU for the future. It is the collective view of the EU, as expressed by the European Commission, that without a functioning, well-informed consumer in the market the full benefits to be gathered from the EU will not be achieved. This is also the collective view of OECD countries (OECD, 2008). In the past, although the consumer was important in many respects, EU policy-making for consumers in general (and including audio-visual products) concentrated more on the supply side than on the demand side of the market (see Chapter 3). It is for this reason that the EU has recently created what is called the 'Consumer Marketwatch': an EU facility (the technical term is 'instrument') to '. . . *investigate markets from a consumer perspective* . . .' (Europa, 2008).

To achieve this, *Marketwatch* will analyse the single market in three ways: first it will instigate sectoral consumer investigations on such matters as '. . . price, complaints, switching, safety and satisfaction . . .'; secondly it will provide for benchmarking of the retail internal market; and lastly it will provide benchmarking data to monitor the national markets in terms of 'enforcement, information, education and redress' (*ibid*).

One reason why this is important came out of the experience of dealing with some of the EU audio-visual telecommunications networks. It was noted at an EU level that international roaming prices for mobile users across the EU were high. What was needed was an opening up of the market for the benefit of the consumer. In other words, the full impact of competition within the EU market was not working properly, or so it was assumed. This led to the 'EU Roaming Regulation' (EU, 2007b) that was able to reduce the cost for consumers using mobiles across borders inside the EU by as much as 70%. The over-riding principle of this case shows that where producers and distributors, especially in the new age of technological development, do not allow for consumer interests through transparent competition, the EU and its regulatory system should step in and protect the interest of the consumer. At the time the decision was controversial.

Involvement of this kind is not just an EU privilege. Such market monitoring already occurs in some of the member states: in Denmark there is an index of consumer conditions for 57 types of products; in The Netherlands a 'scorecard' has been developed to monitor the markets using nine principal indicators; in Italy there is a facility to observe the increase and decrease in prices; and in the UK there is the Office of Fair Trading (OFT) and the Office of Communications (**Ofcom**), specifically designed to make markets work well for consumers. Even so, step by step the EU is building on what it calls 'Ten Basic Principles' that all EU states should try to adhere to (see Point of View 11.2).

Looking forward the OECD (1998) saw the audio-visual world on the verge of technological

Point of View 11.2

European Communities: Health and Consumer Protection Directorate General

The fundamental principles upon which consumer protection in the EU works include the following, all of which could apply to audio-visual industries, both in the sense of bought hardware and the services that are provided by the producers and distributors:

1. Buy what you want, where you want;
2. If it does not work, send it back;
3. High safety standards;
4. Fair contracts;
5. Allow for replacement;
6. Easier means to compare prices;
7. Consumers should not be misled;
8. Effective redress for cross-border disputes . . . etc.

Source: European Commission, *Consumer Protection in the European Union: Ten Basic Principles* (EC, 2005).

This set of principles has now been translated into a series of proposals and a focused 'consumer strategy' for the period 2007–2013:

> Empowering consumers, enhancing their welfare, effectively protecting them [Communication from the European Commission 2007]. Targeted at the retail industry, it has been noted that cross border purchases are increasing with 26% of EU consumers having made at least one purchase across borders in 2006, up from 23% in 2003. Much of the strategy is aimed at an obvious and increasing use of the internet.

Source: *EU Consumer Marketwatch, Questions & Answers* (Europa, 2008).

change. It predicted that policy-makers and consumers alike needed to think through major issues associated with the new 'digital' market in audio-visual products.

- The investment costs for new technology need to be matched by consumer response, rewarding the initial costs and providing for greater reinvestment.
- On the supply side, smaller as well as the larger production companies would now be able to provide content for more localised markets, even though the drive for 'economies of scale' and the 'value chain' (see Chapter 3) still encouraged the 'mass market' culture where producers controlled content.
- On the demand side, would the possible 'interactivity' that the new technology provides change consumer behaviour?

A decade or more on, we can now begin to see some of the trends providing us with indicators as to the future.

- In terms of the consumer reaction to the digital age, the buying of computers, mobiles, high-definition television screens and multi-platform software has been enormous, especially in developed countries such as those of the EU.
- The proliferation of television channels is gathering apace across all the EU nations, depending of course on the economic foundation (GDP and geography) of each member state. The degree to which the smaller players (SMEs – small and medium-sized enterprises) engage in the production and distribution remains a real question.
- Interactivity and content production seem also to have taken off if we are to believe the investments by companies such as Google, Yahoo and Microsoft in such innovations as Facebook, YouTube, MySpace, Bebo and so on. On the latter, even the EU is creating a political MySpace equivalent (Myparl.eu): a social network between EU members of parliament and national members of parliament with the hope of encouraging a new pro-European democratic forum.

Nonetheless, these initiatives are not necessarily European-based but often American. This raises questions about applied European innovation, productivity and competitivity, research and development and, eventually, employment in the new 'information age'. In this the consumer's choice is crucial. The collection and comparable use of audio-visual statistics is one area for development within the EU, and the call for greater transparency has been taken up with initiatives emanating from the European Audiovisual Observatory.

Household measurement: disposable income

As noted before, one of the endearing and enduring statistical variables (categories) often used to explore consumer spending is 'household spend' among other activities such as household 'saving'. All of us live in a 'household' in one form another, from a single person to a many-member family. It is a category that is both fixed and variable and useful for EU consumption because it can be used to compare different societies. The average figure across the EU in household composition was as follows: single adult living alone (12%), two adults without children (25%), three adults with no children (14%), single parent with children (4%), two adults with children (35%) and three adults with children, the rest, at 11% (Eurostat, 2005).

As might be expected, there were differences across the individual member states (Eurostat, 2003). Nevertheless, using the EU overall statistics provides a template for the diversity of societies that can be found across the member states (see Chapter 2) and helps us to compare one set of figures with another. Equally, it relies upon the idea of 'disposable income' beyond the different tax regimes that can be found across the EU, which some would argue distorts consumer choice. This is why you will often see 'household spend' used with percentages allocated for the essentials of food, shelter and water, for luxury goods as well as for audio-visual products. In these statistics we will find trends and choices that 'households' collectively represent (see Source 11.2).

In the audio-visual world in the past, household goods such as television sets and radios were seen as products in their own right with no fundamental connection. In the contemporary age, this cannot

Source 11.2

Definition and use of 'household' in the EU

Household. For surveys on household incomes (e.g. EU-SILC – *Statistics on Income and Living Conditions*) or household budget surveys, households are defined in terms of having a shared residence and common arrangements. A household comprises either one person living alone or a group of people, not necessarily related, living at the same address with common housekeeping, i.e. sharing at least one meal per day or sharing a living or sitting room.

Household consumption/expenditure. The value of goods and services used for directly meeting human needs. Household consumption covers expenditure on purchases of goods and services, own consumption such as products from kitchen gardens, and the imputed rent of owner-occupied dwellings (= the rent that the household would pay if it were a tenant).

Source: *Eurostat Yearbook 2008* (Eurostat, 2008).

now tell the whole story. In a recent special Eurobarometer survey (Eurobarometer, 2006) based on research in the field 2005–2006, the connectivity between us embraced four main categories: fixed and mobile telephone; computers and the Internet; television; and service packages (sometimes known as 'bundled offers'). The results show a Europe diverse but in relative terms very well connected.

From telephony to television to computers to bundled services

As an overall 'snapshot', 97% of households had access to a telephone either by fixed means, 78%, or mobile phone, 80%. Television was present in 97% of households within the EU, of which aerial connection was represented by 48% of households, cable-TV by 32% and satellite by 22%. Over half, 52%, of households had personal computers, with 40% having internet access and 23% using **broadband**. Only 18% of households were using bundled service packages (mixing telephony, television and video-on-demand (VOD) type services). The presence of a telephone and a television has now reached almost all households. The computer, Internet and even bundled services, although still a 'new' industry, showed a trend upwards and, irrespective of the normal highs and lows in the economy, are set to rise over the years to come (see Chapter 10 for more details on broadband developments).

These percentages of course represent overall figures and there were distinct differences between north, south, west and east Europe in some sectors. For example, households with at least one computer reached high proportions in some states (The Netherlands, 83%, Sweden, 79% and Denmark, 77%) while others were much lower (Slovakia, 35%, Portugal, 34% and Greece, 33%). Where there was more than one member in a household the presence of a computer was more likely. The same level of figures was found with Internet access. The computer is no longer an isolated product but one that fits neatly with the integrated telecommunications sector.

Televisions in the survey were divided into standard and wide-screen. The former still dominates the household (77%) and, perhaps not that surprising, there was no north, south, east or west Europe divide with this older type of technology. Where there was a divide it was with the wide-screen television, with the UK leading the way at 44% with the lowest scores in Hungary, 3%, Greece, 5% and Malta, 3%. In 2006 digital TV, digital radio and bundled service packages were not fully developed, but the take-up was significant and on the rise. The future will embrace the whole range of audio-visual products such as IPTV, DTV and cable TV (see Chapter 10): take-up in these sectors has started, and can but only rise.

Stop and consider 11.2

With such a range of statistics how do we make sense of such a wide area and large population as in the EU? Does it make sense to use EU average figures or should we stay within the nation states? There are arguments for and against. This book argues that it makes more sense than not, because the political, economic, regulatory even statistical measurement within the EU has a character all its own despite the differences. See the first five chapters. What do you think?

Radio and wireless in the new wi-fi digital age

Mention has already been made of the importance of 'radio spectrum' control within the EU. In the past this would have been referring to television and radio delivery and consumption. Nowadays, with digital delivery systems, this also means communications that link through to MP3 players and iPods, downloading facilities and mobiles with audio and visual capacity and photography, video clips and live streaming. All these now are part of what might be considered the 'new wireless age' (the wi-fi age). The coming of the mobile everywhere and for everybody, and it is surely one of the consumer's favourite purchases, is set to become one of the major areas of technological growth not only in the EU but globally. If we link this to mobile laptops and new transportable devices then the future is for greater connection not less.

Nor can the household spend on radio be discounted even if its first technology was of the past. New digital radio and greater levels of access are providing significant levels of revenue. As a comparison, a recent UK Ofcom report (Ofcom, 2006) estimated the major global revenues of radio at £21.2 bn compared to television revenue at £104.3 bn and telecoms at £256 bn. Although smaller than the two other categories, radio was still providing notable revenue stream for individual EU nation states such as Germany, £2.3 bn, France, £1.1 bn and the UK, £1.2 bn.

Film, DVD, video and VOD

Not only are the film and television industries increasingly and inextricably linked, the future seems to point toward even greater integration. Films and their revenues through advertising or exhibition are now part of an extended value chain that spreads from the cinema through to television showings, downloads, bundled packages, **CD** and **DVD**, new software provision and the wider concept of VOD. The changes through production and distribution have one aim: to reach out to as many relevant consumers (including customers that are associated with them, such as advertisers) wherever and whenever. In this, the industry may be in 'crisis' as it aims for sound financial models (see André Lange's comments in Point of View 10.1), but the rewards can be high with the right product at the right time. The fundamental relationship between supply and demand, and therefore prices, for audio-visual products (see Chapter 3), places consumption and consumer choice in pole position for economic success.

From some of the latest figures covering 2003–2007 (*Focus 2008, World film Market Trends*, EAO, 2008) some general headlines can be extracted:

- European film production continues to grow with an estimate of 921 theatrical feature films produced in the 27 member states in 2007: 711 were national productions and 210 international co-productions (*ibid.* p. 10). It appears that compared with 2003 film production has increased around 1% per year. However, admissions have shown a slight decrease, just over 1%, with 919 million similar theatre admissions in 2007. This may mean that, at least in the more developed countries, cinema attendance has peaked, although the interest in audio-visual products has not.
- The five major markets for film admissions inside the EU are the UK, Italy, Spain, France and Germany. Although admissions in these major Western European countries are slightly decreasing, in Eastern and Central European countries such as the Czech Republic cinema attendance and film showing has shown large growth (increase in demand: Czech Republic, 11.4%; Lithuania, 34%).

- There appears to be a small increase in market share for European films inside the European market in 2007: audiences watched 28.8% European films, another 6.3% co-productions between the EU and the USA, with the largest share of the market still being dominated by US films at 62.7%.
- The number of VOD services in Europe is on the increase, although only slightly. It is estimated that across Europe there were 258 active services accessible by 293 different platforms in 2007, with France, The Netherlands and Germany the leading countries in providing such services.
- The number of multiplex screens is also on the increase especially in the new market of Eastern Europe.

Concentrating on film admissions, or 'exhibitions', is only half the story for the film, DVD and CD and VOD industries. A film product is now screened through all types of technology access. The future for film and screen showing lies on a path of convergence where television and the computer become indistinguishable: the notion of cinema attendance moving to a complementary, even rival, home-widescreen-high-definition video showing is ever more likely. For the present time, at a moment of transition, convergence has not yet been fully reached even in the most advanced of the EU member states. However, the potential is there, the technology is already being provided and step-by-step consumers are embracing the convergent technology: especially those who can afford it and those who have the competence and attitude to accept it, as the mainly young audiences suggest.

There are EU national differences in the use of the Internet for entertainment, let alone work practices and changed shopping habits, with Northern Europe, especially the Scandinavian countries, The Netherlands, Luxembourg and Denmark, indicating through consumer polls (Eurobarometer, 2006) that the Internet is 'very important' in their lives. It is expected that as broadband use increases across the EU, especially when bandwidth increases and Internet speeds accelerate, with a resulting higher quality product, this tendency will spread across most of the EU.

Even so, there are elements of the industry where take-up by consumers of products remains as much a prediction and a guess as it is a science. For example, Ofcom, the UK regulatory authority recently published a report (Ofcom, 2006) indicating that it considered there were 'major uncertainties' about the future of IPTV among the proliferation of new technologies and delivery systems. In considering consumers and their market, it is a good idea to use EU, national and international sources of commentary to make definitive judgements.

Consumption: national trends – an indication

As previously suggested, no matter how useful the EU and international comparisons are there is still much to be learnt about consumer attitudes by using the national agencies of consumer activity. Each EU nation state will have means by which they can assess consumer behaviour and attitudes. Some national organisations are more developed than others, but most major television, film and audio-visual companies, both private and public, will use statistical and qualitative material to explore trends in their industry.

Stop and consider 11.3

This book has not dwelt upon the importance of audience ratings or their fundamental relationship to both public and private sector assessments of consumer behaviour. In EU terms, this is somewhat logical because there is no standard European audience so there will be no corresponding European audience rating. However, this is not to say that the idea of 'ratings' is unimportant: the opposite is the case. For many in the industry ratings are crucial. Bearing in mind the power and influence of the advertisers (both in the AV and other entertainment industries) and the agencies that surround the media market, it is argued that 'ratings' are the lifeblood of competition, finance, investment and production. Few TV channels survive without a weather eye on the 'ratings'. This book is not primarily about 'audiences' per se*, but it is an interesting question to* *pose: what is the relationship between 'consumers' on the one side and audience 'ratings' on the other? When we investigate national consumption, how much is made of the importance of audience 'ratings'? Some argue that 'ratings' are so important in our understanding of the industry not because they illustrate 'consumer choice' or 'user satisfaction', but because they are the tool used by marketing agencies for product advertising and this underlines the present state of our media markets. Do you agree? (See Case Study 11.2 on the proposed new French TV channel and use it in thinking through this question.)*

Some of the corporations which are heavily committed to audio-visual, multi-platform production and trans-national delivery will be assessing the material at a global, European, national or even regional level, depending on the sector, and that may well include a look at the 'ratings'. They will be assessing not only individual and household consumer trends through purchases of technology, programmes or games and music, but also the different contexts in which audio-visual products are consumed, including the EU legal and regulatory environment in which the EU consumer operates.

As we have seen, the EU varies in these contexts. There are differences in national markets in programming (see Chapter 9), the degree of catch-up technologies (see Chapter 10) and attitudes which go beyond the product into a cultural background which must always, in the EU especially, be a part of market analysis.

Each country will have different forms of organisation as can be seen in Source 11.3 and it is to be

Source 11.3

National sources: seeking out consumer-related information on the audio-visual sector – examples

UK: the UK National Statistics Office site is full of established data including details on the audio-visual industry. Some data can be quite detailed, such as that which illustrated the interest among all ages in the UK for the watching of news and factual programmes, with religious programmes being of least interest. It also shows such matters as cinema attendance, which from 1982 has shown a gradual increase for all age groups. For consumer behaviour there are also organisations such as Mintel although they can be costly for the individual researcher and are better accessed through university or library facilities. Equally for the digital age there is *Screendigest*, but full subscriptions for individuals could also be considered high although the analysis is fascinating. There are also regulatory authorities such as Ofcom that often publish details on consumption, and these are most useful.

France: For national statistics the INSEE (Institut National de la Statistique et des Etudes Économiques) is excellent with data available on the audio-visual industries, showing for example a rise of audience participation across the range of products from television to film since the mid-1990s. The Conseil Supérieur de l'Audiovisuel (CSA) provides a thorough overview of the audio-visual industries in France. In its various 'dossiers' there will also be details of consumer reaction, watching and listening behaviour: for example, recent reports on the importance of 'sports' within French scheduling.

Germany: The Federal Statistical Office in Germany (Satistisches Bundesamt Deutschland) publishes, like most national statistics offices, a 'yearbook' with a range of data, but unlike the UK and France, German audio-visual developments are more likely to be, at the state (Lander) level than national. There is also excellent data available at various universities including the well-known Hans Bredow Institute with a series of high-quality data-based analyses of the German audio-visual environment. Recently the Institute has been researching areas such as children's TV and other matters via academic links with other research universities across Europe.

For further sources see the European Journalism Centre web site located in Maastricht, the Netherlands, or the European Audiovisual Observatory.

remembered that those mentioned are only indicative. Seeking out sources is one of the trials and pleasures of research work.

EU national statistical agencies and the public–private divide

Each country of the EU, as can be seen above (Source 11.3), will have dedicated 'national' statistical offices: by locating them much general information about the factors surrounding the national audio-visual environment becomes accessible. There will also be private sources, used by the industry, or general agencies for the analysis of consumer behaviour. In market analysis terms it is very useful to combine work on international and European trends with more detailed analysis of the national or even regional settings (see Case Study 11.1).

The national trends in the EU are also deeply touched by the public–private sector divide as we have seen in previous chapters. It is of course highly debatable whether from a consumption point of view it really matters who the provider is or how they are financed. However, as we have seen with the work of Sonia Livingstone *et al.* at the beginning of the chapter, the media is not just about finance or corporate business models but also arguments over content and freedom of expression and the role of journalism, as well as the wider entertainment field. This is not the place for a profound discussion, and there has been much comment throughout the book on this topic, but as researchers in the European field we need be sensitive to the arguments (see Case Study 11.2).

Across the EU this public–private debate is a 'hot topic' and one that will need to be resolved. The impact of the new delivery systems could, in theory, undercut the fundamental role of public broadcasting if consumers move away to new private-sector provision. Either public broadcasters invest heavily in

Case Study 11.1

National reports into consumer behaviour

To illustrate the degree of research into 'national' consumer behaviour in the audio-visual sector, the following is an extract from the 'summary' of the Ofcom report. Note the range of questions posed and the answers provided in what is now a complicated audio-visual sector.

> This report covers many aspects of the consumer experience. The following is a summary of the key themes and highlights from this year's research.
>
> - Take-up trends are positive
> - Increase in the take-up of broadband across all groups
> - Increase in the take-up of digital TV, driven by Freeview
> - Increase in take-up of mobile, broadband and digital TV among over 65s (although take-up among this group is still lower than the general population)
> - For the first time households with mobiles overtake the percentage of households with fixed-lines
> - Increase in take-up of bundled services
> - There has been continued downward pressure on prices . . .
> - There has also been an increase in the choice consumers are able to exercise in the communications market
>   - General increase in awareness of suppliers
>   - Increase in the number of operators across the markets
> - Although low income consumers are affected by affordability when taking up communications services, they are more likely to be affected by income variability and other financial issues such as not having a bank account
>   - These factors influence decisions to commit to contracts and pay by direct debit
> - While consumers are actively participating in the broadband market there are some issues that could impact on behaviour
>   - The percentage of consumers who are very satisfied with their broadband supplier is decreasing
>   - The proportion who state switching internet service providers (ISP) is easy is also decreasing

Source: Ofcom (UK), *The Consumer Experience – Research Report 07* (Ofcom, 2007), http://www.ofcom.org.uk/research/tce/ce07/.

Case Study 11.2

Public broadcasting in France 2009

The television consumers of France have recently been confronted with the proposed launch of a non-advertising funded channel FTV (France Télévision), similar to the BBC. This has often been demanded in French left-of-centre circles, but it is the more right-wing President Sarkozy who has launched the new initiative (2008). To pay for this there was an additional proposal for a levy (tax) on telecommunication and Internet operators and even a further tax on advertising revenue upon existing private sector television providers. The private sector (e.g. TF1, M6 and Canal+) immediately complained that this was distorting the market. Yet, M. Sarkozy argued: 'We have to allow the private channels to develop and at the same time we have to give France Télévision the means of offering quality programmes to as many viewers as possible.' Defining what is meant by 'quality' programming of course remains very difficult in consumer terms. This is especially relevant in the French context where it was rumoured that the President of the French Republic could become the president of the new French television channel with the accompanying fear that the interests of the ruling government could supplant wider consumer interests.

Sources: France scraps public TV adverts, *FT.com* (Hollinger, 2008); Le chef de l'état veut pouvoir nommer lui-même le président d France Télévisions et annonce le fin de la publicité après 20 heures dès janvier 2009, *Libération.fr* (Garrigos and Roberts, 2008).

the new technology, burdening themselves with investment costs, or they limit their offerings to their public: or as we might now call them 'consumers'.

There is an alternative approach that suggests that the public broadcasting systems merge facilities across borders, offering a more trans-European 'public consumer space' in which to operate – widening their consumer base and sharing costs. So far, across the national public broadcasting systems in the EU this has not happened to any noticeable degree: political restraint, organisational inertia, language and cultural differences, competition between public-sector 'brands' and differences in revenue models have negated any efforts to create a European as opposed to a national broadcasting system.

For the foreseeable future, unless the EU changes its status and its working practices, the public broadcasting system will remain national. Customers will rely on it as a 'national' semi-official resource. Its success will depend upon consumer loyalty and reactions to a changing market. In the private sector, though, the pressure may well be to create co-productions across the spectrum, generating further mergers and takeovers, meaning possibly greater trans-national consumption as well as production. The future is in question and ultimately the consumers will decide.

The future: a comment

What the consumption of audio-visual products will look like in the future is intriguing. It appears that the flow of goods across borders, often classified as 'cultural goods and services', is stretching the international media scene and encouraging a new agenda. This should not come as any surprise as the global 'cultural' trade in such products as film and television programmes, games and music combines with the print and publishing industry of books, magazines and online newspapers to create 'cultural trade flows' with an economic impact that one estimate (UNESCO UIS, 2005) puts as high as 7% of the world's GDP. If the trends are to be believed will this increase or decrease in the years to come? It is an interesting question.

The same report saw the USA, the UK and Germany in the period 1994–2003 as prime national markets in global and European terms, both in production and consumption of cultural products and services. This was linked to their perceived status as 'high-income' economies of that time. However, there are also regional trade, financial and continental movements taking place within the market from the wider Asia to China and beyond whose impact is already beginning to be felt around the world, including within the EU markets. The EU market too, with enlargement and technological change as an impetus, is also changing. As a result, and conceded by most serious commentators, in a market place changing so quickly there is an expressed need for even more accurate statistical knowledge of the consumer experience. As researchers in the field there is much for us to do.

Chapter summary

➤ Convergence of audio-visual products is occurring at some pace, but the EU remains in a period of transition.

➤ There remains lively interest in television, CD, DVD and other screen products and this appears to be continuing through the normal outlets for screening – the television and the cinema – but may alter as the worlds of television, computing and telecommunications merge even further in the very near future.

➤ There are national differences across the EU in consuming habits, mainly based on political, economic and even historical factors, which are important in the market. Even so, it is expected that taken as a whole and over the mid- and long-term the market will rise with the overall EU economy and so too will the convergence of consumption, even though this may take longer than many believe.

➤ The role of consumer knowledge and pressure in the EU market, as with other OECD markets, is being seen as crucial in encouraging the market towards further competition, meeting supply and demand, and therefore controlling price. Moves are afoot to gather and publish data to illuminate the market and make it more transparent. The use of the new technology and the consumption of products, in all its forms, through broadband technology, will be a spur to the market for years to come.

Key terms

Audio-visual: (sometime spelt audiovisual) a term used to bring together all products that fall into the categories of audio (e.g. radio) and visual (screen products including television).

Broadband: a signalling method used in Telecommunication Technology: Often associated with the cable industry and the growth of the internet.

CD: compact disc – a storage device for recording and keeping digital material.

DVD: a storage device for recording and keeping digital material with greater capacity than a CD.

Ofcom: UK regulator Office of Communications.

Video: similar as a word to above mentioned 'audiovisual' and is used in different settings in different ways. Sometimes it is referring to the technology of video cassettes but more likely nowadays is referring to the general audiovisual products with an emphasis on the visual.

Discussion questions

1. Why is the 'consumer' so important in the audio-visual market?
2. What sorts of organisations are used to monitor and assist the consumer in the EU?
3. How has the new technology changed or how will it change the behaviour of EU consumers?
4. Locate three sources of material for assessing EU and national consumer behaviour and reflect on why they may be different?

5. After the many decades of new technology development, what are the principal trends in EU consumption of audio-visual products?
6. Why is 'household spending' used for measuring consumer interest in audio-visual products?
7. What are the 'headline' trends in the film and VOD industries in the EU?

Assignments

1. Using one or more of the statistics-led works (EU, OECD and UNESCO) compare European consumer behaviour in one of the following: television, film or video.
2. Whilst using statistical material about EU or even global media what are the strengths and weaknesses of the analysis? Refer back to Chapter 2 on statistics with reference to the detail mentioned in this chapter, supplementing your work by looking at statistics from EU and other global sources.

Further reading

Brooker W., Jermyn D. (eds) (2002) *The Audience Studies Reader*, London: Routledge.

EAO (2008) *Focus 2008 – World Film Market Trends*, Strasbourg: European Audiovisual Observatory.

Eurobarometer (2006) *E-communications Household Survey*, Luxembourg: European Commission.

Eurostat (2007) *European Business: Facts and Figures*, Luxembourg: European Commission.

Eurostat (2007) *Consumers in Europe, Facts and Figures on Services of General Interest*, Luxembourg: European Commission.

Jakubowicz K. (2004) Ideas in our heads: introduction of PSB as part of media system change in central and Eastern Europe, *European Journal of Communication*, **19**: 53–74.

Livingstone S. (2003) On the challenges of cross-national comparative media research, *European Journal of Communication*, **18**: 477–500.

Livingstone S. (ed.) (2005) *Audiences and Publics: When Cultural Engagement Matters for the Public Sphere*, Changing Media, Changing Europe, Vol. 2, Bristol: Intellect Books.

Maier J., Rittberger B. (2008) Shifting Europe's boundaries: mass media, public opinion and the enlargement of the EU, *European Union Politics*, **9**: 243–267.

Mediametrie (2008) *Audience ratings for cable, Canalsat and TPS channels From September 3rd 2007 to February 17th 2008*, press release, 11 March, Levallois.

Nightingale V., Ross K. (2003) *Critical Readings: Media and Audiences (Issues in Cultural & Media Studies)*, Buckingham: Open University Press.

Ruddock A. (2000) *Understanding Audiences*, London: Sage.

Ruddock A. (2007) *Investigating Audiences*, London: Sage.

Schroder K.C., Philips L. (2007) 'Complexifying media power: a study of the interplay between media and audience discourses on politics, *Media, Culture and Society*, **29**: 890–915.

Walgrave S., Soroka S., Nuytemans M. (2008) 'The mass media's political agenda-setting power: a longitudinal analysis of media, parliament, and government in Belgium (1993 to 2000), *Comparative Political Studies*, **41**: 814–836.

For a widening review-based search use contemporary journals: and there are many. See the references section for just a small part of what is available.

Online resources

http://www...

There are many sources open to us online. As a starting point use the following and follow through the many resources that are cited and developed within the various web sites mentioned in previous chapters but include:

- *CultureObservatory (Culture Statistics Observatory)* www.culturestatistics.net
- *European Audiovisual Observatory (EAO)* www.obs.coe.int
- *Organisation for Economic Co-operation and Development (OECD)* www.oecd.org
- *UNESCO* www.unesco.org
- *United Nations Institute of Statistics* www.uis.unesco.org

Locate the many national agencies available for statistics and reports on the audio-visual industry across the EU, e.g. Ofcom or OFT in the UK. The European Journalism Centre web site is particularly useful in this regard.

References

EAO (2008) *Focus 2008 – World Film Market Trends*, Strasbourg: European Audiovisual Observatory.

EC (2005) *Consumer Protection in the European Union: Ten Basic Principles*, Luxembourg: European Commission, DG Health and Consumer Protection.

EU (1987) Single European Act, *OJ*, **L169**, 29.06.1987, 1–29.

EU (1989) Council Directive 89/552/EEC of 3 October 1989 on the coordination of certain provisions laid down by Law, Regulation or Administrative Action in Member States concerning the pursuit of television broadcasting activities, *OJ*, **L298**, 17.10.1989, 23–30.

EU (1997) Directive 97/36/EC of the European Parliament and of the Council 30 June 1997 amending Council Directive 89/552/EEC on the coordination of certain provisions laid down by Law, Regulation or Administrative Action in Member States concerning the pursuit of television broadcasting activities, *OJ*, **L202**, 30.7.1997, 60–70.

EU (2007a) Directive 2007/65/EEC of the European Parliament and of the Council of 11 December 2007 amending Council Directive 89/552/EEC of 3 October 1989 on the coordination of certain provisions laid down by Law, Regulation or Administrative Action in Member States concerning the pursuit of television broadcasting activities, *OJ*, **L332**, 18.12.2007, 27–45.

EU (2007b) Regulation (EC) No 717/2007 Of The European Parliament and of the Council of 27 June 2007 on roaming on public mobile telephone networks within within the Community and amending Directive 2002/21/EC, *OJ*, **L171**, 29.6.2007, 32–40.

Eurobarometer (2006) *E-Communications Household Survey*, Luxembourg, European Commission.

Europa (2008) *EU Consumer Marketwatch, Questions & Answers*, Brussels, 31 January.

Eurostat (2003) *The European Union labour force survey – Methods and definitions 2001*, Luxembourg, European Commission.

Eurostat (2005) *Statistics in Focus: Population and Social Conditions, The European Consumer in the Enlarged Union*, Luxembourg: European Commission.

Eurostat (2008) *Eurostat yearbook 2008*, Luxembourg, European Commission.

Garrigos R., Roberts I. (2008) Le chef de l'Etat veut pouvoir nommer lui-même le président de France Télévisions et annonce la fin de la publicité après 20 heures dès janvier 2009, *Libération.fr*, juin 26.

Hollinger P. (2008) France scraps public TV adverts, *FT.com* June 26.

Livingstone S. (ed.) (2005) *Audiences and Publics: When Cultural Engagement Matters for the Public Sphere*, Changing Media, Changing Europe, Vol. 2, Bristol: Intellect Books.

Livingstone S., Lunt P. (2007) Representing citizens and consumers in media and communications regulation, *The Annals of the American Academy of Political and Social Science*, **611**: 51–650.

Mellgren D. (2008) Digital media growing fast, study says, *Associated Press*, June 4.

OECD (1998) Working party on the Information Economy *Content as a New Growth Industry*, Paris: Organisation for Economic Co-operation and Development.

OECD (2008) *Enhancing Competition in Telecommunications: Protecting and Empowering Consumers*, Ministerial background report, Paris: Organisation for Economic Co-operation and Development.

Ofcom (2006) *The Communications Market*, London: Ofcom, http://www.ofcom.org.uk/research/cm/cm06/.

Ofcom (2007) *The Consumer Experience – Research Report 07*, London: Ofcom, http://www.ofcom.org.uk/research/tce/ce07/.

Telefonica (2008) *Spirit of Progress*, Mobile World Congress, Barcelona, 11–14 February.

UNESCO UIS (2005) *International Flows of selected Cultural Goods and Services, 1994–2003*, Montreal: Institute for Statistics.

Index

(Page numbers in *italics* refer to Figures; those in **bold** refer to Tables)